A Field Manual of the

FERNS &
FERN-ALLIES
of the United States & Canada

A Field Manual of the

FERNS &

FERN-ALLIES

of the United States & Canada

David B. Lellinger

with photographs by A. Murray Evans

SMITHSONIAN INSTITUTION PRESS

Washington, D.C.

Library of Congress Cataloging in Publication Data
Lellinger, David B.
A Field manual of the ferns and fern-allies of the United
States and Canada.
Bibliography: p.
Includes index.
1. Ferns—United States—Identification.   2. Ferns—
Canada—Identification.   3. Pteridophyta—United
States—Identification.   4. Pteridophyta—Canada—
Identification.   I. Title.
QK524.5.L45   1985   587   84-22216
ISBN 0-87474-602-7
ISBN 0-87474-603-5 (pbk.)

Designer: Christopher Jones
Editor: Donald C. Fisher

Contents

Preface

Although ferns and fern-allies number only slightly more than 10,000 species compared to over 200,000 species of flowering plants, no plants on earth exceed them in beauty and symmetry. In the past many were thought to have curative or magical properties, but only a few have true medicinal value. Interest in ferns peaked during the Victorian era (Allen, 1969), when a craze for fancy forms of ferns led collectors to comb the woods of England and western Europe. Many fancy forms of ferns were cultivated. After the mania faded early in the twentieth century, the number of kinds of fancy forms in cultivation dwindled; today some of them are known only from herbarium specimens. In the last decade gardeners and nature lovers have shown a reawakened interest in ferns.

The purpose of this book is to aid in identifying all of the species of ferns and fern-allies that are native to or naturalized in Canada and the United States, excluding the state of Hawaii. This amounts to 406 described species, subspecies, and varieties. The hybrids, which mostly do not reproduce vegetatively and which are seldom encountered, in general are only mentioned under the names of their parents or in the chapter on hybrid complexes. Subspecies and varieties are fully treated only if they are relatively common and wide ranging and have few intermediates; those that are poorly distinguished are merely mentioned under their parent species. Most of the species are illustrated by a color photograph. Some of the photographs show the plants in their native habitats; others are close-ups to illustrate important diagnostic features.

The descriptions in the text are numbered consecutively, as are the species names in the keys and the illustrations. Thus, it is easy to move back and forth through the book, comparing illustrations with text or vice-versa. An asterisk before the species number indicates that it is not illustrated.

Because ferns and fern-allies are complex plants, a rather large number of technical terms are needed to describe them accurately and succinctly. These terms are defined in the Glossary, with helpful illustrations. Throughout the text, I have included references to useful literature, which readers may wish to consult for further information.

In preparing this book, I have tried to look at the specimens of North American ferns north of Mexico with the same critical eye that is necessary when working on poorly known tropical ferns. In so doing, I have found some characteristics of the plants useful for identification that were not noticed by previous observers. On the other hand, my knowledge of North American ferns as they grow in the wild is minimal. Therefore, I have been particularly fortunate to have Prof. A. Murray Evans, Dr. James D. Montgomery, and Prof. Warren H. Wagner, Jr., as readers for the entire manuscript. Their many years of field experience and laboratory study have been distilled into the pages of this book, and I am ever grateful for their help. In addition, the following colleagues have provided data or ideas in their areas of specialty: Prof. David S. Barrington, Dr. Joseph Beitel, Dr. Brian M. Boom, Mr. Thomas J. Carlson, Prof. Gerald J. Gastony, Mr. R. James Hickey, Dr. Francis M. Hueber, Dr. Laima S. Kott, Mr. Thomas A. Lumpkin, Dr. Sergius Mamay, Prof. Raymond L. Petersen, Dr. Timothy Reeves, Dr. Harold E. Robinson, Dr. Edith Scott, Prof. Judith E. Skog, Dr. Alan R. Smith, Dr. W. Carl Taylor, Dr. Alice F. Tryon, Prof. Rolla M. Tryon, Jr., Ms. Sherry Whitmore, and Mr. Michael D. Windham. I am indebted to Ms. Mary Monsma, who prepared the line drawings found throughout the book, to Ms. Andrea Sessions, who assisted with the research and helped to prepare the glossary, to Mr. Brian Kahn, who helped to prepare the figures, and to Ms. Marian Skedgell, formerly of E. P. Dutton & Co., Inc., for many helpful editorial suggestions, and to E. P. Dutton & Co., Inc., who first suggested this book and who aided materially in the early stages of its production. Most of the color photographs are the work of Prof. A. Murray Evans. Photographs of those species that Prof. Evans could not photograph personally were contributed by Mr. Edward R. Alverson (194, 197, 242, 278, 353), Dr. Joseph Beitel (20, 93, 135, 333, 406), Dr. Judith E. Gordon (361), Mr. David Johnson (22, 77, 286), Dr. David B. Lellinger (61), Dr. James D. Montgomery (89, 102, 166, 188, 373), Mr. Clifton E. Nauman (228), Dr. Timothy Reeves (47, 236, 337), Dr. W. Carl Taylor (68, 71, 90, 101), Dr. Florence S. Wagner (98, 109, 114, 365, 388, 391), Mr. Kerry S. Walter (21, 246, 326), and Mr. George Yatskievych (86, 145, 170, 182, 284, 314, 370). Their contributions, which have added much of value to this book, are deeply appreciated.

David B. Lellinger
Curator of Ferns
Smithsonian Institution

A note about the photographs

Whenever possible, photographs were taken in the field—from northern Vermont to the Florida Everglades, and in the west from Alaska to southern California. I used two Nikkormat FT2 cameras, primarily with a 55 mm MicroNikkor lens, but occasionally with a 35 mm Nikkor or an 80–200 mm Nikkor zoom lens. Usually a Nikon A2 amber filter was used to correct for excessive blue light in the shade. The cameras were always mounted on a tripod; I used three different sizes and backpacked two of them in the field. Natural light was favored, but when flash was required, I used two or three small strobe lights with slaves, or else a more powerful Vivitar 283 bounced into a reflective, silver umbrella, an effective but cumbersome combination. The film was Kodachrome 64 processed by Kodak. All equipment was packed in a custom, foam-lined, waterproof, fiberglass case adapted for packframe or hand carrying.

Desert ferns and fern-allies were a particular challenge, because when dry they usually curl up beyond recognition or esthetic satisfaction. To wet them in the field, I watered them, often several times, or I removed a few fronds, wetting them with paper towels in plastic bags, and photographed them later in camp or in a motel. Some herbarium specimens were reconstituted the same way. Close-ups were taken with the 55 mm MicroNikkor lens with either an accessory ring or a Nikon bellows on a copy stand or heavy tripod, and multiple flashes or photofloods.

My primary caveats for achieving satisfactory results with ferns are that it takes lots of film (often half a roll or more per subject), usually too much time to travel and work with companions, always a tripod-mounted camera, and consistency in film and equipment.

In order to locate plants to photograph, I used field manuals, herbarium specimen labels, state and county Floras, and personal contacts. I am grateful to many wonderful plantsmen who helped me hunt ferns or pointed out localities to visit. They include Prof. Daniel F. Austin, Mr. George N. Avery, Ms. Susan Black, Dr. Brian M. Boom, Prof. Kenton L. Chambers, Dr. Donovan S. Correll, Dr. Frank C. Craighead, Sr., Dr. C. E. Delchamps, Mr. Charles D. Evans, Prof. David E. Fairbrothers, Prof. Ernest S. Ford, Mr. Roger L. Hammer, Prof. Arthur R. Kruckeberg, Prof. Olga Lakela, Prof. Robert W. Long, Mr. Clifton E. Nauman, Ms. Merilyn Osterlund, Dr. John Popenoe, Dr. Timothy Reeves, Dr. Andrew F. Robinson, Mr. John W. Short, Dr. Alan R. Smith, Mr. Charles Stevens, Prof. R. Dale Thomas, Prof. T. M. C. Taylor, Prof. Warren H. Wagner, Jr., and the rangers, naturalists, and directors of state parks and forests and national parks, monuments, and forests all over the country.

A. Murray Evans
Professor of Botany
University of Tennessee

Introduction

STUDYING AND COLLECTING FERNS

The study of ferns and fern-allies can be as casual or as complex as you wish. On the most basic level you can compare the plants that you find with the photographs in the book. The illustrations will help you to recognize almost all the ferns and fern-allies growing naturally in the United States and Canada.

You can also learn to identify the fern families that grow in your area. This is easier than it might seem, unless you live in Florida. Since 12 of the 25 families of ferns and fern-allies that grow in the United States and Canada are found almost exclusively in tropical and subtropical portions of the continent or are aquatic, you are unlikely to encounter them. That leaves only 13 families. The key to the families and illustrations will help you to understand the differences among the families.

In order to use the keys to genera and species, you will need to become familiar with the terms used to describe ferns. The terms used in this book are explained in the Glossary. Although the Glossary looks formidable, relatively few of the terms are necessary to describe most ferns and fern-allies; many of the terms are specialized and apply to only a few of the plants in this book.

An inexpensive 10× hand lens is very useful for examining small structures such as glands, hairs, scales, sori, indusia, and sporangia. If you have access to a dissecting microscope, it will reveal to you a marvelous world of small and beautiful details, but such costly equipment is not necessary for the study of ferns.

Probably you already know the common names of some ferns. As you use the keys and double-check the plants you identify by means of the photographs, you will learn the common or Latin names of more and more species. Variation in size or structure within a species caused by habitat or growth stage may puzzle you at first, but you will soon learn to allow for it in making identifications. Many of the genera in North America have only a few species, and these are easily distinguished. On the other hand, learning the species of the larger genera and those that form many intermediate hybrids takes careful study and a lot of experience. Usually comparison with correctly named specimens found in a university or museum herbarium is necessary to identify such plants.

1

The best way to study ferns and fern-allies is in the field. Sometimes a frond or two can be clipped or cut (never broken) from the rhizome or near the stipe base, but it is important not to collect plants unnecessarily, especially if they are rare or are growing in a protected area such as a state or national park. However, serious students having a particular research objective may be able to obtain a permit to collect otherwise protected plants. Where documentation of a rare species is necessary, a frond or even just a pinna can be removed carefully without disturbing the plant.

Transplanting ferns from the wild is often difficult, and so it is best to rely on nursery stock, especially for horticultural purposes. Some species are difficult or impossible to cultivate (see the notes accompanying the species). Inexperienced gardeners, therefore, should first try species that are easy to transplant and grow before attempting to transplant difficult species from the wild. Growing ferns from spores is an excellent way to start a wide variety of plants, although it may take several years to get large plants by this method.

Finding ferns in the wild in order to study or collect them is rewarding. However, the rewards are proportional to your knowledge of fern habitats (see Geography, Habitats, and Ecology of Ferns and Fern-allies). In learning to interpret the landscape and habitats, experience is everything; the more carefully you observe, the more you will find.

Some ferns are very common, and others are very rare. Sterile hybrids are almost always rare unless they have a vegetative means of increasing the size of their colonies or of distributing themselves. In the description of each species there is an estimate of its abundance to give you some idea how difficult the species is to find. Of course, all species are more common in some places than in others in the same kind of habitat, and most species tend to be rare toward the edge of their range. *Very rare* signifies that only one or a few populations are known in the United States and Canada. *Rare* means that the plants will be found in about 1/10 or fewer of the habitats in which they could be found. *Occasional* means they will be found in about 3/10 of the habitats, *frequent* in about 1/2, *common* in about 9/10, and *abundant* means they are conspicuous in 9/10 or more of the suitable habitats.

Collecting botanical specimens is a rather exacting procedure. The plants must be properly pressed and informative labels written. This is usually done by botanists or advanced amateurs who have a specific study purpose in mind. Figure 1 shows a properly prepared herbarium specimen. A portion of the rhizome has been collected. (If the rhizome is absent, the rhizome habit should have been noted on the specimen label.) The rhizome was shaken or washed free of soil before the plant was pressed. The fronds have been placed on the sheet so that both the adaxial and abaxial surfaces are visible. Some fronds have been clipped off so that it is possible to see the outlines of the remaining fronds and of several pinnae. The scales or hairs at the base of the stipes are visible.

Because ferns and fern-allies lack delicate flowers and often are rather tough, many collectors put their specimens into plastic bags in the field; but as soon as convenient after collecting, the specimens should be transferred to a plant press (Fig. 2). The press is loaded by putting two straps

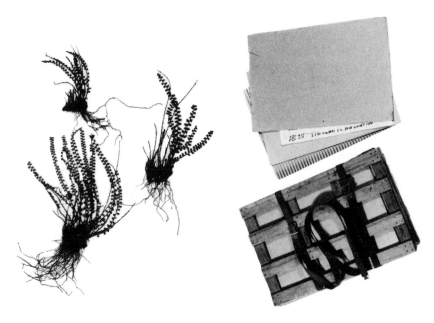

Fig. 1. A herbarium specimen. Fig. 2. A plant press.

or ropes and a press end on a flat surface with a blotter on top. A sheet of newspaper is put on the blotter, the plant is carefully arranged on the newspaper, and the sheet is folded over. The plant is then pressed. The collection number is written on the newspaper, and the collection data are written either on the edge of the newspaper or in a fieldbook. A blotter, a corrugate (made of aluminum or single-faced corrugated cardboard), and another blotter are added, and the process is repeated. The press is closed by squeezing it, sitting or standing on it if necessary, and by tightening the straps or ropes. A press can be made up without blotters, but the specimens will be ridged by the corrugates, which makes them unattractive. A press can be made up without corrugates, but the blotters must be exchanged daily for others that have been dried, usually in the sun, a tedious process. As the plants dry, it is necessary to keep tightening the press. The press usually is put over a mild source of heat (camp lantern or catalytic heater) or, in dry areas, is lashed to the top of a car or truck so that air can blow through. When the plants are dry, they are removed from the press and kept in the newspaper folders until mounted.

The specimen label with the data it contains is nearly as important as the specimen itself. The name of the plant (or space to insert it), the state or province, county, and other locality data to enable the collecting locality to be found all must be recorded. The date of collection always is given. Because route numbers change, it is better to refer to roads by the names of the towns on either side of the collecting locality and to add the distance to the locality from one town or the other or from a county boundary or river crossing, all of which are relatively fixed points. Habitat information is also extremely useful, especially the kind of soil or rock on which the plant grew, exposure to sunlight, and the moisture available. In wilderness areas, the latitude and longitude should be given, and in areas of great relief, the elevation should be stated. Each plant or gathering is given a collector's number, usually starting with 1 and working upwards. (The most prolific collectors in tropical America have collection numbers approaching or over 100,000; their strenuous efforts have been of inestimable value to the science of botany.) People who collect plants on a regular basis maintain fieldbooks in which all of this information is written for permanent reference and for later transfer to specimen labels.

Plants to be placed in univerity or museum herbaria should be mounted on stiff, 100% rag herbarium paper that is 11.5 inches wide and 16.5 inches long. They can best be affixed with strips of gummed linen and with specially formulated cellulose adhesive that will not deteriorate with age. Thick stems are often tied to the sheet with white thread, and the knot on the underside of the sheet covered with gummed paper tape so that it cannot catch on another specimen. For temporary collections, it is possible to use white glue, but that adhesive softens in high humidity. Cellulose tape definitely should not be used. Once the plants are dry, mounted, and labelled, they can be preserved indefinitely by protecting them from fire, insects, and water. They are safest in air-tight cabinets where insecticides or repellants like dichlorvos (Vapona) or paradichlorobenzene can be maintained around them. Keeping the plants in air-conditioned space (less than 72°F and 50% relative humidity) also will deter most attacks of dermestid and anobiid beetles.

FERN NAMES AND CLASSIFICATION

The number of jokes about scientists and their use of Latin- and Greek-derived scientific names is surely endless. To the uninitiated, these names look like unpronounceable jaw-breakers, and a few of them, like *Eriosorus warscewiczii*, are. (Fortunately for students of North American ferns, that particular species grows in Central America.) Like any foreign language, scientific names are decipherable; most have meanings that explain the plants and also help you to remember them.

The more common ferns and fern-allies of the United States and Canada have true common names bestowed on them over the generations. So that people who prefer not to use scientific names have a ready reference to an English name, the common name of every species, subspecies, and variety in this book is given. The rarer and more inconspicuous species have had common names manufactured for them by botanists. Usually these paraphrase the scientific name; Wooton's Lip Fern for *Cheilanthes wootonii*, for instance. Although scientific names are used for stability, common names do have a life of their own, and sometimes a very long one. A few common names have been used in Europe for hundreds of years, far longer than the scientific names. In many more cases, however, common names are ambiguous and of uncertain application, and so cannot be used reliably in scientific work.

Common names in one language are not meaningful to botanists who use other languages, which further restricts their utility. Scientific names are the same the world over and are not ambiguous in their application. Every species is known by its generic name (a noun) and a specific epithet (usually an adjective, sometimes a noun acting as an adjective). For instance, the Eastern Bracken belongs to the genus *Pteridium* and bears the epithet *aquilinum*. Since this species has been further divided into varieties, it also bears the varietal epithet *latiusculum*. The full name of the plant is *Pteridium aquilinum* var. *latiusculum* (Desv.) Underw. The two abbreviations at the end of the name refer to the first person to publish the epithet *latiusculum*, Desvaux, and the first person to publish that epithet as a variety of *Pteridium aquilinum*, Underwood. The names of authorities are abbreviated according to a standard system, usually to the first consonant of the second syllable. Sometimes initials are used to distinguish people with the same surname, such as D. H. Wagner and W. H. Wagner, Jr.

It was Linnaeus' intention, and an axiom today, that scientific epithets should describe the plant, commemorate its discoverer or someone who had something to do with the plant, or make reference to the region where the plant occurs. Numerous examples of all of these occur in North American ferns. For instance, *Onoclea sensibilis* is the Sensitive Fern (in this case the common name is descriptive, too) and *Blechnum serrulatum* has finely serrate pinnae. *Notholaena lemmonii* was discovered by J. G. Lemmon, an early plant collector in the southwestern United States, and *Asplenium herb-wagneri* honors W. H. Wagner, Jr., who investigated the Appalachian Asplenium complex in great detail. *Aspidotis californica* grows in California and *Polypodium virginianum* occurs in the northeastern United States, including Virginia in its modern and pre-revolutionary war area.

From the time of the Middle Ages until the middle of the sixteenth century, European botanists named each plant they knew in the European flora with a phrase-name (polynomial) such as "*Asplenium frondibus pinnatis: pinnis subrotundis crenatis*," which translates from Latin as "Asplenium with pinnate fronds, the pinnae nearly round, crenate." At the time, this system served reasonably well because the number of plants recognized in the European flora was small. However, when expeditions began to bring back plants from the American and Old World tropics in ever-increasing numbers, the phrase-name system could not accommodate them. New species that were similar to old species required that the old phrase-name be changed and another name be coined for the new species. Thus, there was no continuity of names from one book to another. This caused a crisis in nomenclature until the famous Swedish botanist Carl Linnaeus invented the binomial (genus and species) system of nomenclature, replacing the phrase-name or polynomial with a single-word epithet. This sytem has proved useful to the present time, and there is no indication that it will ever lose its utility.

Linnaeus and the botanists who followed him in establishing the binomial system of nomenclature were primarily interested in the suitability of the names to the plants they represented. Linnaeus himself wrote philosophical treatises on giving plants appropriate names. Although the binomial system of nomenclature was a big step forward, it did not completely solve the problem of different names being used for the same plant. In fact, different names proliferated, especially when wars between the nations of Europe made communication between scientists in different countries difficult. Therefore, botanists quickly established the principle of priority: the first epithet to be published for a species was the one that had to be used. Succeeding epithets were to be placed as synonyms under the earlier epithet. It is possible to trace the course of war and peace in Europe on the basis of the number of synonyms produced.

About the middle of the nineteenth century, botanists began to compile their thoughts and practices regarding nomenclature into a formal document, which today is called the International Code of Botanical Nomenclature (Voss, et al., 1983). The principal focus of the Code is on the stability of names, although some names do continue to change. Because many mistakes were made in naming plants during the past 200 years, it takes a great deal of time and effort to research each name carefully. In addition, it is always possible that a rare book or forgotten paper will turn up that upsets previous conclusions, and so requires a different name to be used. Sometimes, for technical reasons, it is necessary to change the specific epithet when changing the genus. These changes are doubly annoying to non-specialists. However unfortunate or inconvenient they may be, in fact it does not take long to become accustomed to the new names and even to forget the old ones.

TABLE 1.   Hierarchy of botanical scientific names.

Kingdom Plant*ae*
 Division Cormo*phyta*
  Class Polypodi*opsida*
   Subclass Hymenophyll*idae*
    Order Asplen*iales*
     Family Dryopterid*aceae*
      Genus Polystich*um*
       Species imbric*ans*
        Subsp. curt*um*

All plant names fit into a hierarchy of categories, beginning with the kingdom Plantae at the top and descending through many ranks to levels below that of species. Table 1 illustrates this hierarchy, although not all possible ranks are shown; it gives examples of the Latin endings of the names that distinguish the different levels of the hierarchy. The names of genera and specific epithets derived from Latin mostly end in *-us, -a,* or *-um.* Those derived from Greek mostly end in *-os, -is, -ma,* or *-on.* The most commonly used categories are the family, genus, and species. To provide names for minor variation within a species, the categories of subspecies, variety, and form are used. These categories each have a definite meaning (Wagner, 1960b, 1963b) and are by no means interchangeable. Subspecies have distinct or only slightly overlapping ranges and few intermediates; varieties have less distinct ranges and more intermediates; and forms have individuals scattered over the range of a species, subspecies, or variety and may or may not have intermediates.

Linnaeus' classification of the ferns was based largely on characteristics of the sori. His classification brought together unrelated plants into single genera. As botanists of the nineteenth century looked more closely at ferns and especially at characteristics of the fronds and other parts in addition to the sori, they realized that sori of relatively unrelated plants may look quite alike and that it is necessary to refer to several other characteristics to distinguish related species. In the nineteenth century, there were six major attempts, by Presl, Fée, Hooker, Mettenius, T. Moore, and Engler and Prantl, to refine the classification of ferns and fern-allies. In the twentieth century, data from anatomy and cytology and, more recently, from chemistry (reviewed by Cooper-Driver and Haufler, 1983) permitted further refinements to be made by Christensen, Ching, Alston, and Holttum. Much recent thought on phylogeny and classification in the true ferns is summarized in the book edited by Jermy, Crabbe, and Thomas (1973).

The details of a complete classification using several supra-generic ranks are of interest principally to taxonomic botanists; in this book, the genera are grouped only into families. Table 2 lists the families and some higher categories of the ferns and fern-allies; those not occurring in the United States and Canada are in parentheses. See p. 28 for a discussion of the fossil history and evolution of the subclasses of ferns and fern-allies.

Although not all pteridologists think any one classification is correct, the differences of opinion do seem to be growing smaller as data accumulate. Nowadays, the relationships among ferns are more nearly agreed upon, and the differences of opinion tend to lie in what ranks or categories the various groups are given. Some botanists, called "splitters," want to have more orders and families with fewer genera in each, whereas others, called "lumpers," prefer to add another rank like subfamily to express groupings within fewer orders and families.

The most recent and comprehensive classifications to be published are those of Pichi Sermolli (1977), an avowed splitter, Crabbe, Jermy, and Mickel (1975), who tend to have broader concepts, and Tryon and Tryon (1982), who for the most part have broad generic concepts. In time, additional data will permit the present classifications to be refined, and new ones eventually will take their place. As additional evidence is uncovered from fossils, changes in classification or strengthening of the present classification will result.

GEOGRAPHY, HABITATS, AND ECOLOGY OF FERNS AND FERN-ALLIES

Geography and habitats

Ferns and fern-allies naturally do not grow everywhere. On a worldwide basis, most of the over 10,000 species thrive only in moist or wet regions that are not subject to freezing temperatures. About 15% of the world's species grow in temperate deciduous and coniferous forests or in alpine or tundra areas. Only 5% grow in temperate grasslands, semideserts, and deserts. The remaining 80% grow in tropical regions: 10% in tropical deciduous forests and scrublands, 30% in tropical rain forests, and 40% in subtropical and montane rain forests. Because peninsular Florida is the only moist tropical and subtropical region in the United States, nearly 50 of the species recorded for the United States and Canada occur only in Florida; and because the deserts and dry areas of the southwestern United States are a rigorous habitat for ferns, the specialized ferns found there for the most part do not occur elsewhere in the United States and Canada.

Some ferns and fern-allies are widespread; others have restricted ranges. Most, however, have rather continuous areas of distribution in one part or another of North America. These distributions are determined by the dispersability of the spores and the ability of the plants to establish

TABLE 2. The classes, subclasses, and families of living ferns and fern-allies. (Groups not represented in the United States and Canada are in parentheses.)

Rhyniopsida	Rhyniidae	Psilotaceae
Lycopodiopsida	Lycopodiidae	Lycopodiaceae
	Selaginellidae	Selaginellaceae
	Isoëtidae	Isoëtaceae
Equisetopsida	Equisetidae	Equisetaceae
Polypodiopsida	(Marattiidae)	(Marattiaceae)
	Ophioglossidae	Ophioglossaceae
	Osmundidae	Osmundaceae
	(Plagiogyriidae)	(Plagiogyriaceae)
	Schizaeidae	Schizaeaceae
		Parkeriaceae
		Sinopteridaceae
		Vittariaceae
		Pteridaceae
	Gleicheniidae	(Gleicheniaceae)
		(Matoniaceae)
		(Cheiropleuriaceae)
		(Dipteridaceae)
		Polypodiaceae
		(Grammitidaceae)
	Hymenophyllidae	(Cyatheaceae)
		(Loxsomaceae)
		(Hymenophyllopsidaceae)
		Hymenophyllaceae
		Dennstaedtiaceae
		Thelypteridaceae
		Aspleniaceae
		Woodsiaceae
		Dryopteridaceae
		Lomariopsidaceae
		Davalliaceae
		Blechnaceae
	Marsileidae	Marsileaceae
	Salviniidae	Salviniaceae
		Azollaceae

themselves and thrive over the years, although the ability of fern spores to be carried by wind or animals to new regions may not be a major factor. Fern spores are capable of being carried vast distances and probably are dispersed very widely. For instance, they ride hurricane winds from the Caribbean to the southeastern United States. Spores carried long distances can germinate wherever they land if the temperature and moisture are correct; but unless the conditions for growth of the gametophyte after spore germination are satisfactory, the young gametophytes die and sporophytes never appear. Furthermore, sexuality of the gametophytes (Warne & Lloyd, 1980) and sporophyte formation also depend upon certain temperatures, which differ for different species. The probability of successful long-distance dispersal in some fern species, such as *Asplenium platyneuron*, is enhanced by their genetic system, which allows variability to be carried in the chromosomes of a single spore (Crist & Farrar, 1983).

Sometimes spores do germinate and sporophytes are produced far out of the usual range of a species. The outstanding example of an out-of-range distribution in the United States is *Grammitis nimbata*, a Cuban species that was found behind a waterfall in North Carolina, both as gametophytes and sporophytes (Farrar, 1967). This plant survived as sporophytes for a number of years, presumably because the falling water protected the plants from freezing temperatures during the winter. However, it is now likely that the plant is present only as gametophytes, if, indeed, it is present at all.

Out-of-range distributions can be considered as accidentals, the way ornithologists regard birds that are found far from their usual haunts. There have been a large number of accidentals in the United States in the past hundred years. Most of them have been found in tropical or subtropical Florida. Table 3 lists 21 accidentals that apparently are no longer found in the United States (*Grammitis nimbata* may be present only as gametophytes), along with their recorded localities and dates of occurrence or collection. There is no current evidence that these accidentals still occur in the United States, and so they are not included in the floristic treatment in this book. Most of these plants presumably arrived as a result of high winds and hurricanes, established themselves for a number of years, were collected at least once by botanists, and later died out as a result of drought or unusual cold. Doubtless such occurrences will continue, especially during times of climatic shifts that produce mild winters. When the climate turns decidedly colder for a few years, many of the accidentals will disappear.

A few species ascribed to the United States have never been recorded here. *Nephrolepis pectinata* (Willd.) Schott (Darling, 1982) and *Vittaria graminifolia* Kaulf. (Gastony, 1980), formerly thought to occur in Florida, have been shown to be *N. exaltata* and *V. lineata*. One species is not recorded elsewhere in this book because it was discovered for the first time in the United States so recently: *Rumohra adiantiformis* (Forst.)

10

TABLE 3. Accidental ferns and fern-allies formerly escaped (E) or naturalized (N) in the United States.

Adiantum hispidulum Swartz	Rough Maiden-hair	E	GA	(1901)
Adiantum macrophyllum Swartz	Broad-leaved Maiden-hair	N?	FL	(1925)
Campyloneurum latum Moore	Broad Strap Fern	N	FL	(1903)
Ceratopteris richardii Brongn.	Triangle Water Fern	E?	LA	(19??)
Cheilanthes notholaenoides Desv.	—	N	TX	(19??)
Dicranopteris flexuosa (Schrad.) Underw.	Forked Fern	N	AL	(1913)
			FL	(1957)
Diplazium esculentum (Retz.) Swartz	Vegetable Fern	E?	FL	(1959)
Grammitis nimbata (Jenm.) Proctor	—	N	SC	(1966–76?)
Hymenophyllum hirsutum (L.) Swartz	—	N	SC	(1936)
Maxonia apiifolia (Swartz) C. Chr.	Climbing Wood Fern	E	FL	(1921)
Nephrolepis falcata cv. Furcans Hort.	Fish-tail Sword Fern	E	FL	(1919, 59)
Pityrogramma calomelanos (L.) Link	Silverback Fern	N?	FL	(1931)
Polypodium scolopendria Burm. f.	Hobnail Fern	E	FL	(1933)
Polypodium triseriale Swartz	Angle-vein Fern	N	FL	(1924)
Pteris grandifolia L.	Long Brake	N	FL	(1950, 59)
Pteris quadriaurita Retz.	—	N	FL	(1925)
Stenochlaena tenuifolia (Desv.) Moore	Giant Vine Fern	E	FL	(1932)
Thelypteris patens (Swartz) Small	Grid-scale Maiden Fern	N	FL	(1905)
Trichomanes lineolatum (v.d.B.) Hooker	Lined Bristle Fern	N	FL	(1906)
Trichomanes membranaceum L.	Scale-edge Bristle Fern	N	MS	(1900)
Woodwardia radicans J. E. Smith	European Chain Fern	E	FL	(1938)

Ching has escaped and appears to be naturalizing at one locality in Florida (A. M. Evans, pers. comm.).

Disjunction is another curiosity in fern distributions. Instead of having a continuous range, some species have one or more outlying populations hundreds or even thousands of miles from the area of their principal occurrence. For example, a few species of northwestern North America occur in the Gaspé Peninsula in northeastern Canada. Among these cases, *Aspidotis densa* is notable because this species is confined to serpentine (selenium-bearing) rocks, which occur commonly in northwestern North America and also sporadically in the Gaspé Peninsula. A few species that grow on rocks or in rocky soil in the southwestern United States are found in the mountains or piedmont in the southeastern United States, like *Asplenium septentrionale* and *Cheilanthes castanea*. They must have come from spores blown to the east, and have established themselves, however tenuously, at a few localities on certain types of rocks thousands of miles from the main areas of their distribution. *Cheilanthes castanea*, for instance, is known in the southwestern United States from southern Arizona and New Mexico to trans-Pecos Texas and one locality west of Oklahoma City. It is also known from shale barrens in a few localities in southwestern Virginia and one locality in northeastern West Virginia (Knobloch & Lellinger, 1969). Wagner (1972) mentions these and several other patterns of disjunction in pteridophytes, such as north to south, south to north, and east to west.

The main requirements for the growth of ferns and fern-allies, which ultimately control their distribution, are temperature, moisture, and soil pH or type of rock substrate. The latter factors were first studied extensively by Wherry (1961, 1967), a mineralogist who became an outstanding pteridologist and ecologist. The exact requirements may be different in different parts of a species' range. For instance, some species which are tolerant of pH or rock type in general only grow on limestone in the northern part of their range. Weedy species tend to be the most tolerant of growing conditions, whereas rare species with restricted distributions are usually the least tolerant. Most of the ferns in temperate regions grow in soil or on rocks. However, many tropical species, including some that grow in tropical or subtropical Florida, grow on tree trunks or branches. It is common for such epiphytes to prefer certain kinds of trees to perch on. For example, *Cheiroglossa palmata* prefers Palmetto trunks. Needless to say, epiphytic plants are very exposed to the environment and have special adaptations to it. Nevertheless, they may suffer badly or be killed during cold winters and droughts.

All the plants of a region are called its flora. The flora, looked at from the standpoint of its physical structure, rather than from the kinds of species which comprise it, is called vegetation. In the United States and Canada, the briefest classification of vegetation is tundra, forests, grasslands, and deserts. Because there are many kinds of forests, this classification is not really adequate. It is better to subdivide some of these categories so that each subdivision, or floristic province, is relatively homogeneous. Gleason and Cronquist (1964) use 10 floristic provinces (Fig. 3) to encompass the vegetation of the United States and Canada.

Many different habitats lie within each floristic province. The habitats are more narrowly defined than the provinces, and most are characterized by the presence of certain species (e.g., beech-maple forest, oak-hickory forest, white cedar swamp, sphagnum bog). Some habitats are confined to a single floristic province, but others (rock outcrops and weedy and aquatic habitats) occur in several provinces.

Each floristic province has some habitats in which the pteridophytes are abundant and diverse and some ferns and fern-allies that characterize the province. Of course, there is often some overlap in characteristic species from one floristic province to another, just the way the boundaries of the provinces themselves are not sharp, but rather merge gradually with each other over a distance of a few miles.

The Tundra Province, which is treeless, has few species of ferns and fern-allies. No species are exclusive to it, for all found there also grow in the Northern Coniferous Forest Province. *Dryopteris fragrans, Equise-*

12

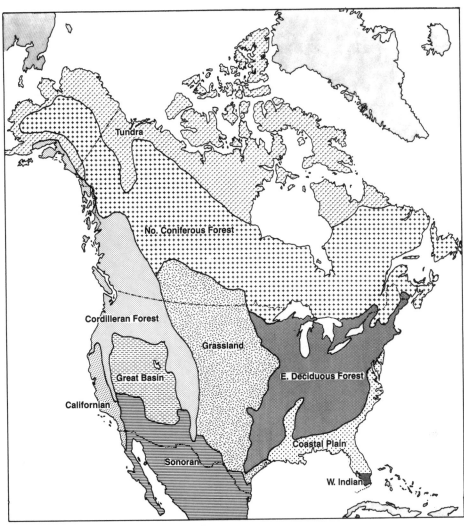

Fig. 3. Floristic provinces of the United States and Canada (after Gleason & Cronquist, 1964, p. 174.)

tum scirpoides, E. variegatum, Selaginella sibirica, Woodsia alpina, W. glabella, and *W. ilvensis* all occur. Alpine areas on mountaintops in eastern and western North America are climatologically akin to tundra, although they differ in being well drained. Some species typical of the Northern Coniferous Forest Province are found in alpine areas, including *Cystopteris montana, Lycopodium complanatum, L. selago,* and *Woodsia glabella*.

The Northern Coniferous Forest Province is a less rigorous habitat than the tundra, and so more species of ferns and fern-allies are found in greater numbers. *Cystopteris montana, Dryopteris fragrans* (also found to the north), *Gymnocarpium robertianum* (also found further south), and *Lycopodium complanatum, W. ilvensis,* and *Woodsia glabella* (all also found further north) are characteristic species.

The Eastern Deciduous Forest Province is yet more temperate, and so shelters even more species. Often they occur in large colonies, especially species of *Athyrium* and *Dryopteris*. *Asplenium rhizophyllum, Botrychium dissectum, Dryopteris marginalis, Lycopodium digitatum* and *Ophioglossum pycnostichum* (both also found on the eastern coastal plain), and *Woodwardia areolata* are all typical. The best habitats for pteridophytes in this province are hardwood swamps with Red Maple, Black Ash, and Yellow Birch trees, white cedar swamps in the northwestern portion of the province, and acid peat or sphagnum bogs.

The Coastal Plain Province has emerged from the ocean only recently in geological time, and so its soils and topography are not very complex; the number of pteridophyte species confined to it is few and includes *Dryopteris ludoviciana* (which also occurs in the West Indian Province), *Lycopodium alopecuroides, L. appressum, L. carolinianum, L. prostratum,* and *Schizaea pusilla*. The most interesting sites for ferns and fern-allies are aquatic: permanent and temporary pools on granite outcrops have several species of *Isoëtes*, and slow-moving streams and sloughs have *Azolla, Ceratopteris,* and *Salvinia*.

The West Indian Province is the most distinctive in the United States for ferns and fern-allies. Many tropical genera are found only in this province in the United States and Canada, where freezing temperatures are rare: *Acrostichum, Actinostachys, Anemia, Campyloneurum, Ctenitis, Lomariopsis, Nephrolepis, Neurodium, Pityrogramma,* and *Sphenomeris*. The hammocks, which are low rises of ground often with moist limestone outcrops that are densely covered with hardwood trees, are the best fern habitat. Many species are rare and many are epiphytes. As in the Coastal Plain Province, aquatic habitats are also interesting.

The Grassland Province is not very ferny; many species are confined to rock outcrops or grow along streams, like *Equisetum laevigatum*. *Marsilea macropoda* and *M. tenuifolia* are characteristic. *Pellaea atropurpurea* and *Selaginella rupestris* both occur on rock outcrops in this province and in the Eastern Deciduous Forest Province. Temporary pools on granite outcrops or muddy depressions provide a good habitat for *Isoëtes*, *Marsilea*, and *Pilularia*.

The Cordilleran Forest Province has for the most part a longer and deeper dry season than does the Eastern Deciduous Forest Province, but along the Pacific coast it is nearly constantly damp to wet. Characteristic species include *Blechnum spicant*, *Equisetum telmateia*, *Pellaea brachyptera* (in drier areas), *Polystichum andersonii*, *P. lonchitis* (also in the Northern Coniferous Forest Province in the eastern United States and Canada), *Selaginella douglasii*, *S. oregana*, and *S. wallacei*. Near the coast of the Pacific Ocean, the best habitat is rich forest containing Douglas-Fir and Vine Maple; *Athyrium*, *Dryopteris*, and *Polystichum* are found abundantly. Low, moist, inland valleys dominated by Western Red Cedar, Black Poplar, and Rocky Mountain Maple support a wide variety of ferns. Serpentine rock outcrops support a peculiar flora of flowering plants and ferns, including *Aspidotis* and some species of *Asplenium*, *Cheilanthes*, *Pellaea*, *Polypodium*, and *Woodsia*.

The Great Basin Province is like the Grassland Province, but is even drier. It has relatively few ferns. Most ferns and fern-allies occur on rock outcrops or along streams. *Selaginella densa* is probably the most common species of pteridophyte, and it is inconspicuous; but only *S. watsonii* is at all characteristic, and it is also found in the Cordilleran Forest Province.

The Californian Province has a Mediterranean climate, with dry summers and wet winters. Many of the ferns, especially in the drier portions of the province, are members of the Sinopteridaceae, able to withstand long periods of drought. Ephemeral species are prevalent, too. *Aspidotis californica*, *Isoëtes orcuttii*, *Ophioglossum lusitanicum* subsp. *californicum*, *Pellaea andromedifolia*, *Pityrogramma triangularis*, *Polystichum dudleyi*, and *Selaginella bigelovii* all are characteristic. Rock outcrops are the best habitat for ferns.

The Sonoran Province is very hot and dry, and so the ferns that are not confined to seepages and streams are adapted to this harsh climate. *Bommeria*, many species of *Cheilanthes* and *Notholaena*, *Pellaea intermedia*, *Phanerophlebia*, *Selaginella lepidophylla*, and *S. rupincola* all are characteristic. Because of the lack of freezing temperatures for long periods of time, this province is second only to the West Indian Province in having genera that do not occur in the other provinces of the United States and Canada. Ledges and crevices of cliffs and rock outcrops, talus slopes, and around the bases of boulders are the best places to look for ferns, many of which are *Cheilanthes*, *Notholaena*, and *Pellaea*. *Adiantum* and other genera are found in moist seeps around springs.

Ecology

Most ferns and fern-allies that live in equable climates today do not seem to be greatly stressed, but those that grow in harsh environments show a variety of interesting adaptations which permit them to survive.

A few ferns show physiological modifications. Kruckeberg (1964) lists a dozen species that will or even must grow on selenium-bearing rocks in the Pacific Northwest. Such plants suffer less competition than do those on other rock types where more plants grow. Cliffs and outcrops of granite, sandstone, and schist are acidic (pH 6 or lower), whereas those of dolomite and limestone are alkaline (pH 7 or higher). In general, the two types support markedly different pteridophytes. Keeley (1981) found that two western American species of *Isoëtes* have a metabolic cycle much like that of desert plants. These plants grow submerged in water, which is very low in carbon dioxide during the day. Their peculiar metabolism makes it possible for them to take in and store carbon dioxide when it is abundant at night and to use it in photosynthesis the next day.

Structural modifications are more prevalent, or at least easier to observe. Rhizome scales have been said to help conduct water to epiphytic rhizomes (Potts & Penfound, 1948) and also must protect rhizomes from drying. Ferns of extreme environments typically have fronds that are adapted to their environment. Those of dry places commonly have finely divided laminae with segments that curl under or roll up and expose a whitish or yellowish, wax-like deposit (farina) on the undersurface (Hevly, 1963). The fronds of some species even separate from the rhizome in dry weather to reduce the amount of water lost from the rhizome and roots. In addition, many species have abundant hairs or scales on one or both surfaces of their laminae that shade the surface and help to prevent water loss (Hevly, 1963). According to Pickett (1923), *Cheilanthes gracillima*, which grows in dryish, rocky habitats in the northwestern United States, has roots up to 1.5 m long and its spores are resistant to desiccation for 18 months. Nobel (1978) found that *Notholaena parryi* plants grow shaded by rocks, which also funnel extra water to the soil in which the plants grow. Some species found in forests where the wind velocity is low have dimorphic fronds, with the fertile laminae held well above the sterile ones so that the spores can be borne away on slight air currents. The fronds of ferns found in bright sunlight typically are leathery to prevent drying and perhaps as protection against strong light.

Although it seems strange to think about the behavior of rooted plants, ferns do exhibit behavior in terms of their life cycles. For instance, Lloyd (1974) has studied the relationship between different mating systems and habitat preferences in pioneer and non-pioneer species of *Sadleria* tree ferns in Hawaii. Although only a few species have been investigated, some ferns exude substances that prevent the growth of gametophytes of the same or other species nearby (Petersen & Fairbrothers, 1980; Munther & Fairbrothers, 1980). This is an obvious method of reducing competition. Some desert ferns, which lack water necessary for fertilization most of the time, can have apogamous life cycles that do not require a film of water to enable spermatozoids to swim from antheridia to archegonia (Hevly, 1963). Both apogamous triploid and sexual diploid races are known in several species of the Sinopteridaceae that are adapted to dry habitats. Although the apogamous, triploid plants can succeed where sexual ones may not be able to, over geological time they are unlikely to persist or to evolve as conditions change. They can be thought of as short-term experiments made by the diploid species. Needless to say, most investigations of gametophytes and sexual behavior have been carried out in the laboratory. Reactions of the plants in nature may or may not be similar. Farrar and Gooch (1975) pointed out some of the deficiencies of conclusions based only on laboratory study and have begun a study of fern reproduction in nature that will add much to our knowledge of gametophyte behavior.

Significantly fewer insects (only 465 species) attack ferns compared to flowering plants, according to Hendrix (1980). Gerson (1979) recorded insects belonging to 12 orders plus mites, millipedes, woodlice, and tardigrades as having been collected on various species of ferns and fern-allies. However, damage occurs both in nature and to cultivated ferns. It is even possible to control some weedy ferns, like *Salvinia*, by introducing insect pests which eat the plants. Although insect molting hormones called ecdysones, which occur in large concentrations in some ferns, were once thought to confer insect resistance on the ferns, Gerson (1979) claimed that this is not the case, because these chemicals are poorly absorbed and rapidly broken down or eliminated by the insects. Apparently neither tannins, which are present in quite a few species, nor cyanide-producing compounds, which are present in a few species, deter insect predators (Balick et al., 1978). However, ferns such as *Pteridium*, which attract ants, apparently are protected from other insect predators by the activities of the ants.

STRUCTURE OF FERNS AND FERN-ALLIES

Ferns and fern-allies are more complicated in external structure (morphology) and internal structure (anatomy) than most people suspect. Eames (1936) wrote the classic text dealing with the morphology and anatomy of pteridophytes. Bierhorst (1971), Foster and Gifford (1974), and Sporne (1975) are more recent summaries. Despite the massive amount of information that is known, most pteridophytes have not been examined in detail, and much of interest remains to be discovered.

The traditional tools of morphologists and anatomists are the dissecting and compound microscopes, along with techniques for sectioning and staining plant tissues so that they can be viewed clearly under the light microscope. In recent years, however, the scanning electron microscope has been used to reveal many details of surface structure, especially of spores. Because of the clarity and depth of field of SEM pictures, especially at magnifications near and beyond the limit of light magnification, botanists today are able to see clearly many structures that were unknown or poorly known in the past.

Since the classical Greeks and Romans, a distinctive terminology has developed to describe the structures of ferns. It is a little different from that used to describe flowering plants (generally stems are called rhizomes and leaves are called fronds, for instance). Some people object to using these specialized terms, but it is best to do so, because they are more precise and comprehensive than the terms available to describe flowering plants.

Rhizomes

Fern rhizomes tend to be inconspicuous, except in some epiphytes; those of terrestrial species are partially or sometimes entirely subterranean. Ferns with erect rhizomes have a crown of fronds that is vase- or basket-shaped. Erect rhizomes, except in the tree ferns, are rarely more than 10–15 mm in diameter. In tree ferns, they may be 60 cm in diameter and, in a few Asiatic species, up to 12 m tall. Most ferns in the United States and Canada have short-creeping or ascending rhizomes; their fronds are borne in clusters. In a few species, short, ascending rhizomes radiate from a common central point (multicipital). At the other extreme, ferns with long-creeping rhizomes have fronds strung out in lines. Most long-creeping rhizomes are 2–5 mm in diameter. The stipes often arise from the upper side of the rhizome or occur in one or more rows laterally on each side of the rhizome. The smallest long-creeping rhizomes occur in the Hymenophyllaceae and are less than 1 mm in diameter.

Rhizomes grow as new cells are produced at the apex. The cells that are cut off behind the apex mature into all the tissues of the rhizome. Lateral apices become fronds and adventitious roots. Some internal cells differentiate into conducting tissues (xylem and phloem) or strengthening tissues (sclerenchyma fibers). The arrangement or shape of the conducting tissues, which collectively make up the stele, are of particular interest. Juvenile rhizomes or those of small diameter usually have a solid cylinder of xylem surrounded by phloem (protostele). Steles of larger diameter commonly have a tube of xylem with soft and/or hard pith cells in the center (solenostele). Where a branch of the stele becomes a leaf trace and diverges into the stipe, a leaf gap is formed. In steles of yet larger diameter, the leaf gaps overlap (dictyostele). Some genera, like *Pteridium* and some species of *Dennstaedtia* and *Pteris* have two or even three concentric dictyosteles (Troop & Mickel, 1968); needless to say, their structure is very complex and difficult to study. Traditionally, a cross-section was taken every few millimeters along the stem, a drawing was made from the cross-section, and the vascular system was reconstructed on the basis of the sequential drawings. Adams (1977), however, used a movie camera to record these cross-sections, which enabled him to trace the course of individual parts of the vascular system upward from their point of origin in the rhizome to their departure into the stipes, without the trouble of making drawings. The xylem of the stele is bounded inside and/or outside by the phloem, those tissues by the pericycle, and the pericycle by the endodermis, which controls the passage of water radially to and from the stele. In the fern-allies, the xylem in cross-section is circular, star-shaped, consists of several bars or patches mixed with parenchyma, or in *Equisetum* forms a series of bundles. A usually thick storage tissue called the cortex surrounds the pericycle in the ferns and fern-allies, and the surface of the rhizome is an epidermis from which hairs, scales, or glands may arise.

Roots

The roots of ferns and fern-allies are adventitious, being formed from the rhizome or sometimes from the stipe, but not from the primary root. They are most conspicuous in tree ferns, where they clothe, thicken, and strengthen the trunk. Roots anchor the plant in the soil and absorb water and minerals. In most species, they are smooth and medium to dark brown. Especially roots of the Vittariaceae bear abundant root hairs, which are extensions of epidermal cells. Presumably they hold water around the roots, as well as expand the surface used to absorb water.

Roots are anatomically simpler than rhizomes. An irregular or star-shaped group (in cross-section) of xylem cells lies at the center of the root. The xylem is partially or entirely surrounded by phloem cells, and the phloem by a thin pericycle from which the branch roots originate. External to the pericycle is an endodermis, which controls radial water flow. A thick cortex and an epidermis form the outer layers of the root.

Fronds

Typical fern fronds consist of a stipe, which joins the frond to the rhizome, and an expanded lamina. The central axis of the lamina is called the rachis if the lamina is pinnate or more divided or the midrib if the lamina is undivided (simple). The smallest fronds are found in *Azolla*, *Salvinia*, and *Trichomanes*. Some of them are smaller than a small fingernail. The largest fronds in the ferns occur in tree-ferns of the family Cyatheaceae, which may be several meters long; no members of this tropical family are native to the United States and Canada, although a few species are cultivated in greenhouses or are grown outdoors in frost-free seasons.

Fern fronds differ markedly from the leaves of flowering plants in that their cells are actively dividing and growing during the maturation of the frond, rather than many of them being preformed and only expanding during maturation. Fronds mature from the stipe base upward and outward. They originate as a low protuberance below the tip of a rhizome

19

apex. The protuberance becomes an apex and elongates, forming first the stipe and then the lamina. Each axis of the lamina is terminated by an apex of its own. Most ferns maintain the lamina apex in young stages rolled up in the tip of a tightly curled fiddlehead (crozier) while the stipe and rachis are being formed. In pinnate or more divided laminae, each pinna and pinnule makes a small fiddlehead of its own. In this way, the lamina apices are protected from drying and other injury. Loss of apices at a young stage usually causes the mature lamina to be malformed. Such abnormalities even have been named as forms or varieties, although they have no genetic basis.

Fern stipes are surprisingly stiff, considering their diameter, which is often small compared to their length. The vascular bundle in relatively primitive ferns typically is gutter-shaped, a shape which is much stronger than a cylinder of the same size would be. In more advanced families, the bundles may be two in the form of a V or may be a series of round or somewhat elongate bundles. In the latter case, the pattern formed by the bundles is roughly U- or omega-shaped. The stipes of many species are further strengthened by a layer of sclerenchyma fibers just under the epidermis.

Fern laminae vary immensely in shape. A few are small and grass-like; others are a meter or more long and are highly dissected. Fronds that are entire to merely lobed are called simple. Those that are pinnate or more dissected are called compound. Most compound fronds are pinnately divided, with opposite or alternate lateral pinnae. A few species have palmate fronds, with the pinnae radiating from a single, basal point. The terms describing the different degrees of dissection are illustrated in Fig. 19. The laminae of most ferns are papery to leathery, several cells thick, and opaque when dry, but the laminae of the Hymenophyllaceae are much thinner. In most species they are only one cell thick between the veins, and so are translucent. Some fern laminae, especially the dissected ones, have free veins that are simple to several times forked. Less dissected laminae often have a polygonal network of veins. In some ferns, one or more free veins lie within each polygon. These veins may be simple or branched. Laminae may be of the same size and shape whether sterile or fertile (monomorphic), or they may be different (dimorphic), typically with the fertile laminae longer than the sterile ones or with the tissue of the fertile laminae contracted. The evolutionary and taxonomic significance of dimorphy was discussed in detail by Wagner and Wagner (1977).

Sporangia, sori, and indusia

Although it is now known that the distinction is less absolute than was formerly believed, the sporangia of ferns and fern-allies have been divided into those that are large, produce hundreds to thousands of spores, have walls several cells thick, and have a massive stalk (eusporangia) and those that are small, produce many fewer spores (usually 64), have walls only one cell thick, and have a slender stalk only one to a few cells thick (leptosporangia). The fern-allies are all eusporangiate, as are the Ophioglossales, Marattiales, and a few primitive groups of higher ferns (Fig. 5). Eusporangia split open, often into two regular halves, and their spores sift out. Advanced leptosporangia also split open into two regular halves, but the act of splitting, which is caused by stresses in the differentially thickened cells of the annulus, causes the sporangium to rear back and throw the spores forcibly from the sporangium. The thickened annulus cells usually are darker in color than the non-thickened cells of the sporangium and are visible as a vertical or (in primitive leptosporangia) oblique line or ridge on the sporangium.

The arrangement of sporangia varies greatly in living ferns. A few tropical species have them thinly scattered over the lamina with the placement of the stalks bearing no particular relationship to the veins within the lamina. The vast majority of species, however, have the sporangium stalks associated with the veins, presumably for more efficient transfer of metabolic products from the veins to the developing sporangia. In *Acrostichum* and several other tropical genera, the sporangia are thickly spread over the entire abaxial surface of the laminae (acrostichoid); although they appear to be randomly scattered, they are in fact often associated with the veins. In most fern genera found in the United States and Canada, few to many sporangia are aggregated into round or elongate sori. Sometimes the sori are terminal on the veins, usually at or near the margin of the laminae (commonly found in the Sinopteridaceae, especially in *Cheilanthes*), or they may be more in the middle of the lamina and the vein that serves them may continue on toward the margin of the lamina, as is the case in *Polystichum*. In some genera or families, notably in *Diplazium* and the Aspleniaceae, the sori are very long and follow along a straight to slightly curved vein.

Many ferns have a protective flap of tissue covering the sorus, which is called an indusium. But some genera, like *Polypodium* and its allies in the Polypodiaceae, lack indusia. These plants are thought to be relatively primitive among the leptosporangiate ferns (Table 2, Fig. 5). However, since genera and species without indusia are also scattered in clearly advanced families like the Dryopteridaceae, it is apparent that the lack of indusia is not necessarily a sign of primitiveness. Some sort of protection for the young sporangia is more usual. In the Sinopteridaceae and other families of the Schizaeales, lamina margins are often underrolled and slightly to greatly modified to form false indusia. True indusia, on the other hand, grow from the surface of the laminae and are found in most genera of the Hymenophyllidae.

The shapes of indusia vary greatly and often serve as a key to the family or genus. Indusia can be divided into three groups: those that are elongate along a vein and have sporangia protruding from one side, those that form an outward-facing flap, cup, or tube, and those that grow from the center of the receptacle and are umbrella-shaped (peltate). Elongate indusia are found along lateral veins on one side of the vein in the Aspleniaceae, on one side but hooked over and back at one end in *Athyrium*, and back-to-back on both sides of the vein in *Diplazium*. Elongate indusia also are found along veins parallel to the pinna costa or pinnule costule in the Blechnaceae, but these indusia always open towards the costa or costule, and not away from it. Several genera belonging to different families have a short flap opening towards the margin; *Sphenomeris* and *Nephrolepis* are the best examples. If the flap bends backwards a bit on either side of the end of the vein, the indusia become kidney-shaped (reniform), as they are in *Dryopteris*. The flap is modified to form a cup over the lamina and sorus in *Cystopteris*. In *Dennstaedtia*, the flap and a section of lamina beneath it fuse laterally to form a shallow cup. In *Woodsia*, a cup-shaped indusium lies wholly beneath and surrounds the sporangia and is present as a rim of hairs or narrow scales, rather than as a complete cup. The indusia of the Hymenophyllaceae are always marginal; *Hymenophyllum* has two short lips, but *Trichomanes* has an elongated tube with a narrow rim or two short lips at the apex. Because the tube is long and the sporangia are produced at the bottom of the tube, the receptacle is modified into a stiff, filamentous bristle that carries the first-formed, older sporangia to the apex of the tube as younger sporangia are being formed at the base of the tube. Eventually the receptacle protrudes from the tube, often by several millimeters. Peltate indusia are found most notably in *Polystichum*, but occur in some species of *Nephrolepis*, too.

Spores

Spores, which are produced in the sporangia, are a fascinating study in themselves. Those of many species and genera are ornamented with ridges, crests, or wart-like or spine-like protuberances. Formerly, using a light microscope, no one could see spores sharply in their entirety. Now that they can be examined under the scanning electron microscope, much more is known about their structure and development. Normal spores are formed in groups of four in most ferns and fern-allies (megaspores are an exception, as are large spores formed asexually in some ferns; see Life Cycle). They have two basic shapes: subspherical to somewhat triangular in outline with a 3-armed suture (trilete), or somewhat elongate to bean-shaped with a single, straight suture (monolete). Trilete spores result when the four nuclei in a spore mother cell lie equidistant from one another in the form of a tetrahedron; the sutures form on the faces where the spores contact each other as they form. Monolete spores result when the four nuclei lie at the corners of a square in a single plane. Spores contain oil droplets and sometimes chlorophyll in addition to their nucleus. In the fern-allies and those few ferns (*Azolla*, *Marsilea*, and *Salvinia*) where there are both small, male microspores and large, female megaspores, the megaspores are reduced to four or one per megasporangium, whereas the microspores are numerous in each microsporangium.

Trichomes

Hairs, scales, and glands that arise from the epidermis of fern rhizomes and fronds are called trichomes. Apparently these structures serve to protect the plants. For instance, hairs and scales prevent drying of the laminae by maintaining a wind-free layer around the laminae and by shading it from the direct rays of the sun. These structures also may deter insects by their texture and unpalatability.

Hairs are always composed of a single file of cells. Usually they are at least two cells long. They vary from short to long, from straight to contorted, and from flexible to stiff (Fig. 24). Commonly they are translucent or whitish, but they may be tan or pale reddish-brown. Sometimes the cell walls where the cells join are thickened, giving the hairs a speckled appearance when viewed with a hand lens.

Scales are by definition several cells wide, although they may have a long apex that is but one cell wide. Dark-colored bristles, which look like stiff hairs, are found in some of the Schizaeidae. Developmentally, they are related to scales and are more than one cell wide at the base. Like hairs, some scales are flexible and others are stiff. Usually they are pale brown, dark brown, or reddish-brown, and they may be of one color or have a dark central stripe with pale margins. Sometimes the pale, marginal cells are fragile and are worn away in age, making it difficult to observe the true nature of the scale margin.

Glands are almost always difficult to see. Typically they consist of a stalk that is a single file of cells and a slightly to greatly swollen terminal cell. Sometimes they lack a stalk, and so look like drops of resin on the lamina surface. In the Sinopteridaceae, glands on especially the abaxial surface of the laminae are usually hidden by copious amounts of farina. The farina presumably reflects light, but may not deter insect attack (Wollenweber & Dietz, 1981). Some other ferns, especially tropical members of the Thelypteridaceae, have delicate, evanescent glands that secrete mucilage. These glands are rarely visible on dried specimens. According to Hennipman (1968), mucilage may carry excess water from the plant or may absorb additional water. It seems likely that mucilage would make the plant unattractive to insects or other animals that might otherwise find young tissues palatable. The minute glands of *Dryopteris* and *Gymnocarium* can be seen with a hand lens because of their slightly colored terminal cell and the lack of any exudate.

Gametophytes

The ferns people notice actually live side-by-side with inconspicuous, minute plants rarely sought or seen in nature. These minute plants, called gametophytes because they form gametes (sex cells) in their male and female sex organs (antheridia and archegonia), usually are no bigger than a finger nail and typically live for only a few weeks or months. In some of the fern-allies and the Ophioglossidae, the gametophytes are massive, irregularly tuberous or turnip-shaped, subterranean, achlorophyllous, and long-lived. In the higher ferns, they are mostly thin, surficial, chlorophyllous, and short-lived (Fig. 4). Sometimes they can be seen on the surface of the ground under or near the plant whose spores gave rise to them, especially in moist or wet areas. A few are filamentous; many others are heart-shaped, and some, especially in the Vittariaceae, are strap-shaped. Needless to say, these gametophytes do not look anything like the fern plants people are used to seeing. In fact, one strap-shaped gametophyte was once described as a liverwort and another, a filamentous type, was described as an alga.

LIFE CYCLE OF FERNS AND FERN-ALLIES

All plants with a sexual life cycle have a means of dividing and segregating their chromosomes at one stage in their cycle and of recombining them through fertilization at another stage. In this way, variability on which natural selection can work is promoted in the offspring, and evolution can proceed. Of course, there are other mechanisms of reproduction and evolution at work, too. For instance, the presence of more than two sets of chromosomes in sporophyte cells or more than one set in gametophyte cells (polyploidy) is very common in ferns and fern-allies. It is, among other things, a system that maintains genetic variability in plants that self-fertilize, as many ferns do (Klekowski, 1966). The significance of polyploidy in pteridophytes has been discussed in detail by Wagner and Wagner (1980). Although fern life cycles have been studied for more than a century, few ferns are known in detail. New life cycle details still are being found (Morzenti, 1962; Evans, 1964). Some plants have blockages to spore or gamete formation, which prevent a normal life cycle from operating. However, many such plants have developed ways of circumventing these blockages. In so doing, they have opened new evolutionary pathways, especially to hybridization, and so have added to their diversity and potential success. The normal life cycle and some of its variations are diagrammed in Fig. 4. Recent information on life cycles in pteridophytes has been summarized by Dyer (1979).

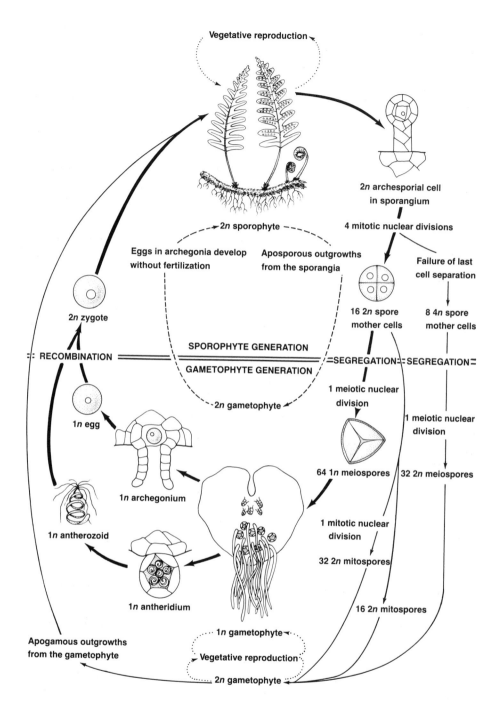

Fig. 4. Life cycles of ferns.

Most ferns and some fern-allies have only one kind of spores (homosporous). In the normal life cycle, sporophyte plants bear sporangia that form spores by meiosis (segregation) of the chromosomes in the spore mother cells (meiospores). The meiotic stage is sought for purposes of chromosome counting; it occurs when the sori are young and pale. Because of meiosis, the spores have half as many chromosomes as the sporophyte plants; diploid sporophytes have monoploid spores, tetraploid sporophytes have diploid spores, etc. The spores germinate and form gametophytes (prothalli) that, depending upon conditions of temperature, light, crowding, and external chemical influences, bear archegonia, antheridia, or usually both (bisexual gametophytes). When the antheridia are mature, spermatozoids are released, which swim in a thin film of water and fertilize the eggs in the archegonia, doubling the chromosome number to what it was in the parent sporophyte. The zygote formed at fertilization divides and grows to form a sporophyte, with a primary root, a short-lived foot attached to the gametophyte, and the beginnings of a rhizome and first frond. In the higher ferns, the gametophyte dies soon after the young sporophyte is formed, and the primary root is supplanted by adventitious roots, which form at the base of each frond as the rhizome elongates. Usually the first few fronds formed by a young sporophyte do not resemble those of mature plants. Not only are they smaller, but often they are less divided or sometimes more divided than the mature fronds. Such fronds are called a heteroblastic series and may yield clues to ancestry or to primitive frond types. For example, the earliest fronds of *Dicranopteris linearis*, an Old World Forked Fern, are not forked, but are pinnate (Wagner, 1957).

Apogamy, the production of a sporophyte from a gametophyte without egg formation or fertilization, is known both in laboratory experiments and in nature. If gametophytes are grown for a long time and are not allowed to form sporophytes because their surfaces are kept dry, eventually they may produce sporophytes from vegetative cells. In nature, such behavior is usually coupled with irregularities in spore production so as to maintain a constant chromosome number from generation to generation.

Apospory, the production of a gametophyte from a sporophyte without meiosis or spore formation, is largely a laboratory curiosity. When plants are starved or parts of plants are grown in nutrient culture, they may, under certain conditions commonly associated with the death of some of their cells, produce gametophytes (Dyer, 1979). Apparently this is a last attempt of a sporophyte to continue the life of the plant under adverse conditions. Aposporous gametophytes produce sporophytes directly from unfertilized eggs.

It is also possible for spores to be formed by a sequence other than the usual four mitotic and one meiotic cell division (Fig. 4). In such cases, 32 or 16 spores form, instead of 64; the spores are likely to be larger than normal and may be spherical. These phenomena of cell division, when coupled with apogamy, result in an agamosporous life cycle, an apomictic alternation of generations. Such life cycles defeat the advantages of segregation and recombination inherent in a sexual life cycle, but polyploid plants maintain variability in their duplicated sets of chromosomes. Agamosporous life cycles permit triploid and pentaploid hybrids, which cannot ordinarily form normal spores, to form spores and hence gametophytes, which can form further polyploids. In addition, some ferns that grow in dry regions have triploid as well as diploid races; this is especially well documented in *Pellaea* (A. F. Tryon, 1968). The triploid plants can pass through an agamosporous life cycle without having water for fertilization, and that is a decided advantage in a dry environment. Only a few species having an odd number of genomes are known to have agamospory. Without it, only vegetative methods like rhizome fragmentation are available, and so such plants are usually very rare.

In addition to reproducing the alternate generation, sporophytes and also gametophytes can reproduce themselves vegetatively. In sporophytes, this is particularly important for sterile hybrids, which otherwise could not live beyond the original hybrid plants. Most ferns and fern-allies reproduce themselves vegetatively by the growth of their rhizomes, which branch occasionally and so form new plants as the older portions of the rhizome die away. Some species of *Equisetum* spread by detached sections of stems, which float and sprout (Wagner & Hammitt, 1970). Some species have bulblets (sometimes called buds or bulbils) on their axes, which germinate before or after dropping from the plant to form new plants.

Many gametophytes will reproduce themselves by outgrowths from their margin if they are old or grown under poor conditions. This is especially true of strap-shaped and filamentous gametophytes. For instance, *Vittaria* gametophytes commonly produce elongate, several-celled gemmae on their margins, which form new gametophytes after they are detached from the parent gametophyte. Six tropical fern species that grow in the southern Appalachians either solely or primarily as gametophytes form extensive colonies by vegetative reproduction. Gametophytes of an unknown species of *Hymenophyllum* subg. *Leptocionium* have been found in western North Carolina, but the sporophytes are unknown. Gametophytes and sporophytes of *Hymenophyllum tunbrigense* are known from South Carolina, and gametophytes and sporophytes of two species of *Trichomanes* are also known from the Carolinas. *Trichomanes* gametophytes are known as far north as northeastern Ohio, Pennsylvania, southeastern New York, and central Vermont (Farrar et al., 1983). Gametophytes of *Grammitis nimbata* have been found behind a waterfall in one locality in western North Carolina. Sporophytes of this species were found when the species was discovered, but have not persisted. Gametophytes of *Vittaria*, perhaps *V. lineata* (Gastony, 1977), occur in grottoes and sheltered crevices, rather commonly in the southern Appalachian mountains, but also in southern Indiana and adjacent Kentucky, as well as in scattered localities in Pennsylvania. The gametophytes of *Hymenophyllum*, *Trichomanes*, and *Vittaria* found in the United States that do not form sporophytes in nature have never been induced to do so under experimental conditions in the laboratory (Farrar, 1978; Gastony, 1977).

Heterosporous fern-allies (Isoëtaceae and Selaginellaceae) and ferns (Azollaceae, Marsileaceae, and Salviniaceae) have life cycles similar to homosporous ferns and fern-allies, but have dissimilar male and female sporangia, spores, and gametophytes. In *Selaginella*, small microsporangia are usually borne toward the apex of the cone and large megasporangia are at the base. In the Selaginellaceae and Isoëtaceae, the megaspores are much larger than the microspores. In some of the water ferns, specialized structures have evolved to insure that fertilization will take place despite water currents that would normally sweep the mega- and microspores and their gametes away from each other.

FERNS AND FERN-ALLIES IN THE PAST

Today ferns and fern-allies do not form a dominant part of the vegetation except in a few tropical and subtropical localities. They were much more important until primitive seed plants (so-called seed ferns, cycads, cycadeoids, and conifers) arose and largely supplanted them during the Mesozoic era, which began 230 million years ago (Table 4). Some fossil ferns and fern-allies lack the gracefulness of living species (they have less lamina tissue, and so their more naked axes are more prominent); nevertheless, they are interesting and important, for they hold clues to the ancestry of living species. Remarkable progress has been made in recent years in the study of fossil ferns and fern-allies, despite the fact that known fossils must be only a very imperfect record of the species that are ancestral to living ferns and fern-allies. T. N. Taylor (1981) summarizes what is currently known; much of the following brief account (but not the construction of Fig. 5) is drawn from his summary.

The ferns and fern-allies have a long, but incomplete fossil record. Some groups can be traced far into the past; others are known only from relatively recent fossils or have no fossil record at all. Not enough fossils are known to fix precisely the origin of the ferns and fern-allies. However, various fern-like plants are known from the Devonian, and the beginnings of the ferns and fern-allies presumably were in these plants and in their progenitors, which probably arose in the late Silurian, some 400 million years ago. The ancestry of the fern-allies and the primitive fern class Marattiidae is better known in the fossil record than is that of the Ophioglossales and the advanced ferns.

TABLE 4.   Geological time table (from van Eysinga, 1975)

Era	Period and estimated age of boundary (*millions of years*)

Cenozoic	Quaternary
	  1.8
	Tertiary
	  65

Mesozoic	Cretaceous
	  141
	Jurassic
	  195
	Triassic
	  230

Paleozoic	Permian
	  280
	Pennsylvanian
	  310 ⎫
	            ⎬ Carboniferous
	Mississippian ⎭
	  345
	Devonian
	  395
	Silurian
	  435
	Ordovician
	  500
	Cambrian
	  600

Precambrian	

To make the transition from water to land in the Silurian, plants had to develop ways of fertilization that required little water. In addition, because land plants are surrounded by air rather than by water, they had to develop an epidermis capable of retarding water loss to the air. At the same time, they had to develop stomata to permit oxygen and carbon dioxide to be exchanged between the plant body and the atmosphere, and land plants of any great size had to develop a conducting system to carry water, minerals in solution, and food throughout the plant. Lastly, they had to develop an internal structure strong enough to hold them erect. By the Devonian, many fern-like fossil land plants had developed these characteristics. These fossils show mixtures of various fern and fern-ally characteristics that are not present in living ferns and fern-allies. Only the more successful combinations of characters escaped extinction over the years. Based on the fossils known at the present time, five classes of fern-allies (Rhyniopsida, Trimerophytopsida, Zosterophyllopsida, Lycopodiopsida, and Equisetopsida) can be distinguished by the position of their sporangia. From these early plants, the ferns and fern-allies as we know

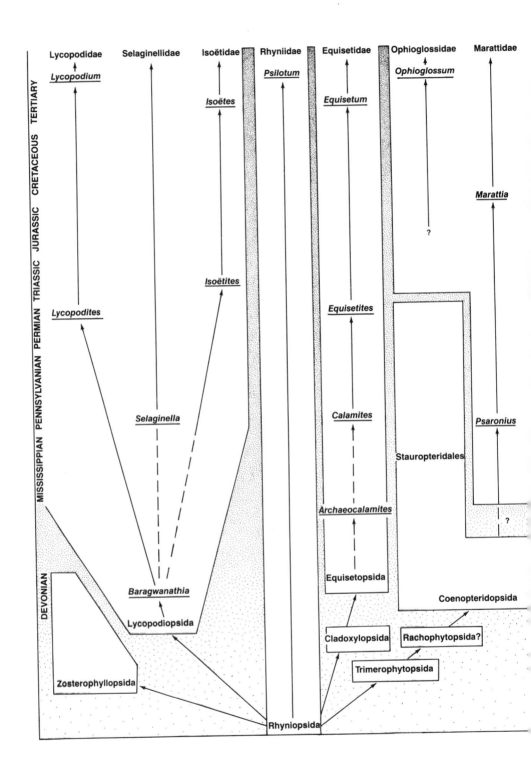

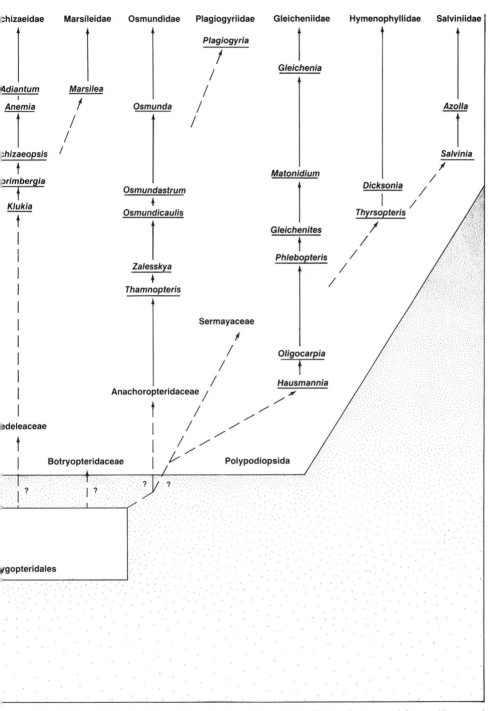

Fig. 5. Possible stratigraphic relationships of the living ferns and fern-allies and their fossil ancestors.

31

them today developed. Figure 5 emphasizes those evolutionary lines that have continued to the present time; some groups known only as fossils are omitted.

Living ferns and fern-allies can be divided into four classes and nine subclasses (Table 2, Figure 5). The classes and subclasses are for the most part distinct well back into the fossil record.

The Rhyniopsida have sporangia borne singly at the tips of main stems in most species. The only living family of the Rhyniopsida, the Psilotaceae, has no fossil record, unlike most other classes and subclasses of ferns and fern-allies. *Psilotum* may be a very advanced and reduced plant in the Rhyniopsida, rather than a primitive one with links to the earliest and simplest genera, as was once thought. Among the Rhyniopsida, *Psilotum* is unusual in having groups of three sporangia laterally fused to form synangia. Because *Psilotum* lacks some of the characteristics of other members of the class and because it exhibits some characteristics of true ferns, it has been suggested that it is more closely related to ancient ferns than to fossil members of the Rhyniopsida (Bierhorst, 1977). The preponderance of evidence, however, indicates that it belongs to the Rhyniopsida, not to the Polypodiopsida (Wagner, 1977).

The Lycopodiopsida, on the other hand, has an extensive fossil record. The members of this class have single sporangia borne in the axil of a scale-like or leaf-like sporophyll. The modern genus *Selaginella* is found little changed in species in the Pennsylvanian. *Lycopodium* also is found in the Pennsylvanian, as *Lycopodites*. The progenitor of this genus may be *Baragwanathia*, found in the lower Devonian and one of the earliest undisputed genera of the Lycopodiopsida. *Isoëtes* is known since the Triassic as *Isoëtites*. The early Lycopodiopsida probably are coordinate with the Zosterophyllopsida, an extinct class of plants found in the Devonian that bore many sporangia laterally along the branches, with or without subtending sporophylls. The sporophylls found in the Lycopodiopsida regularly protect the young sporangia, and so were an evolutionary advance over the Zosterophyllopsida. Apparently the ancient and modern herbaceous Lycopodiopsida were a separate evolutionary line from the tree-like Giant Club-mosses such as *Lepidodendron, Sigillaria,* and their allies, which made up the coal flora forests of the Carboniferous.

The Equisetopsida (Sphenopsida) is represented today only by *Equisetum,* forerunners of which include the tree-sized *Calamites* in the Carboniferous and *Equisetites* in the Triassic. The sporangia in this class are borne in whorls at the tips of lateral branches. The Equisetopsida has been a clearly separate line since the Devonian, and apparently had an origin separate from the Trimerophytopsida, an extinct class of plants that had many sporangia borne in closely dichotomizing clusters on the tips of lateral branches.

The Polypodiopsida (Pteropsida), or true ferns, are more numerous than the fern-allies, both in numbers of plants and in numbers of species. Presumably they are descendants of the Coenopteridopsida through the Trimerophytopsida and possibly the Rachophytopsida, although the latter is of somewhat uncertain position. Living ferns are here divided on the basis of morphology into nine subclasses, of which seven occur in the United States and Canada. It is likely that all nine subclasses belong to five evolutionary lines. The subclasses and evolutionary lines of ferns are separated on the basis of their morphology and cytology, as well as on their separation in the fossil record and their possible connections with fossil ferns. The fossil records of these evolutionary lines vary in their length and completeness. Earlier in this century, it was thought that all ferns with advanced sporangia (leptosporangia) had a common origin, but it is now thought that the development of leptosporangia occurred independently in several evolutionary lines.

The Marattiidae descended from plants like *Psaronius*. The tough synangia of the Marattiidae and the massive eusporangia of the Ophioglossidae make these primitive subclasses of ferns distinct from other ferns.

The Ophioglossidae have a relatively short fossil record. They share some primitive characteristics with the Botryopteridaceae, a primitive and now extinct family of the Polypodiopsida. The ancestry of the Botryopteridaceae, and of the other primitive and now extinct families of the Polypodiopsida, is uncertain; all may have arisen from the Coenopteridopsida, a heterogeneous group of primitive, fern-like plants found from the Devonian into the Permian, but probably not from the known members of this class, which show specializations not found in other true ferns.

Of all the subclasses of ferns, the Osmundidae has the most continuous record, one that dates back to the lower Cretaceous as *Osmundites* (Miller, 1967, 1971), and then to the even older genera *Thamnopteris* and *Zalesskya* (both late Permian). The primitive and enigmatic *Grammatopteris* (also Permian) may be transitional between the other Permian genera of this subclass and members of the very primitive, even earlier, scarcely fern-like Anachoropteridaceae (lower Carboniferous to Permian).

The Anachoropteridaceae may be related to the Sermyaceae, which implies that the Osmundidae are more closely related to the higher ferns than are the Schizaeidae. Although this is an untested hypothesis, because many members of the Schizaeidae do differ in general aspect and in details of their sporangia from the higher ferns, the separation may well prove to be true.

The Plagiogyriidae probably evolved from the Osmundidae, judging by the resemblances between *Plagiogyria* and *Osmunda*. However, there are considerable differences and, in the absence of fossil evidence, the link is by no means certain.

The remaining subclasses cannot be linked firmly with fossil ancestors; the extinct fossil families Tedeleaceae and Sermayaceae may share common ancestors with the modern subclasses, rather than being strictly ancestral to them. Unlike the more primitive ferns, the living subclasses all have leptosporangia.

The Schizaeidae is a large and rather heterogeneous subclass. It has primitive leptosporangia, especially in the primitive families of the subclass. *Norimbergia* (Jurassic) and *Klukia* (Triassic to Jurassic) represent early, now extinct genera in this subclass. Some of the living genera are known as far back as the Mesozoic, such as *Adiantum* (upper Cretaceous) and *Anemia* (mid-Cretaceous).

The Marsileidae, although put in a separate subclass because of the specializations induced by their aquatic habitat, probably arose from the Schizaeidae. If the link between the two subclasses can be established firmly, the Marsileidae should not be considered a subclass separate from the Schizaeidae.

The remaining subclasses, which comprise the bulk of living ferns, all have advanced leptosporangia and probably had a common origin from the extinct family Sermayaceae or closely related plants, perhaps through the Gleicheniidae or through an ancestor of that subclass, which is the only subclass of advanced ferns that can be traced as far back as the Paleozoic.

The Gleicheniidae is known in the Tertiary from fossils that can be placed in existing genera, as well as from several fossil genera that appear to be ancestral to the existing genera. *Hausmannia* and *Oligocarpia*, from the upper Carboniferous, also are attributed to the Gleicheniidae. *Matonidium*, like the present genus *Matonia*, is known from the mid-Jurassic. *Gleichenites* is known from the Triassic.

The Hymenophyllidae is the largest subclass and contains most of the ferns found in the United States and Canada. Its species all have advanced leptosporangia. It has many representatives of modern genera in the Cenozoic. Some modern but primitive members of the subclass, like *Dicksonia* and *Thyrsopteris*, are known virtually unchanged from as early as the Jurassic.

The Salviniidae, another aquatic subclass of greatly modified plants, is known from fossils of *Azolla* and *Salvinia* in the Cretaceous and Tertiary. This subclass may have evolved from the Hymenophyllidae, rather than from more primitive ferns farther back in the fossil record. Until this is known conclusively, the subfamily is best considered to be separate from the Hymenophyllidae.

GROWING FERNS AND FERN-ALLIES

As well as being at home in woodland gardens, native ferns make fine complements to flowering plants in landscape design. Many native species are evergreen, and so make good foundation plants. Some are suitable for borders and rock gardens. Others do well potted on indoor–outdoor terraces and patios. Ferns often require less care than do flowering plants. Their textures, shapes, and shades of green provide interesting contrasts to rocks, paths, fences, foundations, and bright flowers.

Success in raising ferns depends upon how well you can duplicate the soil, water, humidity, and sunlight conditions where they grew in the wild. The more difficult the species is to grow, the closer the cultural conditions must match those in the wild.

Most terrestrial ferns like a slightly acid to neutral soil, the kind that is found in rich woods. The addition of compost or chopped leaves to garden soil is helpful, and sand or gravel may be necessary to lighten hard clay soil. For ferns that require alkaline conditions, reduce soil acidity by adding ground limestone, dolomite, or bonemeal. Those requiring acid soil should have mulched pine needles, oak leaf mold, or superphosphate added to the soil. Garden soil, which is heavy and slow to drain, should not be used for potting ferns in the home or greenhouse. Instead, use a potting mix. One typical mix is four parts by volume perlite and/or white sand and two or three parts of sieved sphagnum moss, peat moss, or leaf mold. Hoshizaki (1975) discusses soil mixes in detail. Epiphytes that are not grown as pot plants commonly are put in hanging baskets filled with sphagnum or tied with sphagnum on slabs of *Osmunda* fiber or Fir bark.

Ordinary mineral fertilizers tend to burn fern fronds and rhizomes. Use only low burn formulations or organic fertilizers like fish emulsion. To be safe, dilute liquid fertilizers more than is recommended for flowering plants. Ferns should be fertilized only when they are making active growth, which means spring and summer for most species.

The water used is important if lime-loving or acid-loving ferns are grown. Tap water may be decidedly alkaline, and so can be harmful to acid-loving ferns. Gardeners used to collect rain to water their ferns. However, rain water is no longer necessarily neutral in some parts of North America, but may be strongly acid and unusable for lime-loving ferns. Tap water should be allowed to remain in an open-topped vessel for a day so that the chlorine it contains evaporates before it is used to water ferns. Water delivered in copper pipes may poison delicate epiphytes. Distilled water can be used, but it is expensive.

Many ferns, especially tropical ones, require high humidity, and so only a few tropical ferns grow really well in the dry atmosphere of an ordinary house. If it is not possible to construct a greenhouse, it is best to grow such plants in a terrarium. Among the ferns that do well in ordinary house conditions, according to Mickel and Fiore (1979), are *Asplenium nidus, Davallia, Humata, Lygodium japonicum, Nephrolepis, Pellaea rotundifolia, Pityrogramma, Phlebodium aureum,* and *Pteris cretica*.

Except for a few leathery sun ferns and many of the Sinopteridaceae adapted to the dry regions and deserts of the southwestern states, most ferns grow in partial sun to full shade. Outdoors they do better under the light shade of trees or a house than they do in full sun. Greenhouses usually need some shading in the summer, and ferns that thrive in a south or west window in the winter often prefer an east or north window in the summer.

A wide variety of ferns and fern-allies can be grown in woodland gardens. For beginning gardeners, it is best to start with species that are easy to grow; usually these are the kinds stocked by nurseries. Excellent instructions for growing hardy ferns are given by Birdseye and Birdseye (1951) and by Mickel and Fiore (1979). Aggressive species with creeping rhizomes that would be difficult to control in formal gardens often can be planted in woodland gardens. On the other hand, species with erect or ascending rhizomes are good choices for formal gardens and as foundation plants. The Ostrich Fern, for example, was often used as a foundation plant at the beginning of this century and still can be seen around old houses in the northeastern United States. Many hardy ferns of the United States and Canada require a cold, dormant period before they will put up a new flush of fronds in spring. Such species cannot be grown indoors or in greenhouses where there is no cold period. If not allowed to become dormant, they slowly dwindle and eventually die. Some terrestrial, hardy ferns have special requirements as to the type of rock present in the soil in which they are planted. Some species grow best on a cobble, which is a mound of earth covered with rocks. Plants are tucked into earth- and pebble-filled crevices between the rocks. Often limestone is chosen for the rock, for there are so many attractive, lime-loving ferns. Cobbles usually are constructed out-of-doors and planted with hardy species, but it is possible to build them in a greenhouse (Wagner & Woodside, 1967) and plant them with tropical species.

For most tropical species, a warm and humid greenhouse during the day is an ideal place to grow. The temperature at night should be 5–10° lower. Large terrestrial ferns, like tree ferns, are too large for most greenhouses, but small and medium-sized ferns can be grown readily in pots. Typically, a soil mixture high in humus is used. Tropical epiphytes are as a rule more difficult to grow than terrestrial species; however, the hardier types will succeed if grown in pots. Epiphytes also can be grown in hanging baskets filled with sphagnum moss or lined with sphagnum moss and filled with a high-humus potting mix. Among the epiphytes, filmy ferns (Hymenophyllaceae) are the most difficult to grow. They require craggy bark with moist sphagnum moss attached with fine plastic line. These and other epiphytes from the mid-altitude tropics prefer cool conditions, and will not tolerate strong sunlight, high heat, or low humidity. It may be necessary to air-condition the greenhouse or bench on which filmy ferns are grown and to provide a nearly constant mist or a supply of dripping water (Farrar, 1968).

Fortunately, ferns are not very susceptible to most insect attack. However, greenhouse and house plants may become infested with scale insects. When a plant is infested, a good method of treatment is to cover it, pot and all, with a plastic bag and put insecticide in the bag. Mild insecticides like pyrethrum are satisfactory when concentrated in a bag and do not endanger the health of the plant being treated. Sanitation is a must if an infested plant is found. Sick plants should be isolated and diseased or insect-ridden fronds cut off and the pests destroyed.

Fungus diseases mostly occur in the greenhouse and are difficult to deal with. Prevention is better than control, which is uncertain. It is important that the fronds be kept relatively dry, particularly in the afternoon and evening as temperatures fall. Also, the soil should not be kept consistently wet unless that is important for the health of the plant. Infected plants should be isolated for treatment or destroyed.

Ferns can be propagated by dividing their rhizomes. This is particularly easy with species that have creeping rhizomes. Newly cut plants may need to be kept in high humidity in a plastic bag until their roots grow and are able to provide water for all the fronds, or some fronds may be cut when the plant is divided. Success is more likely if the plants are actively growing when they are divided. Some species in cultivation have little plants along their rachises that will produce new plants. Growers interested in bringing new species into cultivation usually have to collect their own material from where the plants grow in the wild, or they may grow plants from spores.

Growing plants from spores is not so difficult as one might think, although cleanliness and care are necessary to avoid having the small ferns overcome by fungus diseases. Spores should be sown thinly under fairly sterile conditions onto sphagnum and sand, sterilized soil, or a nutrient solution solidified with agar. The spores must be kept in sealed containers under 100% relative humidity. Germination usually takes a few days to a few weeks. Eventually, small gametophytes (prothalli) are produced. When they are mature, it may be necessary to mist the gametophytes with distilled water to allow fertilization to take place. Young sporophytes will appear shortly thereafter, and should be transplanted to individual pots as they grow. Hoshizaki (1975) gives good instructions for growing plants from spores. A large variety of fern spores is available from the spore banks maintained by several fern societies. A few common species may be obtained from commercial sources.

USES AND MISUSES OF FERNS AND FERN-ALLIES

Ferns and fern-allies have few practical uses and are of relatively slight economic importance. Natural dyes can be made from *Equisetum sylvaticum*, *Lycopodium alpinum*, and *Pteridium aquilinum*. Because of the fats they contain, *Lycopodium* spores have been used to make fireworks; each spore burns with a brief but violent flash. (Try dusting spores from a

Lycopodium cone into a candle or match flame.) Also, *Lycopodium* spores formerly were used like talc to lubricate rubber goods. Several species of Scouring-rush (*Equisetum*) have been used to clean dishes because of the high silica content in their stems. The stems also have been used like fine sandpaper to smooth wood.

American Indians found several uses, among others mentioned by May (1978). *Equisetum telmateia* stems and *Adiantum pedatum* and *Pityro-gramma triangularis* stipes were used for decorating woven baskets. Boiled roots of *Pteridium aquilinum* and rhizomes of *Pteridium* and *Wood-wardia fimbriata* were used in weaving.

Among North American non-Indian people, apparently *Adiantum capillus-veneris*, *Asplenium ruta-muraria*, *Dryopteris filix-mas*, *Equise-tum telmateia*, and *Lycopodium clavatum* have had medicinal uses. Al-though some modern books mention pteridophytes as a source of drugs, such uses should be discouraged. It is impossible to control the dosage or purity of compounds extracted by primitive methods from ferns and fern-allies, and the dangers are likely to outweigh any benefits, most of which apparently are illusory. Some pteridophytes show anti-bacterial or anti-fungal activity (Banerjee & Sen, 1980), but practically none show any anti-cancer activity (Barclay & Perdue, 1976). In all cases, effective drugs come from purification or synthesis of the active compounds the plants contain, not from crude extracts of the plants themselves.

Several—but fortunately not all—uses of ferns for food should be dis-couraged or discontinued. The worst case is that of Bracken (*Pteridium aquilinum*), which is eaten casually in this country but extensively in the Orient, and which apparently is one of the causes of the high incidence of stomach cancer there (Hodge, 1973). Even preparing Bracken fiddle-heads with baking soda and boiling water does not entirely eliminate the carcinogen, which is shikimic acid (Farnsworth et al., 1976). Bracken also causes a variety of cancers in grazing animals, and the carcinogen passes into the milk and to those who drink it (I. A. Evans, 1970). It is clear that Bracken should not be eaten. Also, *Osmunda japonica* Thunb., a close relative of *O. regalis*, is eaten extensively in Japan. Hollenbeak and Kuehne (1974) have isolated osmundalin from North American Royal Fern (*O. regalis* var. *spectabilis*). This compound is an unsaturated lactone and may be carcinogenic, as some other unsaturated lactones are. Some North American books have recommended eating boiled *Osmunda cinnamomea* fiddleheads. Whether or not osmundalin is also present in *O. cinnamomea* is not known at present, but caution is warranted. Most native ferns are likely to be toxic to some degree, and few are eaten. Most ferns are also unpalatable, but a few were eaten by American Indians (May, 1978).

Only one native fern is eaten in quantity, the Ostrich Fern, *Matteuccia struthiopteris* var. *pensylvanica* (Aderkas, 1984). Apparently this fern is safe to eat; there are no reports of toxicity. (However, fiddleheads are such a small part of the normal diet that they have not drawn the interest of investigators.) Ostrich Fern fiddleheads are gathered commercially in upper New England and New Brunswick. They are marketed fresh, canned, and frozen. Gardeners and foragers may want to try this delicacy. The fiddleheads should be picked when they are less than 15 cm tall, and must be cleaned of scales and hairs by rubbing them gently between the fingers. The plants are not harmed by picking unless too many fiddleheads are picked in any one season. After being cleaned, the fiddleheads are ready to be eaten, cooked, or preserved. They taste a little like asparagus, but when fresh are crisper. Fiddleheads may be eaten fresh in salads, simmered for about ten minutes in boiling, salted water and served as a vegetable, folded into omelets, and in general substituted for asparagus. Berglund and Bolsby (1971) give recipes in which fiddleheads are made into soup, steamed in wine, braised, and even made into ice cream. The most comprehensive set of fiddlehead recipes is contained in *Feasting on Fiddleheads,* a publication available for $2.00 postpaid from the American Fern Society at the New York Botanical Garden, Bronx, NY 10458. The pamphlet contains 29 recipes, both original ones and some reprinted from other sources.

Fern societies

The American Fern Society is the oldest scientific society dedicated to the study of ferns. The Society welcomes amateur botanists and horticulturalists, as well as professional botanists. It publishes a bi-monthly newsletter *Fiddlehead Forum* containing information of interest to amateur botanists and horticulturalists, a quarterly scientific periodical *American Fern Journal,* and also has an occasional monograph series *Pteridologia.* The Society maintains an international spore exchange, arranges field trips, and encourages local fern study groups. Information about the Society may be obtained by writing: American Fern Society, Inc., U. S. Nat'l. Herbarium NHB–166, Smithsonian Institution, Washington, D.C. 20560.

Fern societies of aim and scope similar to the American Fern Society exist in several other countries. The British Pteridological Society (c/o British Museum (Nat. Hist.), Cromwell Road, London SW7 5BD, England) publishes the *Gazette,* with technical papers, and the *Pteridologist,* with horticultural notes, as well as a *Bulletin* containing news about the Society. The Schweizerischen Vereinigung der Farnfreunde (c/o Botanischer Garten, Zollikerstrasse 107, 8008 Zürich, Switzerland) publishes the *Farnblätter* with horticultural and scientific papers in German twice a year. The Nippon Fernist Club (c/o Dept. of Botany, National Science Museum, Hyakunin-cho, Shinjuku-ku, Tokyo 160, Japan) publishes scientific papers in its *Journal of the Nippon Fernist Club* in Japanese.

Abbreviations Used in the Keys

Geographical regions of the United States and Canada
N = Northern states and adjacent Canada
    NE = Northeastern states (Maine to Virginia and Ohio to Kentucky) and adjacent Canada.
    NO = Northcentral states (Michigan to Indiana and Minnesota to Missouri) and adjacent Canada
    NP = North plains states (North Dakota to Kansas and eastern Montana to eastern Colorado) and adjacent Canada
    NW = Northwestern states (central Montana to central Wyoming and Washington to Oregon) and adjacent Canada
E = Eastern states and adjacent Canada
    NE = Northeastern states (Maine to Virginia and Ohio to Kentucky) and adjacent Canada
    SE = Southeastern states (North Carolina to Florida and Arkansas to Louisiana)
S = Southern states
    SE = Southeastern states (North Carolina to Florida and Arkansas to Louisiana)
    SP = South plains states (Oklahoma to eastern and central Texas)
    SW = Southwestern states (central Colorado to western Texas and California)
W = Western states and adjacent Canada
    NW = Northwestern states (central Montana to central Wyoming and Washington to Oregon) and adjacent Canada
    SW = Southwestern states (central Colorado to western Texas and California)
P = Pacific states and adjacent Canada
    PN = Pacific northwestern states (Washington to Oregon) and adjacent Canada
    PS = Pacific southwestern states (California)
C = Central states and adjacent Canada
    NO = Northcentral states (Michigan to Indiana and Minnesota to Missouri) and adjacent Canada
    NP = North plains states (North Dakota to Kansas and eastern Montana to eastern Colorado) and adjacent Canada
    SP = South plains states (Oklahoma and eastern and central Texas)
ECP = Eastern coastal plain

ACP = Atlantic coastal plain (Maine to Georgia)
GCP = Gulf coastal plain (Florida to Texas)
SWB = Southwestern border states (western Texas to southern California)
AM = Appalachian mountains
RM = Rocky mountains

Two-letter abbreviations for the states of the United States

AK = Alaska	MT = Montana
AL = Alabama	NB = Nebraska
AR = Arkansas	NC = North Carolina
AZ = Arizona	ND = North Dakota
CA = California	NH = New Hampshire
CO = Colorado	NJ = New Jersey
CT = Connecticut	NM = New Mexico
DE = Delaware	NV = Nevada
FL = Florida	NY = New York
GA = Georgia	OH = Ohio
IA = Iowa	OK = Oklahoma
ID = Idaho	OR = Oregon
IL = Illinois	PA = Pennsylvania
IN = Indiana	RI = Rhode Island
KS = Kansas	SC = South Carolina
KY = Kentucky	SD = South Dakota
LA = Louisiana	TN = Tennessee
MA = Massachusetts	TX = Texas
MD = Maryland	UT = Utah
ME = Maine	VA = Virginia
MI = Michigan	VT = Vermont
MN = Minnesota	WA = Washington
MO = Missouri	WI = Wisconsin
MS = Mississippi	WY = Wyoming

Three-letter abbreviations for the provinces of Canada

ALB = Alberta	NWT = Northwest Territories
BRC = British Columbia	ONT = Ontario
MAN = Manitoba	QUE = Quebec
NBW = New Brunswick	SAS = Saskatchewan
NFL = Newfoundland	YUK = Yukon Territory
NSC = Nova Scotia	

Note: The range indicated in the keys does not or not much exceed the boundaries of the regions, states, or provinces listed above, but very well may not occur completely over the entire region, states, or provinces cited.

How to Use the Keys

Keys, which are a series of paired, contrasting statements, will enable you to identify plants. Most plants will agree with most or all of one statement of a pair and will disagree with most or all of the other statement in the pair. However, hybrids, abnormal plants, and immature plants may not agree well with the statements, and so may not be identifiable using the keys.

If you do not know the family or genus of the plant you wish to identify, start with the Key to the Families of Ferns and Fern-allies. The illustrations cited show in general the kinds of plants found in each family and will help you to confirm the correct identification. Once you know the family, use the key to genera found at the beginning of most families.

To use the keys, read both statements of the first pair to see which one agrees best with the plant at hand. The correct statement will terminate either in the name of the plant or else in another number, which refers you to the next pair of statements that the plant must be tried against. The numbers in parentheses with the statement numbers refer to the preceding statements in the key; this makes it possible to go from the name of a plant all the way back to the beginning of the key. The sum of the statements that apply to a plant often forms a useful, if only partial, description of it.

If you are uncertain which statement of a pair applies to your plant, try continuing on from the more likely statement. If that peters out into all impossible choices, then go back and try the other statement. Use the statements of range in the keys (see Abbreviations Used in the Keys) to include or exclude species by geography when you can.

If you have made a mistake in keying at any level, you still may come up with the name of a plant, although it will be the wrong one. For this reason, when you arrive at a tentative identification, always compare your plant with the illustration and description in this book and with accurately named herbarium specimens if they are available. An asterisk is placed before the species number in the key and description if the species is not illustrated.

Key to the Families of Ferns and Fern-allies

1. Plants bearing expanded fronds (megaphylls) with several vascular strands (only the flattened, needle-like stipe present in *Pilularia* of the Marsileaceae), not needle-like or scale-like; if grass-like, not bearing a single, large sporangium in a swollen base, **6**

1. Plants bearing needle-like or scale-like leaves (microphylls) with a single vascular strand, or the leaves grass- or sedge-like, bearing a single, large sporangium in a swollen base, **2**

2(1). Microphylls grass- or sedge-like, growing in clusters from a 2- or 3-lobed corm or rarely borne singly along short-creeping rhizomes, bearing a single, large sporangium in a swollen base, ISOËTACEAE (**70**), p. 79

2(1). Microphylls not grass- or sedge-like, minute to small, **3**

3(2). Stems obviously jointed, usually fluted, bearing a whorl of scale-like leaves with often deciduous tips above a slightly swollen sheath at each node, EQUISETACEAE (**77, 87**), p. 91

3(2). Stems not or not obviously jointed, not fluted, without a sheath at each node, bearing microphylls spirally arranged along the stem or with two lateral and two smaller dorsal rows of microphylls, **4**

4(3). Stems nearly naked, bearing a few, minute, narrow, scale-like microphylls, PSILOTACEAE (**1**), p. 49

4(3). Stems nearly covered with small, narrow or broad microphylls, **5**

5(4). Sporangia borne in flattened or quadrangular, rarely cylindrical strobili sessile at the branch tips; spores and sporangia of two sizes, the megasporangia larger and basal in the cones, SELAGINELLACEAE (**29, 39**), p. 62

5(4). Sporangia borne in the axils of unspecialized microphylls or in sessile or stalked, cylindrical cones; spores and sporangia of one size, LY-COPODIACEAE (**7, 9, 17**), p. 50

6(1). Plants not floating in water; if rooted in mud, then more than 30 cm long, **10**

6(1). Plants floating in water or sometimes rooted in mud at the edge of water or in dried-up pools; plants less than 30 cm long, **7**

7(6). Laminae at least 5 cm long, dimorphic, the fertile ones pinnate, with narrow segments, held above the broad, entire to deeply lobed (pinnatifid) sterile laminae, PARKERIACEAE (**135**), p. 129

7(6). Laminae less than 5 cm long or absent, monomorphic, **8**

8(7). Stipes several cm long, terminated in laminae resembling four-leaved clover or the laminae absent; sporangia borne in hard, nearly sphericalbodies (sporocarps) on short stalks at the base of the stipes, MARSILEACEAE (**400, 402**), p. 303

8(7). Stipes absent, the laminae sessile on the rhizomes, entire, **9**

9(8). Laminae oval, mostly 5–15 mm long, with obvious, short hairs on the surface exposed to the air, usually bright green, SALVINIACEAE (**403**), p. 308

9(8). Laminae more or less ovate, mostly less than 1 mm long, tightly overlapping (imbricate), lacking obvious short hairs on the surface exposed to the air, often reddish, AZOLLACEAE (**404**), p. 309

10(6). Sporangia small, mostly less than 0.3 mm in diam., delicate, thin-walled, opening into two deciduous, irregular portions (leptosporangia), on expanded laminar tissue, usually borne in separate groups (sori), **12**

10(6). Sporangia large, mostly more than 0.3 mm in diam., firm, thick-walled, opening into two persistent, hemispherical or clamshell-shaped halves (eusporangia), usually scattered on naked axes, **11**

11(10). Fronds mostly 50–150 cm long; laminae medium to dark green, papery, fully dimorphic with the fertile and sterile fronds separate, or partially dimorphic with the fertile pinnae toward the tip or in the middle of otherwise sterile laminae, OSMUNDACEAE (**124**), p. 120

11(10). Fronds mostly 2–40 cm long; laminae pale to medium green (dark green in some species of *Botrychium*), usually somewhat fleshy or leathery, partially dimorphic with the fertile portion a basal, usually erect stalk often taller than the sterile portion, or the fertile portion a short, lateral spike borne along the margins of the stipe just below the expanded portion of the lamina, OPHIOGLOSSACEAE (**94, 97, 106, 112, 116**), p. 101

12(10). Fronds vine-like, scrambling over other vegetation. Pinnae with marginal projections bearing sporangia under protective, indusium-like flaps, SCHIZAEACEAE–*Lygodium* (**128**), p. 122

12(10). Fronds not vine-like, not scrambling over other vegetation, **13**

13(12). Rhizomes very long-creeping, flattened or angled, bearing roots from the lower surface and gently curved stipes from the upper surface. Sterile laminae narrowly oblanceolate, pinnate, the pinnae deeply and sharply serrate, LOMARIOPSIDACEAE (**385**), p. 294

13(12). Rhizomes not as above, **14**

14(13). Fronds erect, grass-like; laminae reduced to a twisted, cylindrical, or angular rachis; fertile fronds terminated by several, small, finger-like, palmately or pinnately arranged, sporangium-bearing segments, SCHIZAEACEAE–*Actinostachys, Schizaea* (**126**), pp. 124, 123

14(13). Fronds not as above, **15**

15(14). Fronds partially dimorphic, with the fertile portion a pair of erect, upright stalks joined to the rachis just below the sterile portion of the frond, SCHIZAEACEAE–*Anemia* (**131**), p. 127

15(14). Fronds monomorphic or fully dimorphic with the fertile and sterile fronds separate, **16**

16(15). Fronds pendent, linear, narrow, grass-like, in compact clumps; sporangia borne in a long, submarginal groove on either side of the midrib, VITTARIACEAE (**217**), p. 179

16(15). Fronds not as above, **17**

17(16). Laminae very thin, only 1 cell thick between the veins, HYMENOPHYLLACEAE (**247, 249, 253**), p. 200

17(16). Laminae relatively thick, more than 1 cell thick between the veins, **18**

18(17). Sori elongate to linear, end-to-end in a single row on each side of the costae (and sometimes the costules); indusia opening toward the costae (or costules), BLECHNACEAE (**390**), p. 298

18(17). Sori round to linear, not end-to-end in a single row on each side of the costae (or costules); indusia present or absent, not opening toward the costae (or costules), **19**

19(18). Sporangia scattered on and between the veins on the entire surface of the fertile pinnae; fronds 1–4 m long, pinnate with simple, unlobed pinnae, PTERIDACEAE–*Acrostichum* (**225**), p. 184

19(18). Sporangia borne in usually distinct but sometimes laterally confluent, marginal or dorsal, round to elongate sori; fronds usually less than 1 m long, often more than pinnately divided, **20**

20(19). Sori marginal or spreading back from the margin along the veins leading to the margin; indusia, if any, not opening toward the margin, often the sori protected by the turned under (reflexed) margin, **31**

20(19). Sori dorsal on the surface of the fronds, occasionally submarginal, round to elongate, rarely confluent, or if marginal, the indusia cuplike, opening toward the margin, **21**

21(20). Sori round (and without or with indusia) or, if slightly elongate, then without indusia, **23**

21(20). Sori greatly elongate, with a flap-like indusium attached along a vein, **22**

22(21). Sori on only one side of a vein; indusia attached to the vein on one side, ASPLENIACEAE (**287, 289, 295, 306**), p. 227

22(21). Sori usually at least partially on two sides of a vein; indusia attached to the vein on both sides or attached principally to one side but curved back across the vein, WOODSIACEAE–*Athyrium, Diplazium* (317, 324), pp. 248, 252

23(21). Laminae fully dimorphic, WOODSIACEAE–*Matteuccia, Onoclea* (315, 316), pp. 246, 247

23(21). Laminae monomorphic or nearly so, 24

24(23). Indusia umbrella-shaped, kidney-shaped, or absent, 26

24(23). Indusia a flap opening toward the lamina margin or a basal cup surrounding the sorus (the cup sometimes dissected into ribbon-like or hair-like trichomes and often appearing absent in *Woodsia*, with persistent stipe bases), 25

25(24). Sori marginal or nearly so; rhizomes (and sometimes the stipes) bearing hairs or bristles, never scaly, DENNSTAEDTIACEAE–*Dennstaedtia, Sphenomeris* (254, 262), pp. 207, 212

25(24). Sori dorsal or submarginal; rhizomes (and often the stipes) bearing narrow to wide scales, WOODSIACEAE–*Cystopteris, Woodsia* (329, 339), pp. 255, 261

26(24). Pinnae or pinnules with stiff, needle-like (acicular) hairs on the upper (adaxial) side of the usually grooved costae or costules (except *T. limbosperma*, with rhombic laminae gradually narrowed at the base), THELYPTERIDACEAE (264, 266, 276), p. 212

26(24). Pinnae or pinnules lacking hairs on the upper (adaxial) side of the often ungrooved costae or costules, or the hairs soft, often with obvious cross-walls, 27

27(26). Laminae ternate or nearly so and 2-pinnate-pinnatifid, the basal pinna pair much the largest, WOODSIACEAE–*Gymnocarpium* (326), p. 254

27(26). Laminae decidedly pinnate, or if ternate, then not 2-pinnate-pinnatifid, 28

28(27). Pinnae articulate; stipe bases with usually a few, small, usually inconspicuous scales; sori borne at the tips of veins in a single, regular row close to the entire to crenate pinna margins, DAVALLIACEAE (388), p. 295

28(27). Pinnae not articulate; stipe bases often with many, large, conspicuous scales; sori borne dorsally on the veins in one or more regular or often irregular rows usually not close to the pinna margins, 29

29(28). Sori indusiate, provided with umbrella-shaped (peltate) or kidney-shaped (reniform) indusia (except *Ctenitis*, with matted, narrow, reddish or blackish scales and jointed hairs at the stipe base), DRYOPTERIDACEAE (345, 350, 352, 381), p. 267

29(28). Sori exindusiate, 30

30(29). Laminae simple to pinnate, POLYPODIACEAE (230, 239, 246), p. 186

30(29). Laminae 2-pinnate or more divided, WOODSIACEAE–*Athyrium* (**322**), p. 250

31(20). Laminae simple. Sori marginal, continuous in the apical portion of the laminae, protected by the reflexed margin, POLYPODIACEAE–*Neurodium* (**227**), p. 187

31(20). Laminae pinnate or more dissected, **32**

32(31). Sori round to somewhat crescent-shaped, marginal, at sinuses between the lobes, protected by a small, tooth-like, reflexed portion of the lamina margin, DENNSTAEDTIACEAE–*Hypolepis* (**257**), p. 208

32(31). Sori not as above, **33**

33(32). Rhizomes hairy; laminae densely hairy (pilose) on the lower (abaxial) surface and/or subternate with the basal pinnae much wider than those above the base; sori protected by the reflexed margin of the segments and by a small, very inconspicuous, flap-like inner indusium facing the margin, DENNSTAEDTIACEAE–*Pteridium* (**260**), p. 209

33(32). Rhizomes scaly; laminae glabrous, scaly, or farinose on the abaxial surface, or if hairy (pilose), then not at all ternate; sori often marginal and protected by the reflexed margin of the segments; inner indusium absent, **34**

34(33). Laminae simply pinnate, with usually linear pinnae 5–25 times longer than wide (pinnate-pinnatifid or 2-pinnate-pinnatifid and with lobes less than 5 times longer than wide in *Pteris multifida* and *P. tripartita*); sori marginal, protected by a continuous, turned under (reflexed) pinna margin, PTERIDACEAE–*Pteris* (**218**), p. 181

34(33). Laminae usually at least 2-pinnate, rarely with linear pinnae; sori marginal or extending back from the margin, protected by a continuous, turned under (reflexed) pinna margin or not, SINOPTERIDACEAE (**136, 156, 161, 163, 166, 168, 174, 196, 203, 207, 209**), p. 130

FERN-ALLIES

PSILOTACEAE
The Whisk-fern Family

There are two genera in the family, *Tmesipteris* (Australasian) and *Psilotum* (pantropical). Of the two or three species of *Psilotum*, only one is found in the United States.

These plants are very primitive; they lack roots and true leaves. Slender, underground rhizomes contain strands of fungal cells between the cells of the outer rhizome layers. The fungi aid in absorbing soil nutrients and may play other physiological roles within the plants. The erect, aerial stems are pale green, glabrous, round, flattened, or fluted, and branch dichotmously several times. In *Psilotum*, minute, narrow, pointed, leaf-like appendages are borne at intervals along the erect stems (in *Tmesipteris* the leaves are larger and more leaf-like). The sporangia are 3-lobed, ca. 1–2 mm in diameter, and are yellowish. The spores are of one size.

The species of Psilotaceae are usually epiphytic in the humid tropics, but mostly grow on fallen tree trunks or stumps in subtropical regions.

1   Psilotum nudum (L.) Pal. Beauv.
Whisk Plant

Rhizome carnose, short-creeping, bearing scattered, erect stems. Erect stems 15–40(75) cm long, repeatedly dichotomous, fluted, glabrous. Scale-like "leaves" minute, subulate, lanceolate, ca. 5–10 mm distant along the erect stems. Sporangia solitary at the tip of very short lateral branchlets along the erect stems, 3-lobed, ca. 1–2 mm in diam., yellowish.

On trees and stumps, on humus hummocks, and palmetto root mounds in damp woods and swamps. Rare. Southern Florida to northeastern South Carolina, southern Georgia, northern Louisiana, and eastern Texas. A disjunct population is known in Sycamore Canyon, Santa Cruz County, Arizona.

LYCOPODIACEAE
The Club-moss Family

There are two traditional genera in the family, *Phylloglossum* (Australia and New Zealand) and *Lycopodium* (world-wide). Some morphological and cytological evidence has accumulated indicating that *Lycopodium* may be broken up into from three to about a dozen genera (Holub, 1964, 1975a; Löve, Löve & Pichi Sermolli, 1977, pp. 1–10) or, more conservatively, into subgenera and sections (Wilce, 1972; Bruce, 1976b). Seven sections belonging to three subgenera are found in the United States and are indicated in the key.

These primitive plants have underground or surficial, long-creeping rhizomes bearing scattered erect stems or short rhizomes bearing clustered erect stems. The creeping rhizomes have few to many scale-like or minute, narrow, simple leaves. The erect stems usually branch dichotomously one to a few times; in a few species they are unbranched or pinnately branched. The leaves are borne in spirals, although sometimes they appear to be in whorls or opposite pairs, and usually are ascending or rather appressed to the stems. Large, yellowish sporangia that are kidney-shaped in outline may be scattered along the erect stems or organized into discrete, sessile or stalked, cones. Each sporangium is borne in the axil of a foliage leaf or a modified, yellowish leaf of a cone. The spores are of one size.

In temperate regions, the species of *Lycopodium* are mostly terrestrial or grow on fallen logs; many tropical species are epiphytic. The temperate species usually are grown in woodland gardens because of the fungi associated with their roots, but some temperate and especially the tropical epiphytic species can be grown in the greenhouse.

The identification of *Lycopodium* specimens sometimes is made difficult because of sun- and shade-forms that exist in various species. In addition, hybrids between terrestrial species are fairly common, perhaps because their gametophytes tend to grow together due to their preference for somewhat disturbed soils.

Key to Lycopodium

1. Erect stems usually not repeatedly dichotomously branched from the base, always scattered along superficial or subterranean, long-creeping stems; plants usually pale green; leaves curved, thin, **2**

1. Erect stems repeatedly dichotomously branched from the base, growing individually or scattered along subterranean, long-creeping stems; plants usually dark green; leaves straight, rather thick (subg. *Urostachya*), **3**

2(1). Largest erect stems not branched or tree-like, with sessile cones; plants not evergreen (subg. *Lepidotis*), **6**

50

2(1). Largest erect stems branched, with upright, sessile or stalked cones; plants evergreen (subg. *Lycopodium*), **11**

3(1). Plants growing on tree branches or trunks; leaves linear-subulate, ca. 1.5 cm long, 1 mm wide (sect. *Phlegmaria*); FL. *8. L. dichotomum*

3(1). Plants growing on soil or rocks; leaves elliptic-oblanceolate or lanceate, acute to acuminate at the apex, less than 1 cm long, usually more than 1 mm wide (sect. *Selago*), **4**

4(3). Leaves reflexed to spreading, of different lengths along the stem (appearing decidedly tufted), 1.5–2.6 mm wide, elliptic-oblanceolate, acute at the apex; E, NO. *9. L. lucidulum*

4(3). Leaves spreading to ascending, of equal length or nearly so (appearing not or only slightly tufted), 0.8–1.2 mm wide, lanceate, acuminate at the apex, **5**

5(4). Sterile leaves 3–5 mm long, 0.6–0.8 mm wide, entire, usually ascending; N. *10. L. selago*

5(4). Sterile leaves 5–8(9) mm long, ca. 1 mm wide, irregularly and distantly serrate-toothed, usually spreading; NC and AL to WI. *11. L. porophilum*

6(2). Cones pendent at the branch tips; erect stems profusely branched well above the base, the branches pinnately divided (sect. *Cernuua*); GCP. *2. L. cernuum*

6(2). Cones erect at the branch tips; erect stems unbranched or scarcely branched near the base, the branches rarely more than 1-forked, **7**

7(6). Fertile stems bearing far fewer and much smaller leaves than the horizontal stems (sect. *Caroliniana*); ECP. *3. L. carolinianum*

7(6). Fertile stems bearing about as many and not or only slightly smaller leaves than the horizontal stems (sect. *Inundata*), **8**

8(7). Leaves entire or nearly so; surface of the erect stems visible, not hidden by the leaves, **10**

8(7). Leaves with conspicuous, spreading, hair-like, marginal teeth; surface of the erect stems hidden by the leaves, **9**

9(8). Horizontal stems arching above the surface of the ground, rooted at wide intervals; erect stems many, equally spaced along the horizontal stems, progressively shorter and sterile towards the apex of the horizontal stems; ECP. *4. L. alopecuroides*

9(8). Horizontal stems creeping along the surface of the ground, rooted more or less continuously; erect stems few, clustered well behind the apex of the horizontal stems, mostly fertile and subequal in length; ECP. *5. L. prostratum*

10(8). Erect stems 5–40 cm long, 1.5–5(7) mm in diam. including the leaves; fertile leaves appressed to ascending, the cones 3–8 mm in diam.; ECP to NE. *6. L. appressum*

10(8). Erect stems 2–7(10) cm long, 4–10 mm in diam. including the leaves; fertile leaves spreading to ascending, the cones 6–12 mm in diam.; N. *7. L. inundatum*

11(2). Leaves slightly to greatly adnate to the branchlets along 1 edge (except not adnate and in 5 ranks in *L. sitchense*), often borne in a single plane; rhizomes in leaf litter or usually shallowly buried in the soil (deeply buried in *L. tristachyum*), usually yellowish, somewhat leafy (sect. *Complanata*), **15**

11(2). Leaves not adnate to the branchlets along 1 side, borne all around the branchlets in 6 or more ranks; rhizomes deeply buried, pinkish or tan, and slightly leafy, or else surficial, green, and very leafy (sect. *Lycopodium*), **12**

12(11). Horizontal stems creeping on or near the soil surface, not deeply buried, leafy like the erect stems; erect stems sparsely branched, not tree-like, **14**

12(11). Horizontal stems deeply buried in the soil, not creeping at or near the surface, with the leaves few and much shorter than those of the erect stems; erect stems profusely branched, tree-like, **13**

13(12). Leaves along the lower portion of the erect stems spreading at a 30(45)–90° angle to the stem; leaves of the lateral branches arranged in 6 equal ranks spaced uniformly around the branches; N, AM. *12. L. dendroideum*

13(12). Leaves along the lower portion of the erect stems appressed or ascending at ca. a 30° angle to the stem; leaves of the lateral branches arranged in 4 long, lateral ranks and 2 shorter ranks, 1 dorsal and 1 ventral; NE, AM. *13. L. obscurum*

14(12). Cones sessile at the tips of leafy, erect branches; leaves acuminate at the apex; N. *14. L. annotinum*

14(12). Cones decidedly stalked, solitary or more commonly in groups of 2–6; leaves with a long, hair-like tip; N. *15. L. clavatum*

15(11). Leaves adnate only at their base, in 5 equal ranks spiralled around the terete stems; N. *19. L. sitchense*

15(11). Leaves slightly to greatly adnate to the flattened stems along 1 side, in 4 ranks, often borne in a single plane, *16*

16(15). Lateral leaves (as seen from the abaxial surface of the branchlets) with recurved, falcate apices; abaxial leaves large, trowel-like, widest above the base; cones subsessile, the stalks almost as leafy as the sterile branches; NFL to NW. *20. L. alpinum*

16(15). Lateral leaves (as seen from the abaxial surface of the branchlets) lacking falcate apices; abaxial leaves triangular from a broad or narrow base; cones distinctly stalked, the stalks scarcely leafy, **17**

17(16). Erect stems monopodial, bearing several dichotomizing branchlets; ultimate branchlets mostly completing their growth in 1 year, so without lateral constrictions; free, apical portion of the abaxial rank of leaves shorter than that of the lateral leaves; NO, NE, AM. *16. L. digitatum*

17(16). Erect stems dichotomous or nearly so; ultimate branchlets mostly growing for more than 1 year, and so with lateral constrictions; free, apical portion of the abaxial rank of leaves shorter than or about equalling that of the lateral leaves, **18**

18(17). Sporangia present in the axil of some leaves along the fertile stalks; adaxial and abaxial branch surfaces both convex; abaxial rank of leaves identical to the adaxial rank of leaves; NE. *21. L. sabinifolium*

18(17). Sporangia absent from the axil of leaves along the fertile stalks; adaxial branch surface convex, abaxial branch surface concave; abaxial rank of leaves different in size and/or shape from of the adaxial rank of leaves, **19**

19(18). Sterile branchlets (1.8)3–4 mm wide including the leaves, not glaucous on the abaxial surface; abaxial leaves much smaller than the lateral ones, their free, apical portion acuminate from a broad base; N. *17. L. complanatum*

19(18). Sterile branchlets 1.0–1.8(2.2) mm wide including the leaves, glaucous on the abaxial surface; abaxial leaves about equal to the lateral ones, their free, apical portion narrowly triangular to nearly linear from a narrow base; NO, NE, RM. *18. L. tristachyum*

2   Lycopodium cernuum L.

Nodding Club-moss

Horizontal stems arching well above the surface of the ground, up to 1 m long or longer, 3–5 mm in diam. including the sparse leaves, rarely forking, rooting only at large intervals. Erect stems 20–80 cm long, 5–9 mm in diam. including the scattered leaves, freely pinnately branched and shrub-like. Leaves 3–5 mm long, 0.2–0.4 mm wide, linear-subulate, spreading to ascending with incurved tips, entire. Cones nodding, slender, 3–10 mm long, ca. 2.5 mm in diam.

Terrestrial in wet meadows, swamp margins, drainage ditches, road cuts, and pine lands in strongly acid soil. Very rare. Southern Florida north to southern and eastern Georgia and west to central Louisiana, always on the coastal plain.

Not cultivated.

3   Lycopodium carolinianum L.

Slender Club-moss

Horizontal stems creeping on the soil surface, 8–12 mm wide including the leaves, freely forking, rooting throughout, densely covered with lanceolate to narrowly ovate-acuminate, entire leaves 3–7 mm long, 1.3–2.1 mm wide, the midribs not obvious under 10× magnification. Erect stems

5–30 cm long, 1.5–3 mm in diam. including the scattered, appressed-ascending leaves, unbranched. Leaves 3–5 mm long, 0.5–0.7 mm wide, linear-lanceate, entire. Cones 1–9(12) cm long, 2.5–5(7) mm wide, the fertile leaves ovate-acuminate, ascending or with spreading tips.

Terrestrial in sphagnous meadows and bogs, roadside ditches, and sandy pine lands in strongly acid soil. Rare. Florida west to eastern Texas and northeast to North Carolina, and in scattered localities to Long Island and central Massachusetts, mostly on the costal plain.

Not cultivated. This species looks superficially like the species of *Lycopodium* sect. *Inundata*, but differs in having more sharply distinct cones and in other characters, which led Bruce (1976a) to separate it and its relatives into *Lycopodium* sect. *Caroliniana*. No hybrids form between the species of these two sections.

4 Lycopodium alopecuroides L.
Foxtail Club-moss

Horizontal stems up to 6 dm long, arching along the surface of the ground, 7–16 mm in diam. including the leaves, occasionally forking, rooting only at intervals, densely covered with spreading, linear-subulate, strongly ciliate-toothed leaves 6–7 mm long 0.6–1 mm wide, the midrib usually not obvious under 10× magnification. Erect stems 10–25(45) cm long, 0.5–1.5 cm in diam. including the ascending leaves, unbranched or with a few branches. Leaves 6–11 mm long, 0.6–1 mm wide, linear-subulate, toothed. Cones 2–6(11) cm long, 0.6–2(2.5) cm in diam.

Terrestrial in bogs, seeps, and moist, sandy pine lands in strongly acid soil. Frequent. Central Florida west to Louisiana and eastern Texas and northeast to Long Island, Connecticut, Nantucket Island, and Cape Cod. Disjunct in the Cumberland Mountains of eastern Tennessee and adjacent Virginia and in western Kentucky.

Not cultivated. This species hybridizes with *L. appressum* to form *L.* ×*copelandii* Eiger and with *L. inundatum* and *L. prostratum*. Hybrids, especially with *L. prostratum*, are difficult to identify.

5 Lycopodium prostratum Harper
Feather-stem Club-moss

Horizontal stems creeping on the soil surface, up to 5 dm long, 7–16 mm in diam. including the apparently distichous leaves, occasionally forking, rooting throughout, densely covered with spreading, linear-lanceolate, slightly ciliate-toothed leaves 3–6 mm long, 0.5–1 mm wide, the midrib usually obvious under 10× magnification. Erect stems 15–35 cm long, 4–8 mm in diam. including the ascending leaves, unbranched or rarely with a few branches. Leaves 7–10 mm long, 0.4–0.8 mm wide, linear-subulate. Cones 4–8 cm long, 1–2 cm in diam.

Terrestrial in sandy and sphagnous bog margins, meadows, and ditches, and in damp, open, coniferous woods. Frequent. Central Florida north to central Georgia, North Carolina, western Kentucky, and west to eastern Texas, mostly on the coastal plain.

Not cultivated. This species hybridizes with *L. appressum* and *L. alopecuroides*. Hybrids, especially with the latter species, are difficult to identify.

6 Lycopodium appressum (Chapm.) Lloyd & Underw.

Southern Club-moss

Horizontal stems creeping along the surface of the ground, up to 6 dm long, 3–15 cm wide including the leaves, occasionally forking, rooting nearly throughout or at intervals, sparsely covered with narrowly lanceolate, sparingly toothed leaves 5–8 mm long, 1–1.2 mm wide, the midribs usually scarcely visible under 10 × magnification. Erect stems 8–30(40) cm long, 1.5–5(7) mm in diam. including the strongly appressed leaves, unbranched. Leaves like those of the horizontal stems, but not toothed. Cones slender, 2.5–7.5(11) cm long, 3–8 mm in diam., the fertile leaves ascending to appressed.

Terrestrial in bogs, sphagnum meadows, wet shores, and sand barrens in strongly acid soil. Common. Central Florida west to western Kentucky, eastern Arkansas, eastern Texas, and southeastern Oklahoma, and northeast to Massachusetts, southeastern New Hampshire, and Newfoundland, on or near the coastal plain. Disjunct at scattered localities in Kentucky, Tennessee, the mountains of North Carolina, and in southwestern Michigan.

Not cultivated. This species hybridizes with *L. alopecuroides, L. inundatum*, and *L. prostratum*, forming a complex of species and hybrids that has been fully researched only in the Great Lakes region and the eastern coastal plain by Bruce (1975), who found that Great Lakes specimens of *L. appressum* belong to two undescribed tetraploid species, at least one of which is present on the Atlantic coastal plain.

7 Lycopodium inundatum L.

Bog Club-moss

Horizontal stems creeping along the surface of the ground, up to 2 dm long, 4–5 mm in diam. including the leaves, rarely forking, the growing tips extending only a few cm beyond the upright fertile stems, rooting nearly throughout or at intervals, sparsely covered with linear-subulate, entire or occasionally sparingly toothed leaves 5–6.5 mm long, 0.5–0.7 mm wide, the midribs obvious under 10× magnification. Erect stems 3–7(10) cm long, 4–10 mm in diam. including the rather scattered leaves, unbranched. Leaves spreading, like those of the horizontal stems, but not toothed. Cones (0.8)2–4 cm long, 6–12 mm in diam., the fertile leaves spreading.

Terrestrial in bogs, on shores of ponds, streambanks, and in meadows, in peaty, sandy, or occasionally clayey, highly acid soils that sometimes are periodically inundated. Frequent. Newfoundland to Alaska south to Maryland, southwestern Virginia, Ohio, Indiana, northern Illinois, Wisconsin, Minnesota, Manitoba, Saskatchewan, Alberta, Montana, Idaho, and northern California.

Not cultivated. This species hybridizes with *L. alopecuroides* and *L. appressum*.

8   Lycopodium dichotomum Jacq.
Hanging Club-moss

Rhizomes short. Hanging stems few, up to 15 cm long, 15 mm in diam. including the leaves, 2- or 3-times dichotomously forking, densely covered with linear-subulate, entire, appressed-ascending leaves ca. 1.5 cm long, 1 mm wide, the midribs prominent under 10× magnification. Sporangia rather inconspicuous at the base of the fertile leaves towards the apex of each branch. Cones absent.

Epiphytic on tree branches and trunks. Very rare. Known only from Fakahatchee Strand, Collier County, Florida.

Not cultivated.

9   Lycopodium lucidulum Michx.
Shining Club-moss

Horizontal stems sprawling and eventually covered by leaf litter, ascending to erect at the tips. Erect portions 10–25(45) cm long, 8–16 mm in diam. including the leaves, 1–3-times dichotomously forking, densely covered with irregularly reflexed to spreading, elliptic-oblanceolate, shiny, evergreen leaves 0.6–1.5 mm long, 1.5–2(2.6) mm wide that are sparsely toothed at the acute apex and are persistent even when dead and brown. Gemmae minute, flattened, apiculate-lobed, borne on small branch-like structures along the stems. Sporangia in distinct zones along the stems. Differentiated cones absent.

Terrestrial in cool, wet woods, on stream banks, and at swamp margins in rich, humusy, subacid soil or epipetric. Common. Newfoundland to the mountains of Ontario south to Georgia, Alabama, Tennessee, Illinois, eastern Missouri, Iowa, and Minnesota, with a disjunct population in northwestern Arkansas.

Attractive in partial sun in the woods garden, but difficult to establish. This species hybridizes with *L. porophilum* and with *L. selago* to form *L. ×buttersii* Abbe.

10   Lycopodium selago L.

Fir Club-moss

Horizontal stems short-creeping on the soil surface, tufted, ascending to erect at the tips. Erect portions 3–30 cm long, 8–10 mm wide including the leaves, unbranched or 1- or 2-times dichotomously forked, densely covered with lanceate-acuminate, ascending, dark green to yellow-green, entire leaves 3–5 mm long, 0.6–0.8 mm wide, the midribs not obvious under 10× magnification. Erect stems 3–30 cm long, 0–2-times equally forking, densely covered with spreading to strictly ascending leaves like those of the horizontal stems. Gemmae minute, flattened, acuminate-lobed, borne on small, branch-like structures along the stems. Sporangia borne singly at the base of fertile leaves ca. 3 mm long. Cones absent.

Epipetric on damp, mossy, acid rocks and in barrens; terrestrial in woods and at bog margins in usually strongly acid soil. Frequent. Baffinland, Newfoundland, and Alaska south to the higher peaks of New England, New York, the mountains of Virginia, West Virginia, North and South Carolina, Georgia, and Tennessee, Michigan, Wisconsin, Minnesota, Colorado, Montana, and Oregon.

Not cultivated. Specimens growing in exposed habitats are compact, with closely appressed leaves, whereas those in sheltered habitats may have ascending or even spreading leaves, and so look somewhat like specimens of *L. porophilum*. This species hybridizes with *L. lucidulum* to form *L.* ×*buttersii* Abbe. This species can be roughly divided into var. *selago* from high-elevation cliffs and mountain tops in eastern North America, var. *appressum* Desv. (Fig. 10) from the tundra regions and western mountains, and var. *miyoshianum* Makino from forests and swamps of northwestern North America.

11   Lycopodium porophilum Lloyd & Underw.

Rock Club-moss

Horizontal stems short-creeping on the soil surface, ascending to erect at the tips or pendent when growing on cliffs. Erect portions 4–12(18) cm long, 8–15(18) mm in diam. including the leaves, 1–3-times dichotomously forking, densely covered with spreading, lanceate-acuminate, slightly shiny, medium green leaves 5–8(9) mm long, ca. 1 mm wide that are irregularly and distantly serrate-toothed. Sporangia borne singly at the base of fertile leaves ca. 5 mm long. Cones absent.

Epipetric on shaded sandstone cliffs and ledges on acidic substrate. Rare. Maryland to southwestern Wisconsin and Iowa south to North Carolina, Tennessee, Alabama, and eastern Missouri.

Not cultivated. This species has been confused with *L. selago* specimens having spreading leaves, but *L. porophilum* has longer sterile leaves, grows at lower altitudes primarily on sandstone, and occupies a more southern range. See *L. lucidulum* for a discussion of hybrids with that species.

12 Lycopodium dendroideum Michx.

Round-branch Ground-pine

Horizontal stems long-creeping, deeply buried, occasionally forking, 1.5–2 mm in diam., rooting throughout, sparsely covered with scale-like leaves. Erect stems 12–30 cm long, tree-like, with several sets of spreading, many-forked branches; erect stems below the branches with mostly spreading leaves. Leaves of the branchlets linear, acute at the apex, in 6 equal ranks spaced uniformly around the stem, with no rank lying straight along the dorsal or ventral side of the branchlet axis. Cones 1.25–6 cm long, solitary or in groups of 2 or 3, sessile.

Terrestrial in moist to rather dry woods, mossy barrens, rocky or sandy areas, and bogs in poor, acid soil. Common. Newfoundland to Alaska south to Virginia, West Virginia, the mountains of eastern Tennessee, Ohio, Indiana, northern Illinois, Iowa, South Dakota, Montana, and Washington.

Forms attractive patches in the woods garden, but difficult to establish and easily damaged by disturbance or over-fertilization.

13 Lycopodium obscurum L.

Princess-pine

Horizontal stems long-creeping, deeply buried, occasionally forking, 1.75–2.25 mm in diam., rooting throughout, sparsely covered with scale-like leaves. Erect stems 15–30(40) cm long, tree-like, with several sets of spreading, many-forked branches; erect stems below the branches with mostly appressed leaves. Leaves of the branchlets linear, acute at the apex, in 4 long, lateral ranks and 2 shorter ranks, 1 dorsal and 1 ventral. Cones 1–6(7.5) cm long, solitary, sessile.

Terrestrial in moist woods, clearings, and sometimes bog margins in fairly rich, subacid soil, and rarely epipetric. Common. Nova Scotia to Ontario south to North Carolina, Tennessee, Alabama, eastern Missouri, Ohio, northern Illinois, and Minnesota.

Forms attractive patches in the woods garden, but difficult to establish and easily damaged by disturbance or over-fertilization. Hickey (1977) has divided this species into var. *isophyllum* Hickey (Fig. 13A), with the ventral row of leaves about the same size as the lateral ones, and var. *obscurum* (Fig. 13B), with the ventral row about 1/2–2/3 as large as the lateral ones. Sun forms of var. *obscurum* are easily confused with specimens of var. *isophyllum*. This species is close to *L. dendroideum*, and it takes some experience and close observation to distinguish the two unfailingly.

14 Lycopodium annotinum L.

Stiff Club-moss

Horizontal stems creeping in the leaf litter, occasionally forking, 1.5–2.5 mm in diam., rooting at intervals, sparsely covered with leaves like those of the erect stems. Erect stems 6–30 cm long, unbranched to narrowly 2-forked. Leaves spreading or reflexed to ascending, 3–11 mm long, linear-subulate to acuminate at the apex, subentire to coarsely toothed. Cones 0.6–4.5 cm long, solitary, sessile.

Terrestrial in swampy to rather dry coniferous, mixed, or rarely deciduous woods, or among rocks in exposed places, in strongly acid soil. Abundant. Labrador to Alaska south to Maryland, the mountains of Virginia, West Virginia, Tennessee, and North Carolina, Pennsylvania, Michigan, Wisconsin, Minnesota, Montana, Wyoming, Colorado, Idaho, and Oregon. Disjunct in northern New Mexico.

Not cultivated. This species has been divided into several rather poorly differentiated varieties on the basis of leaf toothing and posture.

15 Lycopodium clavatum L.

Running Club-moss

Horizontal stems creeping or arching on the soil surface, occasionally forking, 2–3 mm in diam., rooting at intervals, densely covered with ascending leaves like those of the erect stems. Erect stems 10–25(40) cm long, broadly 1–3(4)- times forked. Leaves spreading, 3.5–7 mm long, 0.5–0.8 mm wide, linear-subulate, entire or remotely serrulate, with a long, hair-like, ascending tip. Cones 1.5–11 cm long, solitary or in groups of 2 or 3, on stalks 1.5–15 cm long.

Terrestrial in open woods and grassy areas, rocky barrens, and bog margins, in acid or subacid soil. Abundant. Labrador to Alaska south to Maryland, Pennsylvania, the mountains of Virginia, West Virginia, Tennessee, and North Carolina, Michigan, Wisconsin, Minnesota, Iowa, Montana, Idaho, and northern California.

Cultivated with difficulty in well-drained, acid garden soil; difficult to transplant or establish. In North America, the species is divided by many authors into several, rather dubious varieties based on the number and size of the cones and the length of their stalk.

16 Lycopodium digitatum Dillen. ex A. Braun

Fan Club-moss

Horizontal stems creeping in the leaf litter or on the soil surface, 1.3–2.7 mm in diam., rooting at intervals, sparsely covered with scale-like leaves. Erect stems 15–30 cm long, with several groups of fan-shaped sterile branchlets, these regularly branched usually 4 times. Branchlets close, flattened, dark green, not glaucous, 2–4 mm wide including the leaves. Leaves adnate to the branchlets more than half their length, in 4 ranks, the upper rank narrow, appressed, the lateral ranks broad, erect at the apex, the lower rank smaller than the others, with only the minute, acuminate tips free. Cones 0.5–5 cm long, borne mostly in groups of 3 or 4, on stalks 3–11 cm long.

Terrestrial in dry woods, abandoned fields, clearings, and grassy slopes in rich, subacid soil. Abundant. Newfoundland to Ontario south to Virginia, the mountains of North Carolina, Tennessee, Alabama, and Georgia, Pennsylvania, Ohio, Indiana, Illinois, western Kentucky, Iowa, and Minnesota.

Desirable in the woods garden because of its attractive habit, but transplanted and cultivated with difficulty. Occasionally this species hybridizes with *L. tristachyum* to form *L. × habereri* House, which is intermediate in branchlet width, coloration, and annual constrictions between the parents, according to Wilce (1965). Although this species was long known as *L. flabelliforme* (Fern.) Blanch., Hickey and Beitel (1979) have shown that the earlier epithet *digitatum* must be restored for this species.

17 Lycopodium complanatum L.

Northern Running-pine

Horizontal stems buried deep in the soil, 1–2.7 mm in diam., sparsely covered with scale-like leaves. Erect stems (5)10–30 cm long, with several groups of sterile branchlets, these irregularly branched usually 3 or 4 times. Branchlets flattened, (2)3–4 mm wide including the bright green, not glaucous leaves, with conspicuous annual constrictions. Leaves adnate to the stem more than half their length, in 4 ranks, the upper rank narrow, appressed, the lateral ranks broad, spreading or incurved, the lower rank smaller than the others, appressed, with only the acuminate tip free. Cones 1–3 cm long, solitary or in groups of 2–5, on stalks 3–6 cm long.

Terrestrial in dry woods and clearings, sand barrens, and bog margins, in cool, acid soil. Common. Labrador to Alaska south to New York, Michigan, Wisconsin, Minnesota, Manitoba, Saskatchewan, Montana, northeastern Wyoming, Idaho, and Washington.

Not cultivated. This species rarely forms hybrids with *L. digitatum*, with *L. alpinum* to form *L. × issleri* (Rouy) Lawalrée, and with *L. tristachyum* to form *L. × zeilleri* (Rouy) Beitel.

18 Lycopodium tristachyum Pursh

Ground-cedar

Horizontal stems creeping deep beneath the soil surface, 1.5–3.2 mm in diam., rooting at intervals, sparsely covered with scale-like leaves. Erect stems 15–30(40) cm long, with several groups of fan-shaped sterile branchlets, these regularly 4–6-times branched. Branchlets flattened, blue-green, glaucous, 1–1.8(2.2) mm wide including the leaves, with conspicuous annual constrictions, the leaves adnate to the stem more than half their length, in 4 ranks, the upper rank narrow, appressed, the lateral ranks larger, erect or incurved at the apex, the lower rank smaller, with an appressed, very long, linear, free tip. Cones 1–3 cm long, borne mostly in groups of 2–6, on stalks (3)4.5–9(12) cm long.

Terrestrial in dry, sandy barrens, abandoned fields, clearings, and in usually coniferous woods in strongly acid soil. Frequent. Newfoundland to Ontario south to Maryland, Virginia, the mountains of North Carolina, South Carolina, Georgia, Alabama, Kentucky, and Tennessee, West Virginia, Pennsylvania, Indiana, Michigan, Wisconsin, and Minnesota.

Desirable because of its attractive habit, but transplanted and cultivated with difficulty. Occasionally this species hybridizes with *L. digitatum* to form *L. × habereri* House, which is intermediate between the parents, according to Wilce (1965). Rarely it hybridizes with *L. complanatum* to form *L. × zeilleri* (Rouy) Beital.

19   Lycopodium sitchense Rupr.

Sitka Club-moss

Horizontal stems superficial or slightly buried in the leaf litter, 1–2.7 mm in diam., rooting at intervals, sparsely covered with scale-like leaves. Erect stems 3–10(18) cm long, 2- or 3-times dichotomously forking. Sterile branchlets round, the leaves in 5 spiralled ranks, all similar, adnate to the stem for much less than half their length, with a long filiform-acuminate apex. Cones (0.6)1–2(3.3) cm long, solitary or rarely in pairs, sessile or on stalks up to 3 cm long.

Terrestrial in barrens, montane slopes, and open thickets in acid soil. Frequent. Labrador to Alaska south to Maine, New Hampshire, Quebec, Ontario, Manitoba, Saskatchewan, Montana, Idaho, and Oregon.

Not cultivated. This species rarely forms hybrids with *L. alpinum*, according to Wilce (1965, p. 160).

20   Lycopodium alpinum L.

Alpine Club-moss

Horizontal stems superficial or shallowly buried in the leaf litter, 1.1–2.2 mm in diam., rooting at intervals, sparsely covered with scale-like leaves. Erect stems 3–8(15) cm long, 3- or 4-times dichotomously forking. Leaves in 4 ranks, the ventral ones shorter than the dorsal ones and both ranks appressed, the lateral ones adnate for about half their length, the free portion spreading or appressed with a round to acute, straight tip and the lower lateral edge strongly rolled under. Cones 0.6–2 cm long, solitary, sessile.

Terrestrial on cold, mossy banks, in meadows, woods, and talus slopes in acid soil. Rare. Labrador to Quebec. Also Alberta to Alaska south to Montana, Idaho, and Washington. Disjunct in the upper peninsula of Michigan.

Not cultivated. According to Holub (1975b), who has examined type material, this species hybridizes with *L. complanatum* to form *L.* ×*issleri* (Rouy) Lawalrée, a hybrid more common in Europe than it is in North America, where it is known only from a single collection in Maine.

21 Lycopodium sabinifolium Willd.
Savin-leaved Club-moss

Horizontal stems superficial or shallowly or rarely deeply buried in the leaf litter, 0.7–2.5 mm in diam., rooting at intervals, sparsely covered with scale-like leaves. Erect stems 5–20(25) cm long, 3–5-times dichotomously forked. Leaves in 4 ranks, the dorsal and ventral ranks appressed, slightly adnate, the lateral ranks slightly larger, adnate for about half their length, the free part of the leaves spreading or occasionally appressed, with an acuminate, incurved tip. Cones 1.5–2.5(5) cm long, solitary or in pairs, usually on stalks 1–8 cm long bearing scattered sporophylls with sporangia in the axils, or rarely the cones sessile.

Terrestrial in clearings and disturbed areas. Rare. Labrador to Ontario south to Maine, New Hampshire, Vermont, New York, Pennsylvania, and Michigan.

Not cultivated.

SELAGINELLACEAE
The Spike-moss Family

There is a single genus in the family, *Selaginella* (world-wide), which has been divided into subgenera, sections, and series, most recently by Horner and Arnott (1963). Their classification is followed in the key. Partly it is based on Tryon's (1955) monograph of most western North American species of the genus.

These primitive plants have surficial, usually widely creeping, horizontal, occasionally branched rhizomes. Those species with predominantly creeping rhizomes and branches look a little moss-like at first glance. Other species have scattered, erect stems and resemble miniature trees or fern-like fronds. A few species (Resurrection Plants) have a very short, erect rhizome bearing a rosette of prostrate or ascending, densely leafy stems that curl inward when dry. In most species with erect stems, these branch dichotomously once or a few times or have pinnate branches that branch dichotomously. The leaves along the stems in subg. *Selaginella* are all equal or nearly so and are borne in spirals. In subg. *Stachygynandrum* they are dimorphic, with two larger, ventral ranks spreading and two smaller, dorsal, ranks ascending and appressed to the stems. Aerial roots typically grow from near the base of erect stems or all along creeping rhizomes. These roots repeatedly branch dichotomously near their end. The large, kidney-shaped to nearly spherical sporangia are each borne in the axil of an unmodified foliage leaf or a modified, usually smaller leaf; the terminal cones formed by these leaves are therefore weakly or sharply distinct from the foliage leaves. The spores are of two distinct sizes; single, large megaspores are borne proximally in megasporangia and many, small microspores are borne distally in microsporangia.

The species of the western United States mostly are terrestrial or grow on rocks. In the eastern United States, they are terrestrial, but only occasionally occur on rocks, commonly among mosses. A few species of subg. *Stachygynandrum* are cultivated in Florida; some of these have escaped and become naturalized in the southeastern United States. Virtually all species of this subgenus are suitable for greenhouse cultivation. The species of subg. *Selaginella*, except for the Resurrection Plants, are not commonly cultivated because of their undistinguished appearance and their need for specialized, rocky habitats.

Key to Selaginella

1. Sterile leaves all alike, equally spirally arranged around the stems, in most species with a midrib impressed in the adaxial surface of the leaf; fertile branch tip slightly different (except in S. *selaginoides*) from the sterile portions of the stems (subg. *Selaginella*), **12**

1. Sterile leaves dimorphic, in 4 ranks, the ventral pair spreading and the dorsal pair appressed and ascending; cones sharply distinct from the sterile portions of the stems (subg. *Stachygynandrum*), **2**

2(1). Plants creeping, ascending, or tree-like; lateral branches creeping, spreading, or ascending, not curling inwards when dry (ser. *Decumbentes*), **4**

2(1). Plants forming dense, compact rosettes; lateral branches prostrate or ascending, curling inwards when dry (ser. *Circinatae*), **3**

3(2). Leaves broadly ovate, obtuse to barely apiculate at the apex; leaf margins near the apex with a conspicuous, white band ca. 0.1 mm wide, finely and evenly ciliate near the apex; SWB. *22. S. lepidophylla*

3(2). Leaves narrowly elliptic-lanceolate, acute to acuminate with a very long terminal seta at the apex; leaf margins with an inconspicuous, white band 0.05–0.1 mm wide, entire or finely and evenly ciliate near the apex; SWB. *23. S. pilifera*

4(2). Main stems creeping or ascending, the plants not tree-like or high-climbing, **6**

4(2). Main stems erect, the plants tree-like or high-climbing, **5**

5(4). Plants high-climbing, scrambling over other vegetation, not tree-like, up to 10 m or more long; smaller stems glabrous; lateral leaves thin, ca. 3 times longer than wide; FL. *24. S. willdenovii*

5(4). Plants tree-like, less than 0.5 m long; smaller stems pilosulous; lateral leaves rather thick, ca. 2 times longer than wide; SE. *25. S. braunii*

6(4). Lateral leaves of the main stems 1–2.5 mm long, **8**

6(4). Lateral leaves of the main stems 3–4 mm long, **7**

7(6). Lateral leaves of the main stems 1 mm wide, lanceolate, acute at the apex, ca. 3 times longer than wide, very minutely and evenly ciliolate; SE. 26. *S. kraussiana*

7(6). Lateral leaves of the main stems 1.5 mm wide, ovate, obtuse or round at the apex, ca. 2 times longer than wide, entire; GCP. 27. *S. uncinata*

8(6). Lateral leaves broadly ovate with a round or rarely obtuse apex, ciliate at the base; erect branches from the main horizontal stems (1)2–5 cm distant, the plants forming loose mats; NW. 28. *S. douglasii*

8(6). Lateral leaves ovate-lanceolate with an acute or rarely obtuse apex, entire or ciliolate at the base; erect branches from the main horizontal stems 0.5–1(2) cm distant, the plants forming mats, **9**

9(8). Plants forming small mats usually less than 6 cm in diam.; plants minute, the largest lateral leaves up to 1.25 mm long, 0.8 mm wide; FL. 29. *S. eatonii*

9(8). Plants typically wide-creeping, forming mats much larger than 6 cm in diam.; plants not minute, the largest lateral leaves at least 1.5 mm long, 1 mm wide, **10**

10(9). Leaves obviously white-margined under 10× magnification; lateral branches mostly ascending or erect; GCP. 30. *S. ludoviciana*

10(9). Leaves not noticeably white-margined under 10× magnification; lateral branches mostly prostrate, **11**

11(10). Median leaves elliptic-ovate, acute-acuminate at the apex with the midrib not extending to the apex; E. 31. *S. apoda*

11(10). Median leaves lanceolate, acuminate-attenuate at the apex with the midrib extending to near the apex; MO to MI & QUE. *32. *S. eclipes*

12(1). Sterile leaves spreading to ascending, lacking an impressed midrib visible on the adaxial surface of the leaf; cones distinct from the sterile portions of the branches, their leaves loosely spreading, longer than the sterile leaves (sect. *Selaginoides*); N. 33. *S. selaginoides*

12(1). Sterile leaves appressed-ascending, with an impressed midrib visible on the adaxial surface of the leaf; cones not distinct from the sterile portions of the branches, their leaves appressed-ascending, not longer than the sterile leaves (sect. *Tetragonostachys*), **13**

13(12). Stems mostly creeping or turned up at the apex, forming a loose to dense mat usually less than 4 cm high; aerial roots present all along the stems or the stems pendent, forming loose festoons in *S. oregana*, **19**

13(12). Stems mostly erect or ascending, forming loose or in some species compact clumps usually more than 4 cm high; aerial roots present only at or near the base of the erect stems (ser. *Arenicolae*), **14**

14(13). Leaves of the erect stems 0.15–0.3 mm wide, with the leaf bases about as dark as the stems, long-decurrent on the stems, **16**

14(13). Leaves of the erect stems 0.25–0.35 mm wide, with the leaf bases paler than the dark stems, abruptly attached to the stems, **15**

15(14). Cilia along the margins of the sterile leaves ca. ¼ as long as the leaves are wide; leaf margins and apical seta often white, the setae persistent; SWB. *34. S. rupincola*

15(14). Cilia along the margins of the sterile leaves ⅛ to less than ¼ as long as the leaves are wide; leaf margins and apical seta rarely white, the setae usually not persistent; CA. *35. S. bigelovii*

16(14). Apical seta with a curled and contorted, sometimes deciduous tip; leaf midrib poorly developed and not visible throughout on the abaxial surface of the leaves; NC to GA. *36. S. tortipila*

16(14). Apical seta stout and straight throughout or absent; leaf midrib well developed and clearly visible throughout on the abaxial surface of the leaves, **17**

17(16). Leaves acute at the apex, lacking an apical seta; TX. *37. S. viridissima*

17(16). Leaves acuminate at the apex, with a prominent apical seta, **18**

18(17). Erect branches 5–15 cm long, sometimes pendent, forming loose mats, the branches with 2-pinnate branchlets, wide-spreading, at a 30–45° angle; CO to NM. *38. S. weatherbiana*

18(17). Erect branches 1.5–7 cm long, not pendent, forming tight clumps, the branches appearing to have dichotomous branchlets, strongly ascending, at less than a 30° angle; SE, SP. *39. S. arenicola*

19(13). Leaves on the underside of the stems below the apex gradually attached at a narrow angle by a usually unthickened base, usually not paler than the pale stems, **24**

19(13). Leaves on the underside of the stems below the apex abruptly attached at nearly a right angle by a thickened base, paler than the dark stems (ser. *Sartorii*), **20**

20(19). Leaves of the sterile stems alike, all evenly disposed around the stems, **22**

20(19). Leaves of the sterile stems slightly dimorphic, the ventral ones slightly longer, appressed to the stem and turning upwards at the apex, the dorsal ones slightly shorter, ascending or erect and not appressed to the stems, **21**

21(20). Fertile leaves very short-ciliate at the base; older sterile, ventral leaves occasionally red; marginal cilia of the dorsal leaves antrorse; CA. *40. S. hansenii*

21(20). Fertile leaves long-ciliate at the base; older, sterile, ventral leaves not red; marginal cilia of the dorsal leaves spreading to ascending; TX. *41. S. wrightii

22(20). Sterile leaves acute to round at the apex, thick, distinctly cupped or keeled at the apex; SW. *42. S. mutica

22(20). Sterile leaves acuminate at the apex, thin, plane throughout, **23**

23(22). Terminal seta present on the sterile leaves; sterile branches 1.25–2 mm in diam. including the leaves; cones 1–3 cm long; plants gray-green; NW. 43. S. wallacei

23(22). Terminal seta absent on the sterile leaves; sterile branches ca. 1 mm in diam. including the leaves; cones 2–4 mm long; plants pale gray; CA. *44. S. cinerascens

24(19). Branch tips remaining straight or curling only slightly when dry; branches radially symmetrical or slightly dorsiventrally asymmetrical (ser. *Rupestres*), **27**

24(19). Branch tips curling up when dry; branches always strongly dorsiventrally asymmetrical (ser. *Eremophilae*), **25**

25(24). Apical seta of the leaves irregularly twisted, delicate, usually deciduous, the leaves appearing acute or round at the apex; AZ to CA. 45. S. eremophila

25(24). Apical seta of leaves straight, stiff, usually persistent but sometimes broken off, the leaves appearing acuminate-attenuate at the apex, **26**

26(25). Apical seta of the leaves 0.5–1 mm long, persistent; leaves on the ventral side of the stems linear-lanceate, broadest at or very near the base; OK to NM. *46. S. peruviana

26(25). Apical seta of the leaves 0.1–0.3 mm long, mostly persistent, but sometimes broken off; leaves on the ventral side of the stems linear-lanceolate, broadest above the base; TX to AZ. 47. S. arizonica

27(24). Plants epiphytic or rarely epipetric, usually forming long, loose, pendent festoons; branches distant, gently curved; PN. 48. S. oregana

27(24). Plants usually epipetric or terrestrial, forming loose to dense mats, **28**

28(27). Plants forming mostly loose or compact mats 2–5 cm high; branches mostly 1–3 cm long, not or only slightly intertwined, not fragile and readily fragmenting, **31**

28(27). Plants forming mostly dense, very compact mats ca. 1 cm high; branches mostly 0.5(1) cm long, greatly intertwined, fragile and readily fragmenting, **29**

29(28). Sterile leaves with apical setae absent or less than 0.25 mm long and lacking cilia; SW. *49. S. utahensis

29(28). Sterile leaves with apical setae 0.2–1 mm long and bearing short, ascending to appressed cilia, **30**

30(29). Leaves at the apex of sterile branches each with a seta up to ⅓ as long as the leaf, the setae 0.2–1 mm long, forming a rather conspicuous, whitish tuft; PS. *50. S. asprella*

30(29). Leaves at the apex of sterile branches each with a seta less than ¼ as long as the leaf, the setae ca. 0.25 mm long, not forming a conspicuous, whitish tuft; PS. *51. S. leucobryoides*

31(28). Plants forming open, loose, flat mats; branchlets rather distant, **33**

31(28). Plants forming dense, flat, or rounded mats; branchlets closely spaced, **32**

32(31). Apical seta of the sterile leaves ca. 1 mm long, white or whitish; mats flat; leaves on the ventral sides of the stems decidedly longer than those of the dorsal side; W. 52. *S. densa*

32(31). Apical seta of the sterile leaves ca. 0.25(0.5) mm long, pale green like the lamina; mats rounded, cushion-like; leaves on the ventral sides of the stems not or only slightly longer than those of the dorsal side; W. 53. *S. watsonii*

33(31). Apical seta of the sterile leaves greenish, 1–2 mm long, entire or with a few very short, ascending cilia; sterile leaves long-acuminate at the apex, very gradually tapering into the terminal seta; SW. *54. S. underwoodii*

33(31). Apical seta of the sterile leaves white to tan, 0.25–1 mm long, with many short to long, ascending cilia; sterile leaves acute or acuminate at the apex, abruptly tapering into the terminal seta, **34**

34(33). Apical seta of sterile leaves 0.75–1 mm long, with spreading to laxly ascending lateral cilia; E, C. 55. *S. rupestris*

34(33). Apical seta of sterile leaves 0.25–0.5 mm long, with ascending lateral cilia; AK. *56. S. sibirica*

22   Selaginella lepidophylla (Hook. & Grev.) Spring
Resurrection Plant

Plants rosettes, with lateral stems radiating from a short, central, erect rhizome. Lateral stems mostly prostrate, up to 10 cm long, pinnately branched, the branch tips curling inwards when dry. Ventral 2 longitudinal rows of leaves broadly ovate, ca. 1.25 mm long, 1 mm wide, obtuse at the apex, finely and evenly ciliate along the margin, tightly imbricate, commonly dark orange-brown shading to pale margins. Dorsal 2 longitudinal rows of leaves orbicular to broadly ovate, 0.75–1.25 mm long and wide, round to cuspidate at the apex, finely and evenly ciliate along the margin, tightly imbricate, green except for the conspicuous, white, marginal band ca. 0.1 mm wide. Cones 2–10 mm long, tetragonal.

Terrestrial on dry, north-facing limestone talus slopes, bluffs, and ledges, especially under and around boulders. Rare. Western Texas to southern and central New Mexico.

Occasionally cultivated in greenhouses, or even maintained when it is dead, since it uncurls and appears to revive when wetted.

*23   Selaginella pilifera A. Braun
Resurrection Plant

Plants rosettes, with lateral stems radiating from a short, central, erect rhizome. Lateral stems mostly prostrate, up to 8 cm long, dichotomously branched, the entire lateral stems forming an erect cluster when dry. Ventral 2 longitudinal rows of leaves elliptic-ovate, ca. 2 mm long (excluding the apical seta), 1 mm wide, acute to acuminate at the apex with a terminal seta 0.5–1 times as long as the remainder of the leaf, entire to finely and evenly ciliate near the apex, always ciliate towards the base, imbricate but not tightly so, pale green with an inconspicuous, white marginal band 0.05–0.1 mm wide. Dorsal 2 longitudinal rows of leaves elliptic-lanceolate, slightly asymmetrical, medium green with an inconspicuous white marginal band, otherwise like the leaves of the ventral surface. Cones 5–10 mm long, tetragonal.

Epipetric on dry, limestone rocks and cliff faces. Occasional. Western Texas to southeastern New Mexico.

Not cultivated. Morton (1939) divided this species into var. *pilifera*, with the branches including the leaves ca. 3 mm wide and the terminal leaf setae ca. ⅓ as long as the leaves, and var. *pringlei* (Baker) Morton, with the branches including the leaves ca. 4 mm wide and the terminal leaf setae ca. ½ as long as the leaves.

24   Selaginella willdenovii (Desv. in Poir.) Baker
Vine Spike-moss

Plants vine-like, the main stems high-climbing or scrambling over vegetation, up to 10 m long. Branches and branchlets pinnate, the smaller axes glabrous. Lateral leaves quadrangular, slightly auriculate at the ventral base, round to obtuse at the apex, ca. 3 times longer than wide, membranaceous. Median leaves asymmetrical, acute at the apex. Cones 2–12 mm long, tetragonal, with broadly ovate, scarcely pointed leaves.

Terrestrial. Escaped or naturalized, known only from Chinsegut Hill, Hernando Co., and Paradise Key, Dade Co., in central and southern Florida. Very rare.

Commonly cultivated in Florida and elsewhere in greenhouses.

*25 Selaginella braunii Baker

Treelet Spike-moss

Plants erect, tree-like, in linear groups from a long-creeping underground rhizome, up to 0.5 m long. Branches and branchlets pinnate, the smaller axes pilosulous. Lateral leaves quadrangular-ovate, not at all auriculate at the ventral base, round at the apex, ca. 2 times longer than wide, thick. Median leaves asymmetrical, acuminate-subulate at the apex. Cones 2–8 mm long, tetragonal, with ovate-acuminate, decidedly pointed leaves.

Terrestrial. Naturalized in an old churchyard near St. Marys, Camden Co., southeastern Georgia, according to Maxon (1937), and established in West Feliciana Parish, Louisiana, according to Thieret (1980, p. 41). Also known from New Hanover Co., North Carolina. Very rare.

Commonly cultivated in Florida, southern Georgia, and elsewhere in greenhouses.

26 Selaginella kraussiana (Kunze) A. Braun

Krauss' Spike-moss

Horizontal rhizomes long-creeping, 4–5 mm wide including the very distant lateral leaves. Erect stems 1.5–6 cm long, pseudodichotomously (appearing somewhat pinnately) branched. Branchlets ca. 3.5–4 mm wide including the rather closely spaced lateral leaves. Lateral leaves elliptic-lanceolate, 2.5—3 mm long, 0.8–1 mm wide (ca. ¼ smaller on the branchlets), minutely and evenly ciliolate. Cones tetragonal, 2–12 mm long, 1 mm wide.

Terrestrial on riverbanks, along lake margins, and in well watered lawns. Naturalized in central Georgia and probably farther south and west; adventive as far north as coastal central California and northern Virginia. Very rare.

Cultivated in greenhouses. Several decorative cultivated varieties are known.

27 Selaginella uncinata Spring

Hooked Spike-moss

Horizontal rhizomes long-creeping, 6–8 mm wide including the very distant lateral leaves. Erect stems 1.5–6(9) cm long, pseudodichotomously (appearing somewhat pinnately) branched. Branchlets ca. 4 mm wide including the closely spaced lateral leaves. Lateral leaves ovate-oblong, 3–4 mm long, 1.5–2 mm wide (ca. ⅓ smaller on the branchlets). Cones tetragonal, 3–16 mm long, 1.5 mm wide.

Terrestrial. Escaped from cultivation or naturalized in southern Louisiana, Decatur Co., Georgia, and perhaps eastward into Florida. Very rare.

Cultivated outdoors in the southeasternmost United States and elsewhere in greenhouses.

28   Selaginella douglasii (Hook. & Grev.) Spring
Douglas' Spike-moss

Horizontal rhizomes long-creeping, 4–5 mm wide including the distant lateral leaves. Erect stems 2–6(9) cm long, pseudodichotomously (appearing somewhat pinnately branched. Branchlets 3.5–4 mm wide including the rather distant lateral leaves. Lateral leaves ovate-oblong, 2 mm long, 1.25–1.5 mm wide (ca. ⅓ smaller on the branchlets), long-ciliate at the base. Median leaves ca. 1.5 mm long, 0.7 mm wide (ca. ⅓ smaller on the branchlets). Cones 5–18 mm long, 1.5 mm wide.

Epipetric on cliff faces and shady rocks, often along river banks; occasionally terrestrial. Occasional. Lower Columbia River gorge of Washington and Oregon. Disjunct in central Idaho.

Cultivated only in greenhouses.

29   Selaginella eatonii Hieron. ex Small
Eaton's Spike-moss

Horizontal rhizomes creeping, 2–3 mm wide including the rather closely spaced lateral leaves. Lateral stems creeping or ascending, not very erect, 2–10 mm long, unbranched or pseudodichotomously (appearing somewhat pinnately) branched. Branchlets 2–3 mm wide including the closely spaced lateral leaves. Lateral leaves ovate-oblong, 1–1.5 mm long, 0.5–0.75 mm wide on the stems and branchlets, distantly and very minutely serrate-toothed under 25× magnification, faintly white-margined. Median leaves lanceolate-acuminate, 0.75–1 mm long, 0.2–0.25 mm wide on the stems and branchlets, faintly white-margined. Cones rather loose and flattened, ca. 2 mm long, 1.5–2 mm wide.

Terrestrial in hammocks and lime sinks in neutral soil. Very rare. Dade Co., Florida.

Not cultivated.

30   Selaginella ludoviciana A. Braun
Gulf Spike-moss

Horizontal rhizomes long-creeping, 3.5–4.5 mm wide including the very distant lateral leaves. Erect stems 1–3(5) cm long, simple or pseudodichotomously (appearing somewhat pinnately) branched. Branchlets ca. 3 mm wide including the closely spaced lateral leaves. Lateral leaves ovate-oblong, 1.5–2.25 mm long, 1–1.25 mm wide (up to ½ smaller on the branchlets), distantly serrate-toothed with an obvious white margin. Median leaves elliptic-lanceolate with an acuminate apex, ca. 1.5 mm long, 0.75 mm wide (1/2 smaller on the branchlets). Cones somewhat flattened, 2–12 mm long, 1.5–2 mm wide.

Terrestrial along swamp margins and in wet meadows in pinelands in neutral soil. Rare. Northern Florida to central Mississippi and eastern Louisiana.

Not cultivated. According to Somers and Buck (1975), hybrids between this species and *S. apoda* are rarely found within the range of *S. ludoviciana*.

31 Selaginella apoda (L.) Spring

Meadow Spike-moss

Horizontal rhizomes long-creeping, 3–3.5 mm wide including the distant lateral leaves. Lateral stems creeping or ascending, not very erect, 2–10 mm long, unbranched or subdichotomously forked. Branchlets 2 mm wide including the closely spaced lateral leaves. Lateral leaves ovate, 1.5–2 mm long, ca. 1 mm wide (ca. ⅓ less on the lateral branchlets), distantly and very minutely serrate under 25× magnification. Median leaves elliptic-ovate, acute-acuminate at the apex, 1–1.25 mm long, 0.5–0.7 mm wide (ca. ⅓ less on the lateral branchlets). Cones rather loose and flattened, 3–12 mm long, 2.5–3 mm wide.

Terrestrial in swamps, meadows, pastures, damp lawns, light woods, and stream banks, in neutral to subacid soil, or rarely on rocks. Frequent. Southern Maine, New York, Pennsylvania, Ohio, southern Indiana, southern Illinois, southwestern Missouri, and Arkansas south to Florida, Georgia, Alabama, Mississippi, Louisiana, eastern Texas, and eastern Oklahoma.

Rarely cultivated in greenhouses. Buck (1977) separated this species from *S. eclipes*, which grows farther north and west. Somers and Buck (1975) showed that *S. apoda* hybridizes rarely with *S. ludoviciana*.

*32 Selaginella eclipes Buck

Hidden Spike-moss

Horizontal rhizomes long-creeping, 3–3.5 mm wide including the distant lateral leaves. Lateral stems creeping or ascending, not very erect, 2–15 mm long, unbranched or pseudodichotomously (appearing somewhat pinnately) branched. Branchlets 2–3 mm wide including the rather distantly spaced lateral leaves. Lateral leaves elliptic-ovate, 1.5–2 mm long, 0.8–1.3 mm wide (ca. ⅓ less on the lateral branchlets), distantly and very minutely serrate under 25× magnification. Median leaves elliptic-ovate, acuminate-attenuate at the apex, 1.5–1.8 mm long, 0.6–0.8 mm wide (ca. ⅓ smaller on the lateral branchlets). Cones rather loose and flattened, 1–4 cm long, 2.5–3.5 mm wide.

Terrestrial in swamps, meadows, pastures, light woods, or rarely on rocks, in neutral to subacid soil. Common. Southern Quebec, southern Ontario, New York, Michigan, and eastern Wisconsin south to Indiana, Illinois, Iowa, Missouri, northern Arkansas, and eastern Oklahoma.

Not cultivated. According to Buck (1977), this species may prove to be only a subspecies of *S. apoda*, which it closely resembles.

33   Selaginella selaginoides (L.) Link
Northern Spike-moss

Horizontal rhizomes short-creeping, weak, ca. 2 mm in diam. including the scattered leaves, forming small mats. Erect stems 1–6(8) cm long, 2–4 mm in diam. including the leaves. Leaves ovate-lanceolate, 1.5–3 mm long, 0.6–0.8 mm wide, acuminate-subulate at the apex, sparsely toothed along the margins, without a midrib discernable from the upper surface, spreading to loosely ascending, not appressed to the stem. Cones cylindric, (0.5)2–4(5) mm long, 4–6 mm wide, the fertile leaves loose, spreading, slightly larger than the sterile leaves.

Terrestrial among mosses on cold stream banks, lake shores, bogs, rocks, and wet talus slopes in neutral or slightly alkaline soil. Rare. Labrador to Alaska and the Aleutian Islands south to northern Maine, Quebec, southern Ontario, northern Michigan, northeastern Wisconsin, northern Minnesota, Manitoba, Saskatchewan, Alberta, and southern British Columbia. Disjunct in northwestern Colorado, northwestern Wyoming, and Idaho.

Not cultivated.

*34   Selaginella rupincola Underw.
Rock-loving Spike-moss

Plants forming loose clumps usually 4–8 cm high. Rhizomes absent. Leaves abruptly attached to the erect stems, their bases paler than the dark stems, narrowly lanceolate, ca. 2.5 mm long, 0.25 mm wide, with marginal cilia ca. ¼ as long as the leaves are wide, the apex usually plane, the margins and apical seta often conspicuously white. Cones oblong, 4–12 mm long, 1.5–2 mm wide.

Epipetric on cliff ledges, under rocks on slopes, and in seepages, on igneous rocks. Common. Western Texas to southern Arizona.

According to Tryon (1955, p. 20), this species is closely related to *S. bigelovii*. It hybridizes with *S. mutica* to form *S. ×neomexicana* Maxon, which has abortive spores and is intermediate between its parents. The hybrid has a range similar to that of *S. rupincola*.

35   Selaginella bigelovii Underw.
Bushy Spike-moss

Plants forming loose clumps 5–20 cm high from creeping rhizomes. Leaves abruptly attached, their leaf bases paler than the dark stems, narrowly lanceolate, 1.2–1.8 mm long, 0.25–0.35 mm wide, with marginal cilia ca. ⅙ as wide as the leaves, the apex usually keeled, the margins and apical seta not conspicuously white. Cones oblong, 4–15 mm long, 1.5–2 mm wide.

Epipetric on dry, rocky banks in the mountains. Frequent. Central and southern California.

Not cultivated.

36 Selaginella tortipila A. Braun
Kinky-hair Spike-moss

Plants forming large, compact mounds (4)8–15 cm high; rhizomes present. Leaves long-decurrent on the stems, linear, ca. 2 mm long, 0.25 mm wide, with marginal cilia absent, tooth-like, or up to ca. ⅙ as wide as the leaf blade, keeled-acuminate at the apex, the apical seta terminating in a curled and contorted, sometimes deciduous tip. Cones oblong, 3–5 mm long, 1.5–2 mm wide.

Epipetric on seasonally moist granite and sandstone cliffs and rocks, and terrestrial on slopes, in strongly acid soil. Frequent. Piedmont and mountains of North Carolina, South Carolina, and Georgia.

Not cultivated.

*37 Selaginella viridissima Weath.
Slender Spike-moss

Plants forming loose to dense, large mounds ca. 10 cm high; rhizomes present; stems ca. 1 mm in diam. Leaves long-decurrent on the stems, linear, ca. 1.5 mm long, 0.3 mm wide, with marginal, tooth-like cilia ⅛– ⅙ as long as the leaf blades are wide, carinate-acute at the apex, without an apical seta. Cones oblong, ca. 5–10 mm long, 1.25 mm wide.

Epipetric on large boulders and on cliffs and canyon walls on igneous rock in shaded localities. Very rare. Mountains of western Texas.

Not cultivated. This species can be distinguished by its slender stems.

*38 Selaginella weatherbiana Tryon
Weatherby's Spike-moss

Plants forming loose mats 5–15 cm high or pendent; rhizomes present. Leaves long-decurrent on the stems, narrowly elliptic-lanceolate, ca. 2 mm long, 0.5 mm wide, with marginal, tooth-like cilia ca. ⅙ as long as the leaf blades are wide, carinate-acuminate at the apex, with a long, translucent apical seta. Cones sharply oblong, 5–15 mm long, 2 mm wide.

Epipetric in crevices of boulders and cliffs of igneous rock in exposed or protected places. Rare. Rocky Mountains of Colorado and northern New Mexico.

Not cultivated.

39   Selaginella arenicola Underw.
Sand Spike-moss

Plants forming tufts or clumps 5–10 cm high; rhizomes absent. Leaves rather short- to long-decurrent on the stems, narrowly lanceolate, 2–2.5 mm long, 0.2–0.4 mm wide, with marginal cilia ca. ¼ as long as the leaf blades are wide, flat to keeled at the apex, with a long, translucent apical seta. Cones sharply oblong, 1–20 mm long, 1–1.5 mm wide.

Terrestrial in sandy and gravelly places or epipetric in crevices of acidic rocks, in sun and partial shade. Frequent. North Carolina to Florida west to Oklahoma and Texas, mostly on the coastal plain.

Not cultivated. Tryon (1955, pp. 23–27) divided this species into subsp. *arenicola*, subsp. *acanthonota* (Underw.) Tryon, and subsp. *riddellii* (Van Eselt.) Tryon. Because the differences are minor and many intermediates are known, recognition of these subspecies seems questionable.

40   Selaginella hansenii Hieron.
Hansen's Spike-moss

Plants forming tufts or mats ca. 1–2 cm high. Leaves abruptly attached, the leaf bases paler than the dark stems, linear-lanceolate, the lower ones slightly longer than the upper ones and more appressed to the stems, ca. 2 mm long, 0.4 mm wide, with marginal cilia ca. ¼(½) as long as the leaves are wide, the leaf apex plane, the apical seta conspicuous, white. Cones oblong, 3–8 mm long, 1.5–2.5 mm wide.

Epipetric on cliffs and rocky slopes on igneous rock in full sun or partial shade. Frequent. Sierra Nevada of central California.

Not cultivated.

*41   Selaginella wrightii Hieron.
Wright's Spike-moss

Plants forming tufts or mats ca. 1 cm high. Leaves abruptly attached, the leaf bases paler than the dark stems, linear-lanceolate, the lower ones slightly longer than the upper ones and more appressed to the stems, 2.5–3.5 mm long, 0.3–0.4 mm wide, with marginal cilia ca. ⅓–½ as long as the leaf blades are wide, the apex slightly keeled, the apical seta absent or inconspicuous, yellowish. Cones oblong, 5–30 mm long, ca. 1.5 mm wide.

Epipetric on dry rocks and cliffs on limestone in full sun or partial shade. Rare. Western Texas and southeastern New Mexico.

Not cultivated.

*42   Selaginella mutica D. C. Eaton ex Underw.
Blunt-leaved Spike-moss

Plants forming dense mats 1–2 cm high. Leaves abruptly attached, their leaf bases paler than the dark stems, lanceolate to elliptic-lanceolate, all alike around the stems, 1–1.5 mm long, 0.25–0.5 mm wide, with many marginal cilia ¼–⅓ as long as the leaves are wide, the leaf apex distinctly cupped or keeled, the apical seta absent or present and arising abruptly from the leaf apex. Cones oblong, 2–5 mm long 1 mm wide.

Epipetric on cliffs and rocky slopes on rocks in full sun or partial shade. Frequent. Colorado and Utah south to western Texas and Arizona.

Not cultivated. Tryon (1955, pp. 44–46) divided this species into var. *mutica*, with sterile leaves bearing a short or no apical seta and fertile leaves bearing mostly long, spreading lateral cilia, and var. *limitanea* Weath., with sterile leaves bearing a distinct apical seta and fertile leaves bearing mostly short, ascending, or tooth-like lateral cilia. Intermediates between the varieties are known. Variety *limitanea* is confined to the Mexican border region of western Texas to southeastern Arizona.

43 Selaginella wallacei Hieron.
Wallace's Spike-moss

Plants forming loose mats 1–8 cm high. Leaves abruptly attached, their leaf bases paler than the dark stems, linear-lanceolate, all alike around the stems or nearly so, 1.5–3 mm long, ca. 0.5 mm wide, with a few, ascending, marginal cilia ⅕–¼ as long as the leaves are wide, the apex plane, the apical seta short and arising abruptly from the leaf apex. Cones tetragonal, 1–3 cm long, ca. 1.5 mm wide.

Epipetric on cliffs and rocky slopes in dry to wet places in full sun to full shade. Common. Montana to Washington south to Idaho and northern California.

Occasionally cultivated. According to Tryon (1955, p. 44), this species is variable in habit depending upon its habitat. Plants in dry, sunny places form a compact mat and the sterile leaves are closely imbricate on the stems. Those in wet, shady places form loose mats and have somewhat distant leaves.

*44 Selaginella cinerascens A. A. Eaton
Gray Spike-moss

Plants forming loose to somewhat compact mats ca. 1 cm high. Leaves abruptly attached, their leaf bases paler than the dark stems, linear-lanceolate, all alike around the stems, 1–1.5 mm long, 0.25–0.3 mm wide, with a few ascending or antrorse marginal, short, or tooth-like cilia ⅕ as long as the leaves are wide, the leaf apex plane, the apical seta absent. Cones tetragonal, 2–4 mm long, 1 mm wide.

Terrestrial on hillsides and slopes in partial shade; not on rock. Rare. Southern California.

Not cultivated. The low, open, gray mats formed by the plants are characteristic of this species, which is one of the few species of subg. *Stachygynandrum* that does not grow on or closely associated with rocks.

75

45 Selaginella eremophila Maxon
Desert Spike-moss

Plants forming usually dense mats ca. 1 cm high. Leaves linear-lanceate, scarcely tapered at the base, those on the ventral side of the stem 1.5–2 mm long, 0.3–0.5 mm wide, those on the dorsal side of the stem ca. ⅓ smaller, all with straight, strongly ascending, marginal cilia ¼–⅓ as long as the leaves are wide, the apical seta irregularly twisted, delicate, usually deciduous. Cones tetragonal, 5–10 mm long, ca. 1.25 mm wide.

Epipetric in rock crevices or terrestrial at the base of boulders in open deserts. Rare. Southwestern Arizona and adjacent southern California.

Not cultivated. The figures show plants under wet and dry conditions.

*46 Selaginella peruviana (Milde) Hieron.
Peruvian Spike-moss

Plants forming loose mats ca. 1–2 cm high. Leaves linear-lanceate, scarcely tapered at the base, those on the ventral side of the stem 2.5–3 mm long, those on the dorsal side of the stem ca. ⅓ smaller, all with straight, ascending marginal cilia ca. ⅓ as long as the leaves are wide, the apical seta straight, stiff, usually persistent. Cones tetragonal, 5–20 mm long, 1.25 mm wide.

Mostly epipetric in crevices or on ledges of sandstone or igneous cliffs, less commonly terrestrial. Occasional. Central and western Texas and Oklahoma to New Mexico.

Not cultivated.

47 Selaginella arizonica Maxon
Arizona Spike-moss

Plants forming usually dense mats ca. 1–3(4) cm high. Leaves linear-lanceolate, broadest above the base, those on the ventral side of the stem 0.35–0.65 mm wide, ca. 2 mm long, those on the dorsal side of the stem ca. ⅓ narrower, nearly as long, all with straight or curved, strongly ascending marginal cilia ⅕–⅓ as long as the leaves are wide, the apical seta short, straight, persistent but sometimes broken off. Cones tetragonal, 5–10 mm long, 1–1.25 mm wide.

Epipetric in crevices or on ledges of igneous or rarely limestone cliffs. Frequent. Southwestern Texas and southcentral Arizona.

Not cultivated.

48 Selaginella oregana D. C. Eaton in Watson
Oregon Spike-moss

Plants usually forming loose festoons. Branches very distant, gently curved. Leaves lanceolate, decidedly tapered at the base, similar all around the stem, 2–3 mm long, 0.4–0.5 mm wide, rather thin, lacking marginal cilia, the apical seta absent to 0.3 mm long. Cones tetragonal, 10–20 mm long, 1.5 mm wide.

Epiphytic on tree trunks and branches or rarely on rocks. Occasional. Coastal northern California and Oregon to the Olympic Peninsula and west-central Washington.

Not cultivated.

*49   Selaginella utahensis Flowers
Utah Spike-moss

Plants forming dense mats ca. 1 cm high. Branches greatly intertwined, mostly less than 1 cm long, fragile and readily fragmenting. Leaves linear-lanceate, not much tapered at the base, those on the ventral side of the stem 2–3 mm long, 0.4–0.5 mm wide, those on the dorsal side of the stem ca. ⅕ smaller, all with a few, curved, ascending marginal cilia ⅛–⅙ as long as the leaves are wide, the apical seta absent to less than 0.25 mm long. Cones tetragonal, ca. 5 mm long, 1.25–2 mm wide.

Epipetric in crevices and on ledges of sandstone cliffs. Rare. Southwestern Utah and extreme southern Nevada.

Not cultivated.

*50   Selaginella asprella Maxon
Bluish Spike-moss

Plants forming dense mats ca. 1 cm high. Branches greatly intertwined, mostly less than 1 cm long, fragile and readily fragmenting. Leaves narrowly lanceolate, somewhat tapered at the base, all similar around the stem, 1.5–2 mm long, 0.4–0.6 mm wide, with a few stiff, ascending marginal cilia ⅛–⅙ as long as the leaves are wide, the apical seta 0.2–1 mm long, bearing short cilia. Cones tetragonal, 10–20 mm long, 1.25–2 mm wide.

Terrestrial in rocky soil or in crevices at the base of igneous boulders. Rare. Southern California.

Not cultivated.

*51   Selaginella leucobryoides Maxon
Mojave Spike-moss

Plants forming dense mats ca. 1 cm high. Branches greatly intertwined, mostly less than 1 cm long, fragile and readily fragmenting. Leaves lanceate, slightly or not tapered at the base, ca. 1.5 mm long, 0.4 mm wide, with a few stiff, ascending marginal cilia ⅒–⅙ as long as the leaves are wide, the apical seta ca. 0.25 mm long, bearing short cilia. Cones tetragonal, 5–7 mm long, 1.5–2 mm wide.

Terrestrial in rocky soil or epipetric in rock crevices. Rare. Southern California.

Not cultivated.

52   Selaginella densa Rydb.

Rocky Mountain Spike-moss

Plants forming dense, flat mats ca. 1–3 cm high. Branches not much intertwined, closely spaced, ca. 1 cm long, not readily fragmenting. Leaves lanceate, not tapered at the base, those on the ventral side 1.5–2 mm long, 0.4–0.6 mm wide, those on the dorsal side ca. ⅓ smaller, with none or a few straight, ascending marginal cilia up to ⅛ as long as the leaves are wide, the whitish or sometimes greenish apical seta 0.25–1.25 mm long, entire to subciliate. Cones tetragonal, 5–20 mm long, 1.25–2 mm wide.

Terrestrial in sandy or rocky soil or epipetric on rocks in exposed places. Abundant. Manitoba and the Dakotas to New Mexico west to British Columbia, Washington, Oregon, northern California, Idaho, Utah, Arizona, and western Texas.

Not cultivated. This complex species was divided by Tryon (1955, pp. 66–71) into var. *densa*, with white, opaque apical setae and ciliate fertile leaves, var. *scopulorum* (Maxon) Tryon (Fig. 52), with white, opaque apical setae and entire fertile leaves, and var. *standleyi* (Maxon) Tryon, with greenish or translucent apical setae and entire to ciliate fertile leaves. Many intermediates exist.

53   Selaginella watsonii Underw.

Alpine Spike-moss

Plants forming dense, round, cushion-like mats ca. 2–5 cm high. Branches not much intertwined, mostly closely spaced, ca. 1–1.5 cm long, not readily fragmenting. Leaves linear-lanceate, not tapered at the base, both the ventral and dorsal leaves ca. 2 mm long, 0.5 mm wide, with a very few straight, spreading or ascending, marginal cilia up to ¹⁄₁₀(⅕) as long as the leaves are wide, the greenish apical seta 0.1–0.2 mm long, entire. Cones tetragonal, 5–20 mm long, ca. 1.5 mm wide.

Epipetric in crevices of usually igneous cliffs or boulders in exposed or shady places. Rare. Montana, Utah, and northern Arizona west to eastern Oregon and southern California.

Not cultivated.

*54   Selaginella underwoodii Hieron.

Underwood's Spike-moss

Plants forming flat, loose mats ca. less than 1 cm high. Branches not much intertwined, mostly rather distant, 1–3 cm long, not readily fragmenting. Leaves linear-lanceate, not tapered at the base, both the ventral and dorsal leaves 0.2–0.4 mm wide, with spreading to ascending marginal cilia up to ⅕ as long as the leaves are wide, the greenish apical seta 1–2 mm long, entire or with a few very short, ascending cilia. Cones tetragonal, 5–20 mm long, 1–1.25 mm wide.

Epipetric in crevices or among rocks, usually igneous, in usually moist or shady places. Frequent. Southeastern Wyoming and Colorado south to western Texas, southwestern Utah, and central Arizona.

Not cultivated.

55　Selaginella rupestris (L.) Spring
Rock Spike-moss

Plants forming flat, loose to rather compact mats ca. 1.5–4 cm high. Branches not much intertwined, mostly closely spaced, 1–4 cm long, not readily fragmenting. Leaves linear-lanceate, not tapered at the base, both the ventral and dorsal leaves 1.5 mm long, 0.25–0.45 mm wide, with spreading, curved, or ascending marginal cilia ¼–⅓ as long as the leaves are wide, the white apical seta 0.75–1 mm long, with short, ascending cilia. Cones tetragonal, 5–20 mm long, 1–1.25 mm wide.

Epipetric on cliffs and rocks or terrestrial in rocky, gravelly, or sandy soil, usually in exposed places. Frequent. Nova Scotia and Newfoundland, Quebec, Ontario, Manitoba, Saskatchewan, and Alberta south to Georgia, Alabama, Tennessee, Arkansas, and Oklahoma.

Not cultivated. This species forms rather more compact mats than those of *S. underwoodii* and *S. sibirica*. It also resembles *S. densa*, but is unlike that species in having the leaves on the ventral and dorsal side of the stems essentially equal in length.

*56　Selaginella sibirica (Milde) Hieron.
Siberian Spike-moss

Plants forming flat, loose mats ca. 1–2 cm high. Branches not much intertwined, mostly closely spaced, ca. 1–2 cm long, not readily fragmenting. Leaves linearlanceolate, somewhat tapered at the base, the leaves of both the ventral and dorsal sides 1.5–2 mm long, 0.25–0.4 mm wide, with ascending lateral cilia ¼–⅓ as long as the leaves are wide, the white apical seta 0.25–0.5 mm long, with short, ascending cilia. Cones tetragonal, 5–20 mm long, ca. 1.5 mm wide.

Epipetric on cliffs or terrestrial in rocky soil in exposed places. Occasional or rare. Alaska.

Not cultivated.

ISOËTACEAE
The Quillwort Family

Besides several genera known only as fossils (some of them dating back to the Triassic), the Isoëtaceae includes two living genera, *Isoëtes* and *Stylites*. The latter genus is doubtfully distinct from *Isoëtes*; it consists of two species that grow in the Andes Mountains. *Isoëtes* includes about 60 to 75 species and is distributed world-wide; about 19 species occur in the United States and Canada. The genus is being investigated actively, and the number and status of the species will doubtless be revised as studies progress. Several hybrids are known or postulated, especially with *I. engelmannii*.

The number of hybrids between groups, or sections, as Boom (1980) refers to them, is striking. This casts doubt on the txonomic validity of the groups or sections as they are currently understood. Advances in the taxonomy of this genus should come about as a result of examining megaspores and microspores with the scanning electron microscope. Taylor, Mohlenbrock, and Murphy (1975), for instance, found clear differences between *I. butleri* and *I. melanopoda*, species that had previously been confused and that could not be separated by spore characters visible with a light microscope. The most minute details of spore ornamentation, which are the thread-like structures of which the spore surface is made, I have called "micro-ornamentation," and it appears to be consistent within a species and may be fairly consistent within entire species groups or large parts of such groups. However, the final resolution of the species complexes and the limits of species is going to require culture experiments and programs of articificial hybridization. Little is known about the effect of water level, temperature, pH, or nutrients on the morphology of *Isoëtes* plants, including their spores.

The plants of this family are small or medium-sized and resemble rushes, both in their aquatic or amphibious habitat and in their appearance. A compact, bi- or tri-lobed, corm-like rootstock commonly shallowly rooted in mud gives rise to a number of erect or slightly spreading, bright to dull or olive green leaves that resemble quills. The leaves usually are pale at the base and often have a pale ala on each side extending part way up the leaf margin. A single, central vein runs from the base to the apex of the leaf. Longitudinal strengthening strands called peripheral bundles, which look like veins, occur in the leaves, especially in the amphibious species. Unlike any flowering plants, the leaves contain four air chambers with cross-walls at irregular intervals along their length. They are somewhat swollen at the base, and bear within a basal cavity a single, oval to orbicular sporangium that contains either a few hundred large megaspores or many thousands of nearly microscopic microspores. On the adaxial side of the leaf, the sporangia are covered partially or entirely by a pale membrane called a velum. In many species, the sporangium wall is dark-spotted, striped, or entirely dark-colored. The white or gray to brown megaspores are very large, about 0.5–1 mm in diameter, and at maturity are highly ornamented with tubercles, ridges, or crests, which may be seen under the microscope or with a strong hand lens. Scanning electron microscope studies have shown that the gross ornamentation is itself made up of fine, often spine-like strands. Peripheral strand number, velum coverage, sporangium wall pigmentation, megaspore ornamentation, and habitat all are useful taxonomic characters.

The aquatic species of *Isoëtes* grow more or less permanently submerged in lakes and rivers. The amphibious species grow along the margins of lakes and rivers or in vernal pools underlain by clay, limestone, sandstone, or granite. Plants are fairly easily cultivated, although they may require a cold period during the winter. However, they are not especially attractive other than as aquarium plants, and are rarely grown, except for scientific study.

Key to Isoëtes
1. Plants of the Great Plains and east, **7**
1. Plants of the Rocky Mountains and west, **2**
2(1). Velum covering the sporangium 25–50(75)%, **4**
2(1). Velum covering the sporangium 100%, **3**
3(2). Peripheral strands in the leaves 3; leaves 2.5–15(20) cm long; megaspores mostly more than 0.33 mm in diam., tuberculate or with short, low ridges; PAC. *57. *I. nuttallii*
3(2). Peripheral strands in the leaves 0; leaves 3–6 cm long; megaspores mostly less than 0.33 mm in diam., smooth to tuberculate; CA. *58. *I. orcuttii*
4(2). Plants of lowlands and foothills mostly below 5000 ft elevation, mostly around shallow pools; peripheral strands in the leaves 1–4; NW & CA. *59. *I. howellii*
4(2). Plants of montane areas mostly above 5000 ft elevation, mostly in deep lakes and streams; peripheral strands in the leaves 0, **5**
5(4). Plants terrestrial, amphibious, or aquatic, on muddy flats or in temporary pools or shallow ponds, commonly emersed; megaspores with scattered, low tubercles or short ridges; W. *60. *I. bolanderi*
5(4). Plants aquatic, on margins and bottoms of deep lakes, usually submerged; megaspores echinate or with rather long ridges or crests, **6**
6(5). Leaves somewhat recurved, rather flexible; megaspores 0.25–0.50(0.60) mm in diam., echinate or bluntly so with some spines bifid and micro-ornamentation of very short microspines; N. 61. *I. echinospora* subsp. *muricata*
6(5). Leaves strictly erect, rather stiff; megaspores 0.50–0.60 mm in diam., with long, low ridges and micro-ornamentation of short spines joined below; NW. 62. *I. occidentalis*
7(1). Plants terrestrial or amphibious in wet depressions, shallow pools, or temporary ponds; megaspores tuberculate, with low, ridges, or with low, separate crests, **15**
7(1). Plants aquatic or amphibious in lakes, streams, rivers, or estuaries; megaspores with a reticulum of high crests (except tuberculate to

low-ridged in *I. flaccida*, low-ridged in *I. acadiensis* and *I. hieroglyphica*, and spiny in *I. echinospora*), **8**

8(7). Megaspores with a reticulum of high crests, **12**

8(7). Megaspores with sharp spines, low tubercles, or low ridges, **9**

9(8). Megaspores distinctly echinate under low magnification; velum 25–75% covering the sporangium; sporangia brown-spotted; N. *61. I. echinospora* subsp. *muricata*

9(8). Megaspores tuberculate or with low ridges, **10**

10(9). Megaspores with low tubercles or short ridges, appearing smooth under low magnification; velum entirely covering the sporangium; sporangia unpigmented; GA, FL. *63. I. flaccida*

10(9). Megaspores with a sparse reticulum of low, round ridges, **11**

11(10). Leaves 9–35(69), 5–21(27) cm long; sporangia often brown-spotted; microspores 25–31μm in diam.; MA to NSC. *65. I. acadiensis*

11(10). Leaves 10–20, 6–7.5 cm long; sporangia unpigmented; microspores 31–44μm in diam.; ME. *66. I. hieroglyphica*

12(8). Megaspores 0.55–1.00 mm in diam; leaves strongly recurved and fleshy, 5–10(15) cm long; NE, AM. *64. I. macrospora*

12(8). Megaspores 0.25–0.65 mm in diam.; leaves erect or slightly recurved (decidedly recurved in *I. tuckermanii*), not fleshy, 10–50 cm long (except 5–20 cm in *I. tuckermanii*), **13**

13(12). Leaves pale green, with usually 4 peripheral strands; velum covering less than 20% of the sporangium; sporangia not pigmented; megaspore ornamentation a continuous reticulum; E. *67. I. engelmannii*

13(12). Leaves dark to olive green, with 0(2–4) peripheral strands; velum covering 25–50% of the sporangium; sporangia brown-spotted or entirely brown; megaspore ornamentation of irregular crests, **14**

14(13). Plants amphibious; leaves with many stomata, dark green, all straight but slightly twisted to contorted; sporangia oblong, 3–8 mm long; ligule triangular to long-triangular; NE. *68. I. riparia*

14(13). Plants aquatic; leaves with few or no stomata, olive green, the outer ones recurved; sporangia round to oblong, 2–5 mm long; ligule broadly triangular; NE. *69. I. tuckermanii*

15(7). Plants of pools and seepages on granite outcrops, **18**

15(7). Plants of temporary ponds on clay soil or on sandstone or limestone-cemented sandstone, **16**

16(15). Plants terrestrial on thin, seasonally wet soil over limestone or limestone-cemented sandstone; megaspores (0.36)0.48–0.65 mm in diam.; SE. *70. I. butleri*

16(15). Plants amphibious, on seasonally wet clay soil in temporary pools often underlain by sandstone; megaspores 0.25–0.48 mm in diam., **17**

17(16). Leaf bases commonly black; megaspores 0.30–0.40 mm in diam., tuberculate or with short ridges, the micro-ornamentation short, small spines; SE. *71. I. melanopoda*

17(16). Leaf bases commonly brown; megaspores 0.40–0.48 mm in diam., with short ridges and low crests, the micro-ornamentation a close reticulum with short, minutely lumpy microspines; SE. **72. I. virginica*

18(15). Stems short-creeping, proliferous rhizomes, the plants growing in dense mats; SE. *73. I. tegetiformans*

18(15). Stems erect, 2(3)-lobed corms, the plants growing as separate individuals, **19**

19(18). Plants of central Texas; TX. **74. I. lithophila*

19(18). Plants of Georgia, Alabama, and South Carolina, **20**

20(19). Leaves up to 7 cm long; sporangium wall unpigmented; megaspores gray; velum covering 67–100% of the sporangium; SE. *75. I. melanospora*

20(19). Leaves 7–15(20) cm long; sporangium wall brown; megaspores cream; velum covering up to 33% of the sporangium; SE. *76. I. piedmontana*

*57 Isoëtes nuttallii A. Braun ex Engelm.

Nuttall's Quillwort

Corms 3-lobed; leaves (4)8–20 cm long, 0.1–0.5 mm wide, erect, flexible, commonly twisted, bright green, pale toward the base, with long, hyaline alae above the base; peripheral strands 3; ligule small, triangular; sporangia 3–7 mm long, unpigmented, completely covered by the velum; megaspores white, (0.33)0.40–0.50(0.60) mm in diam., with low tubercles or short ridges, the micro-ornamentation of short microspines arising from a loose reticulum.

Terrestrial in wet ground or seepages and in mud near vernal pools. Frequent. Coast ranges from Vancouver Island, British Columbia to southern California.

Not cultivated.

*58 Isoëtes orcuttii A. A. Eaton

Orcutt's Quillwort

Corms 3-lobed; leaves 3–10 cm long, 0.2–0.33 mm wide, erect, flexible, not much twisted, bright green, pale toward the base, with long, hyaline alae above the base; peripheral strands 0; ligule triangular; sporangia 2–5 mm long, unpigmented, completely covered by the velum; megaspores grayish at maturity, 0.20–0.35 mm in diam., smooth or with low tubercles, the micro-ornamentation of long microspines arising from a loose reticulum.

Amphibious in vernal pools. Frequent. Interior valley of central and southern California.

Not cultivated.

*59 Isoëtes howellii Engelm.

Howell's Quillwort

Corms 2-lobed; leaves 5–20(30) cm long, 0.3–0.7 mm wide, erect or somewhat spreading, not or little twisted, bright green, paler toward the base, with hyaline alae up to ca. 5 cm above the base; peripheral strands (1–3)4; ligule lanceate; sporangia 3–6(8) mm long, frequently brown-spotted, up to ⅓ covered by the velum; megaspores white, 0.40–0.50 mm in diam., with short, low ridges, the micro-ornamentation of long microspines arising from a loose reticulum.

Amphibious in wet depressions and along muddy shores. Frequent. Lowlands and foothills from Washington to Montana and California. Disjunct in northern Utah.

Not cultivated.

*60 Isoëtes bolanderi Engelm.

Bolander's Quillwort

Corms 2-lobed; leaves 6–15(25) cm long, 0.6–1.3 mm wide, erect or slightly spreading, not twisted, bright green, paler or stramineous toward the base with hyaline alae up to ca. 1.5 cm above the base; peripheral strands 0; ligule cordate-lanceolate; sporangia 3–4 mm long, not pigmented, up to ⅓ covered by the velum; megaspores white or bluish, 0.30–0.45(0.50) mm in diam., with scattered, low tubercles or short ridges, the micro-ornamentation of short microspines arising from a loose reticulum.

Amphibious or aquatic in gravel or mud in shallow lakes or in temporary ponds in drier areas. Frequent. Southern British Columbia to Wyoming south to northern New Mexico, northern Arizona, and southern California.

Not cultivated.

61 Isoëtes echinospora subsp. muricata (Dur.) Löve & Löve

Spiny-spored Quillwort

Corms 2-lobed; leaves 4–15(25) cm long, 0.5–1.5 mm wide, erect or sometimes spreading, not or slightly twisted, pale green, paler toward the base, with rather narrow, hyaline alae up to ca. 1.5 cm above the base; peripheral strands 0; ligule cordate-lanceolate; sporangia 4–7 mm long, brown-spotted, up to 1/2(3/4) covered by the velum; megaspores white, 0.25–0.60 mm in diam., with many sharp to blunt or bifid spines, the micro-ornamentation of very short microspines.

Amphibious or aquatic in sand or mud in slightly acid sluggish streams, shallow lakes, and ponds. Common. Newfoundland and Nova Scotia to Alaska south to New Jersey, Pennsylvania, Ohio, Michigan, Wisconsin, Minnesota, Montana, Wyoming, Colorado, Utah, Idaho, Oregon, and northern California.

Not cultivated. Among the species of *Isoëtes* in the Flora area, only *I. echinospora* subsp. *muricata* has truly spiny megaspores. Löve (1962) and some other authors divide this taxon into two or more subunits based on geography and morphological differences, but the differences seem to be too slight to warrant recognition, although some western specimens are triploids, and so may be a different species. In addition, specimens from the western United States do tend to have broader spines than those from the eastern United States, and an examination of many megaspores with the scanning electron microscope might reveal consistent differences.

62 Isoëtes occidentalis Hend.

Western Quillwort

Corms 2-lobed; leaves 5–20 cm long, 0.8–1.6 mm wide, erect and somewhat rigid, not twisted, dark green, stramineous toward the base, with narrow hyaline alae up to ca. 1.5 cm above the base; peripheral strands 0; ligule broadly triangular; sporangia 4–6 mm long, not pigmented, up to ½ covered by the velum; megaspores white to cream, 0.40–0.80 mm in diam., with short, rather low crests, the micro-ornamentation of short microspines arising from a loose reticulum.

Aquatic in lakes and ponds, often deeply submerged. Frequent. British Columbia to Colorado, Utah, and northern California.

Not cultivated. According to W. C. Taylor (pers. comm.), *I. occidentalis* is hexaploid, and so is a distinct species from the European *I. lacustris* L., some of which is decaploid. The two species may share a common parent, because they are very similar.

*63 Isoëtes flaccida Shuttlew. ex A. Braun

Florida Quillwort

Corms 2(3)-lobed; leaves 10–60 cm long, 0.5–1.5 mm wide, erect to prostrate, not twisted, medium to dark green, whitish toward the base, usually with hyaline alae up to 2–5 mm above the base; peripheral strands 4; ligule broadly triangular; sporangia 3–5 mm long, not pigmented, entirely covered by the velum; megaspores cream colored, 0.3–0.5 mm in diam., with low tubercles, papillae, or short ridges, the micro-ornamentation a cobwebby reticulum lacking microspines.

Amphibious in clear ponds, streams, and rivers in fresh to brackish water, often rooted in sand. Rare. Southern Georgia and the Gulf Coast side of Florida.

Cultivated only in aquaria. Plants stunted by brackish water have been called var. *rigida* Engelm., and those from one robust population have been called var. *chapmanii* Engelm., but neither variety is worthy of recognition. Boom (1979) has reported presumable hybrids with *I. engelmannii* and with *I. piedmontana*. The hybrids have an incomplete velum, which covers the sporangium as little as ⅔.

64 Isoëtes macrospora Dur.
Large-spored Quillwort
Corms 2-lobed; leaves 3–15 cm long, (0.5)0.7–2 mm wide, erect to recurved, fleshy, twisted, medium green to reddish-green, commonly brownish toward the base, with greenish or brownish alae up to ca. 1.5 cm above the base; peripheral strands 0; ligule deltate; sporangia 3–5 mm long, pigmented, ⅓–½ covered by the velum; megaspores white, 0.55–1.00 mm in diam., with a reticulum of high crests, the microornamentation a cobwebby reticulum with short, minutely lumpy microspines or smooth.

Aquatic in cold ponds, lakes, streams, and rivers, rooted in gravel. Frequent. Newfoundland to Quebec south to New Jersey, New York, Michigan, Wisconsin, and Minnesota, with disjunct tetraploid populations in the mountains of Virginia and Tennessee.

Not cultivated. This species is known to be decaploid in the north and seems allied to *I. tuckermanii* (W. C. Taylor, pers. comm.), but the morphologically similar southern disjunct population is tetraploid (A. M. Evans, pers. comm.). *Isoëtes heterospora* A. A. Eaton is another enigmatic species or hybrid presumably allied to *I. macrospora*. Some of its megaspores are shaped and ornamented like those of *I.* ×*eatonii* (others are hemispherical or dumbell-shaped); these plants also may be sterile diploids with one genome inherited from each parent.

*65 Isoëtes acadiensis Kott
Acadian Quillwort
Corms 2-lobed; leaves 5–21(27) cm long, ca. 0.5 mm wide, mostly spreading and recurved, thin, not twisted, dark green occasionally tinged with red; whitish toward the base, with whitish alae up to ca. 0 cm above the base; peripheral strands 0; ligule broadly triangular to lanceate; sporangia ca. 5 mm long, pale brown or sometimes brown-spotted, covered ⅙–⅓ by the velum; megaspores white, 0.4–0.55(0.65) mm in diam., with a continuous but sparse reticulum of low, round ridges.

Aquatic, up to 1 m deep, in lakes and ponds or occasionally in rivers. Rare. Eastern Massachusetts and New Hampshire to New Brunswick and Nova Scotia.

Not cultivated. This tetraploid species is closely related to *I. hieroglyphica*, which has similar spores. According to W. C. Taylor (pers. comm.), this species and the vegetatively similar *I. tuckermanii* form a wide range of intermediates and differ mostly in megaspore characters (the ridges are lower and more rounded in *I. acadiensis*). It is possible that the two are despeciating, having been brought into proximity by relatively recent environmental changes.

*66 Isoëtes hieroglyphica A. A. Eaton
Puzzling Quillwort

Corms 2-lobed; leaves 6–7.5 cm long, ca. 1 mm wide, erect or the older ones recurved, thin, olive-green, pale brown toward the base, with pale brown alae up to ca. 1 cm above the base; peripheral strands 0; ligule triangular; sporangia ca. 5 mm long, pale brown, covered ⅓ by the velum; megaspores white, 0.45–0.6 mm in diam., with a discontinuous reticulum of low, round ridges.

Aquatic in lakes and ponds. Rare. Maine.

Not cultivated. This species is a decaploid, and may be of hybrid origin, with one parent being *I. acadiensis*. It may be related to the European pentaploid *I. lacustris* L.

67 Isoëtes engelmannii A. Braun
Engelmann's Quillwort

Corms 2-lobed; leaves 6–35(50) cm long, 0.6–2 mm wide, erect, thin, not twisted, pale green, whitish toward the base, with whitish alae up to ca. 5 cm above the base; peripheral strands usually 4; ligule triangular; sporangia 6–13 mm long, not pigmented, less than 1/5 covered by the velum; megaspores white, 0.4–0.6 mm in diam., with a continuous, regular reticulum of high crests and ridges, the micro-ornamentation of short microspines arising from a loose reticulum.

Amphibious in roadside ditches, ponds, lakes, streams, and rivers, rooted usually in mud. Common. New Hampshire to Florida west to Pennsylvania, West Virginia, Kentucky, Indiana, Illinois, Missouri, and Mississippi.

Easily cultivated in aquaria. According to Boom (1979), this species hybridizes in Louisiana with *I. melanopoda* to form *I.* × *louisianensis* Thieret in Landry & Thieret, with *I. riparia* in South Carolina, with *I. piedmontana* in Georgia, and with *I. flaccida* in southern Alabama. The hybrids are not common and are intermediate in charateristics between their parents. For instance, *I. riparia* has pigmented sporangium walls, and so do its hybrids with *I. engelmannii*. Hybrid megaspores viewed with a scanning electron microscope tend to have irregularly distorted crests not quite like those of either parent.

Other North American *Isoëtes* seem to be related to *I. engelmannii*, although the relationships are not well understood at the present time. According to W. C. Taylor (pers. comm.), *I.* × *eatonii* Dodge, from southeastern New Hampshire, adjacent Massachusetts, New Jersey, and Ontario, is fairly common in the localities where it is found. Apparently it is a diploid hybrid with no chromosome pairing, for it is infertile with mostly abortive megaspores of various sizes, and it rarely if ever forms microspores. The parentage is confirmed by isozyme data. Presumably *I. engelmannii* is one parent. *Isoëtes ×foveolata* A. A. Eaton ex Dodge, from southeastern New Hampshire, is another very uncommon diploid. It may be a hybrid with *I. engelmannii* as one parent and *I. tuckermanii* as the other. The crests on the megaspores of *I.* × *foveolata* are thicker and have smaller spaces between them than do those of *I. engelmannii*.

68   Isoëtes riparia Engelm. ex A. Braun
Shore Quillwort

Corms 2-lobed; leaves (4)9–30(50) cm long, 0.5–1.5 mm wide, erect, thin, somewhat twisted, pale to deep green, whitish toward the base with the alae often brown-edged and up to ca. 5 cm above the base; peripheral strands 0; ligule triangular to long-triangular; sporangia 3–8 mm long, brown-spotted to completely brown, covered 1/5–1/3 by the velum; megaspores white, 0.45–0.65 mm in diam., with a reticulum of high crests and ridges, the micro-ornamentation a dense reticulum with short, minutely lumpy microspines.

Amphibious in gravel or mud of ponds, streams, and fresh-water or slightly brackish rivers. Frequent. Quebec to New England, eastern New York, Pennsylvania, New Jersey, Maryland, and West Virginia to South Carolina.

Not cultivated. This tetraploid species hybridizes with *I. engelmannii* in South Carolina.

69   Isoëtes tuckermanii A. Braun ex Engelm. in A. Gray
Tuckerman's Quillwort

Corms 2(3)-lobed; leaves 2.5–18 cm long, 0.25–1.5 mm wide, erect or the older leaves recurved, thin, somewhat twisted, olive green, whitish toward the base with the alae often brown-edged and up to ca. 2 cm above the base; peripheral strands 0; ligule broadly triangular; sporangia round to oblong, 2–5 mm long, mostly brown-spotted, covered 1/5–1/3 by the velum; megaspores white, 0.40–0.65 mm in diam., with a reticulum of high crests and ridges, the micro-ornamentation a close reticulum with short, minutely lumpy microspines.

Aquatic in sand, gravel, or mud of ponds, lakes and sometimes rivers. Occasional. Newfoundland, Nova Scotia, southern Quebec, New Hampshire, Massachusetts, and New York.

Not cultivated. This species is a tetraploid and probably is of hybrid origin.

70 Isoëtes butleri Engelm.
Butler's Quillwort

Corms 2-lobed; leaves 6–20 cm long, 0.3–0.7 mm wide, erect, thin, twisted, pale green, whitish or pale reddish-brown toward the base, with whitish alae up to ca. 2 cm long above the base; peripheral strands 4 or more; ligule narrowly triangular; sporangia oblong, 6–10(14) mm long, mostly with brown lines, covered ⅒–½ by the velum; megaspores white to pale brown, (0.36)0.48–0.65 mm in diam., with low tubercles, the micro-ornamentation a cobwebby reticulum lacking microspines.

Terrestrial on thin, seasonally wet soil over limestone or limestone-cemented sandstone. Occasional. Kentucky, Missouri, central Texas, and southeastern Kansas south to Georgia, Alabama, Tennessee, and Arkansas.

Not cultivated. Taylor et al. (1975) have demonstrated that this species is distinct in its morphology and ecology from *I. melanopoda*.

71 Isoëtes melanopoda Gay & Dur.
Black-footed Quillwort

Corms 2-lobed; leaves 7–40 cm long, 0.3–1.2 mm wide, erect, thin, not or little twisted, bright green, commonly black or blackish toward the base, with pale alae up to ca. 7 cm long above the base; peripheral strands 4 or more; ligule triangular; sporangia 5–30 mm long, brown-spotted, covered ⅕–⅔ by the velum; megaspores white, 0.25–0.45 mm in diam., with tubercles or low ridges, the micro-ornamentation a reticulum with sharp microspines.

Terrestrial or amphibious on clay soils in temporary pools and old buffalo wallows underlain by sandstone. Occasional. Minnesota and South Dakota to eastern Iowa, Illinois, Kentucky, Tennessee, northwestern Georgia, Arkansas, Louisiana, and Texas. Disjunct in southern New Jersey and in Utah.

Not cultivated. Some plants of this species, especially aquatic ones, lack black pigment in the leaf bases and have been designated f. *pallida* (Engelm.) Clute. This form occurs sporadically throughout the range of the species. A pale line down the middle of the adaxial surface of most leaves helps to distinguish this species from its relatives. It hybridizes with *I. engelmannii* to form *I. × louisianensis* Thieret in Landry & Thieret.

*72 Isoëtes virginica Pfeiffer
Virginia Quillwort

Corms 2-lobed; leaves 15–30 cm long, ca. 0.5 mm wide, recurved, thin, somewhat twisted, pale green, commonly brown toward the base, with pale alae up to ca. 1 cm above the base; peripheral strands 4 or more; ligule long-triangular; sporangia broadly oblong, 3–5 mm long, brown, covered ca. ¼ by the velum; megaspores white, 0.40–0.48 mm in diam., with low but rather short, crest-like ridges, the micro-ornamentation a dense reticulum with short, minutely lumpy microspines.

Amphibious on clay soils in temporary pools often underlain by sandstone. Rare. Piedmont of Virginia, North Carolina, and South Carolina.

Not cultivated. Judging by the micro-ornamentation of its megaspores, this species is related to *I. riparia* and its allies, although in gross morphology the megaspores do show similarity to those of *I. melanopoda*. This species forms spores in spring and early summer.

73 Isoëtes tegetiformans Rury
Merlin's-grass

Stems short-creeping, proliferous, prostrate rhizomes; leaves 2–4 cm long, ca. 0.25 mm wide, erect to spreading, thin, not twisted, bright green, with pale, very short alae; peripheral strands 0; ligule triangular; sporangia broadly elliptic, ca. 2 mm long, pigmented, covered entirely by the velum; megaspores dark brown, 0.28–0.37 mm in diam., with low tubercles, the micro-ornamentation presumably a cobwebby reticulum lacking microspines.

Amphibious on thin, strongly acid soil in temporary pools on granite outcrops. Very rare. Georgia.

Not cultivated. This species of *Isoëtes* is unique in its creeping rhizomes, adventitious plantlets, non-dichotomizing roots, and distichous leaves.

*74 Isoëtes lithophila Pfeiffer
Rock Quillwort

Corms 2-lobed; leaves 3–20 cm long, 0.25–0.75 mm wide, erect, thin, not or slightly twisted, pale green, whitish to brown toward the base, with pale or brown-tinted alae up to ca. 1 cm above the base; peripheral strands 0 or 3; ligule cordate-triangular; sporangia round to oblong, 2.5–4 mm long, not pigmented, covered completely by the velum; megaspores gray, 0.29–0.65 mm in diam., with low tubercles sometimes prolonged into short ridges, the micro-ornamentation a nearly smooth, tightly fused reticulum bearing minute cavities and short projections.

Amphibious in temporary pools on granite outcrops. Rare. Texas.

Not cultivated.

75 Isoëtes melanospora Engelm.
Black-spored Quillwort

Corms 2-lobed; leaves 2–7 cm long, ca. 0.5 mm wide, erect, thin, not twisted, pale green, whitish toward the base, with narrow, pale alae up to ca. 0.5 cm above the base; peripheral strands 0; ligule triangular; sporangia round, 1–2 mm long, not pigmented, covered entirely by the velum;

megaspores gray, 0.40–0.48 mm in diam., with low tubercles or very short, sharp ridges, the micro-ornamentation a dense reticulum.

Amphibious in temporary pools on granite outcrops. Frequent. Georgia and South Carolina.

Not cultivated. The leaves of this species are shorter and their sporophylls less enlarged at the base than are those of *I. piedmontana*, with which it hybridizes, according to Matthews and Murdy (1969). A continuum of forms between these two species was detected by those investigators, which Rury (1978) hypothesized were ontogenetic phases of a single species. Dark megaspores are found only in this species and in *I. tegetiformans*.

76   Isoëtes piedmontana (Pfeiffer) Reed
Piedmont Quillwort

Corms 2-lobed; leaves 7–15(20)cm long, 0.5–1 mm wide, erect, thin, not twisted, medium green, whitish toward the base, with pale alae up to ca. 3 cm above the base; peripheral strands 0, 4, or 6; ligule triangular; sporangia oblong, 3–5 mm long, brown, covered up to ⅓ by the velum; megaspores cream, 0.40–0.48 mm in diam., with short ridges, the micro-ornamentation a loose reticulum bearing short projections.

Amphibious in temporary pools on granite outcrops. Rare. South Carolina to Alabama.

Not cultivated. This species hybridizes with *I. engelmannii, flaccida,* and *melanospora*.

EQUISETACEAE
The Horsetail Family

Among the genera of this ancient family, only *Equisetum* survives. It is known almost unchanged since the Carboniferous, some 200 million years ago. *Equisetum* is a genus of 15 living species, of which 11 are found in the United States and Canada. Three others occur in tropical America, and one other in Asia. All have greenish, silica-laden stems very characteristically divided into distinct, sheath-bearing nodes and hollow internodes, with branches occurring at the nodes in some species.

Some authors have divided the genus into *Hippochaete*, the Scouring-rushes, and *Equisetum*, the Horsetails. However, Hauke (1963, 1966, 1978, 1979), the most recent monographer of the genus, considers these to be subgenera of a single genus.

The plants are small- to medium-sized and conspicuous in their usually upright habit and distinct stem morphology. Their subterranean stems are black and usually rather wide-creeping; round, black tubers occur along the stems occasionally, especially in subg. *Equisetum*. Erect, aerial stems are borne at intervals, and in some species branch repeatedly close to the rhizome, sending up erect stems in clusters. The stems are ribbed in the internodal areas. In subg. *Equisetum*, a whorl of branches usually forms at most nodes. The nodes are covered with an adherent to slightly flaring sheath of laterally fused, scale-like leaves. The sheath is tipped with a row of sometimes deciduous teeth, which are usually white with dark brown to black centers. At least the principal stems terminate in a black, brown or yellowish cone. The cone consists of a principal axis bearing lateral sporophylls (greatly transformed leaves) that are peltate and have sporangia in a ring on the underside, facing the central axis of the cone. Each sporangium contains many spores of 1 size. The spores are green and have a pair of strap-shaped elaters that are thought to help disperse the spores by their curling and uncurling motions, which are a response to changes in humidity.

The species are terrestrial, often in disturbed ground or waste places, and sometimes in wet locations. They are most numerous and diverse in the northern tier of the United States and in adjacent Canada. Some of the species and hybrids reproduce vegetatively from stem fragments and so occur widely. Hybrids occur between some of the species of each subgenus (but not between subgenera) and can be detected by their abortive spores, sporangia, or cones. Because they are widespread and persistent, several hybrid Equisetums are included in the key and are treated as if they were sexual species. Plants of *Equisetum* are coarse and weedy and are rarely cultivated, except in wet, woodland gardens.

Key to Equisetum

1. Stems perennial, evergreen (except in *E. laevigatum*), stiff (except in *E. scirpoides*); sterile and fertile stems monomorphic and usually unbranched (except in *E. ramosissimum* subsp. *ramosissimum*); cones apiculate at the apex (except in *E. laevigatum* and *ramossimum* subsp. *ramosissimum*) (subg. *Hippochaete*), 8

1. Stems annual, deciduous, at least the sterile ones flexible; sterile and fertile stems dimorphic or monomorphic and at least the sterile ones irregularly to regularly branched (often unbranched in *E. fluviatile*); cones round at the apex (subg. *Equisetum*), 2

2(1). Sterile and fertile stems dimorphic; sterile stems copiously branched and green; fertile stems branched or unbranched and lacking chlorophyll, commonly pink or pale brown, 5

2(1). Sterile and fertile stems monomorphic; sterile and fertile stems sparsely and often irregularly branched and green, 3

3(2). Sheaths on the main stems parallel-sided, ca. 1.5× longer than wide including the teeth, scarcely distinct from the stem at the base; teeth with inconspicuous white margins; ridges on the main stems 12–24, often obsolete; N. 78. *E. fluviatile*

3(2). Sheaths on the main stems flaring outward toward the apex, ca. 2× or more longer than wide including the teeth, distinct from the stem at the base; teeth with conspicuous or inconspicuous, white, scarious margins; ridges on the main stems 5–14, prominent, **4**

4(3). Teeth on the sheaths of the main stems with conspicuous, white, scarious margins; main stems with 5–10 ridges; spores not abortive; N. *77. E. palustre*

4(3). Teeth on the sheaths of the main stems with inconspicuous, white margins; main stems with 10–14 ridges; spores abortive, NE. *79. E. × litorale*

5(2). Sheaths 10–30 (50 in fertile stems) mm long, the teeth reddish-brown or pale brown, lacking white margins, **7**

5(2). Sheaths 3–10 (20 in fertile stems) mm long, the teeth dark brown with white margins, **6**

6(5). Teeth on the sheaths of main, erect stems with white margins narrower than the dark brown central portion of the teeth; sterile branches ascending, the sheaths with lanceate-attenuate teeth much longer than wide; N, E, S, W. *80. E. arvense*

6(5). Teeth on the sheaths of main, erect stems with white margins wider than the dark brown central portion of the teeth; sterile branches spreading, their sheaths with deltate teeth about as long as wide; N. *81. E. pratense*

7(5). Stems 4–15 mm in diam.; sheaths 10–30(50) mm long (in fertile stems) including the more than 14 teeth; lateral branches not branched; P. *83. E. telmateia* subsp. *braunii*

7(5). Stems 1.5–3 mm in diam.; sheaths 10–25 mm long including the fewer than 12 teeth; lateral branches themselves branched; N. *82. E. sylvaticum*

8(1). Main erect stems usually with 2 or 3 branches at the nodes; NC, FL, LA. *84. E. ramosissimum* subsp. *ramosissimum*

8(1). Main erect stems unbranched, lacking branches at the nodes unless injured, **9**

9(8). Stem sheaths entirely green; stems annual, with smooth ridges; N,W. *85. E. laevigatum*

9(8). Stem sheaths all, or at least the lower ones, with a black band or entirely black or dark brown; stems perennial or evergreen, with minutely toothed or tuberculate ridges, **10**

10(9). Erect stems 0.3–2.5 mm in diam.; teeth of the stem sheaths persistent, **12**

10(9). Erect stems 2.5–17.5 mm in diam.; teeth of the stem sheaths deciduous (tardily so in *E. hyemale* var. *affine* from the southern and western United States), **11**

11(10). Cones normal in structure, releasing normal spores; most stem sheaths with a narrow to broad blackish band well below the teeth; N,E,S,W. 87. *E. hyemale* var. *affine*

11(10). Cones not releasing spores or the spores aborted; most stem sheaths lacking a blackish band well below the teeth; N,W. 86. *E.* ×*ferrissii*

12(10). Erect stems straight or slightly curved, mostly 15–30 cm long, 0.7–2.5 mm in diam., with a central cavity; N. 88. *E. variegatum*

12(10). Erect stems slightly curved to irregularly contorted, mostly 6–15 cm long, 0.3–0.6 mm in diam., lacking a central cavity; N. 89. *E. scirpoides*

77 Equisetum palustre L.

Marsh Horsetail

Sterile and fertile stems monomorphic, annual, green or greenish, 1–3(5) mm in diam., with 5–10 ridges and sheaths at least 2× longer than wide including the black teeth with white, scarious margins; branches simple, rarely forked, irregularly or regularly borne by the central nodes of the erect stems, bearing irregular tubercles on the ridges; cones 9–35 mm long, borne on stalks 5–32 mm long.

Terrestrial in marshes, swamps, stream banks, ditches, and open, wet woods, usually in circumneutral soil. Rare. Greenland to Alaska south to Vermont, Connecticut, New York, Michigan, Illinois, Minnesota, North Dakota, Montana, Idaho, and California.

Not cultivated. Sterile, unbranched stems of this species resemble those of *E. variegatum*, but lack the horizontal, raised bars in the longitudinal grooves of the stems that characterize the latter species.

78 Equisetum fluviatile L.

Water Horsetail

Sterile and fertile stems monomorphic, annual, deciduous, greenish, 2.5–9 mm in diam., the tissues very thin and papery, with 12–24 often obsolete ridges (the stems then nearly smooth) and sheaths up to 1.5× longer than wide including the blackish teeth with very narrow white margins; branches simple, irregularly or regularly borne by the central and upper nodes of the erect stems or sometimes absent, bearing blocky tubercles on the ridges; cones 12–20 mm long, borne on stalks 8–20(37)mm long.

Terrestrial in marshes, swamps, ponds, and sluggish streams in shallow to deep water and circumneutral soil. Common. Labrador to Alaska south to Virginia, West Virginia, Ohio, Indiana, Illinois, Iowa, Nebraska, Wyoming, Idaho, and Oregon.

Not cultivated. This species is unusual in subg. *Equisetum* for commonly having unbranched sterile stems that resemble those of subg. *Hip-*

pochaete, except that they are deciduous and not nearly so stiff. This species hybridizes with *E. arvense* to form *E. × litorale*.

*79 Equisetum × litorale Kuehl. ex Rupr.
Shore Horsetail

Sterile and fertile stems monomorphic, annual, greenish, 1.25–4 mm in diam., with 10–14 ridges and sheaths ca. 2× longer than wide including the blackish teeth with very narrow white margins; branches simple, irregularly or regularly borne from the central or upper nodes of the erect stems, bearing somewhat irregular, blocky tubercles; cones rather rare, 6–15 mm long, borne on stalks 5–22 mm long; spores abortive.

Terrestrial on tidal river banks, stream banks, lake margins, and occasionally in ditches. Very rare. St. Pierre and Miquelon to Quebec south to New England, New York, Pennsylvania, Ohio, Illinois, Iowa, and Minnesota.

Not cultivated. This is the hybrid of *E. arvense* and *E. fluviatile*. Peck (1980) studied the distribution, ecology, and stand dynamics of this hybrid. He found that colonies, although they occur only sporadically, maintain themselves successfully over long periods of time because their dense growth prevents competing species from becoming established.

80 Equisetum arvense L.
Field Horsetail

Sterile and fertile stems dimorphic, annual, 0.8–4.5 mm in diam.; sterile stems greenish, with 4–14 ridges and sheaths ca. 1.25× longer than wide including the dark brown teeth with white margins, the branches simple, regularly borne from the central nodes to the apex of the erect stems, bearing irregular, block-like or rounded tubercles; fertile stems pale to dark brown, with 4–14 ridges and sheaths ca. 2× longer than wide including the dark brown teeth with white margins, branches lacking; cones 17–40 mm long borne on stalks 22–55 mm long.

Terrestrial in damp woods, meadows, swamps, on stream banks, and along railroad tracks and roadsides, often in disturbed ground in subacid soil. Abundant. Throughout the United States and Canada.

Not cultivated. Hauke (1966) concluded that the many varieties and forms into which this species has been divided are only superficial modifications and none deserves taxonomic recognition. This species hybridizes with *E. fluviatile* to form *E. × litorale*.

*81 Equisetum pratense Ehrh.
Meadow Horsetail

Sterile and fertile stems dimorphic or subdimorphic, annual, 1–3 mm in diam.; sterile stems greenish, with 6–18 ridges and sheaths 1.5–2× longer than wide including the dark brown teeth with white margins, the branches simple, regularly borne from the central nodes to the apex of the erect stems, bearing low, round tubercles; fertile stems pale pinkish to dark brown, with 8–18 ridges and sheaths 2–2.5× longer than wide including the dark brown teeth with white margins, branches lacking; cones 20–25 mm long, borne on stalks 20–48 mm long, the stems later developing and becoming like the sterile stems.

Terrestrial in damp woods in rich, mostly circumneutral soil. Frequent. New Brunswick to Alaska south to New Jersey, New York, Michigan, Wisconsin, Iowa, South Dakota, Alberta, and British Columbia.

Not cultivated.

82 Equisetum sylvaticum L.
Woodland Horsetail

Sterile and fertile stems dimorphic, annual, 1.5–3 mm in diam.; sterile stems stramineous to greenish, with 8–18 ridges and sheaths ca. 2× longer than wide including the reddish-brown, connate teeth with brownish margins, the branches themselves branched, regularly borne from the central nodes to the apex, smooth or bearing irregular or round tubercles or projections on the ridges; fertile stems stramineous to pale brown, with 8–18 ridges and sheaths ca. 3× longer than wide including the reddish-brown, connate, clumped teeth with brownish margins, branches lacking; cones 15–30 mm long, borne on stalks 20–65 mm long, the stems later developing and becoming like the sterile stems.

Terrestrial in moist, open woods, meadows, and swamps in mostly sub-acid soil. Common. Newfoundland to Alaska south to Maryland, Pennsylvania, West Virginia, Ohio, Michigan, Wisconsin, Iowa, South Dakota, northern Wyoming, Montana, Alberta, British Columbia, and Washington.

Not cultivated because of difficulty in transplanting, but clearly the most interesting and beautiful hardy species of the genus because of its large, colorful sheath teeth and delicate branches.

83 Equisetum telmateia subsp. braunii (Milde) Hauke
Giant Horsetail

Sterile and fertile stems dimorphic, annual, 4–15 mm in diam.; sterile stems greenish, with 20–40 ridges and sheaths 1–2× longer than wide including the reddish-brown, connate teeth with brownish margins, the branches simple, regularly borne from the central nodes to the apex of the erect stems, bearing sharp, sometimes almost hooked tubercles on the ridges; fertile stems pale pinkish to dark brown or reddish-brown, with 20–30 ridges and sheaths 2–3× longer than wide including the reddish-brown, connate teeth with brownish margins, branches lacking; cones 40–80 mm long, borne on stalks 30–70 mm long.

Terrestrial in ravines, wet woods, stream banks, and ditches. Common. British Columbia to California.

Not cultivated. Hauke (1978, p. 434) has distinguished the American material as a subspecies separate from Eurasian specimens. He considers the species to be extirpated from the Great Lakes region, because the plants are not known from there now and it is unlikely that several old reports of their occurrence are all in error.

*84 Equisetum ramosissimum Desf. subsp. ramosissimum

Branched Horsetail

Stems sparingly branched with usually 2 or 3 branches at each node, evergreen, greenish, 1.5–7 mm in diam., with 8–24 ridges and sheaths ca. 3× longer than wide including the entirely white or brown-centered, triangular, shriveling but persistent teeth, the lower sheaths light brown with a black band, the upper sheaths entirely green, branches simple, irregularly borne from the central nodes, bearing rows of tubercles or transverse bands on the ridges; cones 12–18 mm long, obtuse to apiculate at the apex.

Terrestrial in wet fields, sandy flats, and ditches. Very rare. Wilmington, New Hanover Co., North Carolina, Pensacola, Escambia Co., Florida, and Pointe Coupee Parish, Louisiana.

Not cultivated. Introduced and persisting at the site of old ship ballast dumps. Hauke (1979) concluded that the plants were more likely undiscovered until recent years, rather than recent introductions.

85 Equisetum laevigatum A. Braun

Smooth Scouring-rush

Stems not branched, annual, greenish, 2–7 mm in diam., with 10–32 ridges and sheaths ca. 2× longer than wide including the brown-centered, long-triangular, teeth with deciduous tips, the sheaths greenish turning pale brown with a dark brown median band in age; ridges of the main stems smooth; cones 10–20 mm long, obtuse or with a slight apiculum.

Terrestrial in meadows, pastures, riverbanks, ditches, and embankments, usually in circumneutral to subacid, sandy or clayey soil. Abundant. Ontario to British Columbia south to Ohio, Indiana, Illinois, Missouri, Oklahoma, Texas, New Mexico, Arizona, and California.

Not cultivated. This species hybridizes with *E. variegatum* var. *variegatum* to form the hybrid *E.* ×*nelsonii* (A. A. Eaton) Schaffn., known from scattered localities in Quebec, Ontario, New York, Michigan, Illinois, and Montana. According to Hauke (1963, pp. 107–110), the hybrid is intermediate in morphology between its parents, although the hybrid plants most resemble *E. variegatum* but have deciduous stems. The species also hybridizes with *E. hyemale* var. *affine* to form *E. ×ferrissii*.

86   Equisetum ×ferrissii Clute

Ferriss' Scouring-rush

Stems not branched, partially evergreen (the lower portions overwintering), greenish, 3–11 mm in diam., with 14–32 ridges and sheaths ca. 2.5× longer than wide including the brown-centered, long-triangular, deciduous teeth, the sheaths greenish turning white toward the apex and sometimes with a brown median band in age; ridges of the main stems regularly and distantly tuberculate; cones 3–10 mm long, apiculate; spores abortive.

Terrestrial on roadsides, lake shores, riverbanks, railroad embankments, and in meadows, in sterile, circumneutral, often disturbed, soil. Common. Vermont, New York, Ontario, Michigan, Wisconsin, Minnesota, North Dakota, Idaho, and Washington south to North Carolina, West Virginia, Ohio, Indiana, Illinois, Arkansas, Oklahoma, Texas, Colorado, Utah, Arizona, Nevada, and California.

Not cultivated. This is the hybrid between *E. hyemale* var. *affine* and *E. laevigatum*, and is easily confused with either parent. According to Hauke (1963, pp. 95–101), it is intermediate in most of its characters of morphology between its parents. It has rough rhizomes, and so can be distinguished from *E. laevigatum* × *variegatum* var. *variegatum* (*E. ×nelsonii* (A. A. Eaton) Schaffn., which has nearly smooth rhizomes.

87   Equisetum hyemale var. affine (Engelm.) A. A. Eaton

Scouring-rush

Stems not branched, evergreen, greenish, 2.5–17.5 mm in diam., with 14–50 ridges and sheaths ca. 1–2× longer than wide including the brown-centered, long-triangular, deciduous teeth, the sheaths white toward the apex and usually with a brown median band in age; ridges of the main stems regularly and distantly tuberculate; cones 10–30 mm long, apiculate.

Terrestrial in woods, fields, swamps, roadsides, riverbanks, and railroad embankments, in moist, circumneutral, often disturbed soil. Abundant. Labrador to Alaska south throughout the United States.

Not cultivated. This variety hybridizes with *E. variegatum* var. *variegatum* to form the hybrid *E. ×trachyodon* A. Braun, known from scattered localities in Newfoundland, Quebec, Ontario, Maine, Vermont, New Hampshire, New York, New Jersey, Ohio, Illinois, Michigan, Indiana, Illinois, Wisconsin, Montana, Idaho, Oregon, Washington, and British Columbia. According to Hauke (1963, pp. 101–107), the hybrid is intermediate in morphology between its parents. Young stems are likely to resemble those of *E. variegatum* var. *variegatum*, but older stems tend to resemble those of *E. hyemale* var. *affine*. It also hybridizes commonly with *E. laevigatum* to form *E. ×ferrissii*.

88   Equisetum variegatum Schleich. ex Weber & Mohr

Variegated Scouring-rush

Stems not branched, evergreen, bright green, 0.7–2.5 mm in diam., with 3–14 ridges and sheaths ca. 2× longer than wide including the dark brown-centered, cuspidate, rather persistent teeth, the sheaths commonly with a blackish apical band; ridges of the main stems regularly tuberculate; cones 5–13 mm long, apiculate.

Terrestrial along lake shores, stream banks, ditches, and in wet meadows in usually sandy, circumneutral to subalkaline soil. Frequent. Newfoundland to Alaska south to New Hampshire, Vermont, Connecticut, New York, New Jersey, northwestern Pennsylvania, Michigan, northern Illinois, Wisconsin, Minnesota, Manitoba, Saskatchewan, Montana, Wyoming, Colorado, Utah, Idaho, and Oregon.

Not cultivated. This species hybridizes with *E. laevigatum* to form *E. × nelsonii* (A. A. Eaton) Schaffn., which is discussed under *E. laevigatum*. It also hybridizes with *E. hyemale* var. *affine* to form *E. ×trachyodon*, which is discussed under *E. hyemale* var. *affine*. Some specimens from coastal Alaska and British Columbia have sheath teeth entirely black or with only narrow, white margins. Many intergradations with var. *variegatum* exist, and so the coastal specimens have been given only varietal status as var. *alaskanum* A. A. Eaton in Harriman.

89   Equisetum scirpoides Michx.

Dwarf Scouring-rush

Stems tufted, not branched, evergreen, slightly curved to irregularly contorted, 0.3–0.6 mm in diam., with 6 or sometimes fewer ridges and sheaths ca. 3× longer than wide including the dark brown-centered, lanceate, persistent teeth, the sheaths usually with a blackish apical band; ridges of the main stems regularly tuberculate; cones 2–3 mm long, apiculate.

Terrestrial in the tundra, on swamp hummocks, and especially in coniferous woods, in wet, usually subacid soil. Frequent. Newfoundland to Alaska south to Connecticut, New York, Michigan, Wisconsin, northern Illinois, Minnesota, South Dakota, eastern Wyoming, Montana, Idaho, and Washington.

Easily cultivated as a pot plant or in a terrarium. The small, bent or contorted stems are distinctive.

FERNS

OPHIOGLOSSACEAE
The Adder's-tongue Family

Conservatively the family contains four genera, *Helminthostachys* (southern China to Malesia and Australia), *Cheiroglossa* (tropical America, Réunion, and Indo-China), and *Ophioglossum* and *Botrychium* (both world-wide). *Botrychium* subgenus *Sceptridium*, the Grape Ferns, is considered by some authors to be an independent genus, but morphologically and ecologically it is very close to subgenus *Botrychium*, the Moonworts. A third subgenus, *Osmundopteris*, includes the Rattlesnake Ferns. All the genera except *Helminthostachys* occur in the United States. The taxonomy of *Botrychium* and to some extent *Ophioglossum* is not thoroughly understood, for the species are variable and little is known about the effect of habitat on the form of the plants.

These plants are among the most primitive of living ferns. The small, unbranched, subterranean stems are short, erect, and cylindrical to bulbous. They bear a few, fleshy roots that lack root hairs, but which contain filaments of fungal cells (hyphae) that presumably contribute carbohydrates to their metabolism. Each stem bears one to a few minute to small fronds, the sterile portion of which is undivided in *Ophioglossum*, palmately divided in *Cheiroglossa*, and pinnately dissected in *Botrychium*. The fronds of the first two genera are presumed to be pseudolaminae that originated by the progressive flattening and widening of a frond that had been reduced to a single midrib without a lamina or that never had a lamina. This is shown by their growth patterns and the fact that the fronds of *Ophioglossum* and *Cheiroglossa* have no midrib. The basal, yellowish or greenish fertile portion of the frond is erect and held above the sterile portion in the terrestrial species to allow dispersal of the spores by the wind. Developmentally, the fertile portion of the frond of *Botrychium* and *Ophioglossum* is a pair of basal, fused, transformed sterile pinnae. Large, yellowish, nearly round sporangia are closely spaced along the apical parts of the fertile portions of the laminae. Each sporangium bears thousands of spores of one size.

The species of Ophioglossaceae are almost all terrestrial. Because of the poorly understood relationship between the root fungi, the ferns, and the soil they grow in, cultivation is difficult or impossible for all members of the family, except for *Ophioglossum petiolatum*. Because the subterranean stems contain buds for at least the following years fronds, it is possible to collect only the fronds for scientific purposes without seriously injuring the plants, although in *Ophioglossum* some entire plants with stems may be necessary for identification. The family was monographed by Clausen (1938), although many of his taxonomic concepts have been superseded in recent years.

Key to the Genera of the Ophioglossaceae

1. Sterile portion of the laminae pinnate-pinnatifid or more divided, or absent (in *B. paradoxum*); fertile stalks decidedly branched, the branches bearing numerous individual sporangia *Botrychium*, p. 102

1. Sterile portion of the laminae unlobed or palmately lobed; fertile stalks unbranched, bearing a single row of sporangia embedded on each side, 2

2(1). Fertile fronds with a single, erect fertile stalk; sterile portion of the fronds unlobed; plants terrestrial, *Ophioglossum*, p. 115

2(1). Fertile fronds with one or more pairs of fertile stalks at the base of the sterile portion of the frond; sterile portion of the fronds palmately lobed; plants epiphytic, *Cheiroglossa*, p. 119

BOTRYCHIUM
The Grape Ferns, Rattlesnake Ferns, and Moonworts

Unlike *Cheiroglossa* and *Ophioglossum*, the species of *Botrychium*, with few exceptions (like *B. simplex*), have the laminae divided into a pinnate to 4-pinnate, apical, sterile portion 1–15(25) cm long that is stalked and deltate to lanceolate or oblong. (Because of the stalk, the sterile portion is longer than its lamina.) The basal, fertile portion of the frond is an erect spike that is slightly to many times longer than the sterile portion. The spike is pinnately branched at its apex, and each branch and branchlet bears two rows of sporangia not or only slightly embedded in the branch or branchlet.

Botrychium is divided into three subgenera. Subgenus *Sceptridium* contains the Grape Ferns. The sterile portion of the fronds are medium-sized, pinnate to 3-pinnate, rather fleshy, and decidedly evergreen. The other two subgenera are not evergreen. Subgenus *Osmundopteris* contains *B. virginianum*, the Rattlesnake Fern, the only representative in our flora. The sterile portion of the lamina is large and highly divided. Subgenus *Botrychium* contains the Moonworts, which have the sterile portion of their fronds small and pinnate or 2-pinnate.

Botrychium species are often only subtly distinct, and so have been much confused in herbaria and in books. They vary considerably, depending upon the conditions under which they grow. Shade forms have been described as separate varieties or species. Juvenile and depauperate specimens, especially of the Moonworts, are difficult to identify correctly because the characters of lamina division are lost as the laminae become smaller and less divided.

In the wild, plants of *Botrychium* are hard to see and usually are missed by casual observers. Those of subgenus *Sceptridium* are best sought in autumn and winter, when they are more easily seen among the dead grasses and herbs. Those of subgenus *Botrychium* are above ground during the spring and summer and are very inconspicuous. Plants of subg. *Sceptridium* commonly grow above the roots of wild cherry and apple trees in meadows and in orchards in the eastern United States or are associated with wild strawberries. A little disturbance, by grazing for instance, seems to favor their establishment and continuation in any habitat. Often several species with plants in various stages of development are found together; small specimens are especially difficult to identify.

Key to Botrychium
   1. Fertile stalk joined to the sterile stalk near the base of the sterile portion of the lamina, far above the rhizome and usually above the ground (except in some specimens of *B. simplex* from the western United States); main roots mostly 0.5–1 mm in diam. when dry, **8**
   1. Fertile stalk joined to the sterile stalk near the rhizome, far below the base of the sterile portion of the lamina and usually below ground; main roots mostly (1)1.5–4 mm in diam. when dry (subg. *Sceptridium*), **2**
   2(1). Sterile pinnae entirely divided into short, round or acute pinnules; lateral pinnules with a rudimentary or inconspicuous central axis; plants often forming 2 or more fronds per season (usually 1 frond in *B. multifidum* and *B. rugulosum*), **5**
   2(1). Sterile pinnae (or their terminal half or third) elongate, entire or slightly lobed, not divided into pinnules; lateral pinnules with a well-developed, conspicuous central axis; plants usually forming 1 frond per season, **3**
   3(2). Sterile pinna apices and those of most lateral segments obtuse to round; NE. *90. B. oneidense*
   3(2). Sterile pinna apices and those of most lateral segments acute, **4**
   4(3). Sterile portion of the laminae mostly 3-pinnate, the segments toothed to highly dissected; E. *91. B. dissectum*
   4(3). Sterile portion of the laminae 2-pinnate, the segments finely toothed but never highly dissected; SE. *92. B. biternatum*
   5(2). Sterile pinna and pinnule apices round, rarely obtuse, **7**
   5(2). Sterile pinna and pinnule apices obtuse to acute, rarely round, **6**
   6(5). Stalk of the sterile laminae less than 2 mm in diam.; basal sterile pinnae distant from the suprabasal ones, some laminae therefore ternate;

segments of the sterile portion of the laminae acute, concave in living specimens; NE. *93. B. rugulosum*

6(5). Stalk of the sterile laminae 2 mm or more in diam.; basal sterile pinnae not distant from the suprabasal ones, none of the laminae ternate; segments of the sterile portion of the laminae obtuse, plane in living specimens; N. *94. B. multifidum*

7(6). Stalk of the basal sterile pinnae (10)15–70 mm long; roots irregularly ribbed; apical segments of sterile pinnae longer than wide, with a weakly developed midrib; SE. *95. B. jenmanii*

7(6). Stalk of the basal sterile pinnae 4–15(20) mm long; roots smooth; apical segments of sterile pinnae about as long as wide, subflabellately veined, the midrib absent; SE. *96. B. lunarioides*

8(1). Sterile portion of the laminae 3-pinnate or more compound; plants (15)30–50 cm long (subg. *Osmundopteris*); N, E, S, W. *97. B. virginianum*

8(1). Sterile portion of the laminae 1–2-pinnate or the sterile portion transformed into a second fertile portion; plants commonly less than 20 cm long (subg. *Botrychium*), **9**

9(8). Sterile portion of the laminae usually absent, transformed into a second, short, fertile portion; MT, ALB. *98. B. paradoxum*

9(8). Sterile portion of the laminae always present, never transformed (except in *B.* ×*watertonense*), **10**

10(9). Sterile pinnae (or pinnules in 2-pinnate sterile laminae) contracted at the base, entire to deeply cleft, **17**

10(9). Sterile segments (or pinna segments in 2-pinnate sterile laminae) not contracted at the base, oblong or elongate, entire to lobed, **11**

11(10). Sterile pinnae obtuse to round at the apex, their segments (and undivided pinnae) about as long as wide, round, obtuse, or truncate at the apex, **13**

11(10). Sterile pinnae acute at the apex, their segments (and undivided pinnae) at least twice as long as wide, mostly lanceolate, acute at the apex, **12**

12(11). Sterile pinna segments mostly acute, 1–2 mm wide; NE. *100. B. lanceolatum* subsp. *angustisegmentum*

12(11). Sterile pinna segments mostly acute, 1–2 mm wide; NE. *100. B. lanceolatum* subsp. *angustisegmentum*

13(11). Sterile portion of the laminae divided into lobed pinnae, **15**

13(11). Sterile portion of the laminae with merely entire to toothed or lacerate lobes, **14**

14(13). Laminae shiny, yellow-green, succulent, the lobes entire to shallowly crenate; NO. *101. B. mormo*

14(13). Laminae dull, bluish-green, herbaceous, the lobes decidedly toothed to lacerate; NW. *102. B. montanum*

15(13). Pinnae nearly at right angles to the central axis of the lamina; ultimate sterile divisions (pinnae or pinnules) approximate; sterile portion of the lamina usually short-stalked 0.5 cm or less; NW. *104. B. pinnatum*

15(13). Pinnae ascending, **16**

16(15). Ultimate sterile divisions (pinnae, pinnules, or pinnule lobes) distant; sterile portion of the laminae usually long-stalked (0.5)1 cm or more; N. *103. B. matricariifolium*

16(15). Ultimate sterile divisions (pinnules) approximate; sterile portion of the laminae usually short-stalked 0.25–0.5 cm; RM. **105. B. hesperium*

17(10). Stalk of the sterile portion of the laminae ⅓–½ as long as the lamina itself; N. *106. B. simplex*

17(10). Stalk of the sterile portion of the laminae less than ¼ as long as the lamina itself, **18**

18(17). Sterile pinnae entire at the apex, sometimes cleft or irregularly incised, **20**

18(17). Sterile pinnae crenate or deeply and irregularly dentate at the apex, **19**

19(18). Sterile pinnae crenate at the apex; plants thin and delicate, pale yellow-green, less than 10 cm long; SW. *107. B. crenulatum*

19(18). Sterile pinnae deeply and irregularly dentate at the apex; plants often more than 10 cm long; NW. *109. B. ascendens*

20(18). Pinnae imbricate, gray-green, dull; fertile portion of the laminae not much exceeding the sterile; NW. *108. B. pumicola*

20(18). Pinnae approximate to distant, rarely imbricate, not gray-green (except in *B. hesperium*), shiny (dull in *B. hesperium*); fertile portion of the laminae usually greatly exceeding the sterile, **21**

21(20). Lower segments lanceolate to oblong or rhomboidal, not completely flabellate, a central midrib present, **24**

21(20). Lower segments fan-shaped or square, with completely flabellate venation, the central midrib absent, **22**

22(21). Pinnae imbricate to approximate, subflabellate to nearly round; N, RM. *110. B. lunaria*

22(21). Pinnae distant to approximate, oblong or oblanceolate to subflabellate, **23**

23(22). Sterile portion of the laminae trough-shaped in living material; pinnae mostly entire; branches of the fertile portion of the laminae mostly spreading; N, RM. *111 B. minganense*

23(22). Sterile portion of the laminae plane in living material; sterile-pinnae mostly deeply bi- to trifid; branches of the fertile portion of the laminae mostly strongly ascending; no. RM, NP. *112. B. campestre*

24(21). Sterile portion of the laminae subsessile, the lower segments lanceolate to oblong, the common stipe lacking a brown stripe; AR, UT, CO. *113. B. echo*

24(21). Sterile portion of the laminae long-stalked, the lower segments rhomboidal, the common stipe bearing a conspicuous, brown stripe; ALB, SAS. *114. B. pedunculosum*

90 Botrychium oneidense (Gilb.) House
Blunt-lobed Grape Fern

Stems producing 1 frond per season, bearing main roots mostly 1.5–2 mm in diam.; stipes 1–6 cm long; fertile portion of the laminae 14–38 cm long; sterile portion of the laminae 6–20 cm long, the laminae 8–19 cm long, 6–15 cm wide, obtuse to truncate at the base, acute to obtuse at the apex, 2–3-pinnate, with coarse, entire to shallowly lobed, obtuse to round pinna and sometimes pinnule apices, the segments ovate or subrhombic, the margins finely serrate.

Terrestrial in low, wet, shady woods and swamps, in acid soil. Rare. New Brunswick, Quebec, and Ontario south to North Carolina, eastern Tennessee, Kentucky, Indiana, Michigan, and Wisconsin.

Not cultivated. According to Wagner (1961), the roots of this species are thinner and predominantly ivory-gray to tan, compared to the thicker, gray-brown roots of *B. dissectum*. In addition, the fronds of *B. oneidense* are lime green when unfolding and are mostly green when exposed in the winter, whereas those of *B. dissectum* are reddish if exposed when unfolding and are often bronze when exposed in the winter. (They are green in either season if covered by leaf litter.)

91 Botrychium dissectum Spreng.
Lace-frond Grape Fern

Stems producing 1 frond per season, bearing main roots mostly 1–3 mm in diam.; stipes 2–6 cm long; fertile portion of the laminae 15–38 cm long; sterile portion of the laminae 4–27 cm long, the laminae deltate, 4–25 cm long, 5–18(27) cm wide, truncate at the base, obtuse at the apex, 3-pinnate to 4-pinnate-pinnatifid, with entire, lobed, or lacerate, acute pinna and pinnule apices, the segments irregular, the margins finely serrate to deeply lacerate.

Terrestrial in moist to rather dry woods, swamps, and pastures or old fields, commonly under somewhat disturbed conditions. Abundant. Nova Scotia, Quebec, Ontario, Wisconsin, and southeastern Minnesota south to northern Georgia, Alabama, Mississippi, Louisiana, Arkansas, eastern Kansas, and Iowa.

Cultivated with difficulty in humus-rich, acid, loamy soil. This highly variable species is more wide-ranging and grows in a greater variety of habitats than does *B. oneidense*, with which the less divided forms often are often confused. Several infraspecific taxa will likely be distinguished as a result of further study in the southeastern United States.

92 Botrychium biternatum (Sav.) Underw.
Sparse-lobed Grape Fern

Stems producing 1 frond per season, bearing main roots mostly 1.5–3 mm in diam.; stipes 2–6 cm long; fertile portion of the laminae 8–32 cm long; sterile portion of the laminae 5–22 cm long, the laminae broadly deltate, 2.5–10 cm long, 3–13 cm wide, truncate at the base, obtuse at the apex, 2-pinnate, with entire or sometimes serrate, acute pinna and pinnule apices, the segments irregular, the margins finely serrate.

Terrestrial in woods, pinelands, swamps, and old fields in subacid soil. Frequent. Florida to eastern Texas north to South Carolina, southern Ohio, Indiana, Illinois, and Missouri.

Not cultivated.

93 Botrychium rugulosum Wagner
Ternate Grape Fern

Stems producing 2 or more fronds per season, bearing main roots mostly 1.25–2.5 mm in diam.; stipes 1–3.5 cm long; fertile portion of the laminae 6–19 cm long; sterile portion of the laminae 3.5–13 cm long, the laminae deltate-lanceolate, 2.5–9(15) cm long, 2.5–9(15) cm wide, obtuse at the base, obtuse or nearly so at the apex, 3-pinnate or 3-pinnate-pinnatifid, with entire to lobed, acute pinnae and pinnule apices, the segments lanceate, the margins entire to irregularly toothed or finely lobed.

Terrestrial in old, brushy pastures, meadows, and wet woods, in sandy, acid soil. Frequent. Quebec, Ontario, and northern Wisconsin south to northern Vermont, southern Michigan, and eastern Minnesota.

Not cultivated. The long-stalked pinnae and the rather large space between the basal pair of pinnae and the upper pairs will distinguish this species from *B. lunarioides* and *B. multifidum*. Wagner (1960a) and Wagner and Wagner (1982b) have shown that differences in phenology and development also exist between these species and *B. rugulosum*, which formerly was thought to be the Asiatic species *B. rugulosum*.

94 Botrychium multifidum (Gmel.) Rupr.
Leathery Grape Fern

Stems producing usually 1 frond per season, bearing main roots mostly 2–4 mm in diam., the older roots contracted and wrinkled transversely; stipes 1.5–6 cm long; fertile portion of the laminae 8–40 cm long; sterile portion of the laminae 6–30 cm long, the laminae deltate-lanceolate, 4–

28 cm long, 3.5–20 cm wide, obtuse to nearly truncate at the base, obtuse or nearly so at the apex, 3–4-pinnate, with entire, acute, obtuse, or rarely round pinna and pinnule apices, the segments ovate to oblong, the margins entire or slightly crenate.

Terrestrial in old pastures, meadows, woodland margins, riverbanks, and bottom lands in subacid soil. Common. Labrador to Alaska south to Virginia, Ohio, Indiana, Illinois, Iowa, Nebraska, Colorado, northern New Mexico, Arizona, and California.

Cultivated with difficulty in humus-rich, acid, loamy soil. Commonly plants of this species are very robust. According to Stevenson (1975), they are long-lived perennials and may live for more than 100 years.

95 Botrychium jenmanii Underw.

Alabama Grape Fern

Stems producing 1 or more grayish-green fronds per season, bearing main roots mostly 1.5–2.5 mm in diam.; stipes 1.5–3.5 cm long; fertile portion of the laminae 15–32 cm long; sterile portion of the laminae 7–24 cm long, the laminae deltate, 6–15 cm long, 7–18 cm wide, obtuse to nearly truncate at the base, obtuse at the apex, 3–4-pinnate, with entire to lobed, round pinna and pinnule apices, the segments commonly obovate, the margins entire to minutely lacerate-denticulate.

Terrestrial in old fields, pastures, and light woods, in subacid soil. Frequent. Virginia to Tennessee south to Florida and Alabama.

Not cultivated. This species is a fertile hybrid between *B. biternatum* and *B. lunarioides*. W. H. Wagner (pers. comm.) recently discovered that *B. alabamense* Maxon is a synonym of this species.

96 Botrychium lunarioides (Michx.) Swartz

Winter Grape Fern

Stems producing 2 or more fronds per season, bearing main roots mostly 1–1.5 mm in diam.; stipes 1–2 cm long; fertile portion of the laminae 7–16 cm long; sterile portion of the laminae 3–10 cm long, the laminae deltate, 3–8 cm long, 5–13 cm wide, cordate at the base, obtuse to round at the apex, 3–4-pinnate, with entire, round pinna and pinnule apices, the segments flabellate to obovate, the margins mostly regularly dentate.

Terrestrial in old fields, pastures, mowed roadsides, and light woods, in dry, sandy, subacid soil. Very rare. South Carolina to northern Florida, eastern Mississippi, eastern Texas, and southeastern Oklahoma.

Not cultivated. This species is unlike most Grape Ferns in that its leaves die in early spring, and new leaves appear in mid-autumn.

97 Botrychium virginianum (L.) Swartz

Rattlesnake Fern

Stems producing 1 frond per season, bearing main roots mostly 1–2 mm in diam.; stipes 10–31 cm long; fertile portion of the laminae 5–26 cm long; sterile portion of the laminae 11–37 cm long, the laminae 5–25 cm long, 7–30 cm wide, truncate to subcordate at the base, obtuse or occasionally acute at the apex, 3-pinnate-pinnatifid to 4-pinnate, with lacerate, acute pinna apices and acute, obtuse, or truncate pinnule apices, the segments ovate to oblong, lacerate-toothed, the margins entire.

Terrestrial in thickets and deciduous woods in rich, circumneutral to subacid soil. Common. Newfoundland to British Columbia south to Florida and California.

Cultivated in rich garden soil. This species is not evergreen, but dies back in winter. It is one of the few fern species found nearly throughout the United States and adjacent Canada, being absent only in northern Canada and the drier parts of the western United States.

98 Botrychium paradoxum Wagner

Two-spiked Moonwort

Stems producing 1 frond per season; stipes 0.5–2 mm in diam., glaucous, ca. 6.5–11 cm long; fertile portions of the laminae twinned, the larger 0.5–4 cm long, the smaller about ⅔ as long; sterile portions of the leaf usually absent.

Terrestrial in both sunny meadows and shady patches of Fireweed. Very rare. Montana and Alberta.

Not cultivated. This peculiar species normally lacks a sterile portion of the lamina. The shorter fertile portion is homologous with the sterile portion of typical *Botrychium* species. Presumably, the plant's needs for carbohydrate are met partially through its endophytic fungus, rather than its own photosynthesis. This species hybridizes in southwestern Alberta with *B. hesperium* to form *B.* ×*watertonense* Wagner.

99 Botrychium lanceolatum (Gmel.) Ångstr. subsp. lanceolatum

Lance-leaved Moonwort

Stems producing 1 frond per season, bearing main roots mostly 0.5–1 mm in diam.; stipes 3–14 cm long; fertile portion of the laminae 1.5–8 cm long; sterile portion of the laminae 1–6 cm long, the laminae 1–6 cm long, 1–6.5 cm wide, obtuse at the base, acute or round at the apex, pinnate-pinnatifid to 2-pinnate-pinnatifid, with scarcely lobed to pinnatifid, acute pinna apices and acute to round pinnule and segment apices, the segments lanceolate to oblong, the margins entire.

Terrestrial on rocky slopes, in meadows and woods, in cold, mostly sub-acid soil. Rare. Alaska to Oregon; Colorado, Utah, New Mexico, and Arizona at high elevations.

Not cultivated.

100 Botrychium lanceolatum subsp. angustisegmentum (Paese & Moore) Clausen

Narrow Lance-leaved Moonwort

Stems producing 1 frond per season, bearing main roots mostly 0.5–1 mm in diam.; stipes 2–21 cm long; fertile portion of the laminae (1)1.5–9 cm long; sterile portion of the laminae 1.5–4.5 cm long, the laminae ovate-lanceate, 1.5–4.5 cm long, 1.5–6 cm wide, truncate to obtuse at the base, acute at the apex, pinnate-pinnatifid to 2-pinnate, with incised, acute pinna apices and entire, acute pinnule and segment apices, the segments narrowly triangular, the margins entire.

Terrestrial in woods and on hummocks in swamps, in cool to warm, mostly rich, subacid soil. Rare. Newfoundland to Ontario south to Virginia, West Virginia, Ohio, Michigan, Wisconsin, and Minnesota. Disjunct in Macon Co., North Carolina.

Not cultivated.

101 Botrychium mormo Wagner

Little Goblin Moonwort

Stems producing 1 frond per season; stipes ca. 5 cm long; fertile portion of the laminae linear, 2.4–7.5 cm long; sterile portion of the laminae 1.3–4.1 cm long, the laminae oblong, 0.8–2.5 cm long, 0.3–0.7 mm wide, obtuse at the base, obtuse to round at the apex, pinnatifid, with entire to shallowly crenate, obtuse to truncate lobes.

Terrestrial on forest floors in full shade. Rare. Michigan to Minnesota.

Not cultivated. This is the smallest North American Moonwort known. Its size doubtless accounts for its having remained undiscovered for so long. Apparently it does not put forth growth above the ground in dry seasons.

102 Botrychium montanum Wagner

Mountain Moonwort

Stems producing 1 or 2 fronds per season; stipes 3–6 cm long; fertile portion of the laminae 1–6.5 cm long; sterile portion of the laminae 0.7–4 cm long, the laminae oblong-lanceate, 0.7–4 cm long, 0.2–0.9 cm wide, acute to obtuse at the base, round to obtuse at the apex, pinnatisect, with irregular, oblong, often confluent segments, the distal margins irregularly toothed to lacerate.

Terrestrial in western red cedar forests and along grassy trail edges. Frequent. British Columbia, Washington, Oregon, and Montana.

Not cultivated.

103   Botrychium matricariifolium A. Braun
Daisy-leaved Moonwort

Stems producing 1 frond per season, bearing main roots mostly 0.5–1 mm in diam.; stipes 3–19 cm long; fertile portion of the laminae 3–12(20) cm long; sterile portion of the laminae 1.5–11 cm long, the laminae lanceolate to ovate, 1–8 cm long, 0.8–4 cm wide, obtuse to truncate at the base, acute to round at the apex, pinnate or pinnate-pinnatifid, with incised or entire, obtuse or round pinna apices and entire, obtuse or truncate segment apices, the segments oblong, the margins entire.

Terrestrial in woods, thickets, and rarely in pastures, in rich, subacid or circumneutral soil. Very rare. Newfoundland to Alberta south to the mountains of North Carolina, Tennessee, Kentucky, and West Virginia, and Ohio, Michigan, northern Illinois, Wisconsin, Minnesota, and North Dakota.

Not cultivated. Hybrids between this species and *B. simplex* have been found in central Michigan, according to Wagner (1980).

104   Botrychium pinnatum H. St. John
Northern Moonwort

Stems producing 1 frond per season, bearing main roots mostly 0.5–1 mm in diam.; stipes 3.5–14 cm long; fertile portion of the laminae 3–12 cm long; sterile portion of the laminae 2–7.5 cm long, the laminae lanceate to oblong, 1.5–7 cm long, 1–4.5 cm wide, truncate at the base, acute, obtuse, or slightly round at the apex, 1–2-pinnate, with entire or incised, round pinna and pinnule apices, the segments oblong to obovate, the margins entire.

Terrestrial on grassy slopes, streambanks, and in mossy woods, in moist to wet soil. Rare. Alaska and Yukon Territory south at higher elevations in the mountains of eastern Montana, northern Nevada, and northeastern Oregon.

Not cultivated. W. H. Wagner (pers. comm.) has distinguished between this American species and the Eurasiatic *B. boreale* Milde.

*105   Botrychium hesperium (Maxon & Clausen) Wagner & Lellinger
Western Moonwort

Stems producing 1 frond per season, bearing main roots mostly 0.5–1 mm in diam.; stipes 3–13 cm long; fertile portions of the laminae 3–10 cm long, the laminae short-stalked, ovate-oblong to deltate, 1–5 cm long,

0.5–4 cm wide, obtuse to truncate at the base, acute at the apex, pinnate to nearly 2-pinnate with deeply lobed pinnae, the pinnae approximate to imbricate, broadly attached, ovate to lanceolate, the basal ones commonly exaggerated, the lobes with rounded apices.

Terrestrial in exposed, dry fields and on roadsides, at high elevations. Rare. Southwestern Alberta, western Montana, and central Colorado.

Not cultivated. This species hybridizes with *B. paradoxum* to form *B. × watertonense*, which is known from southwestern Alberta (Wagner et al., 1984).

106 Botrychium simplex E. Hitchc.

Least Moonwort

Stems producing 1 frond per season, bearing main roots mostly 0.5–1 mm in diam.; stipes 3–13 cm long; fertile portion of the laminae 1.5–12 cm long; sterile portion of the laminae highly variable, 1–7 cm long, the laminae oblong to long-elliptic, 1–6 cm long, 0.3–2 cm wide, truncate to round at the base, round at the apex, pinnate or sometimes nearly simple, with entire, round pinna apices, the pinnae subflabellate to oblong, the margins entire.

Terrestrial in meadows, barrens, and woods in usually subacid soil. Frequent. Newfoundland to British Columbia south to New Jersey, Pennsylvania, Virginia, Michigan, Indiana, Wisconsin, Iowa, South Dakota, Wyoming, Colorado, northern New Mexico, Utah, Nevada, and California.

Not cultivated. This species hybridizes with *B. matricariifolium* in Michigan. Eastern, western, and Colorado forms exist in this species; additional study is needed.

107 Botrychium crenulatum Wagner

Crenulate Moonwort

Stems producing 1 frond per season, bearing main roots mostly 0.5–1 mm in diam.; stipes 3–5 cm long; fertile portion of the laminae 2–3.5 cm long; sterile portion of the laminae 1.5–2 cm long, the laminae oblong, ca. 1.5 cm long, 0.5–0.75 cm wide, truncate at the base, obtuse at the apex, pinnate, with round pinna apices, the pinnae subflabellate, the margins crenate.

Terrestrial in marshy places at rather low elevations. Rare. Central and southern California to central Arizona and Montana.

Not cultivated. This species has been found growing with *B. lunaria* in Clark Co., Nevada and, although the plants look very much like small plants of *B. lunaria*, they differ in having thin, pale green fronds and more spathulate pinnae with decidedly crenate pinna apices.

108 Botrychium pumicola Coville
Pumice Moonwort

Stems producing 1 frond per season, bearing main roots mostly 0.5–1 mm in diam.; stipes 4–10 cm long; fertile portion of the laminae 2–7(9) cm long; sterile portion of the laminae 1.5–5 cm long, the laminae deltate with very large basal pinnae, 2–4 cm long, 2–6 cm wide, obtuse to truncate at the base, round at the apex, pinnate to 2-pinnate, with entire, round pinna and pinnule apices, the segments subflabellate, the margins entire.

Terrestrial on rocky, exposed summits, in pumice gravel. Very rare. Crater Lake National Park, Oregon.

Not cultivated. The restricted range and strange habitat suggest that the specimens of this species may be strongly modified specimens of some other western American *Botrychium*.

109 Botrychium ascendens Wagner
Triangular-lobed Moonwort

Stems producing 1 frond per season, bearing main roots mostly 0.5–1 mm in diam.; stipes 5–10 cm long; fertile portion of the laminae exceeding the sterile portion, 3–7 cm long; sterile portion of the laminae 1.5–3.5 cm long, the laminae yellow-green, shiny, oblong-lanceate, 1–3.25 cm long, 1–1.5 cm wide, obtuse at the base, round at the apex, pinnate with slightly rounded pinnae apices, the pinnae, especially the medial and distal ones, ascending, cuneate, the margins strongly and irregularly dentate.

Terrestrial in grassy places. Rare. British Columbia, Alberta, and Montana to northern California and Nevada.

Not cultivated.

110 Botrychium lunaria (L.) Swartz
Moonwort

Stems producing 1 frond per season, bearing main roots mostly 0.5–1 mm in diam.; stipes 1.5–8 cm long; fertile portion of the laminae 1.5–14 cm long; sterile portion of the laminae 1.5–6.5 cm long, the laminae oblong to ovate, 1–6 cm long, 0.8–2.5 cm wide, cordate to truncate at the base, round at the apex, pinnate, with round pinna apices, the pinnae flabellate, the margins entire.

Terrestrial in grassy or mossy meadows and on sandy or gravelly riverbanks, in acid to circumneutral soil. Frequent. Labrador to Alaska south to Maine, Vermont, New York, Michigan, Minnesota, South Dakota, Colorado, northern New Mexico, Arizona, Nevada, Idaho, and California.

Not cultivated. *Botrychium lunaria* var. *onandagense* (Underw.) House appears to be a shade form not worthy of taxonomic recognition.

111 Botrychium minganense Vict.
Mingan Moonwort

Stems producing 1 frond per season, bearing main roots mostly 0.5–1 mm in diam.; stipes (1.5)3–13 cm long; fertile portion of the laminae 1.5–15 cm long; sterile portion of the laminae 1.5–10 cm long, the laminae oblong, 1–9 cm long, 0.5–2.5 cm wide, truncate at the base, round at the apex, pinnate, with round pinna apices, the pinnae subflabellate, the margins entire but commonly with one or more shallow incisions.

Terrestrial in meadows, prairies, and woods and on sand dunes and riverbanks, in acid to circumneutral soil. Rare. Labrador to Ontario south to Vermont, New York, Michigan, Wisconsin, and North Dakota; Alaska to Alberta south to Montana, Idaho, Utah, Nevada, and Oregon.

Not cultivated. Wagner and Lord (1956) have demonstrated the distinctions between this species and *B. lunaria*. This species also may be difficult to distinguish from *B. crenulatum*, from which it differs in having the distal pinnae progressively smaller than the median ones and usually smooth margins. This character is easily seen in large specimens, but may be obscure in small ones.

*112 Botrychium campestre Wagner
Prairie Moonwort

Stems producing 1 frond per season, bearing main roots mostly 0.5–1 mm in diam.; stipes 3–7(10) cm long; fertile portion of the laminae 1.5–3(4.5) cm long; sterile portion of the laminae 1.5–3 cm long, the laminae oblong, 1.25–3 cm long, 0.5–1.25 cm wide, obtuse at the base, round at the apex, pinnate, the pinnae oblong to oblanceolate with lobed apices, the margins entire.

Terrestrial in prairies among grasses and flowering plants. Very rare. Central Alberta to southwestern Iowa.

Not cultivated. An early spring, possibly ephemeral, species.

*113 Botrychium echo Wagner
Reflected Moonwort

Stems producing 1 frond per season, bearing main roots mostly 0.5–1 mm in diam.; stipes 2–10 cm long; fertile portion of the laminae 1.5–8 cm long; sterile portion of the laminae 1–4.5 cm long, ca. 1–2 cm wide, subsessile, obtuse to truncate at the base, round to acute at the apex, pinnate, with obtuse to acute pinna apices, the pinnae lanceolate to oblong, the margins entire or with 1 or rarely several lobes or incisions on the basal side.

Roadsides, grassy slopes, and along the edges of lakes. Rare. Northern Arizona, northern Utah, and central Colorado.

Not cultivated. This species hybridizes with *B. hesperium*, according to Wagner and Wagner (1983).

114 Botrychium pedunculosum Wagner

Stalked Moonwort

Stems producing 1 frond per season, bearing main roots mostly 0.5–1 mm in diam.; stipes 3–10 cm long, with a conspicuous, pale brown stripe below the sterile portion of the frond; fertile portion of the laminae long-stalked, exceeding the sterile portion, 3–8 cm long; sterile portion of the laminae longstalked, 2–3.5 cm long, the laminae oblong-lanceate, ca. 1.25–3 cm long, 1–1.5 cm wide, obtuse at the base, acute at the apex, pinnate with irregular pinna apices, the pinnae rhomboidal, spreading, the margins entire or lobed.

Roadsides and woods. Rare. Southern Saskatchewan to southern British Columbia. Disjunct in Wallowa Co., northeastern Oregon.

OPHIOGLOSSUM

The Adder's-tongues

All the species of this genus have laminae with a simple sterile portion 2–40 cm long that is elliptic to ovate or nearly so. The fertile portion of the laminae is 2–many times longer than the sterile portion, is fertile at its apex, and bears two rows of sporangia somewhat embedded in it.

The species of *Ophioglossum* are not commonly collected because they are inconspicuous and some of them are winter or spring ephemerals. Woods, roadsides, cemeteries, and undisturbed or slightly disturbed pastures are typical habitats. Especially the smaller species can be found by crawling around on hands and knees in likely habitats during the appropriate season of the year, a procedure that is as hilarious to onlookers as it is effective for collectors.

Key to Ophioglossum

1. Stems globular, spherical or nearly so; fertile spikes commonly with a conspicuous acute or attenuate sterile portion (apiculum) at the apex; SE. *115. O. crotalophoroides*

1. Stems cylindrical or irregularly elongate; fertile spikes without a sterile portion at the apex or the sterile portion inconspicuous, 2

2(1). Sterile portion of the laminae 1–5.5 cm wide, rarely narrower, the venation of small areolae within more prominent, polygonal areolae and with or without free included veinlets, 4

2(1). Sterile portion of the laminae 0.3–1 cm wide, the venation of polygonal areolae usually lacking smaller areolae and free included veinlets, 3

3(2). Sterile portion of the laminae ovate to elliptic, 1–2 times longer than wide; fertile stalks ca. 0.5 mm wide, 3–8(12) cm long; SE. *117. O. nudicaule*

3(2). Sterile portion of the laminae linear-lanceolate to lanceolate, 2–4 times longer than wide; fertile stalks ca. 0.75–1.5 mm wide, 4–12 cm long; CA. *118. O. lusitanicum* subsp. *californicum*

4(2). Large areolae of the sterile portion of the laminae subdivided into smaller areolae containing yet smaller areolae and free veinlets; laminae apiculate; SE. *116. O. engelmannii*

4(2). Large areolae of the sterile portion of the laminae subdivided into smaller areolae lacking free included veinlets; laminae round, obtuse, or acute at the apex, **5**

5(4). Sterile portion of the laminae ovate-lanceate, obtuse to nearly truncate at the base and so broadest very near the base; primary areolae mostly more than 2 mm wide; SE. *119. O. petiolatum*

5(4). Sterile portion of the laminae ovate to elliptical, obtuse to attenuate at the base and so broadest above the base or in the middle; primary areolae mostly less than 2 mm wide, **6**

6(5). Sterile portion of the laminae elliptic, broadest near the middle, acute to attenuate at the base, pale green, dull; basal frond sheath membranaceous, evanescent; N. *120. O. pusillum*

6(5). Sterile portion of the laminae ovate, broadest near the base, obtuse at the base, dark green, shiny; basal frond sheath subcoriaceous, persistent; SE. **121. O. pycnostichum*

115 Ophioglossum crotalophoroides Walter
Bulbous Adder's-tongue

Stems globose, 3–11 mm in diam. Sterile portion of the fronds 2.5–8 cm long, the fertile stalk 1.5–9 cm long, the sporangium-bearing portion 0.5–1 cm long, with a conspicuous, acute or attenuate sterile apiculum; the sterile laminae ovate, the smaller ones sometimes elliptic, borne horizontally near the soil, 1–4 cm long, 0.5–2.5 cm wide, cordate or obtuse and contracted to an acute base, the apex acute or obtuse; venation of areolae with few or no included secondary areolae or free veinlets.

Terrestrial in open pastures, fields, cemeteries, sandy roadsides, and disturbed portions of pine woods, in moist, usually sandy soil. Common. South Carolina to Florida west to southern Louisiana and Texas.

Not cultivated. Found in January in Florida and in February through May in the Carolinas. This species may occur as an ephemeral several times in a single year in response to successive periods of drought.

116 Ophioglossum engelmannii Prantl
Engelmann's Adder's-tongue

Stems cylindrical, 2.5–3.5 mm in diam., with horizontal roots bearing proliferous buds. Sterile portion of the fronds 5–20 mm long, the fertile stalk 4–14 cm long, the sporangium-bearing portion 1.5–3 cm long, with an inconspicuous, acicular apex; the sterile laminae elliptical or nearly so, borne vertically, 2.5–8 cm long, 1.2–3.2 cm wide, acute to acuminate at the base, acute to obtuse or round with a small apiculum at the apex; venation of areolae with abundant secondary areolae and free included veinlets.

Terrestrial in pastures, barrens, and cedar glades, in moist, clayey, limy soils. Frequent. Virginia, Kentucky, Ohio, southern Illinois, Missouri, and Kansas south to Florida, Mississippi, Louisiana, Texas, southwestern New Mexico, and Arizona.

Not cultivated. Found in April or rarely from March to August and to September in Arizona.

*117 Ophioglossum nudicaule L. f.
Slender Adder's-tongue

Stems irregular, up to 2 mm in diam. Sterile portion of the fronds 1–5 cm long, the fertile stalk 1.5–5 cm long, the sporangium-bearing portion 3–7 mm long, with an inconspicuous, acute sterile apex; sterile laminae elliptic or nearly so, borne horizontally, 0.5–2 cm long, 0.2–1 cm wide, the base and apex acute; venation of areolae with few or no secondary areolae or free included veinlets, except in luxuriant forms.

Terrestrial in open, somewhat disturbed meadows and pine woods, often in association with Palmetto plants. Occasional. North Carolina to Florida west to southeastern Oklahoma and Texas.

Not cultivated. An ephemeral found from November to June. Large, lax plants of this species, which grow in marshy places, have been called O. dendroneuron E. P. St. John, but Wagner, Wagner, Leonard, and Mesler (1981) and Wagner, Allen, and Landry (1984) have found that this species (and others) described by St. John from Florida are all populations of the variable species O. nudicaule.

118 Ophioglossum lusitanicum subsp. californicum (Prantl) Clausen
California Adder's-tongue

Stems irregular, up to 3 mm in diam. Sterile portion of the fronds 2.5–8 cm long, the fertile stalk 2.5–12 cm long, the sporangium-bearing portion 0.5–1.5 cm long, with an inconspicuous, attenuate sterile apex; the sterile laminae narrowly elliptic or elliptic-lanceolate, borne vertically, 1.5–5 cm long 0.4–1 cm wide, attenuate at the base, acute at the apex; venation of areolae with few or no secondary areolae or free included veinlets.

Terrestrial in wet, grassy areas in moist or wet soil. Occasional. Amador to Mariposa and Monterey Counties and San Diego County in California.

Not cultivated. Found from December through April, but may not appear in dry years.

119 Ophioglossum petiolatum Hooker
Stalked Adder's-tongue

Stems cylindrical, up to 3 mm in diam., bearing long, horizontal roots commonly provided with buds that give rise to new plants. Sterile portion of the fronds 3–18 mm long, the fertile stalk 2.5–13 cm long, the sporangium-bearing portion 1–2 cm long, with an inconspicuous, acute or acuminate sterile apex; the sterile laminae thick, lanceolate, borne vertically, 1–6 cm long, 0.5–2.5 cm wide, obtuse to subtruncate at the base, acute at the apex; venation of areolae with secondary areolae lacking free included veinlets.

Terrestrial in meadows, roadside ditches, edges of swamps, woods, lawns, and gardens, in moist, usually sandy soil. Frequent. North Carolina to Oklahoma south to Florida and Texas.

Occasionally cultivated in woodland gardens or as a greenhouse pot plant. Found from November through September.

120 Ophioglossum pusillum Raf.
Northern Adder's-tongue

Stems irregular or cylindrical, 2–4 mm in diam. Sterile portion of the fronds 6–24 cm long, the fertile stalk 4–23 cm long, the sporangium-bearing portion 1.5–5 cm long, with a conspicuous, attenuate sterile apex; sterile laminae elliptic, broadest near the middle, borne vertically, 2.5–10 cm long, 1–4 cm wide, acute to attenuate at the base, acute to round at the apex; venation of areolae with secondary areolae and a few free included veinlets.

Terrestrial in pastures, old fields, roadside ditches, and flood plain woods in seasonally wet, rather acid soil. Common. New Brunswick to British Columbia and Alaska south to Virginia, Ohio, Illinois, North Dakota, Montana, and Washington.

Not cultivated. Found from June to September. Wagner (1971a) has found that this species grows mostly north of the southern boundary of Wisconsin glaciation. It has been called *O. vulgatum* var. *pseudopodum* (Blake) Farw., but the differences between it and *O. pycnostichum* seem substantial enough to warrant recognizition as a separate species.

*121 Ophioglossum pycnostichum (Fern.) Löve & Löve
Southeastern Adder's-tongue

Stems irregular to cylindrical, 2–4 mm in diam. Sterile portion of the fronds 6–24 cm long, the fertile stalk 4–23 cm long, the sporangium-bearing portion 1.5–3 cm long, with an inconspicuous, acute or attenuate sterile apex; the sterile laminae ovate, broadest near the base, borne vertically, 2.5–10 cm long, 1.5–5.5 cm wide, obtuse at the base, obtuse to broadly round at the apex; venation of areolae with secondary areolae and a few free included veinlets.

Terrestrial in shady flood plain woods in seasonally wet, circumneutral soil. Common. Southern New Jersey, Delaware, Virginia, West Virginia, Ohio, southern Michigan, Indiana, Illinois, Missouri, and Oklahoma south to Florida, Georgia, Mississippi, Louisiana, and eastern Texas.

Not cultivated. Found from November to August. Wagner (1971a) has found that this species grows mostly south of the southern boundary of Wisconsin glaciation. It has been called *O. vulgatum* var. *pycnostichum* Fern. (see *O. pusillum*).

CHEIROGLOSSA
The Hand Ferns

Unlike *Ophioglossum*, this genus has large, pendent, irregularly palmately lobed laminae with several fertile spikes on each side near the base of the lamina. The plants are epiphytic, a character in *Ophioglossum* found only in the Old World *O. pendulum*. Generally a single species of *Cheiroglossa* has been recognized, although sometimes the African and Brazilian material has been segregated into rather poorly marked varieties. *Cheiroglossa* is known from Florida, tropical America, Réunion, and Indo-China. It apparently occurs in scattered localities over its very wide range.

122 Cheiroglossa palmata (L.) Presl
Hand Fern

Stems subglobular to elongate, up to 1 cm long. Stipes 3.5–17 cm long, 1–2 mm wide, with a sparse tuft of whitish, jointed hairs at the base. Sterile portion of the laminae irregularly and coarsely subdichotomous-palmately lobed with a greatly narrowed, long-tapering base bearing the fertile spikes, 6–15 cm long, 2.5–20 cm wide, usually more or less obdeltate, with 1–4 pairs of lobes, sometimes unevenly lobed; veins forming polygonal, elongate areolae, the major ones containing minor areolae with few or no free included veinlets; fertile portions of the lamina stalked spikes, the stalks 1–2 cm long, the spikes 1–4 cm long, ca. 2 mm wide, often in pairs from the base of the lamina.

Epiphytic mostly or entirely among old leaf bases on palmetto trunks. Very rare. Central and southern Florida.

Not cultivated because it is so difficult to transplant and establish in cultivation. Unfortunately, this species has been overcollected by those who would like to grow it, and many plants have been destroyed by occasional fires.

119

OSMUNDACEAE
The Royal Fern Family

The Osmundaceae have a long and unusually complete history in the fossil record. Both fossil and living species have been treated by Miller (1971), who recognizes, conservatively, three living genera, *Leptopteris* (New Guinea, New Zealand, and Polynesia), *Osmunda* (world-wide), and *Todea* (South Africa, Australia, and New Zealand). The family is in certain respects morphologically transitional between the Ophioglossaceae and other Eusporangiatae, which have short-stalked, thick-walled sporangia, and the higher ferns, or Leptosporangiatae, which have long-stalked, thin-walled sporangia. This intermediateness also extends to spore number per sporangium. The Eusporangiatae have thousands of spores per sporangium, the Osmundaceae have hundreds, and the Leptosporangiatae usually have 64, or sometimes 32.

Osmunda plants have an ascending or decumbent rhizome bearing persistent stipe bases, and so form a massive base. The fronds are erect and form a vase-shaped cluster. In the fully dimorphic species, the fertile fronds are borne on the inside of the cluster of sterile fronds. The sterile fronds (or parts of fronds) are pinnate-pinnatifid or 2-pinnate, with pinnatifid or pinnate pinnae. The fertile fronds (or parts of fronds) lack an expanded, green lamina. The sporangia are borne in clusters on short lobes, and are massive (although with walls only one cell thick) and spherical. The annulus is a lateral group of cells, and the sporangia split open along an indefinite line into two clamshell-like halves.

All the species of *Osmunda* in this Flora are terrestrial and occur most frequently in wet places like marshes, swamps, and stream banks. They are among the most attractive native ferns for the garden and are not at all weedy or invasive.

Key to *Osmunda*

1. Pinnae fully pinnate, the pinnules contracted at the base, sessile; laminae incompletely dimorphic, only the distal pinnae (and/or the median pinnae in hybrid plants) fertile; veins of the sterile pinnules 1–3-forked above the base; E. *123*. *O. regalis* var. *spectabilis*.

1. Pinnae pinnatifid, the segments not contracted at the base, adnate to the costae; laminae completely dimorphic or incompletely dimorphic with the median pinnae fertile; veins of the sterile segments uniformly 1-forked above the base, **2**

3(1). Fronds fully dimorphic, the fertile ones separate from the sterile ones, the sterile ones yellow-green, glossy, with a tuft of reddish-brown, woolly hairs at the base of each pinna; E. *124*. *O. cinnamomea*

2(1). Fronds partially dimorphic, the fertile pinnae median on the otherwise sterile laminae, the sterile pinnae bluish-green, dull, with only a few woolly hairs at the base; E. *125. O. claytoniana*

123 Osmunda regalis var. spectabilis (Willd.) A. Gray
Royal Fern

Stipes (10)20–50 cm long, pinkish, glabrous. Laminae ovate to broadly ovate (1.5)3–13 dm long, 10–55 cm wide, obtuse at the base, obtuse at the apex, with 5–7 pairs of opposite, stalked (ca. 1 cm) pinnae lacking a tuft of reddish-brown hairs at the base. Sterile pinnae oblong, 6–28 cm long, 4–14 cm wide, obtuse at the base, acute at the apex, with 5–13 pairs of alternate to subopposite pinnae, the veins free, 1–3-forked above the base. Fertile pinnae apical, oblong-lanceate, 3–12 cm long, ca. 1 cm wide, 2-pinnate, bearing clusters of brownish sporangia, the pinna axes glabrous or with a few multiseptate, blackish hairs.

Terrestrial in swamps, bogs, and on stream banks in wet, usually strongly acid soil. Common. Newfoundland to Saskatchewan south to Florida, Alabama, Mississippi, Louisiana, Texas, Oklahoma, Kansas, Nebraska, and Minnesota.

Cultivated in full or partial shade in the woods garden in wet, acidic soil. This species hybridizes to form *O. × ruggii* Tryon, which is discussed under the other parent, *O. claytoniana*. Other varieties of *O. regalis* occur in Europe, Bermuda, the Greater Antilles, Central and South America, India, China, and Africa.

124 Osmunda cinnamomea L.
Cinnamon Fern

Stipes 10–20 cm long, pinkish, with reddish-brown, woolly hairs. Sterile laminae elliptic, 3–12 dm long, 13–30 cm wide, tapering to a truncate base, acute at the apex, with 15–25 pairs of opposite, sessile pinnae with a tuft of persistent, reddish-brown hairs at the pinna base, pinnatifid, the pinnae oblong-lanceate, 4–17 cm long, 1–3 cm wide, obtuse at the base, acute at the apex, with 30–40 pairs of pinna lobes, the veins free, uniformly 1-forked above the base. Fertile laminae oblong, 15–45 cm long, 2–3 cm wide, with 8–25 pairs of opposite, essentially 3-pinnate, oblong-lanceate pinnae bearing clusters of brownish sporangia, the rachises with woolly hairs throughout, but becoming glabrous with age.

Terrestrial on stream banks, and in swamps, bogs, and other wet places in rather acid soil. Abundant. Labrador to Ontario south to Florida, Texas, Kansas, Nebraska, and Minnesota.

Cultivated in the woods garden in partial or full shade in wet, rather acid soil.

125 Osmunda claytoniana L.

Interrupted Fern

Stipes 10–30 cm long, pinkish, with early deciduous, reddish-brown, woolly hairs. Laminae elliptic (discounting the contracted, median, fertile pinnae), 2–15 dm long, 15–25 cm wide, tapering to a truncate base, acute at the apex, with 15–20 pairs of opposite to subopposite, sessile pinnae lacking a definite tuft of reddish hairs at the base, but with a few hairs. Sterile pinnae oblong-lanceate, 3–15 cm long, 1.5–3.5 cm wide, truncate at the base, acute at the apex, with 10–20 pairs of subopposite pinna lobes, the veins free, uniformly 1-forked above the base. Fertile pinnae median, oblong-lanceate, 4–6 cm long, 1–1.5 cm wide, essentially 3-pinnate, bearing clusters of brownish sporangia, the pinna axes sparsely covered with woolly hairs.

Terrestrial in woods and on hummocks in swamps, in fairly well-drained, subacid to circumneutral soil. Common. Newfoundland to Manitoba south to western North Carolina, northern Georgia and Alabama, Tennessee, Missouri, Iowa, and Minnesota.

Cultivated in the woods garden in partial or full shade in moist, circumneutral soil. This species hybridizes with *O. regalis* var. *spectabilis* to form *O.* × *ruggii* Tryon, a very rare hybrid known formerly from one locality in Fairfield Co., Connecticut and now known only from one in Craig Co., Virginia. Wagner, Wagner, Miller, and Wagner (1978) have studied the hybrid in great detail. The hybrid has fully pinnate sterile pinnae, as in *O. regalis* var. *spectabilis*, but the pinnules are shorter (mostly only 2–3 times longer than wide) than those of *O. regalis* var. *spectabilis* (4–6 times longer than wide). The spore-producing portions may be apical and/or medial and the veins of the sterile pinnules 1–3-forked, both characteristics intermediate between the parents. The spores are abortive. Because the parents do grow together frequently, the rarity of the hybrids is a fascinating mystery.

SCHIZAEACEAE
The Climbing Fern Family

This family contains five genera, of which all but *Mohria* (Africa) are widespread in the world's tropical and subtropical regions, including Florida. *Schizaea* and *Actinostachys* often grow on sandy soils in wet savannas. Both have sterile laminae that are reduced in area, presumably a response to the high light intensity and evaporation potential of their habitat. *Lygodium*, a climbing fern, grows in woodlands or at their margins. *Anemia* typically grows in rock crevices or on steep banks in rocky soil. Most species grow in full sun, but a few dwell in shade.

The family is considered to be the most primitive of the Schizaeidae because of the peculiar, short-stalked, often pear- or egg-shaped, asymmetrical sporangia that have a terminal annulus and the hairy rhizomes, which lack scales. The small, underground rhizomes are usually much branched and either form a clump or are long-creeping. They bear many fibrous roots that have abundant root hairs. The rhizomes bear several fronds that are under 30 cm long in most species, except for those of the genus *Lygodium*, which are indeterminate and grow to be vines several meters long. Dimorphy, either of entire fronds or parts of fronds, is the rule. The fertile portions are highly contracted and have unprotected sporangia borne in two rows (*Anemia*), or the sporangia are protected by a reflexed margin (*Actinostachys*, *Schizaea*) or a dorsal flap of tissue (*Lygodium*). The sterile laminae or portions of laminae are palmate, pinnate, or pinnately compound in *Lygodium*, pinnate or pinnately compound in *Anemia*, flabellate or reduced to alae lying on either side of the midrib in *Schizaea*, and are absent or reduced to alae in *Actinostachys*.

Key to the Genera of the Schizaeaceae

1. Plants climbing and twining vines up to several meters long; sterile leaves with fully expanded, palmate or pinnate laminae, *Lygodium*, p. 125

1. Plants small herbs mostly less than 30 cm long with pinnate or flabellate laminae or the laminae absent, **2**

2(1). Expanded laminae obvious, pinnate, *Anemia*, p. 127

2(1). Expanded laminae absent (flabellate in some extralimital species), **3**

3(2). Sterile fronds loosely curled; fertile fronds stiffly erect; fertile portions of the laminae pinnate, *Schizaea*, p. 123

3(2). Sterile and fertile fronds stiffly erect; fertile portions of the laminae palmate, *Actinostachys*, p. 124

SCHIZAEA
The Curly-grass Ferns

The species of *Schizaea* have stipes that are plane or shallowly V-shaped in cross-section. The sterile laminae or sterile portion of the laminae is flabellate, fusiform, or (in the only species occurring in the United States and Canada) reduced to narrow alae bordering the midrib, and so appears to be absent.

Some *Schizaea* species are dimorphic, with separate fertile and sterile fronds; others have specialized fertile portions terminating usually fan-shaped sterile portions of the laminae. Most *Schizaea* species have habitats similar to those of *Actinostachys*, terrestrial in sandy soil, often in full sun.

126 Schizaea pusilla Pursh
Curly-grass

Rhizomes erect or ascending, less than 1 mm in diam., bearing small, yellowish, few-celled hairs. Stipes crowded. Sterile fronds linear, very narrow, ca. 0.5 mm wide, 2–5 cm long, forming delicate curls, pale green, glabrous, with paler and slightly thickened edges. Fertile fronds linear, very narrow, 2.5–12 cm long, ca. 0.5 mm wide, stiffly erect, pale green when young, brown at maturity, glabrous, very shallowly V-shaped in cross-section, with paler and slightly thickened edges. Fertile portion deltate, pinnatifid, with 3–7 decreasing pairs of segments (sorophores) 1–3 mm long, ca. 0.5 mm wide, brown, with sporangia in 2 rows on the ventral side, protected by the slightly thinner lateral segment margins, which bear long, lax, multicellular, yellowish hairs.

Terrestrial on sandy flats usually under *Chamaecyparis* trees and on hummocks or logs in bogs and along riverbanks, especially in highly acid, humus-rich soil. Rare. Newfoundland and Nova Scotia, Long Island, New York, southern New Jersey, and the Bruce Peninsula, Ontario.

Not cultivated.

ACTINOSTACHYS
The Ray Ferns

The species of *Actinostachys* have stipes and midribs that are plane or angular in cross-section. The vegetative portion of the lamina is reduced to very narrow alae bordering the midrib, and usually appears to be absent. The terminal, fertile portion of the laminae is a palmate cluster of filiform, sporangium-bearing segments.

Most of the species of *Actinostachys* are found on the islands of the South Pacific and in tropical South America, where they grow on white sand savannas or among mosses on tree stumps. The loss of lamina is doubtless related to the high light intensity and dry conditions under which most of these ferns grow.

Actinostachys and *Schizaea* are similar in having strongly reduced sterile laminae. For this reason, *Actinostachys* often has been placed in *Schizaea*, but Bierhorst (1968) has shown that sufficient differences exist for the generic distinction to be maintained.

*127 Actinostachys pennula (Swartz) Hooker
Ray Fern

Rhizome erect or ascending, less than 1 mm in diam., bearing small, yellowish, few-celled bristles. Stipes crowded, 1–2 cm long, reddish brown. Sterile portion of the laminae linear, very narrow, 7–11 cm long, 0.4–0.7(1) mm wide, stiffly erect, pale green, glabrous, with thickened margins. Fertile portion of the laminae at the apex of the sterile portion, palmate, with 2–6 segments (sorophores) 3–6 mm long, ca. 0.75 mm wide, brown, with long, multicellular, irregularly bent, yellowish hairs and sporangia in 2 or 3 rows on the ventral side, protected by the slightly thinner lateral segment margins.

Terrestrial on decaying *Persea* stumps and in decomposing litter. Very rare. Recently known only from Pinellas and Palm Beach Counties, Florida. Formerly this was called *Actinostachys germanii* Fée, but Wagner (pers. comm.) has found that this is a juvenile, neotenic form of *A. pennula* that occurs throughout the range of the species.

Not cultivated.

LYGODIUM
The Climbing Ferns

Lygodium is rare among fern genera for its climbing fronds. The underground rhizome gives rise to fronds with rachises that grow to 3–10 m long, usually by twining around other plants. The rachises are themselves unusual because they branch unequally to form a series of short, alternate branches, each of which bears a pair of pinnae. Sometimes a dormant terminal bud is formed at the apex of the short branch where the pinnae are inserted, much as in the Gleicheniaceae. Presumably this is not indicative of a relationship with the Gleicheniaceae, but is merely a parallel development. The pinnae are always short-stalked, may be palmately or pinnately divided, do not have reduced laminae, and have incomplete dimorphy, with a fringe of fertile segments around central, sterile areas of the fertile pinnae or with the pinnae fully fertile. The pinnules or lobes of most pinnately divided species are lobed at the base. Veins are free in most species.

The Climbing Ferns grow in mesic habitats. Almost all the species are tropical. The American Climbing Fern is an anomaly geographically and morphologically, with its north temperate range and fully fertile pinnae.

Key to Lygodium
1. Sterile pinnae simple, palmately lobed with 3–7 broadly adnate segments; linear fertile lobes borne at the tips of repeatedly forked axes, sterile tissue absent; stipes 1–4 cm distant on very long-creeping rhizomes; E. *128. L. palmatum*

1. Sterile pinnae pinnate, the pinnules undivided and lanceate, lobed at the base, or themselves pinnate with segments that are lobed at the base; linear fertile lobes borne like a fringe around the ovate to lanceolate sterile portion of the fertile pinnules or segments; stipes 0.2–0.7 cm distant on short-creeping rhizomes, 2

2(1). Sterile costae not flexuous, bearing lobed to compound pinnules (or pinnules with segments) having basal lobes; SE. *129. L. japonicum*

125

2(1). Sterile costae slightly flexuous, bearing entire, lanceate pinnules lacking basal lobes; SE. *130. L. microphyllum*

128   Lygodium palmatum (Bernh.) Swartz
American Climbing Fern

Rhizome very long-creeping, ca. 1 mm in diam., with short, blackish hairs. Stipes 1–4 cm distant, 9–15 cm long, ca. 1 mm in diam. Rachises twining, up to ca. 3 m long, bearing alternate short branches each with a pair of pinnae. Sterile pinnae stalked (1–2 cm), very broadly ovate, 1–4 cm long 2–6 cm wide, deeply palmately lobed, the lobes 3–7, elongate, mostly 1–2 cm long, 8–12 mm wide, round at the apex, each major lobe with a central axis emitting dichotomously branched, free veins. Fertile pinnae borne towards the apex of the laminae, stalked (up to 1.5 cm), irregularly shaped, 2–4 cm long, 2–8 cm wide, 3–5 times dichotomously forked, the fertile lobes many, linear, 3–7 mm long, 1–2 mm wide, the sporangia covered by indusium-like outgrowths of the leaf surface.

Terrestrial in woods, thickets, and at bog margins, in humus-rich, slightly acid soil. Rare. Southern New Hampshire, New York, southern Ontario, Ohio, and Kentucky south to Florida, Alabama, and Mississippi.

Cultivated with great difficulty in moist, acid soil.

129   Lygodium japonicum (Thunb.) Swartz
Japanese Climbing Fern

Rhizome creeping, 2–3 mm in diam., with short, blackish hairs. Stipes 0.2–0.7 cm distant, 10–35 cm long, 1–2 mm in diam. Rachises twining, up to 3 m long, bearing alternate short branches, each with a pair of pinnae. Sterile pinnae stalked (1.5–3.5 cm), lanceolate to lanceate, 6–15 cm long, 5.5–15 cm wide, 2–3-pinnate, the pinnules lanceolate, 1.5–6 cm long, 1–3 cm wide, lobed or divided at the base, with a long, attenuate apex; short, curved hairs present on the axes beneath. Fertile pinnae stalked (1–2 cm), lanceolate-triangular, 5–18 cm long, 4–14 cm wide, 2–3-pinnate, the ultimate segments ovate to lanceolate, fringed with fertile lobes.

Terrestrial in woods, marshes, and roadside ditches, and on riverbanks, in circumneutral soil. Occasional. Florida to South Carolina west to Georgia, Alabama, Mississippi, Louisiana, and Texas.

Cultivated as a greenhouse plant or in outdoor gardens in the southeastern United States. A native of Japan commonly naturalized or escaped from cultivation.

130   Lygodium microphyllum (Cav.) R. Brown
Small-leaved Climbing Fern

Rhizome creeping, 2–3 mm in diam., with short, blackish hairs. Stipes 0.2–0.5 cm distant, 7–25 cm long, 1–1.5 mm in diam. Rachises twining, up to ca. 10 m long, bearing alternate short branches, each with a pair of pinnae. Sterile pinnae stalked (0.5–1.5 cm), oblong, 5–12 cm long, 3–6 cm wide, pinnate, the pinnules lanceate, truncate to subcordate at the base, with an acute to cuneate apex; glabrous beneath. Fertile pinnae stalked (0.5–1 cm), oblong, 3–14 cm long, 2.5–6 cm wide, pinnate, the ultimate segments ovate to lanceate, fringed with fertile lobes.

Terrestrial on riverbanks, in disturbed sites, and in swamps, in wet soil. Occasional. In the Flora region known only from Martin and Palm Beach Counties, along the east coast of Florida.

Cultivated as a greenhouse plant. A native of southeastern Asia, it has recently naturalized and is spreading, according to Nauman and Austin (1978). It forms dense stands and grows to the tops of the trees on which the ferns climb.

ANEMIA
The Flowering Ferns

The species of *Anemia* are called Flowering Ferns because of the conspicuous, yellow to brown, sporangium-covered fertile fronds or pinnae that are held erect and above the sterile fronds or pinnae. In this character, they superficially resemble *Osmunda*, the genus in which early botanists placed them. The sterile laminae or portions are pinnate to 3-pinnate-pinnatifid, and are small and roughly triangular in most species. In many species they are sparsely to densely covered with long, usually straight hairs.

Like other Schizaeaceae, the Flowering Ferns grow well in dry ground; most species are found on rocks or banks. The center of distribution for the genus is central and southern Brazil. The species found in the United States are basically from the West Indies.

Key to Anemia
1. Laminae fully dimorphic, the fertile frond separate from the sterile, arising directly from the rhizome; sterile laminae usually less than 7.5 cm long. Sterile pinnules mostly cuneate at the base, more than 2 times longer than wide, papyraceous, deeply serrately lobed at the apex; FL. *133. A. wrightii*

1. Laminae not fully dimorphic, the fertile portion arising just below the base of the sterile; sterile portion of the laminae usually more than 7.5 cm long, 2

2(1). Sterile portion of the laminae 3-pinnate, the pinnules ovate, obovate, or oblong; FL. *131. A. adiantifolia*

2(1). Sterile portion of the laminae pinnate, the pinnae lanceolate, obtuse to cordate at the base; TX. *132. A. mexicana*

127

131 Anemia adiantifolia (L.) Swartz

Pine Fern

Rhizomes short- to long-creeping, ca. 2 mm in diam., bearing long, dark brown hairs and incompletely dimorphic fronds 0.5–1 cm distant. Stipes 6–40 cm long, dark brown at the base, tan or greenish towards the apex. Fertile portion of the laminae 7–18 cm long, 1(2) pairs of upright pinnae, the lowest inserted ca. 1 cm below the base of the sterile portion of the laminae. Sterile portion of the laminae lanceolate to triangular, 5–25 cm long, 3–16 cm wide, 2-pinnate-pinnatifid to 3-pinnate; pinnules ovate, obovate, or oblong, sparsely covered with short hairs when young, glabrous at maturity.

Terrestrial in dry, rocky pine woods and in hammocks, in sandy, subacid to limy soil or epipetric on limestone rocks. Frequent. Central and southern Florida.

Cultivated in the greenhouse in moist to dry soil in bright sunlight.

132 Anemia mexicana Klotzsch

Mexican Flowering Fern

Rhizomes short-creeping, ca. 1.5 mm in diam., bearing long, dark brown hairs and incompletely dimorphic fronds closely spaced. Stipes 7–30 cm long, brown at the extreme base, tan towards the apex. Fertile portion of the laminae 8–26 cm long, always a single pair of upright pinnae inserted 1–2 cm below the base of the sterile laminae. Sterile portion of the laminae triangular to suboblong, 8–21 m long, 7–15 cm wide, pinnate; pinnae lanceolate to suboblong, obtuse to subcordate at the base, acute at the apex, glabrous.

Epipetric in ravines and on hillsides on limestone or conglomerate cliffs, ledges, and boulders; occasionally terrestrial. Very rare. West-central Texas.

Not cultivated.

133 Anemia wrightii Baker

Wright's Flowering Fern

Rhizomes compact, ca. 1 mm in diam., bearing long, dark brown hairs and fully dimorphic fronds closely spaced. Fertile fronds taller than the sterile ones. Fertile fronds 5–30 cm long, the stipes 4–22 cm long, the laminae 1–8 cm long. Sterile fronds 3–15 cm long, the stipes 1.5–8 cm long, the laminae narrowly lanceolate to triangular, 1.5–6 cm long, 1.5–3.5 cm wide, pinnate-pinnatifid to 2-pinnate; pinnules narrowly oblanceolate, more than 2 times longer than wide, mostly cuneate at the base, glabrous or with a few long, appressed hairs.

Epipetric on the lips of solution holes in open, brushy glades, on limestone rock, growing with *A. adiantifolia* and *A. wrightii*. Very rare. Dade County, Florida.

Not cultivated. This species was discovered recently, but is well established, although in an area threatened by expanding agricultural lands.

PARKERIACEAE
The Water Fern Family

This family includes only the aquatic genus *Ceratopteris* (world-wide tropics). The Parkeriaceae clearly belongs to the Schizaeales, but its exact position is uncertain. As in some cases of flowering plants, the aquatic habitat has caused great modifications of structure in *Ceratopteris* that obscure therelationships of these plants to the other, non-aquatic families in the order. Variation in water temperature and illumination presumably are the causes of variation within the species of *Ceratopteris*. Lloyd (1974), in his monograph of the genus, studied the confusing assemblage of forms and has concluded that they can best be divided into four species; he also found some hybrids between the species. Earlier authors concluded that from 1 to 12 species exist, which is a measure of the variation in the genus and the difficulty in understanding it.

The plants have small, inconspicuous, erect, sparsely scaly rhizomes. Roots arise near the stipe bases. The fronds are dimorphic. The sterile fronds are broad, glabrous, thin, simple to 3-pinnate, and have finely reticulate veins lacking included veinlets. Buds are present in the pinna sinuses. The fertile fronds are longer than the sterile and are 4- or 5-pinnate in larger specimens. They have very narrow segments with inrolled margins that protect 1–4 rows of sporangia.

All the species are aquatic. Some usually root in mud, and others usually float. The plants are commonly overlooked and only infrequently collected. None are conventionally cultivated, but *C. thalictroides* is widely used in freshwater aquaria.

Key to Ceratopteris

1. Sterile laminae simple to pinnate-pinnatifid, the ultimate segments round, the basal lobes or pinnae opposite; stipes tapering toward the base, usually twice as wide at the apex as at the base; plants usually floating; SE. *134. C. pteridoides*

1. Sterile laminae pinnate to 3-pinnate, the ultimate segments acute, the basal pinnae subopposite to alternate; stipes uniformly wide throughout; plants usually rooted in mud; SE. *135. C. thalictroides*

134 Ceratopteris pteridoides (Hooker) Hieron.
Floating Water Fern

Stipes about half as long as the laminae, mostly 5–10 mm wide, gradually tapering to a narrow base. Sterile laminae ovate to deltate, 4–20 cm long, 4–20 cm wide, lobed to pinnate-pinnatifid, the lobes or ultimate segments round at the apex, the midvein of the basal lobes or the pinna costae opposite. Fertile laminae ovate to deltate, 10–30 cm long, 5–25 cm wide, (2)3–5-pinnate, the lobes attenuate.

Plants usually floating in still or moving water in streams, cypress ponds, and lake margins. Occasional. Central and northern Florida and southern Louisiana.

Not cultivated other than in aquaria or warm-weather lily or fish ponds.

135 Ceratopteris thalictroides (L.) Brongn.
Water Sprite

Stipes half as long as the laminae or less, 2–5 mm wide throughout. Sterile laminae lanceolate to ovate, 5–25 cm long, 3–8 cm wide, usually 2–3-pinnate, less divided in juvenile or depauperate specimens, the ultimate segments acute at the apex, the midvein of the basal lobes or the pinna costae subopposite to alternate. Fertile laminae lanceolate to ovate, 15–45 cm long, 10–25 cm wide, (1)1.5–2 times longer than wide, 3- or 4-pinnate, the lobes attenuate.

Plants usually rooted in mud in quiet or moving water in streams and near the mouths of hot springs. Occasional. Naturalized in Florida and central Texas.

Not cultivated other than in aquaria or warm-weather lily or fish ponds. This species was found on the eastern slope of the Laguna Mountains near Borrego Springs, San Diego Co., California, but the collection probably is of escaped plants, rather than of a naturalized population. According to Petrik-Ott (1976), the plants at the Texas localities are favored by the warm water flowing from hot springs into the rivers where they grow.

SINOPTERIDACEAE
The Maiden-hair Family

The circumscription of this family is a matter of much debate among fern specialists. As defined in this book, it includes about 34 genera world-wide, 8 of which occur in the United States and Canada.

The family is intermediate in evolutionary advancement within the Schizaeales, showing neither the primitive characteristics of the Schizaeaceae nor the extreme modification of the Vittariaceae. Being a large family, it is diverse morphologically; and being dwellers in dry places, many of the genera show parallel adaptations to their harsh environment.

The plants are small, mostly less than 0.5 m long and commonly less than half of that. The rhizomes are scaly with usually stiff and often bicolorous and shiny scales; some genera outside the United States are hirsute or bristly. The rhizomes are either erect or ascending and bear a tuft of fronds or else may be short- to long-creeping and bear scattered fronds. The roots and root-hairs are relatively few. The stipes are as a rule thin, wiry, and often dark-colored. Most often they are glabrous, but a few species are hirsute or bear scales substantially like those of the rhizome. The laminae in all but a few species are 2-pinnate or more divided. In the highly dissected forms, the ultimate segments are elongate or round and are small. Several of the genera have a colored farina extruded from glandular hairs on the abaxial or rarely the adaxial surface of the laminae; others bear hairs or scales. True indusia (i.e., outgrowths from the surface of the lamina, often oriented so that the sporangia they protect face the margin of the lamina) are unknown in this family. In the Sinopteridaceae, the indusia are really only modifications of the lamina margin, and so are most correctly called false indusia. The sporangia are borne on the false indusium itself in *Adiantum*, are marginal and protected by a marginal false indusium in *Aspidotis*, *Cheilanthes*, *Cryptogramma*, and *Pellaea*, spread back a little from the margin in *Bommeria* and *Notholaena*, or occur dorsally along the entire veins in *Pityrogramma*.

The species are mainly epipetric, but some are terrestrial and usually grow in association with rocks. Most grow in the drier portions of the southwestern states. The number of species is even greater in Mexico than it is in the United States. Although some require substantial moisture, and so thrive only in mesic habitats or in seepages or on moist cliffs in otherwise dry places, most occur in seasonally very dry habitats. Consequently, their fronds are adapted to minimize water loss through having small, thick laminae bearing a farinose coating or hairs or scales on the abaxial surface. Some *Cheilanthes*, *Notholaena*, and *Pellaea* species or races are triploid or tetraploid. These can spread in the driest deserts because their gametophytes do not require any water for fertilization, and so can develop new sporophyte plants with viable spores under conditions impossible for sexual species.

Although some species of virtually every genus of Sinopteridaceae are in cultivation, the majority of epipetric species are seldom if ever cultivated because of their supposedly difficult habitat requirements. On the other hand, several species of *Adiantum*, which are terrestrial, have a long horticultural history; many cultivated varieties have been developed. Epipetric species of Sinopteridaceae often can begrown, not by attempting to mimic their epipetric natural habitat, which is difficult to do, but by potting them for the greenhouse in soil mixtures to which sphagnum peat or white sand (for acidity) or gypsum or limestone chips (for alkalinity) has been added. To grow these plants successfully, experimentation is necessary and a good deal of care must be taken, even with the pH of the water.

Key to the Genera of the Sinopteridaceae

1. Laminae lacking a white or yellow farinose coating on the abaxial surface, **3**

1. Laminae with a white or yellow farinose coating on the abaxial surface, **2**

2(1). Sori submarginal and/or marginal, round or slightly elongate along the veins, *Notholaena*, p. 150

2(1). Sori decidedly elongate along the veins, sometimes appearing to cover the abaxial surface (acrostichoid), *Pityrogramma*, p. 170

3(1). Sporangia borne on the reflexed, marginal, false indusia (seen by tearing a false indusium away from the lamina surface); veins of the ultimate segments obvious and often slightly prominulous beneath, usually forking from or near the segment base, *Adiantum*, p. 173

3(1). Sporangia borne at or near the margin of the lamina, but not on the false indusium; veins of the ultimate segments usually not obvious beneath, usually pinnately branched, **4**

4(3). Laminae pentagonal and sparsely strigose on the adaxial surface, *Bommeria*, p. 172

4(3). Laminae not pentagonal and sparsely strigose on the adaxial surface, **5**

5(4). Fronds decidedly dimorphic, the fertile ones taller than the sterile ones, their laminae contracted into nearly linear segments, *Cryptogramma*, p. 133

5(4). Fronds monomorphic or nearly so, **6**

6(5). Laminae hirsute, scaly, or with minute, dark red glands on the abaxial surface (except practically glabrous in *Cheilanthes wrightii*, with long-creeping rhizomes 1–1.5 mm in diam.), **10**

6(5). Laminae glabrous on the abaxial surface, **7**

7(6). False indusia prominent, scarious, in a continuous or discontinuous line along the lateral edges of the segments; margins of the segments thickened, *Aspidotis*, p. 148

7(6). False indusia absent; margins of the segments not thickened, sometimes a little thinner and paler than the submarginal portion, **8**

8(7). Ultimate segments or axes slightly to greatly folding or rolling upward when dry, tending to expose the abaxial surface of the segments, pinnules, or pinnae, *Notholaena*, p. 150

8(7). Ultimate segments slightly to greatly folding or rolling (usually by lateral halves) when dry, tending to enclose the abaxial surface of the segments, **9**

9(8). Segment margins slightly modified, thinner and paler than the submarginal portion; ultimate segments mostly more than 5 mm long, *Pellaea*, p. 161

9(8). Segment margins not at all modified; ultimate segments mostly 1.5–3 mm long, *Notholaena*, p. 150

10(6). Pinnae pinnate-pinnatifid to 3-pinnate; segment margins usually reflexed and the edge modified to form a narrow to broad, scarious, whitish false indusium; sori marginal, round, *Cheilanthes*, p. 135

10(6). Pinnae lobed or pinnatifid (except 2-pinnate in the densely hirsute *N. newberryi* and *N. parryi*); segment margins scarcely reflexed and never modified to form a false indusium; sori submarginal and/or marginal, usually at least somewhat elongate along the vein, *Notholaena*, p. 150

CRYPTOGRAMMA
The Rock-brakes

Cryptogramma includes four or five species that occur in the temperate and cool regions of the northern hemisphere and one species in southern South America. The species of *Cryptogramma* look superficially like very small *Pteris* species, hence the common name Rock-brake.

The plants are small and somewhat dimorphic, with the sterile fronds exceeded by the fertile fronds, which have contracted laminae. Both types of fronds are 2-pinnate, but the fertile pinnules are nearly linear, in contrast to the oblanceolate to obovate sterile ones.

The Rock-brakes grow in rock crevices in the northern states and Canada. They are among the few ferns hardy enough to withstand the climates of Labrador, Alaska, and the region between.

Key to Cryptogramma

1. Rhizomes ascending; stipes persistent, very crowded, forming tufts, pale at the base, with many reddish-brown scales ca. 3 mm long at and above the base; laminae coriaceous; N. *136. C. acrostichoides*

1. Rhizomes long-creeping; stipes not persistent, more scattered, not crowded or forming tufts, reddish-brown at and above the base, with a few golden scales ca. 2 mm long only at the base; laminae membranaceous; N. *137. C. stelleri*

136 Cryptogramma acrostichoides R. Brown in Richards.

American Rock-brake

Rhizomes ascending, covered with very crowded, persistent stipe bases. Sterile fronds spreading, 5–13 cm long; stipes yellowish, glabrous, about as long as the laminae; laminae ovate-deltate, 4–6 cm long, 3–4 cm wide, 2-pinnate, the pinnules oblanceolate to obovate, the margins crenate. Fertile fronds stiffly erect, up to 20 cm long; stipes yellowish, glabrous, ca. 1.5 times as long as the laminae; laminae oblong-lanceolate, 4–8 cm long, 3–6 cm wide, 2-pinnate, the segments linear, their margins underrolled, covering the round or elongate sori.

Epipetric in crevices in subacid rocks, or often terrestrial on talus slopes and rock slides in exposed locations. Common. Northern Quebec to Alaska south to northern Michigan, Montana, Wyoming, Colorado, New Mexico, Utah, northern Nevada, and California.

Cultivated in cool-climate rock gardens in moist soil. Some specimens from Alaska and neighboring areas have broadly deltate, much-divided sterile laminae with obovate, toothed ultimate segments. These have been called *C. acrostichoides* var. *sitchensis* (Rupr.) C. Chr. in Hultén or *C. crispa* var. *sitchensis* (Rupr.) C. Chr. According to Löve, Löve, and Kapoor (1971), it has not been determined whether these specimens belong to *C. acrostichoides* or *C. crispa*, or whether they should be considered a species separate from both. Their spores appear to be insignificantly larger than those of the North American diploid *C. acrostichoides* and the Eurasian tetraploid *C. crispa*, but their concolorous rhizome scales may link them with *C. crispa*.

137 Cryptogramma stelleri (Gmel.) Prantl

Slender Rock-brake

Rhizomes creeping, bearing scattered stipes. Sterile fronds erect, 5–25 cm long; stipes reddish-brown nearly to the apex, glabrous, usually slightly longer than the laminae; laminae lanceolate, 3.5–9 cm long, 2–5.5 cm wide, 2-pinnate, the pinnules mostly broadly obovate, the margins subcrenate to entire. Fertile fronds erect, up to 28 cm long; stipes reddish-brown nearly to the apex, glabrous, equalling to twice as long as the laminae; laminae lanceolate-oblong, 2.5–14 cm long, 2–8 cm wide, 2-pinnate, the segments nearly linear, their margins underrolled, covering the round sori.

Epipetric in crevices in usually vertical, calcareous cliffs in moist, protected locations. Frequent. Labrador to Alaska south to northern New Jersey, Pennsylvania, West Virginia, Michigan, northern Illinois, Iowa, Montana, northern New Mexico, Utah, and Oregon.

Cultivated in cool-climate rock gardens in moist, basic soil.

CHEILANTHES
The Lip Ferns

Cheilanthes is a genus of about 125 species, most of which occur in dry places from the southwestern United States to Peru. A few species are more widely distributed in the United States or occur in the Old World. The species are not always obviously distinct from those of *Notholaena*, which for that reason is combined with *Cheilanthes* by some authors. Those species of *Cheilanthes* that lack false indusia (as is characteristic of *Notholaena*) have 3-pinnate laminae with very small, contracted, bead-like segments. The species of *Notholaena* native to the United States are less divided, and so should not be confused with the native *Cheilanthes* species.

The plants are small to medium-sized, monomorphic, and have stipes about equalling the laminae. Most species have curly hairs and/or scales on the abaxial side of the laminae; a few have only hairs.

The Lip Ferns grow in rock crevices or ledges, at the base of boulders, or otherwise associated with rocks in most cases. A few species range beyond the southwestern deserts to the Pacific Northwest, Florida, or the mid-Atlantic states. Some species are cultivated occasionally, but most are thought to be difficult to maintain in cultivation, perhaps because of their specialized, epipetric habitat.

Key to Cheilanthes

1. Ultimate segments nearly round, often bead-like, with strongly underrolled margins, forming a constricted aperture on the abaxial side of the segments; indusia absent or narrow to wide and continuous, **13**

1. Ultimate segments elongate, not bead-like, mostly with weakly underrolled margins, lacking a constricted aperture on the abaxial side; indusia absent or narrow and discontinuous or wide and continuous, **2**

2(1). Sori discrete, confined to the narrow apex or lateral teeth of the segments; indusia only slightly modified, very narrow (less than 0.25 mm wide), **8**

2(1). Sori discrete to laterally confluent, on the lateral or apical margins of the segments; indusia distinctly modified, narrow (ca. 0.25–0.5 mm wide), **3**

3(2). Ultimate segments acute to mucronate, the indusia confined to the lateral margins of the segments, ca. 0.5 mm wide; AZ. *138. C. arizonica*

3(2). Ultimate segments round, the indusia continuous around the lateral and apical margins of the segments, up to 0.25 mm wide, **4**

4(3). Stipes, rachises, and costae with a few narrow, linear-lanceate, distantly toothed, whitish scales; segments subscabrous, covered on all surfaces with many mostly 3-celled, stiff, whitish, sharp-pointed hairs; TX. *139. C. horridula

4(3). Stipes, rachises, and costae with few to many multicellular, stiff to lax, whitish to tan hairs; segments glabrous or with a few stiff to lax, whitish to tan hairs, 5

5(4). Laminae 7–10 cm wide, broadly lanceolate, ca. 2 times longer than wide, with ca. 6–10 pairs of pinnae, the lowest pair with elongate basal pinnules; TX. 140. C. aemula

5(4). Laminae 1.5–6 cm wide, narrowly lanceolate to elliptic-lanceolate, (2)2.5–5 times longer than wide, with 10–20 pairs of pinnae, the lowest pair usually lacking elongate basal pinnules, 6

6(5). Rhizomes very long-creeping, usually rarely branched; stipes not clustered, usually more than 5 mm distant; lower pinnae spaced 1–2 times their width apart (less in depauperate than in fully developed specimens); FL. 141. C. microphylla

6(5). Rhizomes short-creeping, extensively branched; stipes clustered, usually less than 3 mm distant; lower pinnae approximate or spaced 0.5–1(2) times their width apart, 7

7(6). Laminae with dense, curved hairs on the abaxial surface; stipes brown to atropurpureous; indusia absent, the segment margins weakly underrolled; E. 142. C. lanosa

7(6). Laminae glabrous or with a few short, straight hairs on the abaxial surface; stipes blackish; indusia continuous, ca. 0.25 mm wide; S. 143. C. alabamensis

8(2). Stipes and rachises with mostly capitate hairs; scales absent, 10

8(2). Stipes and rachises with few to many narrow, linear to lanceolate, whitish scales (C. wrightii sometimes glabrescent), 9

9(8). Laminae oblong, 2.5–5 times longer than wide, 3-pinnate or sometimes 3-pinnate-pinnatifid; stipes with an adaxial groove throughout; rachis scales few, much narrower than the rachis; SWB. 144. C. wrightii

9(8). Laminae ovate to lanceolate, 1–1.5 times longer than wide, 3-pinnate-pinnatifid; stipes with a slight groove at the apex, terete towards the base; rachis scales abundant, nearly as wide as the rachis; AZ. 145. C. pringlei

10(8). Stipes stramineous, 1–2 mm in diam.; laminae broadly ovate to pentagonal, about as long as wide, 4-pinnate-pinnatifid; TX. 146. C. leucopoda

10(8). Stipes purplish-black to brown, up to 1 mm in diam.; laminae ovate, lanceolate, or linear-lanceolate, 1.5–5 times longer than wide, 3–4-pinnate, 11

11(10). Rhizome scales black, thick, straight, stiff; laminae lanceolate, broadest near the base; TX. 147. C. kaulfussii

11(10). Rhizome scales brown, thin, slightly contorted, flexible; laminae narrowly elliptic-lanceolate, broadest above the base to near the middle, **12**

12(11). Upper and lower surfaces of the laminae with subsessile, capitate hairs; rhizome scales pale reddish-brown, contorted, 3–5 mm long, forming conspicuous tufts among the stipe bases; laminae 3–5 times longer than wide; CA. *148. C. viscida*

12(11). Dorsal and ventral surfaces of the laminae with long, multicellular, capitate hairs; rhizome scales dark brown, straight, ca. 2 mm long, inconspicuous among the stipe bases; laminae 2–3 times longer than wide; CA. *149. C. cooperae*

13(1). Laminae beneath entirely scaly with broad scales or if also hirsute, the hairs mostly hidden by the many, broad, conspicuous scales, **19**

13(1). Laminae beneath entirely hirsute with twisted hairs or, if also scaly, the hairs not hidden by the few, usually narrow, rather inconspicuous scales, **14**

14(13). Rachises with narrow scales and usually also hairs, **16**

14(13). Rachises only with jointed hairs, lacking scales, **15**

15(14). Rhizomes short-creeping, multicipital, the plants tufted; stipes sparsely pilose; indusia absent, the segment margins reflexed but not modified; laminae 3-pinnate; C,W. *150. C. feei*

15(14). Rhizomes long-creeping, the plants not tufted; stipes villous; indusia ca. 0.3 mm wide; laminae 3- or 4-pinnate; AZ. *151. C. lendigera*

16(14). Laminae linear, mostly less than 1.5(2) cm wide, predominantly 2-pinnate; stipes with a few narrow scales, hairs lacking; P. *152. C. gracillima*

16(14). Laminae linear, usually 2 or more cm wide, predominantly 3-pinnate; stipes with many narrow scales and hairs, **17**

17(16). Laminae glabrous above, appearing dark green; terminal segments of pinnae and pinnules typically 2–3 times longer than wide, obviously elongate; SWB, VA, WV. *153. C. castanea*

17(16). Laminae sparsely to densely villous above, appearing gray-green; terminal segments of pinnae and pinnules typically 1–2 times longer than wide, apparently round or nearly so, **18**

18(17). Largest scales on the stipes and rachises linear, hair-like, up to 0.1 mm wide, rather inconspicuous among the abundant, straight hairs; S. *154. C. tomentosa*

18(17). Largest scales on the stipes and rachises narrowly lanceate, not hair-like, ca. 0.2–1 mm wide, conspicuous among the few, straight hairs and narrow scales; SWB. *155. C. eatonii*

19(13). Costae and costules beneath bearing broad scales with a few, inconspicuous hairs or teeth on the margins and base or lacking hairs, the lamina surface glabrous (except in *C. clevelandii*); rachises with narrow, linear, hair-like scales (except *C. covillei*) in addition to the broader, lanceolate scales, **22**

19(13). Costae and costules beneath bearing broad scales with many, long, conspicuous hairs or teeth on the margins and base, the lamina surface thus appearing hirsute even when it is not; rachises lacking narrow, linear, hair-like scales (except *C. wootonii*), **20**

20(19). Scales on the rachises with long, curly hairs; laminae glabrous adaxially, but appearing arachnoid-villous because of the hairs protruding from beneath; SWB. *156. C. lindheimeri*

20(19). Scales on the rachises with straight teeth or short, nearly straight hairs; laminae glabrous adaxially (sometimes with a few hairs protruding from beneath in *C. wootonii*), **21**

21(20). Rhizomes short-creeping, the stipes clustered; scales on the costae and costules with straight teeth; lamina surface beneath conspicuously hirsute, at least when young; CA. *157. C. intertexta*

21(20). Rhizomes long-creeping, the stipes scattered; scales on the costae and costules with long, curly hairs; lamina surface beneath glabrous; SWB. *158. C. wootonii*

22(19). Rachises lacking narrow, linear, hair-like scales; broad scales with a few short hairs at their base present; SW. *159. C. covillei*

22(19). Rachises with narrow, linear, hair-like scales; broad scales lacking short hairs at their base also present (except in *C. clevelandii*), **23**

23(22). Upper surfaces of the laminae distinctly villous; rhizomes short-creeping; SWB. *160. C. villosa*

23(22). Upper surface of the laminae glabrous; rhizomes long-creeping, **24**

24(23). Scales of the costae and costules without hairs or teeth; lower surface of the laminae glabrous; rhizomes long-creeping, ca. 2 mm in diam.; SWB. *161. C. fendleri*

24(23). Scales of the costae and costules with teeth and sometimes a few hairs; lower surface of the laminae hirsute, the hairs usually hidden by the scales; rhizomes ca. 3 mm thick; CA. *162. C. clevelandii*

138 Cheilanthes arizonica (Maxon) Mickel
Arizona Lip Fern
Rhizomes multicipital, the branches ascending to short-creeping; scales narrowly lanceolate, concolorous, dark brown. Stipes 5–14 cm long, chestnut, with a few scales at the base. Laminae broadly lanceolate to subpentagonal, 5–13 cm long, 2–8 cm wide, 4-pinnate; segments elliptic, 2–7 mm long, 1–1.5 mm wide, acute at the base and apex, sparsely dotted with sessile, red glands on the abaxial surface, strongly underrolled on the lateral margins; indusia continuous on the lateral margins of the segments, ca. 0.5 mm wide, erose-fimbriate.

Terrestrial in soil or epipetric on rock walls in the shade. Occasional. Cochise County, Arizona.

Not cultivated.

*139   Cheilanthes horridula Maxon
Prickly Lip Fern

Rhizomes multicipital, the branches ascending, rarely short-creeping; scales linear, weakly bicolorous, orange-yellow with a broad, brown central band towards the base. Stipes 2–11 cm long, blackish, with many scales like those of the laminae. Laminae narrowly elliptic to narrowly lanceate, 5–20 cm long, 1.5–3 cm wide, pinnate-pinnatifid or 2-pinnate, obtuse at the base, acute to attenuate at the apex; segments oblong, 2–5 mm long, 1.5–2.5 mm wide, entire or lobed, obtuse at the base, round at the apex, rather strongly underrolled on all margins, subscabrous, the hairs whitish, sharp-pointed; indusia continuous on all margins of the segments, ca. 0.25 mm wide, erose.

Epipetric in crevices of limestone and sandstone rocks in shade or sun. Frequent. Central and western Texas.

Not cultivated.

140   Cheilanthes aemula Maxon
Texas Lip Fern

Rhizomes multicipital; scales narrowly lanceolate, concolorous to bicolorous, entirely orange-brown or with a broad, brown to blackish central stripe towards the base. Stipes 6–16 cm long, blackish, glabrous or with a few, long, straight, whitish hairs. Laminae lanceolate, 7–19 cm long, 7–15 cm wide, 3-pinnate-pinnatifid (the basal basiscopic pinnules of the lowest pinna pair elongate), cordate at the base, acute at the apex, the pinnules oblong, lobed, truncate at the base, round at the apex, rather strongly underrolled on all margins, with a few strigose hairs on both surfaces; indusia continuous on all margins, ca. 0.25 mm wide, entire.

Epipetric in crevices, on ledges, and in cavities of limestone rocks, or terrestrial among rocks. Very rare. Central and western Texas.

Not cultivated.

141   Cheilanthes microphylla (Swartz) Swartz
Southern Lip Fern

Rhizomes very long-creeping, the stipes distant; scales narrowly lanceolate, weakly bicolorous, pale to dark brown, sometimes with a broad, dark brown central stripe towards the base. Stipes 4–21 cm long, blackish, with many, deciduous, long, twisted, whitish or yellowish, matted hairs. Laminae narrowly lanceolate to elliptic-lanceolate, 4–27 cm long, 1.5–6 cm wide, 9-pinnate-pinnatifid or 3-pinnate, obtuse at the base, acute to acuminate at the apex, the pinnules oblong to lanceolate, the larger ones with 1–3 basal segments, obtuse to truncate from a short stalk, acute at the apex, rather strongly underrolled on all margins, with scattered hairs on both surfaces; indusia continuous or subcontinuous on all margins, ca. 0.25 mm wide, slightly erose to entire.

Epipetric in crevices of limestone outcrops and terrestrial on shell mounds in partial to full shade. Occasional. Florida.

Not cultivated. According to Evans (1975), depauperate specimens of this species resemble *C. alabamensis*, but are more hirsute and have 64 spores per sporangium.

142   Cheilanthes lanosa (Michx.) D. C. Eaton

Hairy Lip Fern

Rhizomes creeping, rarely branched, the stipes crowded; scales linear-lanceolate, distantly toothed, rather sharply bicolorous, pale brown with a wide, dark brown central stripe. Stipes 3–18 cm long, brown to purplish-black, with many, persistent, long, multicellular hairs having obvious, dark joints. Laminae narrowly elliptic to oblong, 4–24 cm long, 1–4.5 cm wide, 2-pinnate-pinnatifid to barely 3-pinnate, acute to obtuse at the base, acute to acuminate at the apex, the pinnules oblong, usually lobed, sessile, obtuse to round at the apex, the margins weakly to strongly underrolled but not modified, the abaxial surface with straight or bent, multicellular hairs, the adaxial surface sparsely pilose.

Epipetric on ledges in usually igneous or metamorphic rocks or terrestrial in subacid or rarely circumneutral soil. Frequent. Connecticut, New York, Pennsylvania, West Virginia, Kentucky, southern Illinois, Missouri, and Kansas south to Florida, Alabama, Mississippi, Louisiana, and Texas. Disjunct on the Wisconsin-Minnesota border in the driftless area.

Cultivated in rocky, acid soil in partial sun. This species probably is easier to cultivate than most other species of the genus because of its adaptability to many different rock types.

143   Cheilanthes alabamensis (Buckl.) Kunze

Alabama Lip Fern

Rhizomes short-creeping, the stipes crowded; scales narrowly lanceolate, weakly bicolorous, pale orange-brown with a broad, brown central stripe towards the base. Stipes 3–23 cm long, blackish, with long, straight, whitish or yellowish, matted hairs. Laminae narrowly lanceolate or elliptic-lanceolate, 3–31 cm long, 1–6 cm wide, 2-pinnate to 2-pinnate-pinnatifid, obtuse at the base, acute to attenuate at the apex, the pinnules oblong to lanceate, the larger ones lobed or with 1 or 2 basal segments, acute to truncate from a broad base, round at the apex, rather strongly underrolled on all margins, glabrous on both surfaces (except the Texas material with a few, short, stiff hairs on the abaxial surface); indusia continuous on all margins, ca. 0.25 mm wide, crenulate to entire.

Epipetric in crevices of limestone rocks, or terrestrial on shell mounds or among limestone rocks, in shade. Frequent. Mountains of Virginia, North Carolina, Alabama, Georgia, and Tennessee to southern Missouri, northwestern Arkansas, Oklahoma, Texas, New Mexico, and southeastern Arizona.

Not cultivated. According to Evans (1975), this species is apogamous and has 32 spores per sporangium, which clearly separates it from *C. microphylla*, which is not apogamous and has 64 spores per sporangium. Specimens from Texas and west-central Arkansas have broader laminae and pinnae than specimens from elsewhere in the range, have hairs on the abaxial surface of the segments like those of *C. microphylla*, and may represent a species or subspecies different from typical *C. alabamensis*.

144   Cheilanthes wrightii Hooker
Wright's Lip Fern
Rhizomes long-creeping, 1–1.5 mm in diam., often branched, the stipes crowded; scales linear-lanceolate, concolorous to weakly bicolorous, entirely reddish-brown or with a broad, brown central stripe at the base. Stipes 1.5–11 cm long, brown to dark brown, with a few scales like those of the rhizome, glabrescent. Laminae oblong, 3–11 cm long, 1–3.5 cm wide, 3-pinnate or sometimes 3-pinnate-pinnatifid, obtuse at the base, acute at the apex, the pinnules lanceate to oblong, obtuse at the base, acute at the apex, glabrous on both surfaces, the margins plane, the fertile margins underrolled and slightly modified to form discrete or slightly confluent, glandular-erose indusia ca. 0.05 mm wide at the segment and lobe apices.

Epipetric in crevices and on ledges of igneous rocks and terrestrial in gravelly soil on talus slopes. Occasional. Western Texas to southern Arizona.

Not cultivated.

145   Cheilanthes pringlei Davenp.
Pringle's Lip Fern
Rhizomes short- to long-creeping, occasionally branched, the stipes crowded; scales very narrowly lanceolate, bicolorous, stramineous with a broad, brown to dark brown central stripe. Stipes 2–11 cm long, brown, with many, lanceolate, concolorous, stramineous, slightly erose-toothed scales. Laminae ovate to lanceolate, 2–7 cm long, 1.5–4.5 cm wide, 3-pinnate-pinnatifid, obtuse to slightly cordate at the base, acute at the apex, the pinnules oblong, obtuse at the base, acute at the apex, glabrous on both surfaces (only the rachis and costae scaly), the sterile margins plane, the fertile margins underrolled and slightly modified to form discrete, glandular-erose indusia ca. 0.05 mm wide at the segment apices.

Terrestrial around rocks and epipetric in crevices in igneous rocks. Occasional. Southeastern Arizona.

Not cultivated.

146   Cheilanthes leucopoda Link
White-footed Lip Fern

Rhizomes short-creeping, occasionally branched, the stipes crowded; scales linear-lanceolate, concolorous, pale, slightly reddish-brown. Stipes 4–18 cm long, stramineous, with many straight or slightly twisted, 2- or 3-celled, capitate hairs. Laminae broadly ovate to pentagonal, 3–9 cm long, 3–8 cm wide, 4-pinnate-pinnatifid, slightly cordate at the base, obtuse at the apex, the pinnules lanceate-oblong, obtuse at the base, acute at the apex, with a few capitate hairs on both surfaces and the axes more densely hirsute, the sterile margins plane, the fertile margins underrolled and slightly modified to form discrete, mostly entire indusia ca. 0.05 mm wide at the segment apices.

Epipetric in exposed crevices and ledges of limestone rocks. Very rare. West-central Texas.

Not cultivated.

147   Cheilanthes kaulfussii Kunze
Glandular Lip Fern

Rhizomes short-creeping, occasionally branched, the stipes crowded; scales narrowly lanceolate, concolorous, black, thick and straight. Stipes 7–22 cm long, chestnut to purplish-black, with many, long, flattened, 2-celled, capitate hairs. Laminae lanceolate, 3–14 cm long, 2.5–6 cm wide, 4-pinnate-pinnatifid, slightly cordate at the base, acute at the apex, the pinnules lanceate, obtuse at the base, acute at the apex, with many, short, flattened, 2-celled, capitate hairs on both surfaces and the axes with long, multicellular, similar hairs, the sterile margins plane, the fertile margins underrolled and modified to form discrete, mostly entire indusia ca. 0.2 mm wide at the segment and lobe apices.

Epipetric in crevices and on rock ledges, and terrestrial among boulders. Very rare. Central and western Texas.

Not cultivated.

148   Cheilanthes viscida Davenp.
Viscid Lip Fern

Rhizomes short-creeping or ascending, rarely branched, the stipes crowded; scales linear-lanceolate, concolorous, pale reddish-brown, thin and contorted. Stipes 3–12 cm long, brown to purplish-black, with a few, deciduous, short, flattened, multicellular, capitate hairs. Laminae narrowly elliptic-lanceolate, 3–14 cm long, 1–3 cm wide, 3-pinnate-pinnatifid, acute or obtuse at the base, acute at the apex, the pinnules lanceate, obtuse at the base, acute at the apex, with many, short, 2-celled, yellow, capitate glands on the abaxial surface, the sterile margins plane, the fertile margins underrolled but not modified at the margins of the segment and lobe apices.

Epiphytic in crevices and terrestrial around boulders. Occasional. Southern California.

Not cultivated.

149 Cheilanthes cooperae D. C. Eaton
Mrs. Cooper's Lip Fern

Rhizomes erect-ascending, rarely branched, the stipes crowded; scales linearlanceolate, concolorous, pale to dark reddish-brown, thin and contorted. Stipes 1.5–8 cm long, brown or reddish-brown to purplish-black, with many, persistent, long, flattened, multicellular, capitate hairs. Laminae elliptic-lanceolate, 3–15 cm long, 1.5–5 cm wide, 3-pinnate-pinnatifid, acute or obtuse at the base, acute at the apex, the pinnules oblong, truncate to obtuse at the base, round at the apex, with many hairs like those of the stipes on both surfaces, the sterile margins plane, the fertile margins underrolled but not modified at the margins of the segment and lobe apices.

Epipetric in crevices of limestone cliffs. Rare. California.

Not cultivated.

150 Cheilanthes feei Moore
Slender Lip Fern

Rhizomes short-creeping, ascending, multicipital, the stipes crowded; scales linear-lanceolate, sharply bicolorous, pale brown with a blackish central stripe, slightly erose at the margins. Stipes 2–8 cm long, reddish-brown to blackish, with a few rather straight, multicellular hairs. Laminae linear-lanceate, 2.5–7(10) cm long, 1–2(3) cm wide, 3-pinnate, obtuse to truncate at the base, acute at the apex, with many, persistent, multicellular, curved, reddish-brown hairs on the abaxial surface, the segment margins underrolled but not modified.

Epipetric in crevices of limestone, dolomite, or sometimes sandstone or rarely granite cliffs and terrestrial on rocky slopes. Frequent. Wisconsin, Minnesota, South Dakota, Montana, Alberta, and British Columbia, south to Arkansas, Texas, New Mexico, Arizona, and southern California.

Cultivated in moist or dry, basic soil in full sun.

151 Cheilanthes lendigera (Cav.) Swartz
Beaded Lip Fern

Rhizomes long-creeping, occasionally branched, the stipes distant; scales linear, concolorous or sharply bicolorous, golden to pale brown, sometimes with a blackish central stripe, entire. Stipes 4–23 cm long, purplish-black to dark brown, woolly, with many, fine, curled, multicellular hairs. Laminae lanceate to linear-lanceate, 3.5–23 cm long, 1.5–10 cm wide, 3- or 4-pinnate, obtuse to truncate at the base, acute at the apex, glabrous or nearly so but with many hairs like those of the stipes on the axes, the segment margins strongly underrolled, modified to form very broad indusia.

Terrestrial in the shelter of boulders and epipetric in rock crevices. Rare. Southern Texas and adjacent Arizona.

Not cultivated.

152   Cheilanthes gracillima D. C. Eaton
Lace Fern

Rhizomes ascending, multicipital, the stipes tufted; scales linear, concolorous or sharply bicolorous, pale brown, sometimes with a blackish or brown central stripe, entire. Stipes 2.5–14 cm long, medium brown to purplish-black, with a few, narrow, concolorous, pale scales. Laminae narrowly elliptic-lanceolate, 3–10 cm long, 0.6–1.5(2.5) cm wide, 2(3)-pinnate, obtuse to truncate at the base, acute to acuminate at the apex, adaxially glabrous, abaxially and on the axes with many, pale brown, curly, multicellular hairs along with a few narrow scales, the segment margins strongly underrolled, with a very narrow, scarcely visible indusium.

Epipetric in crevices of igneous rocks and on rock ledges. Frequent. Southern British Columbia to California east to Idaho and northern Utah.

Cultivated in moist to dry, subacid soil in full sun. For comments on hybrids between this species and *C. intertexta*, see the latter species.

153   Cheilanthes castanea Maxon
Chestnut Lip Fern

Rhizomes short-creeping, multicipital, the stipes tufted; scales linear-lanceolate, sharply bicolorous, pale brown with a dark brown central stripe, entire. Stipes 4–17 cm long, dark reddish-brown to purplish-black, with narrowly lanceolate, linear, hair-like scales and a few hairs. Laminae elliptic-lanceate to nearly oblong, 5–21 cm long, 1.5–3.5(5)cm wide, 3-pinnate, obtuse to truncate at the base, acute to acuminate at the apex, adaxially glabrous, abaxially with many, reddish-brown, curly, multicellular hairs along with narrowly lanceolate scales on the axes, the segment margins strongly underrolled, with a narrow, continuous, entire indusium ca. 0.1 mm wide.

Epipetric in crevices of igneous rocks, on rock ledges, and terrestrial on talus slopes and among boulders. Southwestern Texas to southern Arizona. Disjunct in central Oklahoma, northern Arkansas, and the mountains of southern Virginia and eastern West Virginia.

Not cultivated.

154 Cheilanthes tomentosa Link
Woolly Lip Fern

Rhizomes multicipital, the stipes tufted; scales nearly linear, sometimes sharply bicolorous, pale reddish-brown with a dark brown central stripe, entire. Stipes 5–20 cm long, purplish-black, with linear, nearly hair-like scales and many straight, pale orangish-brown, often appressed hairs, especially in young fronds. Laminae oblong to lanceate, 5–34 cm long, 1.5–6(8) cm wide, 3-pinnate, obtuse to truncate at the base, acute to acuminate at the apex, adaxially villous, abaxially with many pale brown, curly, multicellular hairs along with linear scales on the axes, the segment margins strongly underrolled, with a narrow, continuous, entire indusium ca. 0.1 mm wide.

Epipetric in crevices and on ledges of various circumneutral to subacid rocks, and terrestrial among boulders on talus slopes. Frequent. Mountains of Pennsylvania south to Kentucky, Alabama, and Georgia. Disjunct in Arkansas, Oklahoma, and Kansas west to New Mexico.

Cultivated in moist to dry, circumneutral garden soil in full sun.

155 Cheilanthes eatonii Baker in Hooker & Baker
Eaton's Lip Fern

Rhizomes short-creeping or multicipital, the stipes tufted; scales narrowly lanceolate, mostly sharply bicolorous, pale brown with a dark reddish-brown central stripe, entire. Stipes 3–16 cm long, reddish-brown to purplish-black, with narrowly lanceolate scales, linear, hair-like scales, and a few hairs. Laminae lanceolate-oblong, 3.5–17 cm long, 1.5–4(5) cm wide, 3-pinnate, obtuse to truncate at the base, acute at the apex, adaxially villous, abaxially with many, pale reddish-brown, curly, multicellular hairs along with lanceolate scales on the axes, the segment margins strongly underrolled, with a very narrow, continuous, entire indusium less than 0.1 mm wide.

Epipetric in rock crevices of igneous or limestone rocks, on rock ledges, and terrestrial among boulders on talus slopes. Frequent. Central Texas and western Oklahoma west to Utah and New Mexico.

Not cultivated. This species hybridizes with *C. villosa* in western Texas and southern New Mexico.

156 Cheilanthes lindheimeri Hooker
Fairy-swords

Rhizomes long-creeping, the stipes scattered; scales lanceate, concolorous or occasionally bicolorous, pale or pale reddish-brown sometimes with a dark brown central stripe, entire. Stipes 4–19 cm long, dark reddish-brown to purplish-black, with lanceolate scales having long, curly hairs especially near their base. Laminae oblong-lanceate, 3–15 cm long,

2–4.5 cm wide, 3-pinnate, obtuse to truncate at the base, acute at the apex, glabrous adaxially but with arachnoid-villous hairs protruding from between the segments, abaxially with many, pale brown, curly, multicellular hairs along with broadly lanceolate scales on the axes having long marginal hairs, the segment margins strongly underrolled, without a noticeable indusium.

Epipetric on dry, shaded boulders and ledges of igneous rocks and terrestrial among boulders on talus slopes. Frequent. Western Texas to southern Arizona.

Not cultivated.

157   Cheilanthes intertexta (Maxon) Maxon in Abrams
Coastal Lip Fern

Rhizomes short-creeping, the stipes clustered; scales lanceate, bicolorous, pale brown with a wide, dark brown central stripe, erose. Stipes 3–13 cm long, dark brown to purplish-black, with lanceolate scales having a few teeth at their base. Laminae oblong-lanceolate, 4–10 cm long, 1–2.5 cm wide, 3-pinnate, obtuse to truncate at the base, acute to acuminate at the apex, adaxially glabrous, abaxially with many, pale brown, curly, multicellular hairs along with lanceolate scales having short teeth at their apex and long hairs near their base, the segment margins strongly underrolled, without a noticeable indusium.

Epipetric in crevices of igneous rocks. Occasional. California.

Not cultivated. According to A. R. Smith (1974a), this species hybridizes with *C. gracillima*, presumably forming what has been called *C. gracillima* var. *aberrans* M. E. Jones. *Cheilanthes intertexta* is itself intermediate between *C. covillei* and *C. gracillima*, although whether or not it is a hybrid between these species is not known at present.

158   Cheilanthes wootonii Maxon
Wooton's Lip Fern

Rhizomes long-creeping, the stipes scattered; scales lanceate, concolorous or bicolorous, pale brown with a dark brown central stripe, entire. Stipes 3–18 cm long, dark brown to purplish-black, with lanceolate scales having long hairs near their base plus linear, hair-like scales. Laminae oblong-lanceolate, 4–17(21) cm long, 1.5–5 cm wide, 3-pinnate, obtuse at the base, acuminate to acute at the apex, adaxially glabrous, abaxially glabrous but with lanceolate scales on the axes beneath having long, curly hairs, the segment margins strongly underrolled, without a noticeable indusium.

Terrestrial around the bases of boulders and sometimes epipetric on rock ledges. Frequent. Colorado, western Oklahoma, and western Texas west to Arizona.

Not cultivated.

159   Cheilanthes covillei Maxon
Coville's Lip Fern

Rhizomes short-creeping, the stipes clustered; scales lanceate, bicolorous, pale brown with a wide, dark brown central stripe, entire. Stipes 3–16 cm long, brown to dark reddish-brown, with wide and narrow lanceolate scales having long hairs near their base. Laminae oblong-lanceate, 3–17 cm long, 1.5–4 cm wide, 3-pinnate, obtuse at the base, acute to acuminate at the apex, adaxially glabrous, abaxially glabrous along with lanceolate scales on the axes having a few long hairs, the segment margins strongly underrolled, without a noticeable indusium.

Epipetric in rock crevices and terrestrial at the bases of granite and sandstone boulders. Frequent. Southwestern Utah and Arizona to southern California.

Not cultivated. According to A. R. Smith (1974a), this species hybridizes with *Notholaena parryi* to form the rare hybrid *C.* × *parishii* Davenp. in southern California and Maricopa Co., Arizona. It also seems likely that it hybridizes with *N. newberryi* to form the equally rare hybrid *C.* × *fibrillosa* (Davenp.) Davenp. ex Underw.

160   Cheilanthes villosa Davenp.
Villous Lip Fern

Rhizomes short-creeping, multicipital, the stipes clustered; scales lanceate, concolorous or sometimes bicolorous, pale reddish-brown with a narrow, blackish central stripe, entire. Stipes 3–14 cm long, purplish-black, with wide and narrow, lanceate scales having a few teeth at the base, plus linear, hair-like scales. Laminae oblong-lanceate, 4–21 cm long, 1.5–4.5 cm wide, 3-pinnate, obtuse at the base, acuminate at the apex, adaxially villous, abaxially glabrous with hairs protruding from above and broad, lanceolate scales on the axes, the segment margins strongly underrolled, without a noticeable indusium.

Epipetric in crevices and on ledges of igneous rocks, and terrestrial at the bases of boulders. Occasional. Western Texas to Arizona.

Not cultivated. This species hybridizes with *C. eatonii* in western Texas and southern New Mexico.

161   Cheilanthes fendleri Hooker
Fendler's Lip Fern

Rhizomes long-creeping, the stipes close to scattered; scales lanceate, concolorous to weakly bicolorous, pale brown sometimes with a dark brown central stripe, entire. Stipes 3–17 cm long, brown to purplish-black, with narrow, lanceate scales having long teeth near their base plus linear, hair-like scales. Laminae oblong-lanceate, 4–14 cm long, 1–4 cm wide, 3-pinnate, obtuse at the base, acuminate at the apex, adaxially glabrous, abaxially glabrous with broad, lanceolate scales and a few linear, hair-like scales on the axes, the segment margins strongly underrolled, without a noticeable indusium.

Epipetric in crevices of igneous rocks and on dry ledges, and terrestrial at the bases of boulders. Occasional. Southern Colorado, Oklahoma, and western Texas to Arizona.

Cultivated in moist to dry, rocky, subacid soil in full sun.

162 Cheilanthes clevelandii D. C. Eaton
Cleveland's Lip Fern

Rhizomes long-creeping, the stipes close; scales lanceate, bicolorous, pale brown with a wide, dark brown central stripe, erose or sometimes slightly distantly toothed. Stipes 5–31 cm long, brown to dark reddish-brown, with wide and narrow, lanceate scales having long hairs near their base plus linear, hair-like scales. Laminae oblong-lanceate, 6–23 cm long, 2–8 cm wide, 3-pinnate, obtuse at the base, acuminate at the apex, adaxially glabrous, abaxially conspicuously hairy along with lanceolate scales on the axes having few to no long hairs or teeth, the segment margins strongly underrolled, without a noticeable indusium.

Terrestrial at the bases of boulders and epipetric in rock crevices. Occasional. Southern California.

Not cultivated.

ASPIDOTIS
The Lace Ferns

This genus includes three species in California and Mexico and another species of dubious affinity in Africa.

Aspidotis is distinct from other Sinopteridaceae genera because of its highly divided, glabrous laminae, which have long, mucronate, distantly toothed segments with thickened margins and a minutely striate or ridged, shiny, adaxial surface.

The plants are small and monomorphic. The stipes usually are 1–3 times as long as the laminae. The highly divided laminae have long ultimate segments. Each frond looks a little like a crude paint brush when it has been dried and pressed.

The Lace Ferns grow in rock crevices or on talus slopes from British Columbia to southern California. A disjunct population occurs in Quebec. The plants, which are restricted to selenium-bearing (ultramafic) rocks and soils, are difficult to maintain in cultivation.

Key to Aspidotis

1. Laminae 3-pinnate, lanceolate to oblong, with linear, continuous sori on the lateral edges of the entire ultimate segments; P. *163.A. densa*

1. Laminae 4-pinnate or 4-pinnate-pinnatifid, lanceolate to deltate, with round, discontinuous sori at intervals on the lateral edges and apices of the toothed to lacerate ultimate segments; CA. *164. A. californica*

163   Aspidotis densa (Brack. in Wilkes) Lellinger
Indian's-dream

Rhizomes multicipital, the branches ascending. Stipes crowded, dark reddish-brown throughout, 5–20 cm long. Laminae lanceolate to oblong, 3–7 cm long, 1.5–4.5 cm wide, 3-pinnate, coriaceous, the ultimate segments linear, 3–8 mm long, the midrib prominulous abaxially, the margins underrolled, entire, bearing a continuous, erose false indusium.

Epipetric in rock crevices and on ledges, and terrestrial on talus slopes, always on or associated with serpentine-bearing rock. Frequent. British Columbia to California east to Idaho, Montana, and Utah. Disjunct in Quebec.

Cultivated with difficulty in well-drained garden soil in full sun; adding selenium-bearing rock to the soil probably would be worthwhile. This species has hybridized with *A. californica* to form *A. carlotta-halliae* (Wagner & Gilbert) Lellinger, a rare, fertile species known only from central coastal California. A. R. Smith (1975) has studied the morphology and cytology of this species and that of its parents. It grows only on serpentine substrates, as does *A. densa*. It has variable, discontinuous indusia usually longer than those of *A. densa* but shorter than those of *A. californica*. Its frond morphology approximates that of *A. californica*.

164   Aspidotis californica (Hooker) Nutt. ex Copel.
California Lace Fern

Rhizomes short-creeping. Stipes crowded, dark reddish-brown throughout, 3–20 cm long. Laminae lanceolate to deltate, 3–11 cm long, 1.5–9 cm wide, 4-pinnate or 4-pinnate-pinnatifid, papyraceous, the ultimate segments narrowly oblanceolate to rhombic, 1.5–4 mm long, the midrib usually obscure abaxially, the margins sparsely toothed or lacerate, plane except underrolled only near the discrete, semicircular, suberose false indusia.

Epipetric in rock crevices or terrestrial among usually granitic rocks. Frequent. California coast ranges and the Sierra Nevada.

Cultivated with difficulty in well-drained garden soil in partial sun. This species hybridizes to form *A. carlotta-halliae*, which is discussed under the other parent, *A. densa*.

NOTHOLAENA
The Cloak Ferns

Notholaena includes about 75 species, mostly in the drier parts of the western United States and Central and South America. About a dozen species grow in the Old World. A few species of *Notholaena* resemble *Cheilanthes* to some extent; see the latter genus for a discussion. Some other species of *Notholaena* resemble *Pellaea* slightly in having rather bead-like segments, but no *Notholaena* has segments that fold longitudinally, a characteristic of almost all Pellaeas that grow in the United States. The Notholaenas commonly fold their segments or pinnae upward to reveal the protective and reflective farinose coating on the abaxial surface.

The plants are small, monomorphic, and have stipes usually as long or longer than the mostly highly divided laminae. Some of the species have a white, cream, or yellow farinose exudate and sometimes also hairs or scales on the abaxial surface of the laminae; other species are glabrous or have only hairs and/or scales.

The Cloak Ferns grow in rock crevices or on rock ledges and at the bases of boulders. None ranges farther east than the Mississippi River or farther north than Nebraska and southern Nevada. Only a few of the species have been cultivated, although several of the farinose species and certainly *N. sinuata* would make attractive greenhouse plants. The genus was monographed by Tryon (1956).

Key to Notholaena
   1. Laminae with hairs, scales, or farina on the abaxial surface, **3**
   1. Laminae lacking hairs, scales, and farina on the abaxial surface, **2**
   2(1). Ultimate segments articulate, the dark color of the stalk stopping abruptly at the base of the segment, the segments deciduous in age; laminae commonly 4-pinnate; rachises slightly flexuous towards the apex; TX, NM. *165. N. parvifolia*
   2(1). Ultimate segments not articulate, the dark color of the stalk passing into the base of the segment, the segments not deciduous in age; laminae commonly 3-pinnate; rachises straight towards the apex; AZ, CA. *166. N. jonesii*
   3(1). Laminae sparsely to densely farinose, the hairs and scales usually few or absent, the farina not hidden, **10**
   3(1). Laminae densely covered with hairs and/or scales on the abaxial surface, lacking farina, **4**
      4(3). Abaxial surface of the laminae densely scaly, **7**
      4(3). Abaxial surface of the laminae densely hirsute, **5**
      5(4). Laminae linear-elliptic, mostly 15–40 cm long, pinnate-pinnatifid, the pinnae cut about half way to the costa; adaxial surface of

the laminae sparsely villous with appressed hairs, appearing green; SWB. *167. N. aurea*

5(4). Laminae lanceate, mostly less than 15 cm long, 2-pinnate; adaxial surface of the laminae mostly densely villous or arachnoid-villous, appearing gray, **6**

6(5). Laminae loosely pilose on both surfaces, the outline of the segments difficult to see; rhizome scales obviously bicolorous with a narrow, black central stripe; stipes and rachises with a few, short, spreading, obviously jointed hairs; SW. *168. N. parryi*

6(5). Laminae appressed arachnoid-villous adaxially, densely villous abaxially, the outline of the segments easy to see; rhizome scales appearing concolorous, with a flexible, yellowish, seta-like apex; stipes and rachises with many, long, matted, obscurely jointed hairs; CA. *169. N. newberryi*

7(4). Pinnae lobed nearly to the costae; rhizome scales black, with many marginal setae about as long as the scale is wide; stipes black to purplish-black; SWB. *170. N. aschenborniana*

7(4). Pinnae unlobed or only shallowly lobed not more than ca. half way to the costae; rhizome scales pale reddish-brown, with a few marginal setae shorter than the scale is wide; stipes pale reddish-brown to dark brown, **8**

8(7). Pinnae up to 0.65 cm long, 1–2 times longer than wide, with 0 or 1 pair of very broad and shallow lobes; rhizome scales entire; scales on the adaxial surface of the lamina persistent, nearly round in outline, the central body scarcely elongate; SWB. *171. N. cochisensis*

8(7). Pinnae 0.65–3.5 cm long, mostly 1.5–2.5 times longer than wide, with 3–8 pairs of very broad and shallow to rather narrow and deep lobes; rhizome scales distantly toothed; scales on the adaxial surface of the lamina lanceolate in outline, the central body clearly lanceolate, **9**

9(8). Pinnae 0.65–1 cm long, unlobed or with 1–3 pairs of broad, shallow lobes; adaxial surface of the laminae bearing persistent, long-toothed scales having a central body ca. 3–4 times as wide as the teeth are wide; SWB. **172. N. integerrima*

9(8). Pinnae 1–3.5 cm long, usually with 3–8 pairs of narrow, rather deep lobes; adaxial surface of the laminae bearing deciduous, long-toothed scales having a central body ca. 1–2 times as wide as the teeth are wide; SWB. *173. N. sinuata*

10(3). All or some ultimate segments petiolulate, bead-like, not adnate, **16**

10(3). All ultimate segments adnate, none petiolulate, **11**

11(10). Laminae pentagonal, about as wide as long; stipes 2–4 times longer than the laminae; SWB. *174. N. standleyi*

11(10). Laminae oblong to lanceolate, at least twice as long as wide; stipes less than 2 times longer than the laminae, **12**

12(11). Rachises and lamina axes with narrow scales, **14**

12(11). Rachises and lamina axes lacking narrow scales, **13**

13(12). Laminae ca. 2 times longer than wide, with 3–8 pinna pairs, shorter than the stipes; basal basiscopic pinnule of the basal pinna pair much longer than the suprabasal basiscopic pinnules; TX. *175. N. candida* var. *copelandii*

13(12). 1Laminae 3–6 times longer than wide, with 8–12 pinna pairs, usually longer than the stipes; basal basiscopic pinnule of the basal pinna pair not much longer than the suprabasal basiscopic pinnules; AZ. *176. N. lemmonii* var. *lemmonii*

14(12). Stipes, rachises, and laminae with reddish-brown, hair-like scales; rhizome scales with spine-like teeth, darker towards the margin than the center; TX. *177. N. schaffneri* var. *nealleyi*

14(12). Stipes, rachises, and laminae with stramineous, narrowly lanceolate scales; rhizome scales with a few weak cilia, the very narrow margins pale, the central portion black or dark brown, **15**

15(14). Adaxial surface of the laminae sparsely dotted with white farina; abaxial surface of the lamina usually densely covered with white farina; laminae 1.5–3 cm wide; SWB. *178. N. grayi*

15(14). Adaxial surface of the laminae sparsely villous with long, pale hairs; abaxial surface of the laminae sparsely covered with pale yellow farina; laminae 1–2 cm wide; TX. *179. N. aliena*

16(10). Lamina axes markedly flexuous; RM. *180. N. fendleri*

16(10). Lamina axes not flexuous; **17**

17(16). Basal pinnae not much larger than the suprabasal ones; basiscopic pinnule not exaggerated, not longer than the suprabasal pinnules and not as long as the basal pinna, **19**

17(16). Basal pinnae much larger than the suprabasal ones; basiscopic basal pinnule exaggerated, longer than the suprabasal pinnules and about as long as the basal pinna, **18**

18(17). Stipes brown to reddish-brown; laminae mostly pentagonal, with yellow or rarely white farina; rhizome scales with a very narrow, slightly toothed, pale margin; AZ, CA. *181. N. californica*

18(17). Stipes purplish-black to black; laminae mostly elongate, usually with pale sulfur yellow farina; rhizome scales with a broad, erose, and slightly toothed, pale margin; SWB. *182. N. neglecta*

19(17). Stipes and rachises grooved; rhizome scales bicolorous, brown with a broad, black central stripe; pinnules mostly stalked ca. 0.5 mm; TX. *183. N. greggii*

19(17). Stipes and rachises terete; rhizome scales concolorous, pale brown, yellowish-brown, or reddish-brown; pinnules mostly stalked 1 mm or more, **20**

20(19). Segments subarticulate, the dark color of the stalk ending abruptly at the segment base; laminae up to 3-pinnate; AZ, NM. *184. N. incana*

20(19). Segments not articulate, the dark color of the stalk passing into the segments; laminae 3–5-pinnate, **21**

21(20). Stipes mostly 0.5 mm in diam. or less, pale to medium brown, rarely reddish-brown; laminae rather thin, the veins visible through the upper surface; NP, SP. *185. N. dealbata*

21(20). Stipes mostly 0.75 mm in diam. or more, purplish-black to black, sometimes reddish-brown or brown; laminae thick, the veins not visible through the upper surface, **22**

22(21). Laminae 4- or 5-pinnate, ca. 2 times longer than wide, the basal pinnae ca. ½ as long as the laminae; SWB. *186. N. limitanea* var. *limitanea*

22(21). Laminae 3- or 4-pinnate, at least 3 times longer than wide, the basal pinnae ca. ¼ as long as the laminae; SWB. *187. N. limitanea* var. *mexicana*

165 Notholaena parvifolia Tryon
Small-leaved Cloak Fern

Rhizome scales narrowly lanceolate, concolorous, brown or reddish-brown, entire. Stipes 3–12 cm long, adaxially grooved, reddish-brown to dark brown, bearing a few scales like those of the rhizome. Laminae triangular, 5–14 cm long, 2–7 cm wide, 3- or 4-pinnate, truncate at the base, acute to acuminate at the apex, glabrous on both surfaces, commonly glaucous, the ultimate segments petiolulate, nearly round, appearing elongate or triangular when dry and curled, the segment margins underrolled.

Epiphytic in crevices and on ledges of limestone and other calcareous rocks. Occasional. Southern Texas to southern New Mexico.

Not cultivated.

166 Notholaena jonesii Maxon
Jones' Cloak Fern

Rhizome scales linear, concolorous, brown or reddish-brown, entire. Stipes 2–6 cm long, terete, reddish-brown to dark brown, glabrous. Laminae lanceolate, 3–7 cm long, 0.8–3 cm wide, 2(3)-pinnate, obtuse at the base, acuminate at the apex, glabrous on both surfaces, not glaucous, dark blue-green, the ultimate segments petiolulate, ovate to deltate, not curled when dry, the segment margins underrolled.

Epipetric in crevices and on ledges of limestone and igneous rocks. Occasional. Southern Utah to southern Arizona west to soutern Nevada and southern California.

Not cultivated.

167 Notholaena aurea (Poir.) Desv.
Golden Cloak Fern

Rhizome scales lanceolate, bicolorous, pale brown with a reddish-brown central stripe, erose. Stipes 4–25 cm long, terete, purplish-black, bearing deciduous, matted hairs. Laminae linear-elliptic, 10–30 cm long, 1–3 cm wide, attenuate at the base, gradually tapered above to an acute or obtuse apex, the adaxial surface sparsely villous with appressed hairs, the abaxial surface densely villous with pale, golden-tan hairs, the ultimate segments broady attached, ovate-triangular, not curled when dry, the segment margins underrolled.

Terrestrial at the base of boulders and epipetric on rock ledges. Occasional. Western Texas to southeastern Arizona.

Not cultivated.

168 Notholaena parryi D. C. Eaton
Parry's Cloak Fern

Rhizome scales narrowly lanceolate, bicolorous, reddish-brown with a narrow, black central stripe, entire. Stipes 2–9 cm long, terete, purplish-black to brown, bearing a few, short, spreading, obviously jointed hairs. Laminae lanceate, 2–12 cm long, 1–4 cm wide, 2-pinnate-pinnatifid, obtuse at the base, acute at the apex, the adaxial and abaxial surfaces loosely pilose with straight to slightly curly, white to tan hairs, the ultimate segments broadly attached lobes on the short-stalked pinnules, not curled when dry, the segment margins scarcely underrolled.

Epipetric in crevices of calcareous and igneous rocks or rarely terrestrial at the bases of boulders. Frequent. Southern Utah and adjacent Nevada to southern Arizona and central and southern California.

Not cultivated. This species hybidizes with *C. covillei* to form the rare *C. ×parishii* Davenp. in southern California.

169 Notholaena newberryi D. C. Eaton
Cotton Fern

Rhizome scales narrowly lanceolate, concolorous, reddish-brown with a flexible, yellowish, setiform apex, entire. Stipes 2–15 cm long, terete, purplish-black to dark brown, bearing many, long, matted hairs. Laminae lanceate-oblong, 3–19 cm long, 1.5–4 cm wide, 2-pinnate-pinnatifid to 3-pinnate, obtuse at the base, acute at the apex, the adaxial surface appressed arachnoid-villous, the abaxial surface matted-villous with pale, reddish-brown to golden hairs, the ultimate segments nearly round, broadly attached on the short-stalked pinnules, not curled when dry, the segment margins scarcely underrolled.

Epipetric in rock crevices or sometimes terrestrial at the bases of boulders. Occasional. Southern California.

Cultivated in full sun in moist to dry potting soil. This species apparently hybridizes with *Cheilanthes covillei* to form the rare *C.* ×*fibrillosa* (Davenp.) Davenp. ex Underw. in southern California.

170 Notholaena aschenborniana Klotzsch
Aschenborn's Cloak Fern

Rhizome scales narrowly lanceolate, concolorous, black, with many, long, marginal teeth. Stipes 3–12 cm long, terete, black to purplish-black, bearing lanceolate, brown, subsetose scales and nearly round, stramineous, highly dissected, nearly stellate scales. Laminae lanceate-oblong, 7–24 cm long, 2–4.5 cm wide, pinnate-pinnatisect, obtuse at the base, acute-acuminate at the apex, the adaxial surface arachnoid-villous, the abaxial surface villous with pale, reddish-brown hairs and with scales on the axes like those of the stipes, the ultimate segments slightly lobed, broadly attached on the costae, not curled when dry, the segment margins underrolled.

Terrestrial at the bases of boulders or epipetric in crevices, perhaps only on limestone rocks. Very rare. Western Texas, southern New Mexico, and southeastern Arizona.

Not cultivated.

171 Notholaena cochisensis Goodd.
Cochise's Cloak Fern

Rhizome scales linear, concolorous or weakly bicolorous, pale reddish-brown, sometimes with a darker, broad, central stripe, entire. Stipes 2–6 cm long, terete or adaxially flattened, reddish-brown to brown, bearing appressed, lanceolate, toothed scales. Laminae linear, 5–23 cm long, 0.8–1.3 cm wide, pinnate, tapering gradually at the base and apex, the adaxial surface with persistent, whitish scales nearly round in outline with long teeth radiating from a scarcely elongate body, the abaxial surface densely scaly with pale reddish-brown, lanceolate, abundantly toothed scales, the ultimate segments nearly oblong, unlobed or with a basal pair of shallow lobes, curled upward to reveal the abaxial surface when dry, the segment margins slightly underrolled.

Terrestrial, often among limestone rocks or epipetric on rock ledges. Frequent. Western Texas to southeastern California.

Not cultivated. Toxic to livestock. This species hybridizes with *N. sinuata* var. *sinuata* to form *N. integerrima*.

*172   Notholaena integerrima (Hooker) Hevly
Hybrid Cloak Fern

Rhizome scales linear, concolorous or weakly bicolorous, pale reddish-brown, sometimes with a darker, broad, central stripe, with a few, short, marginal teeth. Stipes 2–9 cm long, terete, reddish-brown to brown, bearing lanceolate, toothed, appressed scales. Laminae linear, 6–23 cm long, 1.3–2 cm wide, pinnate, tapering gradually at the base and apex, the adaxial surface with persistent, whitish scales lanceolate in outline with long teeth radiating from a lanceolate body ca. 3–4 times wider than the width of the teeth, the abaxial surface densely scaly with pale reddish-brown, lanceolate, abundantly toothed scales, the ultimate segments oblong, unlobed or with 1–3 pairs of broad, shallow lobes, curled upward to reveal the abaxial surface when dry, the segment margins slightly under-rolled.

Terrestrial among limestone rocks or epipetric in rock crevices. Frequent. Oklahoma and Texas west to southern Nevada and Arizona.

Not cultivated. Hevly (1965) demonstrated that this widespread species is an apogamous, fertile hybrid that originated from *N. cochisensis* and *N. sinuata* var. *sinuata*. It is intermediate in pinna morphology and rhizome scale toothing, in particular.

173   Notholaena sinuata (Lag. ex Swartz) Kaulf. var. sinuata
Wavy Cloak Fern

Rhizome scales linear, concolorous or weakly bicolorous, pale reddish-brown, sometimes with a darker, broad, central stripe, with many short, marginal teeth. Stipes 1.5–14 cm long, terete or slightly adaxially flattened, reddish-brown to brown, bearing lanceolate, toothed, appressed scales. Laminae linear, 10–45 cm long, 2–7 cm wide, pinnate, tapering gradually at the base and apex, the adaxial surface with deciduous, whitish scales lanceolate in outline with long teeth radiating from a lanceolate body ca. 1–2 times wider than the width of the teeth, the abaxial surface densely scaly with pale reddish-brown, lanceolate, abundantly toothed scales, the ultimate segments oblong, ovate, or nearly lanceolate, with 3–8 pairs of narrow lobes extending 1/3–1/2 way to the costa, scarcely curled upward to reveal the abaxial surface when dry, the segment margins slightly underrolled.

Terrestrial among usually limestone rocks or epipetric in rock crevices. Frequent. Western Oklahoma and Texas west to southeastern Arizona. Disjunct in Meriwether County, Georgia.

Not cultivated. This species hybridizes with *N. cochisensis* to form *N. integerrima*. Hevly (1965) divided *N. sinuata* into several varieties; all but var. *sinuata* are confined to tropical America.

174 Notholaena standleyi Maxon
Standley's Cloak Fern

Rhizome scales lanceolate, bicolorous, brown with a black central stripe, entire. Stipes 4–25 cm long, terete or slightly adaxially flattened, reddish-brown to brown, with a tuft of concolorous or bicolorous scales like those on the rhizome at the base. Laminae pentagonal, 2–8 cm long, 2–8 cm wide, pinnate-bipinnatifid at the base, bipinnatifid above the base, the adaxial surface glabrous, the abaxial surface with pale sulfur yellow farina, the ultimate segments broad or elongate lobes, curled upward to reveal the abaxial surface when dry, the segment margins underrolled.

Epipetric in rock crevices or terrestrial at the bases of boulders. Occasional. Western Oklahoma, southern Colorado, and southern Nevada south to central Texas and southern Arizona. Seigler and Wollenweber (1983) have found one race with gold farina (principally in Arizona), another with yellow farina (from southeastern Colorado and Oklahoma to northern Mexico), and a third race with yellow-green farina (from northern Mexico to western Texas).

Not cultivated.

175 Notholaena candida var. copelandii (C. C. Hall) Tryon
Copeland's Cloak Fern

Rhizome scales lanceolate, bicolorous, pale brown with a broad, black central stripe, sparsely erose-ciliate at the margin, the broad margins wearing away in age. Stipes 3–18 cm long, terete to shallowly adaxially grooved, black to purplish-black, bearing a few scales like those of the rhizome. Laminae lanceate, 3–11 cm long, 2.5–6 cm wide, 2-pinnate-pinnatifid at the base, pinnate-pinnatifid above the base, the adaxial surface essentially glabrous, the abaxial surface with white farina, the ultimate segments linear-lanceate, slightly curled upward to reveal the abaxial surface when dry, the segment margins underrolled.

Epipetric in crevices in limestone and terrestrial at the bases of boulders. Rare. Southwestern Texas.

Not cultivated.

176 Notholaena lemmonii D. C. Eaton var. lemmonii
Lemmon's Cloak Fern

Rhizome scales narrowly lanceolate, bicolorous, pale brown with a very wide, black central stripe, sparsely ciliate at the margin, the narrow margins not wearing away in age. Stipes 3–12 cm long, shallowly adaxially grooved, purplish-black, bearing a few lanceolate, weakly bicolorous, broad-margined scales. Laminae oblong, 6–18 cm long, 1.5–3 cm wide, pinnate-pinnatifid or pinnate-bipinnatifid, obtuse at the base, acute to acuminate at the apex, the adaxial surface glabrous or slightly farinose, the abaxial surface with sparsely to densely covered with white to pale cream farina, the ultimate segments linear, commonly crenately lobed, slightly curled up when dry, the segment margins underrolled.

Epipetric in crevices of igneous rocks and terrestrial at the bases of boulders. Occasional. Southeastern Arizona.

Not cultivated.

177 Notholaena schaffneri var. nealleyi (Seaton ex Coulter) Weath.

Nealley's Cloak Fern

Rhizome scales narrowly lanceate, concolorous, black, with spine-like teeth along the margin. Stipes 2–5 cm long, terete, purplish-black to black, bearing narrowly lanceolate, brown to dark brown scales with spine-like teeth along the margin and narrower scales lacking spines. Laminae oblong-elliptic, 5–15 cm long, 1–3 cm wide, pinnate-pinnatifid, narrowed gradually at the base and apex, obtuse at the base, acute at the apex, the adaxial surface very sparsely dotted with the abaxial surface sparsely to densely covered with white farina, the axes with hair-like, reddish-brown scales, the ultimate segments linear, crenately lobed, slightly curled upward when dry, the segment margins underrolled.

Epipetric in crevices in limestone rocks and terrestrial at the bases of boulders. Rare. Southwestern Texas.

Not cultivated.

178 Notholaena grayi Davenp.

Gray's Cloak Fern

Rhizome scales lanceate, weakly bicolorous, brown with a very broad, dark brown central stripe, with a few soft teeth along the margin. Stipes 2–13 cm long, terete, pale brown or gray-brown, bearing scales like those of the rhizome and minute, glandular hairs. Laminae oblong, 4–15 cm long, 1–3(4) cm wide, 2-pinnate-pinnatifid, obtuse at the base, acute at the apex, the adaxial surface sparsely dotted with farina, the abaxial surface sparsely to densely covered with white farina, the axes with narrowly lanceolate, straw-colored, entire scales, the ultimate segments nearly oblong, slightly irregularly lobed, curled upward when dry.

Epipetric in rock crevices. Occasional. Western Texas to southeastern Arizona.

Not cultivated.

179 Notholaena aliena Maxon

Foreign Cloak Fern

Rhizome scales lanceate, weakly bicolorous, brown with a very broad, dark brown central stripe, with a few soft teeth along the margin. Stipes 3–6 cm long, terete, gray-brown, bearing scales like those of the rhizome and minute, glandular hairs. Laminae oblong, 3–10 cm long, 1–1.5 cm wide, pinnate-pinnatifid except 2-pinnate-pinnatifid at the base, obtuse at the base, acute to acuminate at the apex, the adaxial surface sparsely villous, the abaxial surface sparsely covered with pale yellow farina, the axes with narrowly lanceolate, straw-colored, weakly ciliate scales, the ultimate segments nearly oblong, slightly irregularly lobed, curled upward when dry.

Epipetric on ledges of igneous rock. Very rare. Southwestern Texas.

Not cultivated.

180 Notholaena fendleri Kunze
Fendler's Cloak Fern

Rhizome scales narrowly lanceate, concolorous, rather pale orange-brown, entire. Stipes 3–16 cm long, terete or slightly adaxially flattened, brown, bearing a few scales like those of the rhizome near the base. Laminae asymmetrically triangular, 5–15 cm long, 5–12 cm wide, 4–6-pinnate, obtuse at the base, acute at the apex, the adaxial surface glabrous or sparsely dotted with white farina, the abaxial surface densely covered with white farina, the ultimate segments ovate to lanceolate, sometimes crenate, slightly curled upward when dry.

Epipetric in crevices in rocky bluffs. Occasional. Southeastern Wyoming to southern New Mexico.

Not cultivated.

181 Notholaena californica D. C. Eaton
California Cloak Fern

Rhizome scales narrowly lanceate, bicolorous, brown with a very broad, blackish central stripe, with a few soft teeth along the narrow margin. Stipes 2–15 cm long, terete, brown to dark brown, bearing a few scales like those of the rhizome. Laminae pentagonal, 1.5–5 cm long, 1.5–4 cm wide, 4-pinnate at the base, 3-pinnate above the base, cordate at the base, acute at the apex, the adaxial surface sparsely dotted with pale to brilliant yellow or rarely white farina, the adaxial surface densely covered with similar farina, the ultimate segments roughly ovate, rather bead-like, the pinna and pinnule axes curled upward when dry.

Epipetric in rock crevices and terrestrial at the bases of boulders. Occasional. Arizona to southern California.

Not cultivated.

182 Notholaena neglecta Maxon
Neglected Cloak Fern

Rhizome scales narrowly lanceolate, strongly bicolorous, brown with a black central stripe, the margins erose and slightly toothed. Stipes 3–12 cm long, terete, purplish-black or black, bearing a few scales like those of the rhizome. Laminae long-pentagonal to lanceolate, 2–6 cm long, 1.5–4 cm wide, 3-pinnate or 3-pinnate-pinnatifid, cordate at the base, acute at the apex, the adaxial surface glabrous or sparsely dotted with pale sulfur yellow farina, the abaxial surface densely covered with pale sulfur yellow farina, the ultimate segments ovate to oblong, rather bead-like, the pinna and pinnule axes curled upward when dry.

Epipetric in crevices of limestone cliffs. Rare. Southwestern Texas to southeastern Arizona.

Not cultivated.

183   Notholaena greggii (Mett. ex Kuhn) Maxon
Gregg's Cloak Fern
Rhizome scales lanceate, bicolorous, brown with a very broad, black central stripe, with erose-toothed margins. Stipes 2–12 cm long, terete, pale reddish-brown, brown, or gray-brown, bearing a few bicolorous scales with pale brown, broad, erose margins. Laminae lanceate, 2–8 cm long, 1–2 cm wide, 2- or 3-pinnate, obtuse at the base, acuminate at the apex, the adaxial surface dotted with white farina, the abaxial surface densely covered with white farina, the ultimate segments ovate to oblong, rather bead-like, the pinna and pinnule axes curled upward when dry.

Epipetric in crevices and on ledges of limestone rock. Very rare. Brewster and Presidio Counties, southwestern Texas.

Not cultivated.

*184   Notholaena incana Presl
Hoary Cloak Fern
Rhizome scales narrowly lanceolate, yellowish brown with some irregular dark brown patches, entire. Stipes 4–12 cm long, terete, purplish-black, sparsely scaly above the base. Laminae lanceolate, 6–15 cm long, 3–6(8) cm wide, 3-pinnate, obtuse at the base, acute to acuminate at the apex, the adaxial surface glabrous, the abaxial surface densely covered with white farina, the ultimate segments ovate, the pinna and pinnule axes curled upward when dry.

Epipetric on canyon walls. Very rare. Santa Cruz County, Arizona and Hidalgo County, New Mexico, according to Mason and Yatskievych (1981).

Not cultivated.

185   Notholaena dealbata (Pursh) Kunze
Powdery Cloak Fern
Rhizome scales narrowly lanceate, concolorous, brown or yellowish brown, entire. Stipes 2–11 cm long, terete, pale to medium brown, bearing a few scales like those of the rhizome at the base. Laminae lanceolate, 2–6 cm long, 1.5–6 cm wide, 4-pinnate, obtuse to acute at the base,

acute at the apex, the adaxial surface glabrous, the abaxial surface densely covered with white farina, the ultimate segments oblong to ovate, the pinna and pinnule axes curled upward when dry.

Epipetric in crevices and on ledges of limestone rock. Frequent. Nebraska and Missouri south to central Texas.

Not cultivated.

186   Notholaena limitanea Maxon var. limitanea
Border Cloak Fern

Rhizome scales linear-lanceate, concolorous, brown or reddish-brown, entire. Stipes 3–12 cm long, terete, purplish-black to black, rarely reddish-brown, bearing a few scales like those of the rhizome at the base. Laminae lanceolate, 2.5–11 cm long, 2–6 cm wide, 4- or 5-pinnate, obtuse at the base, acute at the apex, the adaxial surface glabrous, the abaxial surface densely covered with white farina, the ultimate segments elliptic to ovate, the pinna and pinnule axes curled upward when dry.

Epipetric in crevices or on ledges of calcareous or sometimes acidic rocks or terrestrial at the bases of boulders. Occasional. Southern Utah to New Mexico, southern Arizona, and southeastern California.

Not cultivated.

*187   Notholaena limitanea var. mexicana (Maxon) Broun
Southern Border Cloak Fern

Rhizome scales linear-lanceate, concolorous, brown or reddish-brown, entire. Stipes 3–11 cm long, terete, purplish-black to black, sometimes reddish-brown or brown, bearing a few scales like those of the rhizome at the base. Laminae oblong, 4–9 cm long, 1–2.5 cm wide, 6- or 4-pinnate, obtuse at the base, acute at the apex, the adaxial surface glabrous, the abaxial surface densely covered with white farina, the ultimate segments elliptic to ovate, the pinna and pinnule axes curled upward when dry.

Epipetric in crevices or on ledges of calcareous or sometimes acidic rocks or terrestrial at the bases of boulders. Very rare. Western Texas to southeastern Arizona.

Not cultivated.

PELLAEA
The Cliff-brakes

Pellaea includes 80 species, mostly in dry places from tropical to subtropical regions around the world. The plants look like miniature species of *Pteris* and many grow on cliffs, which accounts for the common name.

The United States species of *Pellaea* can be distinguished from the related genus *Notholaena* by their pinnae, pinnules, or segments, the lateral halves of which fold down to protect the plants from drying. The segments are ovate to elliptic, and never bead-like, as they commonly are in *Cheilanthes*. The segments may be glaucous but are never shiny, as they are in *Aspidotis*. With the exception of the weakly dimorphic *P. atropurpurea*, the fronds of *Pellaea* are monomorphic, rather than strongly dimorphic, as they are in *Cryptogramma*.

The Cliff-brakes are small to medium-sized with short-creeping or multicipital rhizomes bearing tufts of fronds. The stipes are mostly glabrous and about equal the laminae. The laminae are pinnate to 3-pinnate, ovate-lanceolate to oblong, glabrous, and have many pinnae. The pinnae, pinnules, or ultimate segments are glabrous, pale green, and ovate, elliptical, oblong, or rarely nearly round or linear. They are laterally folded and underrolled, especially when dry, and so appear to be linear. Even false indusia are lacking, although the sporangia are somewhat protected by the unmodified underrolled lateral margins of the pinnae, pinnules, or segments on which they are borne. The Pellaeas of the United States and Canada were monographed by A. F. Tryon (1957).

The United States species of the genus, with the possible exception of *P. bridgesii*, all belong to sect. *Pellaea*. Most grow in the drier regions of the southwestern states. Typically they inhabit rock crevices, ledges, and talus slopes. The Old World species belong in one or more other sections of the genus; they may not be closely related, for they grow in more moist habitats and have larger, non-folding segments. Some of these species, notably *P. falcata*, *P. rotundifolia*, and *P. viridis*, are easier to cultivate than the rock-dwelling United States species and may become weeds in greenhouses.

Key to Pellaea
1. Stipes and rachises reddish-brown to black throughout, **5**

1. Stipes and rachises straw-colored or gray, rarely pale brown above the base, **2**

2(1). Costae and distal portion of the rachises strongly flexuous; SWB. *188*.*P. ovata*

2(1). Costae and distal portion of the rachises not or scarcely flexuous, **3**

3(2). Rhizomes short-creeping, multicipital, 5–10 mm in diam.; fronds fasciculate; TX. *189. P. cordifolia*

3(2). Rhizomes long-creeping, sparingly branched, 1.5–3.5 mm in diam.; fronds scattered, **4**

4(3). Veins flush with the laminar surface, clearly visible on the adaxial and abaxial surfaces; larger laminae 3-pinnate nearly throughout; CA. *190. P. andromedifolia*

4(3). Veins immersed in the laminar tissue, not visible on the adaxial and abaxial surfaces; larger laminae 2-pinnate nearly throughout; SWB. *191. P. intermedia*

5(1). Stipes and rachises adaxially grooved, flattened, or convex; rhizome scales bicolorous, **11**

5(1). Stipes and rachises terete or elliptical in cross-section; rhizome scales concolorous, entirely orangish-brown, reddish-brown, or brown (except concolorous or bicolorous in *P. bridgesii*), **6**

6(5). Sori submarginal and spreading along the veins towards the costae, occupying a band usually much more than 0.5 mm wide; stipes of larger fronds usually longer than or equalling the rachises; usually at least a few and commonly most rhizome scales brown with a dark brown to black central stripe; CA. *192. P. bridgesii*

6(5). Sori strictly submarginal, not spreading along the veins, occupying a band less than 0.5 mm wide; stipes of larger fronds mostly shorter than or equalling the rachises; all rhizome scales concolorous; **7**

7(6). Stipes and rachises sparsely pilose, dull; pinnae long-stalked, the basal ones stalked 5–15 mm; fronds dimorphic, the fertile exceeding the sterile ones; N, S, E, W except P. *193. P. ×atropurpurea*

7(6). Stipes and rachises glabrous or nearly so, shiny; pinnae sessile to short-stalked, the basal ones stalked 0–4(6) mm; fronds monomorphic, **8**

8(7). Stipes articulate above the base, the rhizome clothed with many persistent stipe bases; rachises green towards the apex; W. *194. P. breweri*

8(7). Stipes not articulate above the base; rachises entirely dark, **9**

9(8). Lateral pinnae (2)4–6 pairs, the basal ones sessile, the stalk less than 1 mm long; NP. *195. P. occidentalis*

9(8). Lateral pinnae (2)4–6 pairs, the basal ones subsessile to stalked, the stalk 1–14 mm long, **10**

10(9). Pinnae in the basal half of the laminae commonly lobed or pinnate with 1–several pairs of pinnules; basal pair of pinnae never deciduous, stalked (1)3–14 mm; NE, NO. *196. P. glabella*

10(9). Pinnae in the basal half of the laminae sometimes lobed or rarely pinnate with 1 pair of pinnules; basal pair of pinnae commonly deciduous, subsessile, stalked ca. 2 mm; W. *197. P. suksdorfiana*

11(5). Laminae lanceate to lanceolate, rarely suboblong, usually widest near the base; pinnae pinnate or 2-pinnate with more than 4 pairs of pinnules, except in depauperate specimens, **14**

11(5). Laminae oblong or narrowly elliptic, rarely narrowly lanceate, usually evenly wide or widest near the middle; pinnae simple or ternate, rarely pinnate with up to 4 pairs of pinnules, **12**

12(11). Pinnae (except the apical ones) pinnate with 2–4 lateral pairs of pinnules, the margins evenly and deeply crenate; P. *198. P. brachyptera*

12(11). Pinnae (except the apical ones) ternate or pinnate with 2(4) lateral pairs of pinnules, the margins entire, **13**

13(12). Segments mostly 2–4 cm long; pinnae usually simple towards the apex, ternate only towards the base; TX. *199. P. ternifolia*

13(12). Segments mostly 0.5–1.5(2) cm long; pinnae usually ternate nearly to the apex, ternate or normally pinnate towards the base; SP, SWB. *200. P. wrightiana*

14(11). Segments (5)6–12 mm long, the margins whitish, often crenate; rhizome scales distantly toothed; SW. *201. P. truncata*

14(11). Segments 3–5(7) mm long, the margins greenish, usually entire; rhizome scales decidedly erose-toothed; CA. *202. P. mucronata*

188 Pellaea ovata (Desv.) Weath.
Ovate-leaved Cliff-brake

Rhizomes short-creeping, ca. 2 mm in diam., much-branched, the stipes 0.5–1 cm distant; rhizome scales bicolorous, toothed. Stipes 10–30 cm long, adaxially flattened, straw-colored to gray. Laminae lanceate-oblong, 10–60 cm long, 0–18 cm wide, 3- or 4-pinnate, the costae flexuous, the ultimate segments long-ovate to elliptical, long-stalked, articulate, subcordate at the base.

Epipetric on limestone or granite ledges and at the base of boulders. Occasional. Southern Texas and southeastern New Mexico.

Cultivated in moist to dry garden soil in full sunlight. Attractive because of its peculiar rachis and costa structure.

*189 Pellaea cordifolia (Sessé & Moc.) A. R. Smith
Heart-leaved Cliff-brake

Rhizomes short-creeping, 6–10 mm in diam., multicipital, the stipes fasciculate; rhizome scales bicolorous, toothed. Stipes 7–25 cm long, adaxially flattened, straw-colored to gray. Laminae lanceolate, 12–37 cm long, 8–11 cm wide, 2-pinnate, the ultimate segments ovate, elliptic, or nearly circular, short-stalked, subarticulate, cordate at the base.

Epipetric on igneous rock ledges and terrestrial at the base of cliffs. Rare. Southwestern Texas.

Cultivated in moist to dry garden soil in full sunlight. A. R. Smith (1980a, p. 26) has shown this to be an independent species, rather than a variety of *P. sagittata*.

190 Pellaea andromedifolia (Kaulf.) Fée
Coffee Fern

Rhizomes long-creeping, 2–3.5 mm in diam., occasionally branched, the fronds mostly 0.5–1 cm distant; rhizome scales concolorous or bicolorous, slightly toothed. Stipes 8–40 cm long, adaxially flattened, straw-colored to gray. Laminae lanceolate to nearly triangular, 8–40 cm long, 3–18 cm wide, mostly 3-pinnate, the ultimate segments elliptical, sessile to short-stalked, subarticulate, truncate to subcordate at the base.

Terrestrial or epipetric on rock ledges or in crevices. Frequent. California.

Cultivated in moist to dry garden soil in full sun. Evergreen when cultivated and given water year-around. Pray (1968) has distinguished certain pubescent collections of this species from coastal California and its offshore islands as var. *pubescens* D. C. Eaton.

*191   Pellaea intermedia Mett. ex Kuhn
Intermediate Cliff-brake

Rhizomes very long-creeping, 1.5–2 mm in diam., occasionally branched, the fronds mostly 0.5–1 cm distant; rhizome scales sharply bicolorous, toothed. Stipes 5–3 cm long, adaxially flattened, straw-colored to gray, rarely pale brown. Laminae lanceolate to triangular, 8–30 cm long, 4–16 cm wide, mostly 2-pinnate, the ultimate segments ellipical, subsessile, articulate, truncate to subcordate at the base.

Terrestrial among rocks and epipetric on rock ledges. Occasional. Western Texas to central Arizona.

Not cultivated.

192   Pellaea bridgesii Hooker
Bridges' Cliff-brake

Rhizomes multicipital, 2–3 mm in diam., much-branched, the fronds crowded; rhizome scales concolorous or bicolorous, pale brown, some with a dark brown or black central stripe, entire. Stipes 3–18 cm long, terete, brown to dark brown, rarely reddish-brown, glabrous. Laminae oblong, 4–12 cm long, 1–2.5 cm wide, pinnate, the pinnae broadly ovate, sessile, not articulate, folded when dry, truncate to slightly cordate at the base.

Epipetric in rock crevices and under ledges. Frequent. California.

Cultivated in moist to dry potting soil in partial sun. This species hybridizes rarely with *P. truncata* according to W. H. Wagner (pers. comm.), and with *P. mucronata* var. *mucronata* to form *P.* ×*glaciogena* Wagner, Pray & Smith.

193   Pellaea × atropurpurea (L.) Link
Purple Cliff-brake

Rhizomes short-creeping or ascending, 2–3 mm in diam., occasionally branched, the fronds crowded; rhizome scales concolorous, orangish-brown, entire. Stipes 4–20 cm long, terete to elliptical, purplish-black, sparsely pilose, dull. Laminae lanceate to oblong, 5—25 cm long, 3–18 cm wide, 1–3-pinnate, the ultimate segments oblong, sessile or subsessile, subarticulate, obtuse to truncate at the base.

Epipetric in crevices in calcareous cliffs and rock ledges, on limestone walls, in limy mortar on walls, or rarely terrestrial. Common. Vermont, Massachusetts, Rhode Island, New York, upper Michigan, Wisconsin, Minnesota, South Dakota, Wyoming, and Colorado south to Florida, Alabama, Tennessee, Arkansas, Texas, New Mexico, and Arizona. Disjunct in Saskatchewan and Alberta.

Cultivated in moist to dry, alkaline soil in partial shade. This apogamous triploid apparently is the hybrid of tetraploid *P. glabella* and diploid *P. ternifolia*. It apparently hybridizes with *P. occidentalis* to form *P. × suksdorfiana* (see p. 325).

194 Pellaea breweri D. C. Eaton
Brewer's Cliff-brake

Rhizomes short-creeping or ascending, ca. 3 mm in diam. excluding the persistent stipe bases, occasionally branched, the fronds very crowded; rhizome scales concolorous, reddish-brown, entire. Stipes 2–12 cm long, terete, brown or reddish-brown, glabrous, or nearly so. Laminae oblong, 3–12 cm long, 2.5–3(4) cm wide, pinnate, the pinnae often often with 1(2) basal lobes, the lobed pinnae triangular in outline, the unlobed pinnae oblong, all pinnae subsessile, not articulate, obtuse at the base.

Epipetric in crevices of granite rocks and terrestrial at the base of boulders. Occasional. Wyoming to Washington south to Colorado, Utah, Nevada, and California.

Not cultivated.

*195 Pellaea occidentalis (E. Nelw.) Rydb.
Western Cliff-brake

Rhizomes multicipital, ca. 2 mm in diim., much branched, the fronds crowded; rhizome scales concolorous, orangish-brown to brown, entire. Stipes 1–8 cm long, terete, pale brown to dark brown, rarely reddish-brown, glabrous. Laminae oblong, 1.5–8 cm long, 1.25–4 cm wide, pinnate, the pinnae rarely with 1(2) basal lobes, the unlobed pinnae oblong, all pinnae sessile, not articulate, obtuse to truncate at the base.

Epipetric in crevices in calcareous cliffs. Rare. Alberta to South Dakota and Wyoming.

Not cultivated. *Pellaea occidentalis* is an independent sexual diploid species which hybridizes with *P. × atropurpurea* to form *P. × suksdorfiana* (see p. 325).

196   Pellaea glabella Mett. ex Kuhn
Smooth Cliff-brake

Rhizomes multicipital, ca. 2.5 mm in diam., much branched, the fronds crowded; rhizome scales concolorous, orangish-brown, slightly contorted, entire. Stipes 2–17 cm long, terete, brown, reddish-brown, or purplish-brown, glabrous or very sparsely pilose. Laminae oblong, 2–15(20) cm long, 1.5–7.5 cm wide, pinnate or 2-pinnate, the pinnae simple in the apical half of the laminae, pinnate in the basal half of the laminae, the pinnules and simple pinnae oblong, sessile, not articulate, obtuse to truncate at the base.

Epipetric in crevices of vertical limestone cliffs and on ledges. Frequent. Vermont to Ontario and Minnesota south to the mountains of Virginia and Tennessee, Kentucky, Arkansas, Missouri, Oklahoma, and northern Texas.

Not cultivated. According to Wagner, Farrar, and Chen (1965), *P. glabella* exists as a sexual, 64-spored diploid in Missouri. Presumably the more widespread, apogamous, 32-spored tetraploids of this species were produced as a result of chromosome doubling, rather than through hybridization between *P.* × *atropurpurea* and *P. occidentalis*, as A. F. Tryon (1957, p. 140) suggested. Apparently tetraploids of this species hybridize with diploid *P. ternifolia* to form *P.* × *atropurpurea* (see p. 325)

197   Pellaea suksdorfiana Butters
Simple Cliff-brake

Rhizomes multicipital, ca. 2.5 mm in diam., much branched, the fronds crowded; rhizome scales concolorous, orangish-brown, very slightly contorted, entire. Stipes 2–6 cm long, terete, brown, reddish-brown, or purplish-brown, glabrous to sparsely pilose. Laminae oblong, 2.5–10 cm long, 1.5–4 cm wide, pinnae or rarely 2-pinnate at the base, the pinnae almost all simple, except the basal ones sometimes lobed or rarely pinnate with 1 pair of pinnules, the pinnules and simple pinnae oblong, sessile or subsessile, not articulate, acute to obtuse at the base.

Epipetric in crevices of limestone cliffs and on ledges. Rare. British Columbia to Washington, Wyoming, southern Utah, Colorado, northern Arizona, and northwestern New Mexico.

Not cultivated. According to A. F. Tryon (1957, p. 140), this species may have arisen as a hybrid between *P.* × *atropurpurea* and *P. occidentalis*. Because it probably had an origin much different from that of *P. glabella*, it should be considered an independent species, rather than a variety of *P. glabella*.

198 Pellaea brachyptera (Moore) Baker
Sierra Cliff-brake

Rhizomes multicipital, 2–4 mm in diam., much branched, the fronds crowded; rhizome scales concolorous or bicolorous, brown, some with a black central stripe, distantly toothed. Stipes 4–20 cm long, adaxially flattened or shallowly grooved, brown, dark brown, or purplish-brown, glabrous. Laminae oblong, 4–21 cm long, 1.25–3.5 cm wide, 2–pinnate, the pinnules linear, 0.5–2 cm long, sessile, not articulate, strongly underrolled, cordate at the base, mucronate at the apex.

Epipetric in crevices of basalt or serpentine rocks and terrestrial on talus slopes. Occasional. Southern Oregon to northern California and disjunct in Chelan Co., Washington.

Cultivated in moist to dry potting soil in partial sun. This species is known to hybridize with *P. mucronata*.

199 Pellaea ternifolia (Cav.) Link
Ternate-leaved Cliff-brake

Rhizomes multicipital, 4–6 mm in diam., much branched; the fronds crowded; rhizome scales bicolorous, pale brown to straw-colored with a black central stripe, distantly toothed. Stipes 7–22 cm long, adaxially convex to grooved, purplish-black to black, glabrous. Laminae oblong or narrowly elliptic, 14–26 cm long, 3–7.5 cm wide, pinnate or with ternate pinnae, the pinnae and pinnules linear, 1–4 cm long, sessile, not articulate, strongly underrolled, truncate or subcordate at the base, mucronate at the apex.

Epipetric in crevices of igneous rocks or terrestrial on talus slopes. Frequent. Western Texas.

Not cultivated. Diploids of this species have hybridized with diploid *P. truncata* to form *P. wrightiana* and apparently with tetraploid *P. glabella* to form *P. × atropurpurea*.

200 Pellaea wrightiana Hooker
Wright's Cliff-brake

Rhizomes multicipital, ca. 3 mm in diam., much branched, the fronds crowded; rhizome scales bicolorous, pale brown with a black central stripe, distantly toothed. Stipes 2–18 cm long, adaxially flattened or shallowly grooved, purplish-brown or dark brown, glabrous. Laminae oblong or narrowly elliptic, rarely narrowly lanceate, 4–30 cm long, 1.5–7 cm wide, 2-pinnate, the pinnules linear, (0.5)0.75–4 cm long, sessile, not articulate, strongly underrolled, obtuse at the base, mucronate at the apex.

Epipetric in crevices of rocks or terrestrial on talus slopes. Frequent. Oklahoma and Texas to southeastern Colorado, southwestern Utah, and Arizona.

Not cultivated. Wagner (1965) demonstrated that this species is a fertile allotetraploid hybrid between diploid *P. truncata* and diploid *P. ternifolia*. It backcrosses with *P. truncata* to form the sterile triploid *P.* × *wagneri* (see p. 326).

201 Pellaea truncata Goodd.
Spiny Cliff-brake

Rhizomes multicipital or short-creeping, 2–6 mm in diam., usually much branched, the fronds crowded; rhizome scales bicolorous, brown with a black central stripe, sometimes somewhat contorted, distantly toothed. Stipes 3–20 cm long, adaxially flattened or very shallowly grooved, reddish-brown to purplish-black, glabrous. Laminae lanceate to lanceolate, 8–22 cm long, 2.5–10 cm wide, 2-pinnate, the pinnules elliptic, (5)6–12 mm long, sessile, not articulate, strongly underrolled, obtuse to truncate at the base, mucronate at the apex.

Epipetric in crevices of igneous rocks and terrestrial at the bases of boulders in gravelly soil. Common. Colorado and western Texas to southern Nevada, southern California, and southern Arizona.

Not cultivated. This species hybridizes with *P. ternifolia* to form *P. wrightiana* (see p. 326) and backcrosses with *P. wrightiana* to form *P.* × *wagneri* Windham. According to Pray (1967) it hybridizes rarely with *P. mucronata* also.

202 Pellaea mucronata (D. C. Eaton) D. C. Eaton
Bird's-foot Cliff-brake

Rhizomes multicipital or short-creeping, 3–5 mm in diam., much branched, the fronds crowded; rhizome scales bicolorous, brown with a black central stripe, erose-toothed. Stipes 4–20 cm long, adaxially flattened or very shallowly grooved, brown, reddish-brown, or purplish-black, glabrous. Laminae ovate-lanceolate to rarely suboblong, 4–30 cm long, 1.25–11 cm wide, 2- or 3-pinnate, the pinnules simple or ternate, the pinnules or ultimate segments linear, 3–5(7) mm long, sessile, not articulate, strongly underrolled, obtuse to truncate at the base, mucronate at the apex.

In crevices of igneous rocks and terrestrial in rock talus. Frequent. California and Nye Co., Nevada.

Cultivated in moist to dry garden soil in full sun. A. F. Tryon (1957, pp. 157–162) divides this species into var. *mucronata*, with distant, spreading, pinnae having up to 40 commonly ternate pinnules per pinna and var. *californica* (Lemmon) Munz & Johnston (Fig. 202), with imbricate, ascending pinnae having fewer than 20 usually simple pinnules per pinna. According to Pray (1967), var. *mucronata* hybridizes with *P. truncata* and with *P. bridgesii* to form *P.* × *glaciogena* Wagner, Pray & Smith. According to D. M. Johnson (pers. comm.), it also hybridizes with *P. brachyptera*.

PITYROGRAMMA
The Goldback and Silverback Ferns

Pityrogramma includes 14 species in the warm and tropical regions of the world, especially the western hemisphere and Africa, according to R. M. Tryon (1962), who monographed the genus.

The plants of *Pityrogramma* are small or medium-sized and have dark, wiry stipes bearing pinnately organized or pentagonal laminae that are covered with a usually white or yellow exudate, especially on the abaxial surface. Although such ferns are called waxy, the exudate is not a wax and so should be called a farina. False indusia are absent. The sporangia spread over the abaxial surface of fertile fronds and are not confined to or near to the margin. The fronds are not hirsute or scaly. These characters distinguish *Pityrogramma* from *Notholaena*.

The Goldback and Silverback ferns grow in rock crevices, at the bases of boulders, and in soil on dry slopes in the western United States, especially in California. One tropical American species is known in Florida from roadside ditches and similar weedy habitats. The tropical species are readily cultivated, but the rock-dwelling ones may be more difficult to maintain in cultivation.

Key to Pityrogramma

1. Laminae lanceolate to oblong, at least 2 times longer than wide; fronds mostly more than 30 cm long; pinnae twisted out of the plane of the lamina; stipes 2–5 mm in diam., shorter than or equalling the laminae; FL. *203. P. trifoliata*

1. Laminae pentagonal or nearly so, not much longer than wide; fronds mostly less than 30 cm long; pinnae in a single plane; stipes 0.75–1.5 mm in diam., much longer than the laminae, 2

2(1). Distal pinnae entire, not lobed; basal basiscopic lobes of the basal pinnae entire to deeply crenate; laminae viscid on the adaxial surface, white to pale yellow on the abaxial surface; CA. *204. P. viscosa*

2(1). Distal pinnae mostly regularly lobed, seldom entire; basal basiscopic lobes of the basal pinnae pinnatifid, often deeply so; laminae glabrous or glandular on the adaxial surface, 3

3(2). Stipes brown or reddish-brown; laminae glabrous or glandular on the adaxial surface, appearing green, pale to sulfur yellow on the abaxial surface; P. *205. P. triangularis*

3(2). Stipes purplish-black or black; laminae rather densely glandular on the adaxial surface, appearing gray or gray-green; CA. **206. P. pallida*

203   Pityrogramma trifoliata (L.) Tryon
Goldenrod Fern

Plants forming large, dense colonies by root propagation. Rhizomes erect, ca. 1 cm in diam., the scales narrowly lanceate, bicolorous, bronzy with a broad, dark brown central stripe. Stipes 30–50 cm long, purplish-black, densely scaly at the base with narrowly lanceate, concolorous, bronzy scales. Laminae narrowly oblanceolate, 20–90 cm long, 10–20 cm wide, usually 2-pinnate; rachises with a few lanceate scales and appressed, villose hairs; pinnae simple or with 1 or 2 linear lobes or pinnules at the base, glabrous above, covered abaxially with a sparse to dense, pale to brilliant yellow farina.

Terrestrial on roadsides and canal banks. Very rare. Known from Dade County, Florida.

Not cultivated. This species is said to spread and choke out other vegetation. It is readily overlooked because in its rigid, 3-dimensional habit it resembles flowering plants like Goldenrod and various other members of the Aster Family.

204   Pityrogramma viscosa (D. C. Eaton) Maxon
Silverback Fern

Rhizomes short-creeping or ascending, ca. 2 mm in diam., the scales linear-lanceate, bicolorous, brown with a wide, black central stripe. Stipes 4–21 cm long, brown or reddish-brown, glaborus. Laminae pentagonal to broadly lanceolate, 3–12 cm long, 1.5–8(11) cm wide, pinnatifid toward the apex, pinnate-pinnatifid or sometimes pinnate-bipinnatifid at the base; pinnae entire, lobed, pinnatifid, or bipinnatifid, covered abaxially with a sparse to dense, white to yellowish-white farina; adaxially covered with viscid glands.

Terrestrial in sandy soil on hillsides. Occasional. Coastal southern California.

Not cultivated. According to Alt and Grant (1960), this species introgresses with *P. triangularis* and so forms plants that intergrade in frond morphology between the parental types.

205   Pityrogramma triangularis (Kaulf.) Maxon
Goldback Fern

Rhizomes short-creeping or ascending, 1–3 mm in diam., the scales narrowly lanceate, bicolorous, brown with a wide, black central stripe. Stipes 5–23(28) cm long, brown or reddish-brown, glabrous or with a few, scattered, hair-like scales. Laminae pentagonal to broadly lanceolate, 3–14 cm long, 2–11 cm wide, pinnate-pinnatifid toward the apex, 2-pinnate-pinnatifid at the base in large specimens; pinnae entire, lobed, pinnatifid, or pinnate-pinnatifid, covered abaxially with a sparse to dense, bright to pale yellow farina, adaxially glabrous or sparsely yellow-glandular.

Epipetric in crevices of igneous cliffs and among boulders, and terrestrial in dry, low woods, usually in partial shade. Common. British Columbia to southern California, east to southern Nevada, Arizona, and southwestern New Mexico.

Cultivated in dry garden soil in full sun. Alt and Grant (1960) divided this species into var. *triangularis* (Fig. 205), with the adaxial surface of the laminae glabrous, and var. *maxonii* Weath., with the adaxial surface of the laminae bearing sparse, yellowish glands. The two varieties are not sharply distinct. Within var. *triangularis*, diploid and tetraploid cytotypes are known, and within the diploid cytotype, races with large and small fronds exist. Star et al. (1975) have published some data on the chemical patterns of internal flavonoids that correlate with ploidy and which suggest that the tetraploid kaepmferol methyl ether chemotype is of alloploid origin from two diploids and that the tetraploid ceroptin chemotype may be of autoploid origin. D. M. Smith (1980) came to slightly different taxonomic conclusions. Yet more data are needed to understand the taxonomy of *P. triangularis* fully.

*206   Pityrogramma pallida (Weath.) Alt & Grant
Pale Silverback Fern

Rhizomes multicipital, ca. 2 mm in diam., the scales narrowly lanceate, bicolorous, brown with a wide, black central stripe. Stipes 5–26 cm long, purplish-black or black, glabrous or with a little white farina. Laminae pentagonal to broadly ovate-lanceolate, 2–9 cm long, 2–9 cm wide, pinnate-pinnatifid toward the apex, 2-pinnate-pinnatifid at the base in large specimens; pinnae entire, lobed, pinnatifid, or pinnate-pinnatifid, covered abaxially with a sparse to dense, white farina; adaxially covered with white glands.

Terrestrial in dry soil. Rare. Sierra foothills of California.

Cultivated in dry garden soil in full sun or partial shade.

BOMMERIA
The Copper Ferns

Bommeria includes five species that range from the southwestern United States and Mexico to Costa Rica. Only one species is native to the United States. The common name derives from the somewhat copper-colored hairs and scales that abundantly clothe the abaxial surface of the laminae. The hairs are long, stiff, straight, and spreading to nearly appressed to the lamina surface; they are not at all like the curly hairs found in *Notholaena,* the only other genus of Sinopteridaceae in the United States that has pentagonal laminae.

The Copper Ferns are small, with very long-creeping rhizomes bearing scattered stipes. The stipes are brown and have many spreading hairs and scales when young. The pentagonal laminae are 2-pinnate-pinnatifid at the base and have exaggerated basiscopic pinnules or segments. The adaxial lamina surface is sparsely covered with acicular hairs. The abaxial surface is densely covered with hairs and with some scales.

Like many other Sinopteridaceae genera, *Bommeria* grows in the southwestern states from western Texas to Arizona. The plants are found in crevices, on rock ledges, and at the base of boulders. The genus is not in cultivation. Haufler (1979) has published a biosystematic revision of the genus.

207 Bommeria hispida (Mett.) Underw.

Copper Fern

Rhizomes very long-creeping, ca. 0.75 mm in diam., bearing lanceate, concolorous, pale brown to yellowish-brown scales having a long, filiform apex. Stipes 3–23 cm long, terete or slightly flattened, brown or reddish-brown, sparsely covered with appressed to spreading, acicular hairs and scales like those of the rhizome, often glabrous at maturity. Laminae pentagonal, 2.5–9 cm long and wide, 2-pinnate-pinnatifid at the base, pinnate-pinnatifid above the base, lobed at the apex, the adaxial surface sparsely covered with acicular, multicellular hairs, the abaxial surface densely covered with similar hairs and with scales on the rachis and costae like those of the rhizome; sporangia submarginal; false indusia none.

Epipetric in crevices, on rock ledges, and terrestrial at the bases of boulders. Western Texas to southern Arizona.

Not cultivated.

ADIANTUM

The Maiden-hairs

Adiantum includes about 200 species that grow in the tropical and temperate, mostly forested regions of both hemispheres. The common name comes from the classical European species *A. capillus-veneris.* The generic name means not wetted, a reference to the shiny, glabrous fronds, which shed raindrops readily. *Adiantum* is unique among the genera of Sinopteridaceae in bearing its sporangia on the abaxial surface of the distinctive, marginal, false indusium, rather than at the margin of the lamina covered by the false indusium. The general architecture of the plants and the glossy, shiny, usually glabrous fronds are easily distinguished from plants of other genera in the family.

173

The Maiden-hairs are small to moderate-sized, with tufted to scattered, wiry, dark-colored, glossy stipes and rachises. The segments are small, commonly nearly round or oblong, glabrous in most species, and have obvious veins that fork repeatedly, usually from near the base of the segment. The veins are free in all the temperate species and in all but a few tropical ones. The false indusia have veins that underlie the sporangia. The indusia vary from lunulate to elongate and are sometimes linear along the margins of the segments.

The species of *Adiantum* grow in more mesic habitats than do most other genera of the Sinopteridaceae. They are found in woods or along streambanks and seepages in drier climates. Many species of the genus are in cultivation, and many cultivated varieties are known (Hoshizaki, 1970).

Key to Adiantum
   1. Segments round to broadly oblanceolate or trapeziform, usually no more than 2 times wider than long, petiolulate, the stalks 1–7 mm long, **6**

   1. Segments oblong, mostly 2–4 times longer than wide, subsessile, the stalks 0–1(2) mm long, **2**

   2(1). Laminae pinnate, with an unforked central rachis; stipes and rachises with short, curved hairs; pinnules coriaceous, shiny, dark green; FL. *208. A. melanoleucum*

   2(1). Laminae pedate, divided laterally into approximately equal halves, **3**

   3(2). Laminae held horizontally or drooping in life; main rachis branches usually strongly recurved. Pinnae nearly oblong at maturity, abruptly tapering at the apex; pinnules usually not glaucous; WIDE-SPREAD. *209. A. pedatum* subsp. *pedatum*

   3(2). Laminae ascending to erect in life; main rachis branches usually not strongly recurved, **4**

   4(3). Pinnules strongly imbricate, the lower margin curved and somewhat reflexed; laminae 6–12 cm long; BC. *212. A. pedatum* subsp. *subpumilum*

   4(3). Pinnules not or only slightly imbricate, the lower margins nearly straight, **5**

   5(4) Pinnules green, the median ones (10)12–20(23) mm long, frequently deeply incised on the distal margin; indusia inconspicuous; AK to CA. *211. A. pedatum* subsp. *aleuticum*

   5(4). Pinnules glaucous, the median ones 7–12(17) mm long, usually not incised on the distal margin; indusia conspicuous; QUE, VT, WA, and CA. *210. A. pedatum* subsp. *calderi*

   6(1). Segments strongly deciduous, the black stalks terminating in a small disc at the base of the segment; FL. *213. A. tenerum*

6(1). Segments not deciduous or weakly so, the black color of the stalks passing into the base of the segments or ending abruptly, but without a small disc, **7**

7(6). Segments sparsely pilose beneath, mostly less than 1 cm in diam.; laminae 3- or 4-pinnate; rhizomes erect or ascending; TX. *214. A. tricholepis*

7(6). Segments glabrous beneath, mostly 1 cm or more in diam.; laminae (2)3-pinnate; rhizomes short- to long-creeping, **8**

8(7). Segments cuneate, acute, or obtuse at the base; sori discontinuous, sublunulate to elongate; sterile segments irregular and variable in outline, dissected into several round lobes at the apex; S. *215. A. capillus-veneris*

8(7). Segments obtuse to truncate at the base; sori nearly continuous, elongate to linear; sterile segments regular, flabellate to suborbicular, not or scarcely dissected into broad lobes at the apex; CA. *216. A. jordanii*

*208   Adiantum melanoleucum Willd.
Fragrant Maiden-hair

Rhizomes short-creeping, ca. 1.5 mm in diam., the stipes mostly approximate; rhizome scales lanceate, filiform-tipped, concolorous, brown, entire. Stipes 8–25 cm long, purplish-black, with minute, curved, multicellular hairs. Laminae oblong to lanceolate, 10–25 cm long, 3–15 cm wide, (1)2-pinnate, the compound lateral pinnae 0–2 pairs, about half as long as the terminal pinna, the pinnae oblong, truncate at the base, acute at the apex, the pinnules oblong, dark green, the indusia sublunulate-elongate.

Epipetric on the sides of limestone sinks. Very rare. Everglades National Park, Dade County, Florida.

Not cultivated. The fronds of this species are fragrant, which is unusual or perhaps unique in *Adiantum*.

209   Adiantum pedatum L. subsp. pedatum
Northern Maiden-hair

Rhizomes short- to long-creeping, ca. 2 mm in diam., the stipes mostly 0.5–1 cm distant; rhizome scales lanceate, concolorous, bronzy, entire. Stipes 15–45 cm long, purplish-black to reddish-brown, with scales like those of the rhizome at the base. Laminae broadly ovate to nearly orbicular, 15–25 cm long, 15–30 cm wide, the pinnae nearly oblong, slightly tapering towards the base and the apex, then abruptly tapering at the apex, the pinnules not imbricate or deflexed, oblong, usually not glaucous, the indusia oblong to linear.

Terrestrial in rich, moist, circumneutral to subacid soils, usually in the shade. Common. Quebec, Ontario, and Minnesota south to Georgia, Alabama, Mississippi, Louisiana, Oklahoma, Kansas, western South Dakota, and Nebraska. Disjunct in Idaho, Nevada, California, and Arizona.

Commonly cultivated in moist but well-drained woodland gardens in circumeneutral soil in full shade. See subsp. *aleuticum* for notes on discriminating these two subspecies. This subspecies hybridizes with *A. jordanii* to form *A. × tracyi*; see *A. jordanii* for a dicussion.

*210 Adiantum pedatum subsp. calderi Cody
Calder's Maiden-hair

Rhizomes short-creeping, 2–3 mm in diam., the stipes approximate; rhizome scales lanceolate, reddish-brown with bronzy margins. Stipes (6)10–35 cm long, purplish-black to reddish-brown, with a few bronzy scales like those of the rhizome at the base. Laminae broadly ovate to broadly oblanceolate, 5–20 cm long, 4–15 cm wide, the pinnae nearly oblong, slightly tapering at the base, slightly tapering at the nearly round apex, the pinnules approximate or sightly distant, rarely subimbricate, glaucous, the indusia elongate or short and often curved.

Terrestrial or epipetric on serpentine or dolomite rocks, often in full sun. Occasional. Newfoundland, Quebec, northern Vermont, and a few localities in Washington and California.

Not cultivated.

211 Adiantum pedatum subsp. aleuticum (Rupr.) Calder & Taylor
Aleutian Maiden-hair

Rhizomes short-creeping or ascending, ca. 2 mm in diam., the stipes approximate, less than 0.5 cm distant; rhizome scales lanceate, concolorous, bronzy, entire. Stipes 6–60 cm long, reddish-brown to purplish-black, with scales like those of the rhizome at and near the base. Laminae oblanceolate or lanceolate, sometimes very broadly lanceolate, 4–40 cm long, 4–30 cm wide, the pinnae narrowly elliptic-lanceolate at maturity, tapering toward the apex, the pinnules not imbricate or reflexed, oblong, usually glaucous, the indusia sublunulate to oblong.

Terrestrial on high-magnesium, low-calcium soils derived from ultramafic rocks (peridotite, dunite, and serpentine) or rarely on soils derived from granite adjacent to ultramafic rocks. Occasional. Alaska to California, east to Alberta, Idaho, Montana, and Utah. Disjunct locally in northwestern Wisconsin and adjacent Michigan.

Not cultivated. Certain habitat forms of subsp. *pedatum* intergrade with subsp. *aleuticum* and can cause confusion. If possible, all the key characters should be used to distinguish these subspecies, as individual specimens may not agree with the key characters in every respect.

*212 Adiantum pedatum subsp. subpumilum (Wagner in Wagner & Boydston) Lellinger

Dwarf Maiden-hair

Rhizomes short-creeping, ca. 2 mm in diam., the stipes mostly 0.5–1 cm distant; rhizome scales lanceate, concolorous, bronzy, entire. Stipes 3–6 cm long, purplish-black, with scales like those of the rhizome at the base. Laminae broadly ovate to deltate, 3–6 cm long, 4–6 cm wide, the pinnae nearly oblong, slightly tapering toward the base and the apex, then abruptly round at the apex, the pinnules imbricate, suboblong to sublunulate, reflexed, the lower margin curved, not glaucous, the indusia oblong, short.

Epipetric on wet, exposed, crystalline, metamorphic cliffs. Very rare. Vancouver Island, British Columbia and presumably coastal Washington.

Cultivated in cool rock gardens or on limy rocks or perhaps in moist garden soil. The reflexed, imbricate pinnules make this an interesting horticultural novelty. Wagner and Boydson (1978) note that this taxon may be an incipient species in the process of differentiation.

213 Adiantum tenerum Swartz

Brittle Maiden-hair

Rhizomes short-creeping, ca. 2.5 mm in diam., the stipes approximate; rhizome scales lanceolate, bicolorous, pale brown with a wide, dark brown central stripe, erose-toothed. Stipes 15–40 cm long, purplish-black, with scales like those of the rhizome at the base. Laminae deltate to lanceolate, 20–45 cm long, 12–30 cm wide, 3- or 4-pinnate, glabrous, the ultimate segments on stalks 1.5–3.5 mm long that terminate in a flat disc, strongly deciduous, irregularly subtrapeziform to very broadly oblanceolate, 8–25 mm long, 9–25 mm wide, with several distal lobes, obtuse at the base, round at the apex, the indusia elongate.

Epipetric on limestone ledges and in sink holes or terrestrial on soil derived from limestone. Frequent. Peninsular Florida.

Cultivated in moist, basic potting soil in partial to full shade. Several cultivated varieties, in addition to the wild species, are grown.

214 Adiantum tricholepis Fée

Hairy Maiden-hair

Rhizomes erect or ascending, 2–4 mm in diam., the stipes crowded; rhizome scales lanceolate, concolorous, dark brown to blackish, short-toothed. Stipes 6–32 cm long, purplish-black to reddish-brown, with lanceolate, concolorous, brown to bronzy, entire to slightly erose-toothed scales at and near the base. Laminae broadly lanceolate, 15–40 cm long, 10–30 cm wide, 3- or 4-pinnate, the ultimate segments on stalks 1–2(3.5) mm long, weakly deciduous, the dark color of the stalk not passing into the base of the segment, the segments regularly flabellate to suborbicular, 4–13 mm long, 4–15(21) mm wide, sparsely pilose, not lobed at the apex, the indusia elongate.

Epipetric on moist limestone cliffs in partial to full shade. Very rare. Edwards Plateau of central Texas.

Not cultivated.

215 Adiantum capillus-veneris L.
Southern Maiden-hair

Rhizomes long-creeping, ca. 2 mm in diam., the stipes rather crowded, 2–10 mm distant; rhizome scales linear-lanceate, concolorous, pale brown to bronzy, entire, with a long, linear apex. Stipes 5–15(25) cm long, purplish-black to reddish-brown, with scales like those of the rhizomes at and near the base. Laminae lanceolate to narrowly elliptic, 8–30 cm long, 2.5–12 cm wide, 2(3)-pinnate, the ultimate segments on stalks 1–3 mm long, weakly deciduous, the dark color of the stalk passing slightly into the base of the segment, the segments irregular and variable in outline, 5–20(25) mm long and wide, glabrous, with several round lobes at the apex, cuneate, acute, or obtuse at the base, irregular at the apex, the indusia sublunulate to elongate.

Epipetric on moist to wet limestone cliffs and rocks, often in seeps or the spray of waterfalls. Frequent. North Carolina, Kentucky, Missouri, Oklahoma, Texas, New Mexico, southwestern Colorado, Utah, Nevada, and California south to Florida, Georgia, Alabama, Mississippi, Louisiana, Texas, New Mexico, and Arizona. Disjunct in South Dakota and British Columbia. Occasionally found as an escape within or to the north of the usual range.

Cultivated in moist, alkaline soil or on limy rocks in full to partial shade. Fernald (1950) divided the North American plants into var. *modestum* (Underw.) Fern. from Utah, Arizona, and New Mexico, which has small, only slightly cleft segments; and var. *protrusum* Fern. from the entire United States range excluding Arizona and New Mexico, which has larger, more deeply lobed segments. The two varieties are more sharply demarcated by geography than by morphology. Many intermediates exist, which casts doubt on the validity of Fernald's varieties.

216 Adiantum jordanii K. Muell.
California Maiden-hair

Rhizomes short- to long-creeping, ca. 2 mm in diam., the stipes very crowded, 1–5 mm distant; rhizome scales lanceolate, concolorous, brown, entire. Stipes 5–20 cm long, reddish-brown, brown, or purplish-black, with scales like those of the rhizome at the base. Laminae lanceolate, 7–27 cm long, 2–13 cm wide, 2(3)-pinnate, the ultimate segments on stalks 1–7 mm long, weakly deciduous, the dark color of the stalk stopping

abruptly at the base of the segment, the segments usually regularly flabellate to suborbicular, 5–15 mm long, 7–28 mm wide, glabrous, not
lobed at the apex, obtuse to truncate, rarely cuneate at the base, round at
the apex, the indusia elongate to linear.

Terrestrial at the base of trees and rocks, on shaded banks, or rarely
epipetric. Frequent. Oregon and California.

Cultivated in moist to dry potting soil in partial shade. This species
hybridizes with *A. pedatum* subsp. *pedatum* to form the sterile hybrid
A. × *tracyi* C. C. Hall, found occasionally in California. Although intermediate, the hybrid's segments look superficially much like those of *A.
jordanii;* the influence from *A. pedatum* is best seen in the basal pinnae,
which are 2-pinnate only at the base on the basiscopic side; the remainder
of the basal pinnae and the supra-basal pinnae are only pinnate. *Adiantum* × *tracyi* is hardy and grown in moist potting soil in full to partial sun.

VITTARIACEAE
The Shoestring Fern Family

There are seven or eight genera in the family with fewer than ten species plus the larger genera *Antrophyum* (world-wide tropics), *Polytaenium*
(tropical America), and *Vittaria* (world-wide tropics).

Plants of *Vittaria*, the only genus of the family present in the United
States, have short-creeping rhizomes with abundant roots covered
densely with brown root hairs. The stipes are closely spaced and short.
The laminae are rather small, simple, linear, and are commonly underrolled at each edge. The sporangia are borne in one submarginal groove
on each side of the midrib; they are protected by growing among paraphyses and by the reflexed, unmodified frond margin, but false indusia
are absent. Other genera of the Vittariaceae differ from *Vittaria* in having
broader, strap-shaped laminae with several grooves on either side of the
midrib; paraphyses are present in some, but not all, of the other genera.

The Vittariaceae are epiphytic. Their abundant root hairs trap water
and debris. All grow in tropical and subtropical areas, many in the most
humid parts of the lowland tropics. Only *V. lineata* occurs in the United
States. A few species of Vittariaceae are cultivated in tropical regions or
in greenhouses.

217 Vittaria lineata (L.) J. E. Smith
Shoestring Fern

Rhizomes short-creeping, occasionally branched, the fronds crowded;
rhizome scales ca. 0.25–0.55 (4–6 cells) wide, the cells uniformly clathrate, the scales with a filiform apex many cells long. Stipes 1–3 cm long,
not sharply distinct from the laminae, straw-colored, flattened or angular.

179

Laminae linear, 10–50 cm long, 1–3 mm wide, long-acuminate at the apex. Sporangia borne in a submarginal groove, mixed with slender, linear to slightly clavate, tan to reddish-brown paraphyses. Spores monolete.

Epiphytic, especially on the bases of *Sabal palmetto* palm trunks. Frequent. Peninsular Florida, especially from Lake Okeechobee southward. Found once on rocks, presumably as an accidental, in Lincoln Co., east-central Georgia.

Cultivated in well-drained potting soil in full sun. Darling (1982) has shown that reports of *V. graminifolia* Kaulf. from Florida have proved to be *V. lineata*.

PTERIDACEAE
The Brake Family

The Pteridaceae includes three or four small genera plus the large genus *Pteris*. It and *Acrostichum* are the only genera of the family present in the United States.

Plants of this family are medium- to large-sized, with erect, ascending, or short-creeping, hairy or scaly rhizomes bearing robust fronds. The laminae are 1- or 2-pinnate in most species. There is a tendency toward having dimorphic fronds or parts of fronds. This occurs in a few species of *Pteris*, is more pronounced in *Acrostichum*, and is extreme in *Neurocallis* (tropical America). The dimorphic species tend to be pinnate or pinnate-pinnatifid, the monomorphic ones mostly pinnate-pinnatifid with a few pinnate members.

The species of Pteridaceae are terrestrial, although a few *Pteris* species grow epipetrically or on walls. All grow in tropical and subtropical areas. Many are sun ferns and may have very firm laminae. They are easily cultivated, although the larger tropical species are too large to be very useful in ordinary greenhouses. Some of the smaller *Pteris* species have had many cultivated varieties selected from the original wild stock.

Key to the Genera of Pteridaceae
1. Sori confined to the lamina margins, protected by a linear false indusium; laminae papery, pinnate-pinnatifid, or if only pinnate, then the pinnae less than 1 cm wide, *Pteris*, p. 181
1. Sori dorsal on the entire abaxial surface of the lamina, not protected by an indusium; laminae leathery, pinnate, the pinnae 2–5 cm wide, *Acrostichum*, p. 184

PTERIS
The Brakes

Pteris is a large genus of about 250 species widely distributed throughout the warm and tropical regions of the world. The few species found in
the United States grow mostly in Florida. Only *P. bahamensis* is native;
the others are all naturalized. The commonly cultivated species of *Pteris*
were treated by Morton (1957) and by Walker (1970).

The Brakes are medium- to large-sized ferns. Their rhizomes are compact or short-creeping and bear a few to many 1- to 2-pinnate, commonly
glabrescent fronds. The stipes typically are straw-colored except for being
reddish-brown or brown at the base, which bears a few, lanceate, usually
concolorous, tan scales. The pinnae are linear with a few or no lobes or
pinnules or are pinnatisect throughout. The sori are marginal and are covered by a continuous, marginal, reflexed, false indusium. At least the
lower pinnae of many species have elongate lobes or pinnules, and some
species have pinnae which are pinnatisect throughout. This development
may be slight or exaggerated to produce pedate laminae with basal pinnules that curl back on themselves.

The naturalized and native Brakes are mostly terrestrial in woods and
along roads and ditches in Florida. Some species also grow readily on rock
and brick walls. Plants of the latter are smaller than terrestrial ones, but
may have a wider geographical range. All the species are readily cultivated in the greenhouse or in garden beds in frost-free climates.

Key to Pteris
1. Pinnae with 1 to many lobes or pinnules, 4

1. Pinnae strictly simple, without lobes or pinnules, 2

2(1). Pinnae sparsely pilose on the abaxial surface of the costae; stipes
scaly throughout; SE. *218. P. vittata*

2(1). Pinnae glabrous on the abaxial surface of the costae; stipes glabrous or nearly so, except at the base, 3

3(2). Median pinnae 3–10 cm long, the fertile ones 2–3.5 mm wide;
stipes 1.5–3 mm in diam., straw-colored; spores normal; FL. *219. P. ba-*
hamensis

3(2). Median pinnae mostly 10–15 cm long, the fertile ones 4–6 mm
wide; stipes 4–6 mm in diam., pale brown; spores of various sizes or
abortive; FL. **220. P. × delchampsii*

4(1). Pinnae all fully pinnatifid, the many lobes with narrow sinuses
between them; FL. *221. P. tripartita*

4(1). Pinnae, at least the basal ones, with 1–6 widely spaced lobes or
pinnules, 5

5(4). Laminae ternate or pinnate; basal pair of pinnae each with a single basiscopic lobe or pinnule; fertile pinnae (4.5)6–12 mm wide; FL. 222. *P. cretica*

5(4). Laminae always pinnate; basal pair of pinnae each with at least 2 lobes or pinnules, the suprabasal pairs also commonly having 1 or more lobes or pinnules; fertile pinnae 2–5(6) mm wide, **6**

6(5). Fronds monomorphic; lateral fertile pinnae sessile, all but the basal and sometimes suprabasal ones decurrent on the rachis; FL. 223. *P. multifida*

6(5). Fronds dimorphic, the sterile ones much shorter than the fertile ones, with short, round pinna and pinnule apices; all but the apical fertile pinnae stalked and not decurrent on the rachis; FL. *224. P. ensiformis* cv. *Victoriae*

218 Pteris vittata L.
Chinese Ladder Brake
Stipes 1–26 cm long, straw-colored to pale brown, scaly throughout with straw-colored to brown, lanceate, entire scales. Laminae narrowly oblanceolate, 15–80 cm long, 6–25 cm wide, pinnate, the rachis with scales like those of the rhizome and multicellular hairs with obvious cross-walls, the pinnae simple, mostly opposite, linear, 2–18 cm long, 4–8 mm wide, truncate to subcordate at the base, acuminate at the apex, the veins forked above the base, occasionally simple, the veins entirely free.

Terrestrial or epipetric on limestone. Occasional. Naturalized in peninsular Florida, adjacent parts of Georgia, and in Los Angeles, Co., California. Escaped and growing mostly on walls from the District of Columbia to Georgia and Louisiana.

Cultivated in moist garden soil or potting mix in full sun or partial shade. This species hybridizes with *P. bahamensis* to form *P. × delchampsii*.

219 Pteris bahamensis (Agardh) Fée
Bahama Ladder Brake
Stipes 4–25(45) cm long, straw-colored, scaly only at the base, with reddish-brown, linear-lanceate, entire scales. Laminae narrowly oblanceolate to narrowly elliptic, 18–60 cm long, 3–16 cm wide, pinnate, the rachis glabrous, the pinnae simple, opposite at the base to alternate at the lamina apex, linear, 1.5–9 cm long, 1.5–5 mm wide, obtuse at the base, acute or round at the apex, the veins forked above and/or at the base, the veins entirely free.

Terrestrial, often in rocky, limy soil. Common. Broward, Collier, Dade, and Monroe Counties, Florida.

Not cultivated. This species hybridizes with *P. vittata* to form *P. × delchampsii*.

COLOR ILLUSTRATIONS

1 Psilotum nudum

2 Lycopodium cernuum

3 Lycopodium carolinianum

4 Lycopodium alopecuroides

5 Lycopodium prostratum

6 Lycopodium appressum

7 Lycopodium inundatum

8 Lycopodium dichotomum

9 Lycopodium lucidulum

10 Lycopodium selago var. appressum

11 Lycopodium porophilum

12 Lycopodium dendroideum

13A Lycopodium obscurum var. isophyllum

13B Lycopodium obscurum var. obscurum

14 Lycopodium annotinum

15 Lycopodium clavatum

16 Lycopodium digitatum

17 Lycopodium complanatum

18 Lycopodium tristachyum

19 Lycopodium sitchense

20 Lycopodium alpinum

21 Lycopodium sabinifolium

22 Selaginella lepidophylla

24 Selaginella willdenovii

26 Selaginella kraussiana

27 Selaginella uncinata Spring

28 Selaginella douglasii

29 Selaginella eatonii

30 Selaginella ludoviciana

31 Selaginella apoda

33 Selaginella selaginoides

35 Selaginella bigelovii

35 Selaginella bigelovii

36 Selaginella tortipila

36 Selaginella tortipila

39 Selaginella arenicola

40 Selaginella hansenii

40 Selaginella hansenii

43 Selaginella wallacei

45 Selaginella eremophila

45 Selaginella eremophila

47 Selaginella arizonica

48 Selaginella oregana

52 Selaginella densa var. scopulorum

52 Selaginella densa var. scopulorum

53 Selaginella watsonii

53 Selaginella watsonii

55 Selaginella rupestris

55 Selaginella rupestris

61 Isoëtes echinospora subsp. muricata

62 Isoëtes occidentalis

64 Isoëtes macrospora

67 Isoëtes engelmannii

68 Isoëtes riparia

69 Isoëtes tuckermanii

70 Isoëtes butleri

71 Isoëtes melanopoda

73 Isoëtes tegetiformans

75 Isoëtes melanospora

76 Isoëtes piedmontana

77 Equisetum palustre

78 Equisetum fluviatile

80 Equisetum arvense

82 Equisetum sylvaticum

83 Equisetum telmateia subsp. braunii

85 Equisetum laevigatum

86 Equisetum × ferrissii

87 Equisetum hyemale var. affine

88 Equisetum variegatum

89 Equisetum scirpoides

90 Botrychium oneidense

91 Botrychium dissectum

92 Botrychium biternatum

93 Botrychium rugulosum

94 Botrychium multifidum

95 Botrychium jenmanii

96 Botrychium lunarioides

97 Botrychium virginianum

98 Botrychium paradoxum

99 Botrychium lanceolatum subsp. lanceolatum

100 B. lanceolatum subsp. angustisegmentum

101 Botrychium mormo

102 Botrychium montanum

103 Botrychium matricariifolium

104 Botrychium pinnatum

106 Botrychium simplex

107 Botrychium crenulatum

108 Botrychium pumicola

109 Botrychium ascendens

110 Botrychium lunaria

111 Botrychium mnganense

114 Botrychium pedunculosum

115 Ophioglossum crotalophoroides

116 Ophioglossum engelmannii

118 Ophioglossum lusitanicum subsp. californicum

119 Ophioglossum petiolatum

120 Ophioglossum pusillum

122 Cheiroglossa palmata

123 Osmunda regalis var. spectabilis

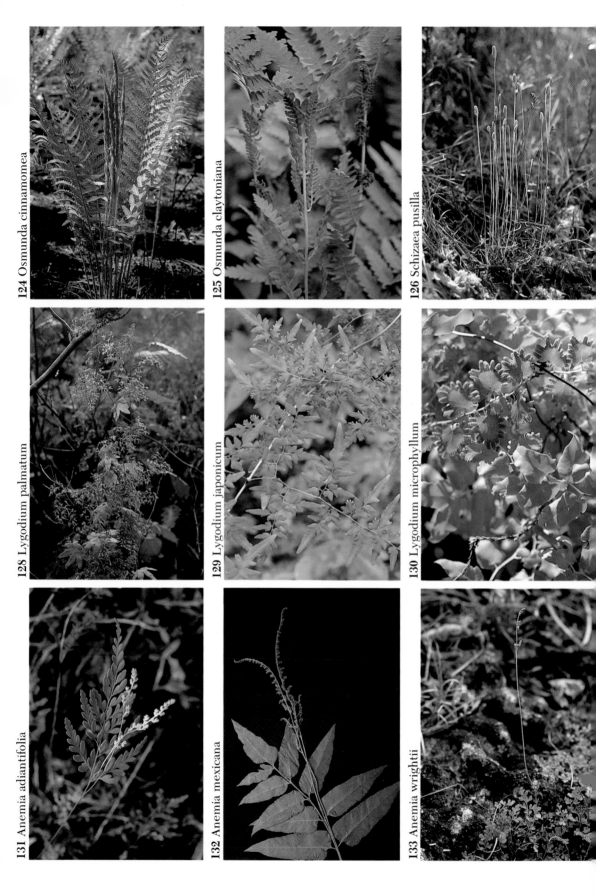

124 Osmunda cinnamomea

125 Osmunda claytoniana

126 Schizaea pusilla

128 Lygodium palmatum

129 Lygodium japonicum

130 Lygodium microphyllum

131 Anemia adiantifolia

132 Anemia mexicana

133 Anemia wrightii

134 Ceratopteris pteridoides

135 Ceratopteris thalictroides

136 Cryptogramma acrostichoides

137 Cryptogramma stelleri

138 Cheilanthes arizonica

140 Cheilanthes aemula

141 Cheilanthes microphylla

142 Cheilanthes lanosa

142 Cheilanthes lanosa

143 Cheilanthes alabamensis

144 Cheilanthes wrightii

145 Cheilanthes pringlei

146 Cheilanthes leucopoda

147 Cheilanthes kaulfussii

148 Cheilanthes viscida

148 Cheilanthes viscida

149 Cheilanthes cooperae

149 Cheilanthes cooperae

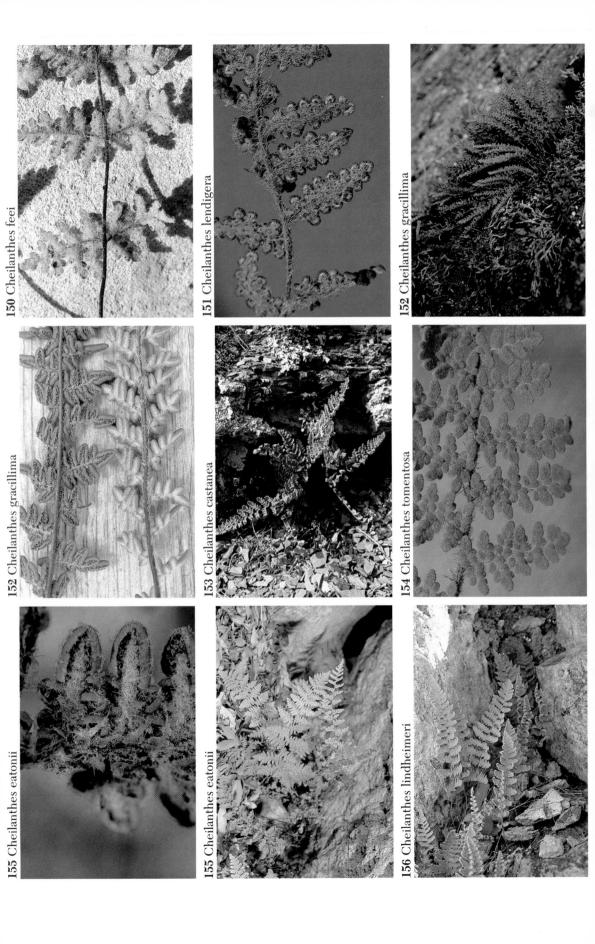

150 Cheilanthes feei

151 Cheilanthes lendigera

152 Cheilanthes gracillima

152 Cheilanthes gracillima

153 Cheilanthes castanea

154 Cheilanthes tomentosa

155 Cheilanthes eatonii

155 Cheilanthes eatonii

156 Cheilanthes lindheimeri

156 Cheilanthes lindheimeri

157 Cheilanthes intertexta

157 Cheilanthes intertexta

158 Cheilanthes wootonii

158 Cheilanthes wootonii

159 Cheilanthes covillei

159 Cheilanthes covillei

160 Cheilanthes villosa

161 Cheilanthes fendleri

161 Cheilanthes fendleri

162 Cheilanthes clevelandii

163 Aspidotis densa

163 Aspidotis densa

164 Aspidotis californica

165 Notholaena parvifolia

166 Notholaena jonesii

167 Notholaena aurea

167 Notholaena aurea

173 Notholaena sinuata

170 Notholaena aschenborniana

168 Notholaena parryi

174 Notholaena standleyi

171 Notholaena cochisensis

168 Notholaena parryi

175 Notholaena candida var. copelandii

173 Notholaena sinuata

169 Notholaena newberryi

176 Notholaena lemmonii var. lemmonii

177 Notholaena schaffneri var. nealleyi

178 Notholaena grayi

179 Notholaena aliena

180 Notholaena fendleri

181 Notholaena californica

182 Notholaena neglecta

183 Notholaena greggii

185 Notholaena dealbata

186 Notholaena limitanea var. limitanea

188 Pellaea ovata

190 Pellaea andromedifolia var. andromedifolia

192 Pellaea bridgesii

193 Pellaea × atropurpurea

194 Pellaea breweri

196 Pellaea glabella

197 Pellaea suksdorfiana

198 Pellaea brachyptera

199 Pellaea ternifolia

200 Pellaea wrightiana

201 Pellaea truncata

202 Pellaea mucronata

203 Pityrogramma trifoliata

204 Pityrogramma viscosa

205 Pityrogramma triangularis var. triangularis

207 Bommeria hispida

209 Adiantum pedatum subsp. pedatum

211 Adiantum pedatum subsp. aleuticum

213 Adiantum tenerum

214 Adiantum tricholepis

215 Adiantum capillus-veneris

216 Adiantum jordanii

217 Vittaria lineata

218 Pteris vittata

219 Pteris bahamensis

221 Pteris tripartita

222 Pteris cretica

223 Pteris multifida

225 Acrostichum danaeifolium

225 Acrostichum danaeifolium

226 Acrostichum aureum

226 Acrostichum aureum

227 Neurodium lanceolatum

228 Campyloneurum angustifolium var. angustifolium

229 Campyloneurum costatum

230 Campyloneurum phyllitidis

231 Micrulogramma heterophylla

233 Pleopeltis astrolepis

234 Phlebodium aureum

234 Phlebodium aureum

235 Polypodium polypodioides var. michauxianum

235 Polypodium polypodioides var. michauxianum

236 Polypodium thyssanolepis

237 Polypodium ptilodon var. caespitosum

238 Polypodium plumula

239 Polypodium dispersum

240 Polypodium virginianum

241 Polypodium hesperium

242 Polypodium amorphum

243 Polypodium scouleri

245 Polypodium glycyrrhiza

246 Polypodium californicum

247 Hymenophyllum tunbrigense

249 Trichomanes boschianum

251 Trichomanes krausii

252 Trichomanes punctatum subsp. floridanum

253 Trichomanes petersii

254 Dennstaedtia punctilobula

254 Dennstaedtia punctilobula

255 Dennstaedtia globulifera

256 Dennstaedtia bipinnata

256 Dennstaedtia bipinnata

257 Hypolepis repens

257 Hypolepis repens

258 Pteridium caudatum

259 Pteridium aquilinum var. pubescens

260 Pteridium aquilinum var. latiusculum

261 Pteridium aquilinum var. pseudocaudatum

262 Sphenomeris clavata

262 Sphenomeris clavata

263 Thelypteris torresiana

264 Thelypteris phegopteris

265 Thelypteris hexagonoptera

266 Thelypteris reticulata

266 Thelypteris reticulata

267 Thelypteris serrata

268 Thelypteris tetragona

269 Thelypteris reptans

270 Thelypteris sclerophylla

271 Thelypteris pilosa var. alabamensis

271 Thelypteris pilosa var. alabamensis

273 Thelypteris totta

274 Thelypteris limbosperma

275 Thelypteris palustris var. pubescens

277 Thelypteris novaboracensis

278 Thelypteris nevadensis

279 Thelypteris dentata

280 Thelypteris hsipidula var. versicolor

281 Thelypteris kunthii

282 Thelypteris grandis var. grandis

283 Thelypteris augescens

284 Thelypteris puberula var. sonorensis

286 Thelypteris ovata var. lindheimeri

287 Phyllitis scolopendrium var. americana

288 Asplenium septentrionale

289 Asplenium serratum

290 Asplenium dalhousiae

291 Asplenium pumilum

292 Asplenium auritum

293 Asplenium trichomanes-ramosum

294 Asplenium trichomanes-dentatum

295 Asplenium verecundum

297 Asplenium abscissum

298 Asplenium cristatum

299 Asplenium palmeri

300 Asplenium monanthes

301 Asplenium resiliens

302 Asplenium × heteroresiliens

302 Asplenium × heteroresiliens

303 Asplenium heterochroum

303 Asplenium heterochroum

304 Asplenium vespertinum

305 Asplenium trichomanes

306 Asplenium platyneuron

306 Asplenium platyneuron

307 Asplenium × ebenoides

308 Asplenium rhizophyllum

309 Asplenium pinnatifidum

309 Asplenium pinnatifidum

310 Asplenium montanum

311 Asplenium bradleyi

311 Asplenium bradleyi

312 Asplenium ruta-muraria

313 Asplenium adiantum-nigrum

314 Asplenium exiguum

315 Matteuccia struthiopteris

316 Onoclea sensibilis

317 Athyrium pycnocarpon

317 Athyrium pycnocarpon

318 Athyrium thelypteroides

318 Athyrium thelypteroides

319 Athyrium alpestre subsp. americanum

320 Athyrium filix-femina subsp. cyclosorum

320 Athyrium filix-femina subsp. cyclosorum

321 Athyrium filix-femina subsp. angustum

321 Athyrium filix-femina subsp. angustum

322 Athyrium filix-femina subsp. asplenioides

322 Athyrium filix-femina subsp. asplenioides

323 Diplazium japonicum

324 Diplazium lonchophyllum

325 Gymnocarpium dryopteris

325 Gymnocarpium dryopteris

326 Gymnocarpium robertianum

327 Cystopteris montana

328 Cystopteris bulbifera

328 Cystopteris bulbifera

329 Cystopteris tennesseensis

331 Cystopteris fragilis

333 Cystopteris protrusa

334 Cystopteris tenuis

336 Woodsia glabella

336 Woodsia glabella

337 Woodsia alpina

338 Woodsia ilvensis

338 Woodsia ilvensis

339 Woodsia scopulina

339 Woodsia scopulina

340 Woodsia oregana

341 Woodsia obtusa

342 Woodsia mexicana

342 Woodsia mexicana

343 Woodsia plummerae

343 Woodsia plummerae

344 Ctenitis submarginalis

345 Ctenitis sloanei

345 Ctenitis sloanei

346 Tectaria heracleifolia

347 Tectaria incisa

348 Tectaria lobata

349 Tectaria coriandrifolia

I Cm.

352 Polystichum acrostichoides

351 Polystichum andersonii

351 Polystichum andersonii

352 Polystichum munitum

353 Polystichum setigerum

354 Polystichum californicum

354 Polystichum californicum

355 Polystichum dudleyi

356 Polystichum braunii

358 Polystichum imbricans subsp. imbricans

359 Polystichum scopulinum

360 Polystichum lemmonii

362 Polystichum lonchitis

362 Polystichum lonchitis

363 Polystichum aleuticum

365 Cyrtomium falcatum

367 Phanerophlebia auriculata

368 Phanerophlebia umbonata

370 Dryopteris rossii

372 Dryopteris expansa

373 Dryopteris campyloptera

374 Dryopteris intermedia

374 Dryopteris intermedia

375 Dryopteris carthusiana

375 Dryopteris carthusiana

376 Dryopteris cristata

378 Dryopteris ludoviciana

379 Dryopteris celsa

379 Dryopteris celsa

380 Dryopteris goldiana

380 Dryopteris goldiana

381 Dryopteris marginalis

381 Dryopteris marginalis

382 Dryopteris fragrans

383 Dryopteris filix-mas

383 Dryopteris filix-mas

384 Dryopteris arguta

385 Lomariopsis kunzeana

386 Nephrolepis exaltata

387 Nephrolepis cordifolia

387 Nephrolepis cordifolia

388 Nephrolepis biserrata

389 Nephrolepis multiflora

390 Blechnum spicant

391 Blechnum serrulatum

392 Blechnum occidentale

393 Woodwardia areolata

394 Woodwardia virginica

394 Woodwardia virginica

395 Woodwardia fimbriata

396 Marsilea quadrifolia

397 Marsilea mexicana

399 Marsilea macropoda

400 Marsilea vestita

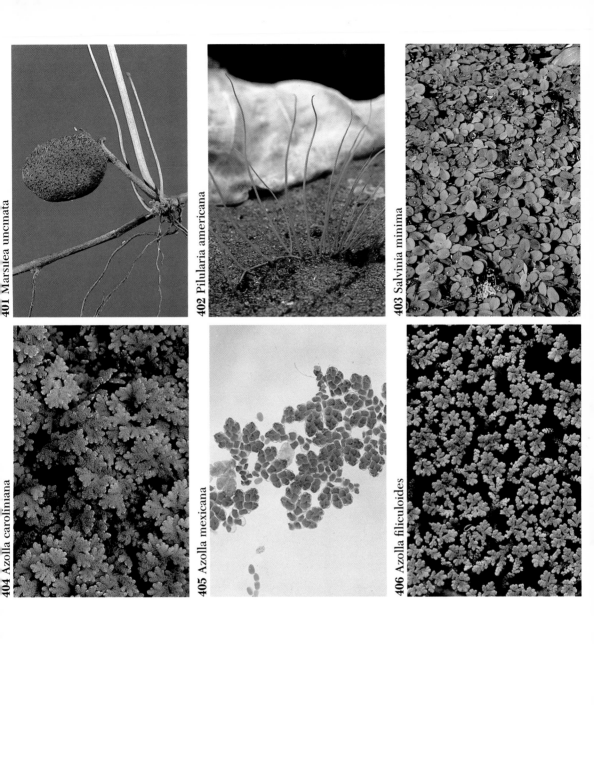

401 Marsilea uncinata

402 Pilularia americana

403 Salvinia minima

404 Azolla caroliniana

405 Azolla mexicana

406 Azolla filiculoides

*220 Pteris × delchampsii Wagner & Nauman
Delchamp's Ladder Brake

Stipes 20–40 cm long, pale brown, scaly with pale brown, linear-lanceate, entire scaly when young, commonly glabrous in age. Laminae narrowly elliptic, 40–120 cm long, 15–30 cm wide, pinnate, the rachises partially scaly with scales like those of the rhizome, also glabrous in age, the pinnae simple, alternate throughout or sometimes opposite towards the base, linear, 7–15 cm long, 4–6 mm wide, truncate to obtuse at the base, acuminate at the sterile, often serrate apex, the veins forked at or above the base, sometimes simple, the veins entirely free; spores of various sizes or abortive.

Terrestrial along roads and canals. Rare. Dade Co., Florida.

Cultivated in moist potting mix or garden soil in partial sun. According to Wagner and Nauman (1982), this is the hybrid of *P. bahamensis* and *P. vittata*.

221 Pteris tripartita (Swartz) Presl
Giant Brake

Stipes up to 1.25 m long, reddish-brown, scaly at the base and with multicellular hairs with obvious cross-walls when young, glabrous in age. Laminae deltate, up to 2 m long and wide, pedate, the basal basiscopic pinnule of the basal pinnae repeatedly subdivided, the rachis glabrous in age, the suprabasal pinnae pinnatifid, the veins along the costae forming usually 2 rows of elongate areoles, the veins along the costules forming usually 1 row of elongate areoles, the veins free toward the margin.

Terrestrial in swamps and woods in circumneutral to acid soil. Rare. Naturalized in Dade, Palm Beach, Broward, and Highlands counties, Florida, and perhaps elsewhere in southern Florida.

Cultivated in moist garden soil in partial sun.

222 Pteris cretica L.
Cretan Brake

Stipes 10–50 cm long, straw-colored and commonly reddish-brown toward the base, scaly at the base with a few linear-lanceolate, concolorous, dark brown, entire scales. Laminae ovate-lanceolate to nearly triangular, 10–30 cm long, 6–25 cm wide, the basal and rarely suprabasal pinnae with a single basiscopic lobe or pinnule, the distal pinnae simple, the veins 1-forked above the base, rarely at the base or the veins simple, all free.

Terrestrial in usually limy soil in moist woodlands. Frequent. Naturalized throughout Florida to south-central Louisiana.

Cultivated in moist potting mix or garden soil in full sun or partial shade. Many distinctive cultivated varieties are known, including the white-striped cv. *Albolineata*, which has become naturalized in Hernando Co., Florida.

223 Pteris multifida Poir.
Spider Brake

Stipes 4–14 cm long, straw-colored and reddish-brown at the base, glabrous. Laminae ovate-lanceolate, 10–30 cm long, 10–24 cm wide, the basal and sometimes distal pinnae with 1 or 2 lobes or pinnules, the distal pinnae simple, the veins 1-forked at or above the base or rarely simple, all free.

Terrestrial in moist, circumneutral soil in woods and along streambanks or epipetric in rock crevices. Occasional. Naturalized in southern Alabama and Louisiana, west-central Arkansas, eastern Texas, and southern California. Escaped and growing on brick walls from Maryland to Georgia and Louisiana, also southwestern Texas.

Cultivated in moist potting mix or garden soil in partial shade. Many cultivars are known.

*224 Pteris ensiformis cv. Victoriae Hort.
Victorian Brake

Stipes 4–30 cm long, straw-colored and reddish-brown at the base, with a few lanceate, concolorous, dark brown, entire scales. Laminae dimorphic, whitish along the costae and costules on the adaxial surface; veins mostly 1-forked above the base, all free. Sterile laminae lanceolate, 10–20 cm long, 4–10 cm wide, 2-pinnate, the pinna and pinnule apices round. Fertile laminae lanceolate, 20–35 cm long, 10–20 cm wide, 2- or 3-pinnate, the pinna and pinnule apices acute to attenuate.

Terrestrial in rocky woods. Rare. Naturalized in peninsular Florida, according to Wherry (1964, p. 208).

Cultivated in moist potting mix or garden soil in partial shade.

ACROSTICHUM
The Leather Ferns

Acrostichum includes two principal species widely distributed throughout the tropics including southern Florida, plus one or possibly more species that are not very distinct in the Old World tropics.

The Leather Ferns are huge, coarse, tough ferns. The rhizomes are massive and bear fronds up to several meters long. The laminae are pinnate, very thick and leathery, and rather narrowly lanceolate; the pinnae are narrowly oblong and their veins form elongate, polygonal areoles and are usually prominulous on the abaxial surface of the lamina. Fertile pinnae are completely covered with sporangia on the abaxial surface, giving them a felt-like appearance. Minute, multicellular paraphyses grow intermixed with the sporangia, presumably to protect the young sporangia from desiccation.

Acrostichum grows in marshes and swamps in brackish water or, in the case of *A. danaeifolium*, in fresh-water swamps, lakes, and canals, as well. All are sun ferns. Florida specimens of *Acrostichum* were studied in detail by Adams and Tomlinson (1979).

Key to Acrostichum
1. Lateral pinnae usually 20–30 overlapping pairs, in fertile fronds almost all of the pinnae fertile; rhizomes erect or ascending, seldom branched; costular areolae no more than 3 times longer than wide; FL. 225. *A. danaeifolium*

1. Lateral pinnae usually no more than 15 distant pairs, in fertile fronds only the upper 3–5 pairs fertile; rhizomes creeping or ascending, frequently branched; costular areolae more than 3 times longer than wide; FL. 226. *A. aureum*

225   Acrostichum danaeifolium Langsd. & Fisch.
Inland Leather Fern
Rhizomes erect or ascending, seldom branched; laminae lanceolate, 1.5–4(5) m long, 15–50 cm wide, pinnate, the pinnae narrowly lanceolate, 7–30 cm long, 2–5 cm wide, obtuse to acute and slightly inequilateral at the base, slightly tapering toward the apex, abruptly acute at the apex; veins on the adaxial surface of the sterile laminae diverging at ca. a 75° angle from the midrib, distinctly prominulous, often stiffly pilose.

Terrestrial in fresh-water marshes and swamps and lake and canal margins in circumneutral soil or in brackish water. Common. Inland and coastal peninsular Florida.

Cultivated occasionally in botanical gardens.

226   Acrostichum aureum L.
Coast Leather Fern
Rhizomes creeping or ascending, frequently branched; laminae lanceolate, 1–2(3) m long, 12–30 cm wide, pinnate, the pinnae 10–20 cm long, 2–3.5 cm wide, acute or obtuse and equilateral at the base, slightly tapering, round at the apex, the veins on the adaxial surface of the sterile laminae diverging at ca. a 55° angle from the midrib, faintly prominulous, glabrous.

Terrestrial in salt water and brackish marshes and mangrove swamps in circumneutral soil. Occasional. Central and southern coastal peninsular Florida.

Cultivated occasionally in botanical gardens.

POLYPODIACEAE
The Polypody Family

The Polypodiaceae includes about 46 genera and at least 665 species, of which 35 genera and at least 350 species are exclusively Old World. Eleven genera are entirely or partially found in the New World, and six of these including only 20 species are found in the United States and Canada.

The plants of this family are small to medium-sized and have short- to long-creeping, scaly rhizomes. The fronds may be scattered or close together along the rhizome. The stipes abcise from the rhizome at a point of articulation, in most species leaving behind a short, cylindrical protuberance on the rhizome called a phyllopodium. The laminae are simple to 1-pinnate in the species native to the United States and Canada, and are glabrous or with short hairs or few to many scales. The veins anastomose in the species with simple laminae or laminae that have rather broad lobes; in those with narrow lobes (*Polypodium* subg. *Pectinatum*), the veins are repeatedly forked and as a rule do not anastomose regularly. The sori are usually round or oval (rarely elongate or linear), exindusiate, and are borne in one to several rows on each side of the costa.

The Polypodiaceae are mostly epiphytic and epipetric, although a few species are terrestrial. Most of the species grow in the moist or wet tropics; a few occur in at least seasonally moist temperate regions. In general, Polypodies are easy to grow. The hardy species do well in northern gardens, and the tropical ones thrive outdoors in warm climates and in greenhouses.

Key to the Genera of Polypodiaceae
1. Laminae pinnatifid, pinnatisect, or pinnate, **5**

1. Laminae simple, entire, not lobed, **2**

2(1). Sori linear, in a continuous line near the margin of the laminae, *Neurodium*, p. 187

2(1). Sori round or elongate, in 1–several rows on the abaxial surface of the lamina, **3**

3(2). Rhizomes short-creeping, the fronds in a tuft; lamina midrib with prominulous, parallel side-veins; sori terminal at the end of a single branch veinlet, 2 or more in each oblong areola lying between the main side-veins, *Campyloneurum*, p. 188

3(2). Rhizomes long-creeping, the fronds distant; lamina midrib lacking prominulous, parallel side-veins; sori at the intersection of several small veinlets, 1 in each polygonal areola, **4**

4(3). Scales absent from the abaxial surface of the lamina; sori round; rhizome scales narrowly rhombic, many times longer than wide, lacking hairs, *Microgramma*, p. 189

4(3). Scales scattered on the abaxial surface of the lamina; sori at least somewhat elongate; rhizome scales ovate, not much longer than wide, with a tuft of reddish hairs on their surface, *Pleopeltis*, p. 190

5(1). Veins entirely areolate; sori at the end of usually 2 included veinlets; rhizome scales 5–15 mm long, *Phlebodium*, p. 192

5(1). Veins entirely free or areolate only along the costae; sori at the end of 1 included veinlet or on a forked, free vein; rhizome scales less than 5 mm long, *Polypodium*, p. 193

NEURODIUM
The Ribbon Ferns

Neurodium, which was formerly called *Paltonium*, contains only one species. It occurs on the islands of the Caribbean, in Central America, northern South America, and southern Florida.

The Ribbon Fern is unique among the genera of the Polypodiaceae found in the United States in having 2 linear, submarginal sori; all the other genera have round or, in a few cases, elongate sori arrayed variously on the abaxial surface of the laminae. The pinnae are shaped like a broad, tapering strap and are narrowed slightly in the fertile portion at and below the lamina apex.

The Ribbon Ferns are epiphytic on tree trunks and large branches. The genus is not in cultivation.

227 Neurodium lanceolatum (L.) Fée
Ribbon Fern

Rhizomes short-creeping, 2–4 mm in diam., with phyllopodia closely spaced, ca. 2 mm long; rhizome scales lanceolate, ca. 1.5 mm long, 0.5 mm wide, subclathrate, blackish with pale, distantly toothed margins. Stipes 2–4 cm long, slightly grooved toward the base, brown. Laminae monomorphic, simple, narrowly elliptic, 10–35 cm long, 1–3 cm wide, attenuate at the base and apex, with the fertile apical portion slightly tapered; veins anastomosing in short, polygonal areolae with included veinlets; sori linear, submarginal near the lamina apex, not protected by the scarcely underrolled lamina margins.

Epiphytic on tree trunks and large branches. Very rare. Key Largo, Monroe Co., and found in 1881 in Dade Co., Florida.

Not cultivated.

CAMPYLONEURUM
The Strap Ferns

Campyloneurum, which is sometimes included in *Polypodium* in the broad sense, includes about 25 species in the American tropics, three of which occur in the United States. The Strap Ferns have strap-shaped fronds borne in a cluster from a compact or short-creeping rhizome. The stipes are short in the United States species. The laminae are simple (or pinnate in a few South American species). Most species have prominulous main lateral veins with less conspicuous transverse veins forming one or more minor areolae; the fertile areolae have an included veinlet bearing the sorus. Usually two sori are present in each major areola formed between two transverse veins. In some species, the veins and sorus number are irregular. In very narrow laminae of small species, the sori may be reduced to a single row on each side of the lamina midrib, in the manner of *Microgramma*.

The Strap Ferns are mostly epiphytic on tree trunks or logs; a few tropical species are terrestrial or epipetric. Many are cultivated as pot plants or in hanging baskets in warm, moist greenhouses or outdoors in frost-free regions.

Key to Campyloneurum

1. Laminae linear or nearly so, less than 1.5 cm wide; FL. *228. C. angustifolium* var. *angustifolium*

1. Laminae narrowly elliptic, more than 2 cm wide, 2

2(1). Main lateral veins and especially the transverse veins between the main lateral veins obscure; laminae dark green, arching to pendent, up to 20(30) cm long, acuminate at the apex; FL. *229. C. costatum*

2(1). Main lateral veins and the transverse veins between the main lateral veins obvious; laminae lime green, erect to arching, at least (25)30 cm long, acute at the apex; FL. *230. C. phyllitidis*

228 Campyloneurum angustifolium (Swartz) Fée var. angustifolium

Narrow Strap Fern

Rhizome short-creeping, 3–4 mm in diam.; rhizome scales lanceolate. Stipes crowded, 2–8 cm long. Laminae linear, 15–50 cm long, (0.3)0.5–1 cm wide, attenuate at the base and apex, the margins revolute, the veins obscure; sori 1 per areola, in 1 row on each side of the midrib.

Epiphytic. Dade and Collier counties, Florida.

Cultivated in moist potting soil or in fiber in hanging baskets in partial sun. Rare. Besides var. *angustifolium*, several other varieties of this species are known elsewhere in tropical America and may be in cultivation, especially var. *ensifolium* (Willd.) Farw., with very narrow, revolute laminae.

229 Campyloneurum costatum (Kunze) Presl
Tailed Strap Fern

Rhizome short-creeping, 2–3 mm in diam., the scales lanceolate. Stipes crowded, 4–5 cm long. Laminae narrowly elliptic, 10–40 cm long, 2–4 cm wide, acuminate at the base, acute at the apex, with an acuminate tip, the margins not or scarcely revolute, the main lateral veins and the transverse veins obscure, the sori 2 per areola, in 4–6 rows on each side of the midrib.

Epiphytic on tree trunks and logs. Rare. Collier Co., Florida.

Cultivated in moist potting soil in partial sun.

230 Campyloneurum phyllitidis (L.) Presl
Long Strap Fern

Rhizome short-creeping, 4–8 mm in diam., the scales lanceolate. Stipes crowded, 2–10 cm long. Laminae narrowly elliptic, 30–90 cm long, 3.5–6.5 cm wide, attenuate at the base, acute at the apex, the margins not revolute, the main lateral veins prominulous, the cross veins rather obscure, regular, with 3 acroscopic veinlets, the sori 2 per major areola, in 6–10 rows on each side of the midrib.

Epiphytic on tree trunks, on logs or mossy hummocks, or rarely epipetric in limestone sink holes. Frequent. Peninsular Florida.

Cultivated in moist potting soil or in fiber in hanging baskets in partial sun. Occasionally this species is identified as *C. latum* Moore, a species which occurred as an accidental in Dade Co., Florida, in 1903, but which is not currently known from the United States. *Campyloneurum latum* differs from *C. phyllitidis* in having irregular veins, with the primary areolae divided into more than 2 irregular areolae and the sori usually more than 2 per primary areola.

MICROGRAMMA
The Clinging Vine Ferns

Microgramma, which is sometimes considered to be a subgenus of *Polypodium*, includes about 20 species in tropical America and Africa, only one of which occurs in the United States.

The Vine Ferns have very long-creeping rhizomes, in most species ca. 1 mm in diameter; the rhizome scales are lanceolate to linear and are rarely clathrate. The stipes are short to absent in most species. The laminae are simple, weakly to strongly dimorphic, with the sterile laminae

189

typically shorter and broader than the fertile laminae. The laminae are glabrous or have a few scales along the midrib; the veins form elongate, polygonal areolae bearing simple or branched included veinlets; the sori are round in most species, but slightly elongate in a few, and are borne one in each areola in a single row on either side of the lamina midrib.

The Vine Ferns all are epiphytic. Their rhizomes usually adhere to tree trunks and branches. Several species are in cultivation as greenhouse plants.

231   Microgramma heterophylla (L.) Wherry
Clinging Vine Fern

Rhizomes long-creeping, 0.6–1.5 mm in diam., phyllopodia 5–10 mm distant, ca. 0.5–1 mm long; rhizome scales narrowly rhombic, 3–8 mm long, 0.25–0.5 mm wide, peltate, blackish at the point of attachment, dark reddish-brown fading to paler brown outward, with pale, irregularly toothed and slightly erose margins. Laminae strongly dimorphic. Sterile laminae exstipitate, elliptic to oblanceolate, 1.2–4 cm long, 0.6–1.4 cm wide, simple, round at the apex, cuneate at the base. Fertile laminae with stipes 5–18 mm long, narrowly lanceolate to linear, 3–9.5 cm long, 0.5–1 cm wide, simple, acute to round at the apex, attenuate at the base, the veins anastomosing in long, polygonal areolae with often branched included veinlets; sori round, in a single medial row on each side of the midrib.

Epiphytic. Rare. Collier and Monroe counties, Florida.

Cultivated in moist potting soil in partial sun.

PLEOPELTIS
The Shielded-sorus Polypodies

Pleopeltis, which is often included in *Polypodium* when that genus is used in a broad sense, includes about 40 species in the tropics of the New and Old World. Only two species occur in the United States. The common name refers to the sori, which are protected by small, peltate scales when immature.

The Shielded-sorus Polypodies have mostly very long rhizomes ca. 1 mm in diameter; the rhizome scales are peltate and usually round or ovate. The laminae are monomorphic or nearly so, and are nearly linear in most species. They bear scattered, round to lanceolate scales on at least the lower surface. The veins form elongate, irregular, polygonal areolae bearing simple or branched included veinlets. The sori are round or rarely elongate and are borne in a single row on either side of the midrib or costa.

The Shielded-sorus Polypodies are epiphytic on tree trunks and branches or sometimes they are terrestrial in rocky places. Only one species is well established in the United States; the other is adventive or naturalized and may prove to be ephemeral. At least the common tropical *P. percussum* (Cav.) Hook. & Grev. is in cultivation.

Key to Pleopeltis
1. Scales on the abaxial surface of the laminae 0.5–2 mm long, many, the lamina surface hidden; sori round to slightly elongate; rhizome scales lanceolate, bicolorous, with a black central stripe and pale, erose-toothed margins; TX. *232. P. erythrolepis*
1. Scales on the abaxial surface of the laminae 0.15–0.35 mm long, few, the lamina surface not hidden; sori rarely round, usually slightly elongate, sometimes linear; rhizome scales ovate, covered with many reddish-brown hairs on the surface; FL. 233. *P. astrolepis*

*232   Pleopeltis erythrolepis (Weath.) Pic. Ser.
Red-scaled Polypody
Rhizomes long-creeping, 1–2.5 mm in diam., with phyllopodia 1.5–6 mm distant, ca. 0.5 mm long; rhizome scales lanceolate, peltate, up to ca. 2.5 mm long, 0.5 mm wide, sharply bicolorous, the central stripe black, the margins pale brown, erose-toothed. Stipes 1–2.5 cm long, alate, the alae folding to form a double adaxial groove, slightly scaly. Laminae monomorphic, linear-elliptic to somewhat linear-oblanceolate, 1.5–4.5 cm long, 0.5–1 cm wide, simple, cuneate at the base, cuneate to somewhat round at the apex, the sori rarely round, usually slightly elongate, sometimes linear, in a single medial row on each side of the midrib.

Terrestrial along streams and in soil pockets on cliffs. Rare. Western Texas.

Not cultivated.

233   Pleopeltis astrolepis (Liebm.) Fourn.
Star-scaled Polypody
Rhizomes long-creeping, 1–1.25 mm in diam., with phyllopodia 3–10 mm distant, ca. 1 mm long; rhizome scales elliptical to ovate, peltate, up to ca. 0.5 mm long, 0.2 mm wide, densely covered with and obscured by many, reddish-brown hairs borne on the surface of the scales. Stipes 1–3 cm long, flattened, slightly scaly. Laminae slightly dimorphic, nearly linear, 5–17 cm long, 0.5–1.5 cm wide, simple, attenuate at the apex and base, the sori slightly elongate to linear, but not continuous, in a single medial row on each side of the midrib.

Epiphytic. Very rare. Found in 1977 in Broward Co., Florida; this species may prove to be an accidental that may not persist.

Not cultivated.

PHLEBODIUM
The Serpent Ferns

Phlebodium, which is sometimes included in *Polypodium* in the broad sense, includes conservatively two species in the New World tropics, although *P. decumanum* (Willd.) J. Smith may be an aggregate subject to division into several species when more is known of its cytology and biochemistry. Only one species of *Phlebodium* occurs in the United States. The common name of the genus reflects the large, conspicuous, creeping rhizomes, which are rather brightly colored by their scales.

The Serpent Ferns have creeping rhizomes 5–15 mm in diameter. The abundant, loose, reddish-brown, toothed rhizome scales are linear-lanceolate from a peltate base. The large, glabrous, sometimes glaucous, oblong-lanceolate laminae are pinnatifid, with 1–several pairs of long, acute to attenuate lobes 2–5 cm wide. The veins are completely areolate, with elongate, polygonal areolae lacking included veinlets, except that the sori are borne on (1)2–3 included veinlets in 1–several rows on each side of the costae.

The Serpent Ferns are all epiphytic on tree trunks and large branches. *Phlebodium decumanum* is not often cultivated, but *P. aureum* and its many cultivars are commonly grown either as greenhouse plants or outdoors in frost-free regions. An unrelated but superficially similar species, *Phymatosorus scolopendria* (Burm.) Pic. Ser. (*Microsorium scolopendrium* (Burm.) Copel.) is widely cultivated in southern Florida and occasionally may escape from cultivation.

234   Phlebodium aureum (L.) J. Smith
Gold-foot Fern

Rhizomes long-creeping, 5–10 mm in diam., with phyllopodia ca. 10 mm distant, ca. 2 mm long; rhizome scales linear-lanceolate, up to ca. 10 mm long, 1.25 mm wide, reddish-brown, toothed along the margins. Stipes 12–42 cm long, with 2 adaxial grooves, glabrous. Laminae monomorphic, oblong-lanceolate, 15–65 cm long, 15–35 cm wide, pinnatifid, acute at the apex with a long, terminal pinna, obtuse to truncate at the base, the veins anastomosing in long, polygonal areolae without included veinlets, except the sori on (1)2 included veinlets in 1(2) rows of areolae on each side of the costae.

Epiphytic, commonly on *Sabal palmetto*. Frequent. Peninsular Florida and the Atlantic coast of Georgia.

Cultivated in moist potting mix in full sun or partial shade. Many cultivated varieties are grown, including glaucous and lacerate-leaved forms.

POLYPODIUM
The Polypodies

Polypodium, used in this book in a rather restricted sense, includes about 160 species. Most occur in the New World tropics, but a few occur in temperate areas, both in the New World and the Old World. Twelve species are found in the United States and Canada. The common name refers to the rhizome habit, which is to creep over rocks or tree branches and tree trunks. The scale-clad side branches and phyllopodia look like many feet. The laminae are all monomorphic and very deeply lobed to simply pinnate, which sets them apart from all other genera of the family in the United States and Canada, except for *Phlebodium*, which has much larger, coarser laminae and conspicuous, large, reddish-brown rhizome scales.

The Polypodies mostly have long-creeping rhizomes that are relatively large in diameter compared to those of *Microgramma* and *Pleopeltis*. The rhizomes bear conspicuous but short phyllopodia in close succession and are commonly somewhat contorted. The rhizome scales are small, lanceolate, concolorous to weakly bicolorous, and medium to dark brown. The lamina surface is glabrous in most species, but may have a few, short hairs in subg. *Pectinatum* or few to many ovate to lanceolate scales in subg. *Marginaria*. The veins are free and simple to several times forked in subg. *Pectinatum* and subg. *Polypodium*, or some of the forks may be united occasionally in those subgenera or regularly in subg. *Marginaria*. Closely set, parallel veins from the costae give off pairs of short, lateral veins that unite to form one to several rows of short areolae in subg. *Goniophlebium*. In the last subgenus, one to several rows of sori may be present as a consequence of the one to several rows of areolae; in the other subgenera, a single row of sori on each side of the costa is the rule. The sori are round or oval, lack indusia, but may have paraphyses intermixed with the sporangia.

The Polypodies grow mostly epiphytically or epipetrically in nature and are relatively easy to cultivate in tropical gardens. Many species are in greenhouse cultivation, where most will adapt to being grown in pots or hanging baskets.

Key to Polypodium

1. Laminae sparsely to densely scaly on the lower surface and stipes, the scales minute (subg. *Marginaria*), **3**

1. Laminae not scaly on the lower surface, other than sometimes a few scales on the costae and/or rachis, **2**

2(1). Rhizomes short-creeping; stipes crowded; laminae pectinate, the segments long, linear, 1.5–8 mm wide, usually more than 25 pairs per lamina (subg. *Pectinatum*), **4**

2(1). Rhizomes long-creeping; laminae not pectinate, the segments elongate, (3)5–20(30) mm wide, usually fewer than 20(25) pairs per lamina (subg. *Polypodium*), **6**

3(1). Scales on the abaxial surface of the laminae ovate to lanceolate, grayish, entire or with a few, irregularly scattered teeth; laminae ca. 2–2.5 times longer than wide, usually longer than the stipe; segments 1.5–4 mm wide; SE. *235. P. polypodioides* var. *michauxianum*

3(1). Scales on the abaxial surface of the laminae lanceolate, reddish-brown, with many, rather regular teeth; laminae ca. 1.5–2(2.5) times longer than wide, usually shorter than the stipe; segments 3–8 mm wide; TX, AZ. *236. P. thyssanolepis*

4(2). Rachises dark reddish-brown; segments 4–8 mm wide at the midpoint, tapering rather uniformly from their expanded base, the sinuses between them V-shaped; rachis scales linear, inconspicuous; FL. *237. P. ptilodon* var. *caespitosum*

4(2). Rachises black; segments 1.5–5(6.5) mm wide at the midpoint, mostly parallel-sided above their expanded base, the sinuses between them U-shaped; rachis scales narrowly lanceolate or broader, hastate or cordate at the base, **5**

5(4). Laminae usually curved and drooping, the rachis wiry; rhizome scales decidedly and evenly toothed; segments 1.5–2.5 mm wide at the midpoint, strictly linear above the slightly expanded base, the basal segments reduced to auricles; veins 1-forked; rachis scales broadly lanceolate, cordate at the base, commonly whitish; FL. *238. P. plumula*

5(4). Laminae straight and erect, the rachis stiff; rhizome scales weakly and unevenly toothed to entire; segments 3–5(6.5) mm wide at the midpoint, often slightly broader at the middle than above the greatly expanded base, the basal segments often reflexed but not reduced to auricles; veins (1)2-forked; rachis scales narrowly lanceolate, hastate at the base, commonly brownish; FL. *239. P. dispersum*

6(2). Sori medial, equidistant from the margin and the costa; laminae ovate-lanceolate to nearly oblong, 1–3 times longer than wide, usually widest above the base, **9**

6(2). Sori supramedial to submarginal, closer to the margin than the costa; laminae lanceate to nearly oblong, (2)2.5–5 times longer than wide, usually widest at or very close to the base, **7**

7(6). Fertile segments mostly 3–5(6) mm wide, much more than 3 times longer than wide; E. *240. P. virginianum*

7(6). Fertile segments mostly 4–9 mm wide, no more than 3 times longer than wide, **8**

8(7). Rhizome scales subentire to erose, dark reddish-brown to orangish-brown in mass; young sori oval, rarely with a few paraphyses like abortive sporangia; W. *241. P. hesperium*

8(7). Rhizome scales erose-toothed, orangish-brown to golden-brown in mass; young sori round, commonly with paraphyses like abortive sporangia; P. *242. P. amorphum*

9(6). Segments 10–20 mm wide, sparsely scaly on the abaxial surface of the rachis and costae; rhizomes pruinose; laminae leathery, the veins partially anastomosing to form fertile areolae; P. *243. P. scouleri*

9(6). Segments 5–13(15) mm wide, not scaly on the abaxial surface of the rachis and costae; rhizomes not pruinose; laminae usually papery, the veins free or sometimes partially anastomosing to form fertile areolae, **10**

10(9). Laminae 1–1.5 times longer than wide, broadest just above the base; inconspicuous, hair-like, branched paraphyses present among the sporangia; CA. *244. P. cambricum*

10(9). Laminae 1.5–3.5 times longer than wide, broadest near the middle; paraphyses absent among the sporangia, **11**

11(10). Segments acute to acuminate at the apex; rhizomes with a licorice taste, mostly less than 5 mm in diam.; veins entirely free; P. *245. P. glycyrrhiza*

11(10). Segments round to acute at the apex; rhizomes with an acrid taste, mostly more than 5 mm in diam.; veins sometimes partially anastomosing to form fertile areolae; CA. *246. P. californicum*

235 Polypodium polypodioides var. michauxianum Weath.

Resurrection Fern

Rhizomes long-creeping, 1.5–2 mm in diam.; rhizome scales lanceolate, up to ca. 2.5 mm long, 0.5 mm wide, concolorous to sharply bicolorous, the central stripe black, the margins pale brown, erose-toothed. Stipes 0.5–3 cm distant, 2–10 cm long, not alate, densely scaly, the scales deciduous in age. Laminae monomorphic, oblong to lanceate, 2–15 cm long, 1–5 cm wide, pinnatisect, truncate at the base, acute at the apex, the adaxial surface glabrous, the abaxial surface with round to ovate, peltate, erose-toothed, grayish scales; sori round, in a single row on each side of the midrib.

Epiphytic and epipetric, forming large mats. Common. Maryland, West Virginia, southern Ohio, Indiana, and Illinois, Missouri, and Oklahoma south to Florida, Georgia, Alabama, Mississippi, Louisiana, and Texas.

Cultivated in moist potting mix or in acidic to circumneutral garden soil in partial sun.

236   Polypodium thyssanolepis A. Braun ex Klotzsch
Scaly Polypody

Rhizomes long-creeping, 2–3.5 mm in diam., phyllopodia obscure; rhizome scales lanceolate, up to ca. 4 mm long, 0.75 mm wide, weakly bicolorous, the central stripe brown, the margins pale brown, erose-toothed. Stipes 0.5–1.5 cm distant, 2–15(25) cm long, not alate, densely scaly, the scales deciduous in age. Laminae monomorphic, triangular to nearly lanceate, 3–10(25) cm long, 2–5(12) cm wide, pinnatisect, truncate to obtuse at the base, acute at the apex, the adaxial surface glabrous, the abaxial surface with broadly lanceolate, peltate, erose-toothed, reddish-brown scales, the sori round in 1(2) rows on each side of the midrib.

Epipetric on cliffs or rocky slopes. Very rare. Western Texas and southeastern Arizona.

Cultivated in moist potting mix or in acidic garden soil in partial sun.

237   Polypodium ptilodon var. caespitosum (Jenm.) A. M. Evans
Comb Polypody

Rhizomes short-creeping, 5–8 mm in diam., the phyllopodia 1–3 mm long; rhizome scales linear-lanceate, ca. 2 mm long, 0.25 mm wide, concolorous, blackish, strongly clathrate with long, irregular cells, entire. Stipes 3–15 cm long, dark reddish-brown. Rachis scales few, linear. Laminae narrowly ovate to linear-ovate, 27–90 cm long, 6.5–18 cm wide, deeply pinnatifid, cuneate at the base, acute to cuneate at the apex, the segments 4–8 mm wide, the basal ones gradually reduced to lobes or auricles, the veins 2–3(4)-forked, the sori oval.

Terrestrial or sometimes epipetric. Peninsular Florida.

Cultivated in moist potting soil in partial sun.

238   Polypodium plumula Humb. & Bonpl. ex Willd.
Plumy Polypody

Rhizomes short-creeping, 3–6 mm in diam., the phyllopodia 1 mm long; scales linear-lanceate, ca. 3 mm long, 0.4 mm wide, concolorous, brown, weakly clathrate with long, irregular cells, regularly toothed along the margin. Stipes 5–15 cm long, black. Rachis scales lanceolate with a caudate base. Laminae narrowly elliptic to linear-elliptic, 15–52 cm long, 3–7.5 cm wide, acute to cuneate at the base and apex, the segments 1.5–2.5 cm wide, the basal ones abruptly reduced to auricles, the veins 1-forked, the sori round.

Epiphytic or occasionally epipetric. Frequent. Peninsular Florida.

Not cultivated.

239   Polypodium dispersum A. M. Evans
Widespread Polypody

Rhizomes ascending, erect or sometimes short-creeping, 4–7 mm in diam., the phyllopodia 2–3 mm long; rhizome scales linear-lanceate, ca. 3 mm long, 0.5 mm wide, concolorous, dark brown, clathrate with long, irregular cells, irregularly toothed along the margin or entire. Stipes 5–21 cm long, black. Rachis scales narrowly lanceolate with a hastate base. Laminae narrowly ovate to narrowly lanceate, 17–48 cm long, 4.5–9 cm wide, slightly reduced and truncate at the base, acute at the apex, the segments 3–5(6.5) mm wide, the basal ones often reflexed but not reduced to auricles, the veins (1)2-forked, the sori round or oval.

Epipetric on limestone rock, or occasionally epiphytic on tree trunks. Frequent. Peninsular Florida.

Not cultivated. Evans (1968, 1969, pp. 203–208) has demonstrated the distinctness of this species, which formerly was confused with *P. plumula* and *P. ptilodon* var. *caespitosum*.

240   Polypodium virginianum L.
Rock Polypody

Rhizomes long-creeping, 2–4 mm in diam., the phyllopodia less than 0.5 mm long; rhizome scales broadly lanceolate, 2–4 mm long, 0.5—1.5 mm wide, concolorous or weakly bicolorous, the central stripe brown, the margins pale brown, erose-toothed. Stipes 0.5–1.5 cm distant, 4–17 cm long, not alate. Laminae lanceate to nearly oblong, 5–25 cm long, (1.5)2–5.5(7) cm wide, pinnatifid, truncate at the base, acute at the apex, the segments 3–5(6.5) mm wide, 3–5 times longer than wide, acute to round at the apex, the young sori round, with abundant, golden, glandular paraphyses like abortive sporangia.

Epipetric on dry rocks, rarely terrestrial or epiphytic. Abundant. Newfoundland to Great Slave Lake and Manitoba south to Georgia, Alabama, Tennessee, Arkansas, Missouri, Iowa, South Dakota, and Minnesota.

Cultivated in moist, subacid potting soil in partial sun. Established with difficulty in woodland gardens. This species is known to have diploid, triploid, and tetraploid phases (Kott & Britton, 1982), which are subtly different morphologically. Diploid plants probably are one of the parents of the European *P. vulgare*. Several casual forms and varieties based on elaborated lamina forms have been described, but now are considered not to merit taxonomic recognition. The best known among these is *P. virginianum* f. *cambricoides* F. W. Gray, with broad, pinnatifid pinnae.

241 Polypodium hesperium Maxon

Western Polypody

Rhizomes long-creeping, 3–4 mm in diam., the phyllopodia 1–2 mm long; rhizome scales broadly lanceolate, 3–6 mm long, 0.5–2 mm wide, concolorous or weakly bicolorous, the central stripe brown, the margins pale brown, subentire to erose. Stipes 2–10(15) cm long, not alate. Laminae lanceate to nearly oblong, 4–13 cm long, 1.5–3.5 cm wide, pinnatifid to pinnatisect, truncate at the base, acute at the apex, the segments 6–9 mm wide, 1.9–3.1 times longer than wide, round to acute at the apex, the young sori oval, with few or no paraphyses like abortive sporangia.

Epipetric on cliff faces and under ledges. Frequent. British Columbia, Montana, and South Dakota south to Oregon, Idaho, Utah, southern California, Arizona, and New Mexico.

Cultivated in moist potting soil in partial sun. This species is the tetraploid hybrid between *P. amorphum* and *P. glycyrrhiza*; see p. 327.

242 Polypdodium amorphum Suksd.

Irregular Polypody

Rhizomes long-creeping, 2.5–3.5 mm in diam., the phyllopodia 1 mm long; rhizome scales lanceolate, 1.5–3 mm long, 0.5–1 mm wide, concolorous or rarely weakly bicolorous, the central stripe brown, the margins pale orangish-brown, erose-toothed. Stipes 2–10 cm long, not alate. Laminae lanceate to nearly oblong, 4–11 cm long, 1.5–2.5 cm wide, pinnatisect, truncate at the base, acute at the apex, the segments 4–7 mm wide, 1.8–3 times longer than wide, round at the apex, the young sori round, commonly with paraphyses like abortive sporangia.

Epipetric in crevices of cliffs and rocks. Rare. British Columbia to California and Arizona. Disjunct in Wyoming and Colorado. Lang (1969) coined the superfluous and illegitimate name *P. montense* Lang for this species.

Not cultivated. This species hybridizes with *P. glycyrrhiza* to form *P. hesperium* (see p. 327). In the past it may have hybridized with *P. virginianum* to form the European *P. vulgare*, but the ranges of these species do not now overlap.

243 Polypodium scouleri Hook. & Grev.

Leather Leaf Polypody

Rhizomes long-creeping, 3–12 mm in diam., pruinose, the phyllopodia 0–1 mm long; rhizome scales lanceolate, 3–12 mm long, 1–1.5 mm wide, concolorous or slightly bicolorous, the central stripe dark reddish-brown, the margins paler reddish-brown, regularly finely toothed. Stipes 6–40 cm long, not alate. Laminae oblong or nearly so, with an apical segment longer than the subtending lateral ones, (5)8–22(28) cm long, (6)8–12 cm wide, pinnatisect, truncate at the base, acute to acuminate at the apex, the segments 10–20 mm wide, round at the apex, the young sori oval, lacking paraphyses.

Epiphytic and epipetric. Frequent. Coastal British Columbia to California.

Cultivated in moist potting soil in partial sun.

*244   Polypodium cambricum L.
Welsh Polypody

Rhizomes long-creeping, ca. 5 mm in diam., the phyllopodia 0–1 mm long; rhizome scales narrowly lanceolate, 2–12 mm long, 0.5–1 mm wide, concolorous, reddish-brown, irregularly toothed. Stipes 3–20 cm long, not alate. Laminae oblong or rarely triangular, 6–13 cm long, 4–7 cm wide, deeply pinnatifid, truncate at the base, acute at the apex, the segments 5–9 mm wide, acute or slightly round at the apex, the young sori oval, with inconspicuous, hair-like, branched paraphyses.

Epipetric on San Clemente Island, Santa Barbara Co., California. Very rare. Introduced with grazing animals from Europe during the 18th and 19th centuries, according to Lloyd and Hohn (1969). The plants are now naturalized.

Cultivated in moist potting mix in partial sun. This species has been known as *P. australe* Fée, a later name which must be displaced according to Nardi (1979).

245   Polypodium glycyrrhiza D. C Eaton
Licorice Fern

Rhizomes long-creeping, 3–5 mm in diam., the phyllopodia 1–2 mm long; rhizome scales lanceolate, 3–8 mm long, 0.5–2.5 mm wide, concolorous or sometimes slightly bicolorous, the central stripe reddish-brown, the margins pale brown, finely toothed, slightly eroding and so appearing entire in age. Stipes 2–18(27) cm long, very narrowly alate. Laminae ovate-lanceolate to nearly oblong, (6)8–23(35) cm long, 2.5–7(12) cm wide, deeply pinnatifid, truncate at the base, acuminate at the apex, the segments 5–11 mm wide, acuminate or sometimes acute at the apex in smaller fronds, the young sori round or slightly oval, lacking paraphyses.

Terrestrial on shaded banks, epiphytic on tree trunks, or occasionally epipetric. Common. Alaska to California along the coast and in the coastal mountains. Disjunct in Gila Co., central Arizona.

Cultivated in moist potting mix in partial sun. This species hybridizes with *P. amorphum* to form *P. hesperium* (see p. 327).

246 Polypodium californicum Kaulf.
California Polypody

Rhizomes long-creeping, (3)5–10 mm in diam., the phyllopodia 1–2 mm long; rhizome scales broadly lanceolate, 3–5 mm long, 1–2 mm wide, concolorous or sometimes slightly bicolorous, the central stripe reddish-brown, the margins pale brown, finely toothed, eroding slightly and becoming entire in age. Stipes 4–20 cm long, sometimes narrowly alate. Laminae ovate-lanceolate to nearly oblong, (6)13–26(40) cm long, (3)6–12(15) cm wide, deeply pinnatifid towards the apex, pinnatisect towards the base, truncate at the base, acute to acuminate at the apex, the segments 6–15 mm wide, round to acute at the apex, the young sori oval, lacking paraphyses.

Epipetric on rock ledges or terrestrial on banks. Common. California.

Not cultivated. Lloyd and Lang (1962) have shown that *P. californicum* var. *kaulfussii* D. C. Eaton is a coriaceous form of the species that intergrades completely with typical *P. californicum*, and so is not worthy of taxonomic recognition.

HYMENOPHYLLACEAE
The Filmy Fern Family

According to the conservative treatment of Morton (1968), there are six genera in the family. Some authors, however, recognize in excess of 30 genera, but these are sometimes ill-defined. Cytological evidence may eventually lead to a more soundly based, revised generic classification of the family. Four of the traditional genera in this family are small and occur only in the southern hemisphere. Only the large genera *Hymenophyllum* and *Trichomanes* (both world-wide largely in warm and tropical regions) are present in the United States.

The plants of this family are small and with few exceptions have laminae only one cell thick between the veins. No other ferns have such thin laminae. The laminae range from simple to several times pinnate. The indusia, which usually are called involucres, are borne at the ends of segments or veins. They consist of two roughly hemispherical halves in *Hymenophyllum* and are tubular or conical in *Trichomanes*. They range from being immersed along their lateral edges in the leaf tissue to short-stalked at the ends of veins protruding from the margin of the lamina.

The Hymenophyllaceae are mostly epiphytic or epipetric, although some tropical species of *Trichomanes* are terrestrial. *Trichomanes* grows mostly in the lowland tropics, with a few species ranging into more temperate areas. Most *Hymenophyllum* species grow in tropical cloud forests, mostly above 500 m altitude. All grow in shady places. Their thin laminae cannot resist desiccation, and so most species are limited to regions that are quite constantly humid or wet. Farrar (1968) has been successful in growing Hymenophyllaceae and other cloud forest species in an artificial greenhouse enclosure utilizing an air-conditioner to control temperature.

Key to the Genera of Hymenophyllaceae
1. Involucres bivalvate; receptacle a low pad, never exserted from between the involucral flaps, *Hymenophyllum*, p. 201
1. Involucres tubular; receptacle bearing the sporangia long, whip-like, often exserted from the mouth of the involucres, *Trichomanes*, p. 202

HYMENOPHYLLUM
The Filmy Ferns

Hymenophyllum is a genus of about 300 species widely distributed in warm and tropical regions. Only two species occur in the United States and Canada. Both occur in very restricted habitats and neither is widely distributed.

The Filmy Ferns are small and sometimes very minute. The rhizomes are wire- or thread-like and very wide-creeping. The fronds are scattered along the rhizomes and have thin stipes, which are at least partially alate in many species. The laminae are pinnate with the pinnae commonly subdichotomously divided into linear segments. The fertile segments bear a terminal sorus. The sporangia are borne on a low mound of tissue and are protected by a pair of involucral lips that may be round, broader than long, or somewhat elongate. Many tropical species bear pale, simple, bifid, or stellate hairs on the axes and margins and sometimes also on the surface of the laminae.

Hymenophyllum grows in warm and tropical areas, most abundantly in mid-altitude cloud forests that are continuously moist and not so hot as the tropical lowlands. The species are difficult to cultivate because of their requirement for moist, moving, not overly hot air. Reports that they can be grown successfully in plastic bags have not been confirmed.

Key to Hymenophyllum
1. Segments and involucres distantly toothed; SC. *247. H. tunbrigense*
1. Segments and involucres entire; AK, BC. *248. H. wrightii*

247 **Hymenophyllum tunbrigense (L.) J. E. Smith**
Tunbridge Filmy Fern
Rhizomes thread-like, very long-creeping, the fronds scattered on the rhizomes but usually appearing matted. Stipes thread-like, 7–20 mm long. Laminae lanceolate, 11–35 mm long, 8–13 mm wide, 2–3-pinnatifid, the rachises entirely alate, the basal pinnae acroscopically and basiscopically branched, the apical pinnae acroscopically branched, the segments

0.5–1 mm wide, mostly emarginate at the apex, distantly toothed, bearing truncate, toothed involucres at the apex of fertile segments.

Epipetric on shaded, moist, granite cliffs and rocks. Very rare. Known in the United States as sporophytes only from Pickens Co., South Carolina, where it has persisted since its discovery in 1935. The unwarranted change of spelling of the epithet to *tunbridgense* was made by J. E. Smith; Linnaeus' original spelling was based on a pre-Linnaean phrase name coined by Petiver.

Not cultivated.

*248 Hymenophyllum wrightii v. d. Bosch
Wright's Filmy Fern

Rhizomes thread-like, very long-creeping, the fronds scattered, but appearing matted. Stipes thread-like, 4–10 mm long. Laminae ovate to lanceolate, 10–25 mm long, 7–13 mm wide, 2–3-pinnate-pinnatifid, the rachises entirely alate, the basal pinnae acroscopically and slightly basiscopically branched, the apical pinnae acroscopically branched, the segments 0.75–1 mm wide, emarginate at the apex, entire, bearing obtuse to round, non-toothed involucres at the apex of fertile segments.

Epiphytic on the bark of old Sitka Spruce trees, terrestrial, or epipetric. Very rare. Coastal Alaska and British Columbia.

Not cultivated. This species produces sporophytes occasionally, but is more widely distributed in North America only as gametophytes, according to Taylor (1967). An alternative name is *Mecodium wrightii* (v. d. Bosch) Copel.

TRICHOMANES
The Bristle Ferns

Trichomanes, if considered in the broad sense, is a genus of about 325 species of world-wide distribution in warm and especially in tropical regions. Two have been found as accidentals in the southeastern United States (Correll, 1939). The common name alludes to the long, bristle-like receptacle, which grows from the base of the involucre as it produces sporangia, and which finally protrudes from the indusium as a short to long bristle.

The Bristle Ferns are usually small to minute plants. A few tropical species have thick, erect rhizomes with a tree-like tuft of fronds at the apex, but most species have wire- or thread-like, long-creeping rhizomes. In such plants, the fronds are scattered along the rhizomes. Commonly the rhizomes branch and cross each other, and so the patch of fronds produced from them is quite dense and matted. The stipes are short and are alate at least at the apex in most species. The laminae are up to 2-

pinnate-pinnatifid with irregular lobes divided into linear segments in subg. *Trichomanes*, but are only pinnatifid or less divided in subg. *Achomanes* and *Didymoglossum*. In subg. *Didymoglossum*, the United States species have black marginal hairs that are mostly bifid or stellate; the other subgenera are glabrous. Fertile segments or laminae bear a terminal sorus. The sporangia are borne on an elongate, bristle-like receptacle and are protected by a conical or tubular involucre that bears a pair of flaring lips in most species.

Trichomanes grows in mostly tropical lowland areas, although a few species extend to merely warm regions. The terrestrial species are perhaps not so difficult to cultivate as the epipetric and epiphytic ones, but conditions of humidity and temperature are likely to be critical, and so very few species are in cultivation.

Key to Trichomanes
1. Laminae up to 2(4) cm long, simple or lobed (pinnatifid in *T. krausii*), with a few, dark, often stellate hairs or paired, pale scales scattered along the margins (subg. *Didymoglossum*), 3

1. Laminae at least (3)4 cm long, pinnatifid or pinnate-pinnatifid, without dark hairs or pale scales along the margins, 2

2(1). Laminae pinnate-pinnatifid or occasionally 2-pinnate-pinnatifid at the base; sori lateral along the sides of the lobes (subg. *Trichomanes*); rhizomes long-creeping, the fronds scattered; involucres not flaring at the mouth, narrowly conical, ca. 3 times longer than wide; SE. 249. *T. boschianum*

2(1). Laminae pinnatifid; sori terminal on the apex of the lobes (subg. *Achomanes*); rhizomes erect, the fronds clustered; involucres flaring at the mouth, broadly conical, ca. 2 times longer than wide; FL. *250. *T. holopterum*

3(1). Laminae more than 1 cm long, pinnatifid, with long, lateral lobes, rhombic to oblanceolate; FL. 251. *T. krausii*

3(1). Laminae less than 1 cm long, with short, irregular lobes or unlobed, circular, oblanceolate, or spathulate, 4

4(3). Sterile laminae essentially lacking a midrib; involucres not immersed in the laminar tissue; veins ca. 0.2 mm distant; FL. 252. *T. punctatum* subsp. *floridanum*

4(3). Sterile laminae with a midrib extending to or nearly to the apex of the lamina; involucres immersed in the laminar tissue; veins ca. 0.5 mm distant; SE. 253. *T. petersii*

249 Trichomanes boschianum Sturm
Appalachian Bristle Fern

Rhizomes delicate, long-creeping, not intertwining, bearing scattered fronds. Stipes 1–5 cm long. Laminae nearly lanceate, slightly if at all narrowed at the base, 2–15 cm long, 1–4 cm wide, pinnate-pinnatifid or rarely 2-pinnate-pinnatifid at the base, the pinnae deeply pinnatifid, the segments deeply divided into linear lobes; involucres terminal on lateral veins at the base of the lobes, conical, ca. 3 times longer than wide, not flaring at the mouth.

Epipetric on moist, usually sandstone cliffs under overhangs or in shallow caves in deep shade. Occasional. Western South Carolina, Georgia, Alabama, and Arkansas north to southern Ohio, Kentucky, and southern Illinois.

Not cultivated.

*250 Trichomanes holopterum Kunze
Entire-winged Bristle Fern

Rhizomes erect, occasionally branched, bearing clustered fronds. Stipes 1–3.5 cm long, with a broad ala at the apex, gradually narrowed toward the base. Laminae lanceate-oblong, slightly narrowed at the base, 1.5–6 cm long, 0.6–2 cm wide, pinnatifid, the segments shallowly and broadly lobed, the involucres terminal on apical veins at the apex of the lobes, broadly conical, ca. 2 times longer than wide, flaring at the mouth.

Epiphytic on cypress stumps and logs in shade. Very rare. Monroe and Collier counties, Florida.

Not cultivated.

251 Trichomanes krausii Hook. & Grev.
Krauss' Bristle Fern

Rhizomes long-creeping and intertwining, bearing scattered fronds, but the fronds appearing matted. Stipes 1–10(17) cm long. Laminae rhombic to oblanceolate, 13–28 mm long, 4–10 mm wide, pinnatifid, the lobes themselves shallowly and irregularly lobed, with stellate or bifid, black hairs scattered along the margin; involucres terminal on the lobes toward the lamina apex, tubular, flaring at the mouth, alate and slightly immersed in the laminar tissue.

Epiphytic on tree trunks and roots, rarely on fallen trees or epipetric in limestone sinks. Frequent. Dade Co., Florida.

Not cultivated.

252 Trichomanes punctatum subsp. floridanum W. Boer

Florida Bristle Fern

Rhizomes long-creeping and intertwining, bearing scattered fronds, but the fronds appearing matted. Stipes 2–8 mm long. Laminae spathulate, oblanceolate, elliptic, nearly circular, or rhombic, sometimes broadly so, 3–13 mm long, 2–9 mm wide, entire to slightly lobed at the apex, with stellate, black hairs scattered along the margin; involucres 1–6, terminal on the lamina, long-conical to somewhat tubular, flaring at the mouth, very slightly alate and only slightly immersed in the laminar tissue.

Epipetric in limestone sinks or occasionally on rocks in hammocks, rarely on the bases of tree trunks. Occasional. Dade and Sumter counties, Florida.

Not cultivated.

253 Trichomanes petersii A. Gray

Dwarf Bristle Fern

Rhizomes long-creeping and intertwining, bearing scattered fronds, but the fronds appearing matted. Stipes 3–7 mm long. Laminae narrowly oblanceolate to elliptical with a cuneate base, 3–9 mm long, 2–5 mm wide, entire, with bifid or a few, simple, black hairs scattered along the margin; involucre usually 1, teminal on the lamina, short-conical, flaring at the mouth, entirely immersed in the laminar tissue.

Epipetric on cliffs and overhanging ledges or sometimes epiphytic on the bases of tree trunks. Occasional. Mountains of North Carolina, South Carolina, and Tennessee, southern Illinois, and Arkansas south to Georgia, Florida, Alabama, Mississippi, and Louisiana.

Not cultivated.

DENNSTAEDTIACEAE
The Bracken Family

There are conservatively 16 genera in this family, most of which are confined to the New World and/or Old World tropics, and three of which extend to the tropical and subtropical regions of the United States. Only the widespread, weedy genus *Pteridium* is found widely in the United States and adjacent Canada.

The plants of this family are medium- to large-sized. Most have long-creeping rhizomes, which are tenacious and deeply buried in *Pteridium*. The rhizomes bear a few to many, multicellular, articulate hairs, rather than scales. According to Troop and Mickel (1968), dormant or active buds are present near the stipe bases of many species of this family. In some, like *Hypolepis*, the rhizomes terminate in an upright stipe base and are continued horizontally through actively elongating buds on the stipe bases. The stipes of the Dennstaedtiaceae roughly equal the laminae and are straw-colored or sometimes pale brown, except for the dark brown bases. The stipes and laminae are glabrous in some genera, but have hairs like those of the rhizome, although the articulations are less conspicuous in *Hypolepis*. The laminae are broadly triangular or ovate; they are papery in most genera, but are leathery in *Pteridium*. The sori are marginal or nearly so. In *Hypolepis*, they lack indusia or more usually are protected slightly by a reflexed lamina lobe or tooth. In most other genera of the family, the indusia are an extrorse flap of laminar tissue, and the sori open toward the margin. In *Dennstaedtia*, this flap and a portion of the lamina margin form a cup-like indusium; in *Sphenomeris*, the flap is more distinct from the margin in shape and texture, and in *Pteridium*, the flap is minute and not usually seen, but the margin forms a rather thin, continuous false indusium resembling that formed in *Pteris* and in some cheilanthoid ferns (Sinopteridaceae).

The Dennstaedtiaceae are predominately terrestrial, but a few species are epipetric. Those with thin laminae tend to grow in shadier and more protected places than the tough plants of *Pteridium*. Most species can be cultivated successfully in garden soil in frost-free regions, although they tend to spread. *Pteridium*, however, is a noxious weed nearly everywhere it grows, and so is seldom cultivated.

Key to the Genera of Dennstaedtiaceae

1. Ultimate segments narrowly wedge-shaped, up to 10 mm long, 2 mm wide; fronds all less than 0.5 m long; rhizomes 1–2 mm in diam., *Sphenomeris*, p. 212

1. Ultimate segments not wedge-shaped, usually larger than 10 mm long, 2 mm wide; fronds usually more than 0.5 m long; rhizomes 2–10 mm in diam., **2**

2(1). Indusia continuous along the lamina margins; laminae broadly triangular, sometimes ternate, leathery, *Pteridium*, p. 209

2(1). Indusia discrete, marginal or submarginal; laminae usually not broadly triangular, rarely if ever ternate, papery, commonly with articulate hairs on the axes, at least when young, **3**

3(2). Indusia cylindrical, globular, or clamshell-like, *Dennstaedtia*, p. 207

3(2). Indusia a reflexed, marginal flap, *Hypolepis*, p. 208

DENNSTAEDTIA
The Cuplet Ferns

Dennstaedtia is a pantropical genus of about 70 species, of which 11 occur in the New World and three are known from the United States, according to Tryon (1960). All are large forest ferns or form thickets. The common name refers to their cup-like indusia.

The Cuplet Ferns have very long, straight or contorted, subterranean rhizomes, which bear copious, small, articulate, pale hairs with short cells and dark, conspicuous transverse walls. The adaxially grooved stipes are scattered along the rhizomes and typically are straw-colored but darker at the base. The stipes, rachises, and axes bear at least a few hairs like those of the rhizome when young. The laminae are large, usually highly dissected, free-veined, and have terminal sori protected by cylindrical, globular, or clamshell-like indusia.

The Cuplet Ferns are all terrestrial. Because of their creeping rhizomes, they tend to form large colonies or even thickets, in the case of *D. bipinnata*. A few species are cultivated in garden beds or as pot plants, but most are too large and weedy for horticultural use.

Key to Dennstaedtia

1. Laminae yellow-green, 30–80 cm long, 9–22 cm wide, mostly 2-pinnate-pinnatifid; E. *254. D. punctilobula*

1. Laminae dark green, commonly more than (1)2 m long, (0.5)0.75 m wide, mostly 3-pinnate-pinnatifid, **2**

2(1). Sori globular, wider than long; laminae rather dull below, the veins flush or slightly prominulous; tertiary segments (divisions of the pinnules) obtuse at the base, broadly round at the apex, ca. 2 times longer than wide; TX. *255. D. globulifera*

2(1). Sori cylindrical, longer than wide; laminae rather shiny below, the veins distinctly prominulous; tertiary segments (divisions of the pinnules) acute at the base, acute or sometimes round at the apex, ca. 3 times longer than wide; FL. *256. D. bipinnata*

254 Dennstaedtia punctilobula (Michx.) Moore
Hay-scented Fern

Rhizomes very long-creeping, straight, 1.5–2.5 mm in diam. Stipes scattered along the rhizome, 1–4 cm distant, 10–45 cm long. Laminae lanceolate to elliptic-lanceolate, 30–80 cm long, 9–22 cm wide, 2-pinnate-pinnatifid to barely 3-pinnate at the base, truncate at the base, acute at the apex, the pinnae lanceate-oblong, the proximal ones subopposite, the distal ones alternate, the costae with a few articulate hairs, the pinnules obtuse at the base, round at the apex, the indusia globular, whitish, cup-like.

207

Terrestrial or rarely epipetric in full sun or partial shade in acid to strongly acid soil. Common. Newfoundland, Quebec, Ontario, Michigan, Wisconsin, Ohio, southern Indiana, southern Illinois, and southeastern Missouri south to South Carolina, the mountains of Georgia and Alabama, Tennessee, and Arkansas.

Cultivated in moist garden soil in full sun or partial shade, but spreading too rapidly by the creeping rhizomes to be used in most gardens.

255 Dennstaedtia globulifera (Poir.) Hieron.
Beaded Cuplet Fern
Rhizomes long-creeping, contorted, (3)6–15 mm in diam. Stipes scattered along the rhizome, 1–5 cm distant, 30–100 cm long. Laminae deltate, 1–3 m long and wide, 3-pinnate-pinnatifid, truncate at the base, acute at the apex, the pinnae lanceate, the ultimate segments right-angled at the base, round at the apex, the indusia globular, greenish, wider than long.

Terrestrial in deep sink holes. Very rare. Val Verde Co., Texas.

Not cultivated.

256 Dennstaedtia bipinnata (Cav.) Maxon
Bipinnate Cuplet Fern
Rhizomes long-creeping, straight, 5–6 mm in diam. Stipes scattered along the rhizome, 1–5 cm distant, 30–75 cm long. Laminae lanceolate-ovate, 50–150 cm long, 25–100 cm wide, mostly 3-pinnate-pinnatifid, obtuse at the base, acute at the apex, the pinnae oblong-lanceolate, the ultimate segments acute at the base, round at the apex, the indusia cylindrical, greenish, longer than wide.

Terrestrial in deep, muck soil in full shade. Rare. Palm Beach and Seminole counties, Florida.

Cultivated in moist garden soil or potting mix in shade.

HYPOLEPIS
The Bramble Ferns

Hypolepis is a pantropical and subtropical genus of about 45 species, of which some 25 occur in the New World. Only one species, *H. repens*, occurs in the United States, and it is confined to peninsular Florida. This species has rather stiff hairs, but lacks the spines that characterize many of the tropical species and that are responsible for the common name.

The Bramble Ferns have very long, straight, subterranean rhizomes, which bear articulate, pale to dark hairs with short cells and conspicuous transverse walls. Each rhizome terminates in a horizontal stipe that turns erect and bears two buds near the base. Each bud normally produces another rhizome segment or petiolar shoot, as Troop and Mickel (1968) called it. The adaxially grooved stipes are pale reddish-brown, but darker near the base, and bear large, highly dissected laminae. The stipes, rachises, and axes bear few to many hairs like those of the rhizome. The laminae are free-veined, with round, marginal sori slightly protected by a reflexed, slightly modified, sometimes toothed or fimbriate segment lobe, which forms an indusial flap.

The Bramble Ferns are all terrestrial. They are easily cultivated in beds or as pot plants, but many species are too large for small gardens and greenhouses.

257 Hypolepis repens (L.) Presl
Creeping Bramble Fern

Rhizomes very long-creeping, 2.5–4 mm in diam., with articulated hairs. Stipes scattered, usually producing two rhizomes from buds near the base, 20–60 cm long. Laminae lanceolate to deltate, 25–100 cm long, 12–60 cm wide, to 4-pinnate-pinnatifid, obtuse at the base, acute at the apex, the pinnae lanceate, the ultimate segments broadly attached at the base, round at the apex, the indusia pale, irregularly toothed, reflexed, and marginal.

Terrestrial in subacid to circumneutral soil in full shade. Occasional. Central peninsular Florida.

Readily cultivated in moist garden soil or potting mix in partial sun.

PTERIDIUM
The Brackens

Pteridium is a world-wide genus in tropical and temperate regions. Both the Latin and the common name are diminutives and mean a small *Pteris* or little Brake.

The Brackens have very long, usually straight, subterranean rhizomes with small, articulate, pale to dark hairs with short cells and conspicuous transverse walls. The stipes are shallowly to deeply grooved on the adaxial side and are scattered alternately along the rhizome. Hairs with conspicuous transverse walls are not found on the laminae, but are confined to the rhizomes and stipe bases. The laminae are small to large, free-veined, with marginal sori protected by a continuous, small, inconspicuous inner indusium arising from the surface of the lamina plus a continuous, larger, conspicuous outer indusium formed at the margin of the lamina.

The Brackens are all terrestrial and tend to form thickets in full sun. They are easily cultivated in garden beds, but are too aggressive for most horticultural use. The genus was monographed by R. M. Tryon (1941).

Key to Pteridium

1. Laminae stiff and wiry; fertile ultimate segments only decurrent or more decurrent than surcurrent, mostly 1–2.5 mm wide; hairs on the abaxial surface of the axes and laminae straight and stiff; FL. *258*. *P. caudatum*

1. Laminae papery to leathery; fertile ultimate segments adnate or equally decurrent and surcurrent, mostly 2.5–6 mm wide; hairs on the abaxial surface of the laminae twisted and flexible, **2**

2(1). Pinnules at nearly a 90° angle to the pinna costa; indusia pilose on the margin and often on the surface; W. *259*. *P. aquilinum* var. *pubescens*

2(1). Pinnules at a 45–60° angle to the pinna costa; indusia glabrous, **3**

3(2). Terminal segments of the pinnules 2–4 times longer than wide, mostly 5–8 mm wide; segment margins and abaxial surface of the lamina axes villous; E, C. *260*. *P. aquilinum* var. *latiusculum*

3(2). Terminal segments of the pinnules ca. 6–15 times longer than wide, mostly 2–4.5 mm wide; segment margins and abaxial surface of the lamina axes sparsely pilose to glabrous; E. *261*. *P. aquilinum* var. *pseudocaudatum*

258 Pteridium caudatum (L.) Maxon
Lacy Bracken

Stipes scattered along the creeping rhizomes, 20–75 cm long. Laminae broadly ovate to triangular, 30–100(500) cm long, 20–80(100) cm wide, 2- or 3-pinnate-pinnatifid, obtuse at the base, acute at the apex, the pinnae narrowly to broadly triangular, the terminal segment of each pinna ca. 10 times longer than wide, the longer ultimate segments several times their width distant, ca. 1–2.5 mm wide, the abaxial surface of the axes usually densely covered with straight, stiff, subappressed to spreading hairs, the outer indusia entire, not ciliate.

Terrestrial in barren areas, pine woodlands, and at the edges of deciduous woods in strongly acid to circumneutral soil. Occasional. Southern peninsular Florida.

Cultivated in moist to dry garden soil in full sun, but too weedy for most gardens.

259 Pteridium aquilinum var. pubescens Underw.
Western Bracken

Stipes scattered along the creeping rhizomes, 10–100 cm long. Laminae ovate-triangular to subpentagonal, 30–200(ca. 400) cm long, 15–100(ca. 200) cm wide, 3-pinnate to 3-pinnate-pinnatifid, obtuse to subcordate at the base, acute at the apex, the larger pinnae triangular, the smaller ones oblong, the terminal segment of each pinna ca. 4 times longer than wide, the longer ultimate segments less than their width distant, ca. 1.5–5 mm wide, the abaxial surface of the axes usually densely covered with contorted, lax, spreading hairs, the outer indusia entire, but with a few hairs like those of the axes.

Terrestrial in both dry and moist woods and open areas in partial to full sun. Abundant. Alaska to California east to Alberta, Montana, Wyoming, Colorado, New Mexico, and western Texas. Disjunct in the upper peninsula of Michigan and the corresponding Bruce Peninsula, Ontario.

Cultivated in moist to dry garden soil in partial to full sun.

260   Pteridium aquilinum var. latiusculum (Desv.) Underw.

Eastern Bracken

Stipes scattered along the creeping rhizomes, 15–90 cm long. Laminae broadly triangular to sometimes ovate, 20–80 cm long, 25–50 cm wide, 3-pinnate or 3-pinnate-pinnatifid at the base, obtuse at the base, obtuse below the apex with a short, acute terminal apex, the larger pinnae broadly triangular, the smaller pinnae narrowly triangular or oblong, the terminal segment of each pinna ca. 2–4 times longer than wide, the longer ultimate segments less than their width distant, ca. 3–6 mm wide, the abaxial surface of the axes glabrous or sparsely pilose, the outer indusia entire or somewhat erose, glabrous.

Terrestrial in barrens, pastures, and open woodlands in moderately to strongly acid soil. Abundant. Newfoundland to Manitoba south to Georgia, Tennessee, Mississippi, Louisiana, Arkansas, Kansas, Colorado, Wyoming, and South Dakota; more common in the northern part of the range than in the southern.

Cultivated in moist to dry garden soil in full sun, but too weedy for most gardens.

261   Pteridium aquilinum var. pseudocaudatum (Clute) Heller

Tailed Bracken

Stipes scattered along the creeping rhizomes, 10–55 cm long. Laminae broadly triangular to sometimes ovate, 20–75 cm long, 20–70 cm wide, 2–3-pinnate-pinnatifid at the base, obtuse at the base, obtuse below the apex, with a short, acute terminal portion, the larger pinnae ovate-lanceolate or triangular, the smaller pinnae oblong with an abruptly narrowed, acuminate apex, the terminal segment of each pinna ca. 6–15 times longer than wide, the longer ultimate segments (0.8)1–2(2.5) times their width distant, ca. (1.5)2.5–5 mm wide; the abaxial surface of the axes sparsely pilose to glabrous, the outer indusia entire to somewhat erose, glabrous.

Terrestrial in barrens and open pine or oak woods in acid, often sandy soil. Abundant. Massachusetts, southern New York, New Jersey, Maryland, Virginia, West Virginia, southern Ohio, southern Michigan, Indiana, Illinois, Missouri, and Oklahoma south to Florida, Alabama, Mississippi, Lousiana, and Texas; more common in the southern part of the range than in the northern.

Cultivated in moist to dry garden soil in full sun.

SPHENOMERIS
The Wedgelet Ferns

Sphenomeris includes 18 species, one in Florida and the Bahamas, two in Colombia, and the others principally in the tropics of the Old World. The common name and Latin name both refer to the small, wedge-shaped lamina segments.

The Wedgelet Ferns have short-creeping, thin rhizomes with blackish, articulate hairs and closely spaced stipes. The fronds are 10–45 cm long, with highly divided laminae bearing small, narrowly wedge-shaped ultimate segments. Each sorus is borne terminally on an ultimate segment; the indusia are extrorse, small, almost round flaps, look much like the lamina margin, and so appear nearly like those of *Hymenophyllum*.

The Wedgelet Ferns are epipetric or terrestrial. They are cultivated occasionally because of the peculiar shape of their segments.

262 Sphenomeris clavata (L.) Maxon
Wedgelet Fern

Rhizomes short-creeping, 1–2 mm in diam., twisted, copiously covered with blackish, articulate hairs. Stipes 1–4 mm distant, 5–20 cm long, straw-colored except brown at the base, shallowly grooved, glabrous. Laminae ovate-lanceolate, 5–25 cm long, 2–10 cm wide, 3–4-pinnate, acute at the base, narrowly acute at the apex, the pinnae conspicuously alternate throughout, the pinnules subdichotomously forked, the ultimate segments narrowly clavate, up to 10 mm long, 2 mm wide, cuneate at the base, truncate at the apex, the sori on a transversely elongate receptacular vein terminating 2–several segment veins, protected by an extrorse, erose indusial flap not much differentiated from the segment margin.

Epipetric on limestone ledges, cliffs, and sinks, in circumneutral soil. Rare. Dade and Monroe counties, southern peninsular Florida.

Cultivated in moist, basic potting mix in partial shade.

THELYPTERIDACEAE
Marsh Fern Family

The family contains, conservatively, a single genus, *Thelypteris*. Although Holttum (1971) has proposed a logical system of 23 genera of Thelypteridaceae for the Old World (some of which also occur in the New World), it is not possible to extrapolate from Holttum's work to all the New World species. Therefore, the United States species are placed in a single genus and divided, following Holttum (1971) and Morton (1963), into informal groups, rather than into formal taxonomic units like subgenera and sections. Several subgenera of *Thelypteris* in the broad sense have been monographed by A. R. Smith (1971, 1974b, 1980b). Additional research should eventually result in a unified, world-wide system of classification of the family.

The plants of this family mostly are medium- to large-sized. The rhizomes are generally short- to long-creeping and bear approximate to distant fronds, but are erect in a few species, or even trunk-like and so bear a terminal tuft of fronds. The stipes are typically straw-colored with a dark base, and in species with creeping rhizomes the stipes are often curved at the base because of their lateral attachment to the rhizome. The laminae of most species are pinnate-pinnatifid, but in the *Macrothelypteris* group they are 2-pinnate-pinnatifid and in the *Meniscium* group they are simply pinnate. Most species are hairy, at least on the axes of the abaxial surface, and a few species are also scaly on the costae and/or rachis. Except for the *Meniscium* and *Stegnogramma* groups, which have elongate, exindusiate sori, the other species have round and mostly indusiate sori. The sori are always dorsal on the abaxial surface of the laminae. The indusia, when they are present, are reniform rather than peltate, for they have a small and sometimes inconspicuous sinus. In many species, the indusia are pilose or pilosulous.

The species are terrestrial for the most part, with a few epipetric. They are well distributed in moist to wet habitats throughout the United States and Canada, with the subtropical areas having the greatest diversity and number of species. For the most part, they are tolerant of a variety of soil, light, and moisture conditions, and several species are weedy, both in nature and in cultivation. The spores of some species germinate readily on greenhouse soils, and so the plants are weeds in many greenhouses.

Because of their aggressive nature, few species of Thelypteridaceae are cultivated except in greenhouses, although the native species of the northeastern United States are suitable for woodland gardens.

Key to Thelypteris
1. Pinna midrib with an adaxial groove, **4**
1. Pinna midrib lacking an adaxial groove, **2**

2(1). Laminae 2-pinnate-pinnatifid, (30)40–100 cm long, bearing scattered, simple, thin, straight hairs 0.5–1.5 mm long on the abaxial surface; pinnae short-stalked; sori medial (*Macrothelypteris* group); SE. 263. *T. torresiana*

2(1). Laminae pinnate-pinnatifid or bipinnatifid, 7–25(30) cm long, bearing scattered, simple, acicular, straight hairs 0.1–1 mm long on the abaxial surface; pinnae mostly expanded at the base and adnate to the rachis; sori marginal or nearly so (*Phegopteris* group), 3

3(2). Basal pinnae not surcurrent; laminae mostly longer than wide; costae and costules bearing tan to brown, lanceate scales and acicular hairs 0.5–1 mm long on the abaxial surface; NE. *264. T. phegopteris*

3(2). Basal pinnae surcurrent; laminae mostly wider than long; costae and costules bearing white to pale tan, narrowly lanceate scales and acicular hairs 0.1–0.25 mm long on the abaxial surface; E. *265. T. hexagonoptera*

4(1). Sori usually round (elongate in *T. pilosa* var. *alabamensis*); pinnae pinnatifid or lobed, rarely entire or nearly so, **6**

4(1). Sori elongate on transverse veins between the main veins; pinnae entire, undulate, or serrate (*Meniscium* group), **5**

5(4). Pinna margins irregularly undulate throughout; rhizomes bearing reddish-brown scales at the apex; FL. *266. T. reticulata*

5(4). Pinna margins hooked-serrate, especially towards the pinna apex; rhizomes with few or no scales at the apex; FL. *267. T. serrata*

6(4). Hairs of the rhizome scales and stipes all simple or absent, **9**

6(4). Hairs of the rhizome scales and stipes all or at least some of them minute, stalked, and stellate (*Goniopteris* group), **7**

7(6). Laminae mostly more than 10 cm wide, abruptly narrowed to a nearly conform apex, the apical pinna similar to the lateral ones; FL. *268. T. tetragona*

7(6). Laminae mostly less than 8 cm wide, very gradually narrowed to a pinnatifid apex, the apex not similar to the lateral pinnae, **8**

8(7). Pinnae entire or with low, round lobes; rhizomes short-creeping to ascending; lamina hairs minute, stalked, stellate mixed with long, simple hairs; laminae usually drooping or pendent, stoloniferous, and producing bulblets on the rachis; FL. *269 T. reptans*

8(7). Pinnae with rather pointed lobes; rhizomes erect; lamina hairs all minute, subsessile, stellate; laminae erect, not rooting at the apex or producing bulblets; FL. *270. T. sclerophylla*

9(6). Sori elongate, exindusiate; pinnae crenate or crenately lobed, long- pilose (*Stegnogramma* group); AL. *271. T. pilosa* var. *alabamensis*

9(6). Sori round, indusiate; pinnae pinnatifid (sometimes crenately lobed in *T. totta*), **10**

10(9). Rhizomes erect, forming a small trunk in age; laminae with spherical, sessile, reddish-brown glands on the abaxial surface (*Amauropelta* group); basal pinnae reduced to mere auricles; FL. **272. T. resinifera*

10(9). Rhizomes short- to long-creeping; laminae eglandular or with yellowish to reddish glands on the abaxial surface, **11**

11(10). Basal veins from adjacent lobes or segments united and producing a long excurrent vein running to the base of the sinus; rhizomes black, very long-creeping; stipes distant, black at the base (*Cyclosorus* group); SE. 273. *T. totta*

11(10). Basal veins free (except uniting to produce a short excurrent vein in *T. dentata* and partially uniting in *T. hispidula* var. *versicolor*); rhizomes usually dark brown (purplish in *T. dentata*), short- to long-creeping; stipes approximate to distant, dark brown at the base, **12**

12(11). Stipes congested at the apex of the short-creeping rhizomes, rather densely covered with ovate to linear scales; rachises sometimes scaly; laminae acute to attenuate at the base (*Oreopteris* group); PN. 274. *T. limbosperma*

12(11). Stipes approximate to distant along the short- to long-creeping rhizomes; rachises not conspicuously scaly; laminae truncate to acute at the base (attenuate in *T. nevadensis* and *noveboracensis*), **13**

13(12). Rhizome scales linear to lanceate, 2–6 mm long, yellowish-brown, reddish-brown, or brown, usually pilosulous, stiff and rather thick (*Christella* group), **17**

13(12). Rhizome scales lanceate to ovate, 1–4 mm long, pale brown to golden, glabrous, flexible and very thin (*Parathelypteris* and *Thelypteris* groups), **14**

14(13). Laminae acute to attenuate at the base, abruptly or rarely gradually tapered, the basal pinnae much smaller than the median ones, **16**

14(13). Laminae truncate to obtuse at the base, not or little tapered, the basal pinnae rarely much smaller than the median ones, **15**

15(14). Veins in sterile lobes forked; fertile lobes strongly underrolled; laminae eglandular abaxially; E, C. 275. *T. palustris* var. *pubescens*

15(14). Veins in sterile lobes simple; fertile lobes plane to slightly underrolled; laminae with minute, sessile, globular, golden to reddish glands abaxially; NE, WI. *276. *T. simulata*

16(14). Costae conspicuously pilose on the abaxial surface, the hairs ca. 1 mm long; laminae eglandular on the abaxial surface; E. 277 *T. noveboracensis*

16(14). Costae glabrous or inconspicuously pilosulous on the abaxial surface, the hairs ca. 0.25 mm long; laminae with small, yellow or orange glands on the abaxial surface; P. 278. *T. nevadensis*

17(13). Basal veins from adjacent pinna segments free or connivent at the sinus between the segments, **19**

17(13). Basal veins from adjacent pinna segments united and producing an excurrent vein which runs to the base of the sinus between the segments, **18**

18(17). Rachises and stipes usually purplish; costae densely pilosuluous on the abaxial surface, the hairs ca. half as long as the costa width; SE. *279. T. dentata*

18(17). Rachises and stipes straw-colored; costae sparsely pilose on the abaxial surface, the hairs ca. as long as the costa width; SE. *280. T. hispidula* var. *versicolor*

19(17). Costae and costules pilosulous on the adaxial surface, the hairs never much longer than the width of the costae, **21**

19(17). Costae and costules pilose or sparsely pilose on the adaxial surface, the hairs much longer than the width of the costae, **20**

20(19). Laminae lanceate, broadest at or very near the base, the basal pinnae not or only slightly shorter than the distal ones; GCP. *281. T. kunthii*

20(19). Laminae lanceolate, broadest above the base, the basal and suprabasal pinnae noticeably shorter than the distal ones; SE. *280. T. hispidula* var. *versicolor*

21(19). Lower pinnae ca. 2.5 cm wide, with 12–15 pairs of veins per segment; FL. *282. T. grandis* var. *grandis*

21(19). Lower pinnae 0.5–2 cm wide, with 5–11 pairs of veins per segment, **22**

22(21). Pinnae usually more than 12 times longer than wide, usually less than 10(13) mm wide; FL. *283. T. augescens*

22(21). Pinnae usually less than 10 times longer than wide, usually more than (10)15 mm wide, **23**

23(22). Basal basiscopic segments of the pinnae at ca. a 45° angle to the rachis; rachises not scaly or the scales few, less than 1 mm long; PS. *284. T. puberula* var. *sonorensis*

23(22). Basal basiscopic segments of the pinnae usually at no more than a 30° angle to the rachis; rachises sparsely scaly, the scales more than 1 mm long, **24**

24(23). Hairs on the abaxial surface of the costae usually as long or a little longer than the width of the costae; SE. **285. T. ovata* var. *ovata*

24(23). Hairs on the abaxial surface of the costae always shorter than the width of the costae; TX. *286. T. ovata* var. *lindheimeri*

263 Thelypteris torresiana (Gaud.) Alston
Mariana Maiden Fern

Rhizomes short-creeping, scaly, the scales brown, large, not clathrate. Stipes approximate, 15–70 cm long, adaxially grooved, straw-colored above the dark brown base, scaly at the base. Laminae lanceate, 25–100 cm long, 25–65 cm wide, 2-pinnate-bipinnatifid, broadest at or near the base, the pinnules not contracted at the base but sharply and deeply serrate, herbaceous, with whitish, acicular hairs ca. 0.5 mm long on the axes

216

of the adaxial side and scattered, thin, straight hairs 0.5–1.5 mm long on the axes of the abaxial side; sori round, dorsal on the veins, in 1 medial row between the pinnule axis and margin; indusia minute, flap-like, hairy like the axes, not persistent.

Terrestrial along streams or in wet woods or hammocks, often in soil underlain by limestone. Rare. South Carolina to Florida west to Louisiana, Arkansas, and eastern Texas.

Cultivated in moist garden soil in full shade. Leonard (1972) demonstrated the spread of this fern in the United States since it was first known in central Florida during the first third of the 20th century, perhaps as an escape from cultivation. Although native to the Old World tropics, the plant is well naturalized now, both in the southeastern United States and in scattered localities in the New World tropics.

264   Thelypteris phegopteris (L.) Slosson
Narrow Beach Fern

Rhizomes long-creeping, 1–3 mm in diam., scaly, the scales ovate to lanceolate, 3–5 mm long, pale brown, not clathrate. Stipes distant, 8–35 cm long, straw-colored above the brown base, scaly at the base. Laminae narrowly deltate, 6–25 cm long, 4–15 cm wide, pinnate-pinnatifid or bipinnatifid, the lowest pinna pair reflexed, the lobes ascending, round at the apex, herbaceous, with acicular, straight hairs 0.5–1 mm long on the axes and veins of both surfaces and on the margins, and with lanceolate, tan to pale brown scales on the abaxial surface of the costae and costules; sori round, dorsal near the end of a vein, in 1 submarginal row; indusia absent.

Terrestrial in moist, strongly to moderately acid soil or, especially in the southern portion of the range, epipetric in shaded rock crevices. Common. Alaska to Washington and Saskatchewan. Labrador to Ontario south to Pennsylvania, West Virginia, the mountains of Virginia, North Carolina, and Tennessee, northern Ohio, Michigan, Illinois, Wisconsin, and Minnesota.

Cultivated in moist, acid soil or on acid rocks in full shade. According to Mulligan and Cody (1979), this species usually is triploid, but hybridizes with *T. hexagonoptera* at a few localities in Quebec, New Brunswick, and Nova Scotia to form tetraploids that usually have larger and wider laminae with the lowest pinna pair less deflexed than triploid *T. phegopteris*.

265   Thelypteris hexagonoptera (Michx.) Weath.
Broad Beach Fern

Rhizomes long-creeping, 2–3.5 mm in diam., scaly, the scales lanceolate, 3–4 mm long, pale golden brown, not clathrate. Stipes distant, 7–40 cm long, straw-colored or greenish above the brown base, scaly at and above the base. Laminae broadly triangular or triangular-deltate with the lowest pinna pair usually not or not much reflexed, 8–30 cm long and wide, pinnate-pinnatifid or bipinnatifid, the lobes of the pinnae or segments slightly ascending (the larger ones themselves pinnatifid), round at the apex, herbaceous, with acicular, straight hairs 0.1–0.25 mm long mostly on the costae but also the costules and veins of both surfaces and on the margins; sori round, dorsal near the end of a vein, in 1 submarginal row; indusia absent.

Terrestrial in moist, moderately acid soil, usually in full shade. Common. Quebec and Ontario south to Florida, Georgia, Alabama, Louisiana, Texas, Oklahoma, southeastern Kansas, Missouri, Iowa, southeastern Minnesota, and Wisconsin.

Cultivated and rapidly spreading in shady woods gardens.

266 Thelypteris reticulata (L.) Proctor
Lattice-vein Fern

Rhizomes short-creeping, 3–10 mm in diam., the apical scales reddish-brown, not clathrate. Stipes (30)50–100 cm long, longer in fertile than in sterile fronds, pale brown above the brown base, densely tomentose but only sparsely scaly at the base. Laminae lanceolate to elliptic, 30–120 cm long, 20–60 cm wide, pinnate with a conform terminal pinna; pinnae lanceolate or narrowly elliptic- lanceolate, 10–30 cm long, 1.7–5 cm wide, sessile or the lower ones sometimes short-stalked, the margins irregularly undulate throughout, the transverse veins in ca. 10–20 rows between the costa and the margin, the costae and veins strigulose; sori elongate, the sporangia glabrous or occasionally setulose; indusia absent.

Terrestrial in hammocks in subacid, swampy soil in full shade. Very rare. Everglades of southern peninsular Florida.

Not cultivated.

267 Thelypteris serrata (Cav.) Alston
Toothed Lattice-vein Fern

Rhizomes short-creeping, 3–8 mm in diam., with few or no scales at the apex. Stipes ca. 50 cm long, longer in fertile than in sterile fronds, pale brown above the brown base, sparsely tomentose, scarcely scaly at the base. Laminae lanceolate, 50–90 cm long, 15–45 cm wide, pinnate with a conform terminal pinna; pinnae linear-lanceolate, 10–25 cm long, 1–3.5 cm wide, at least the basal ones short-stalked, the margins hooked-serrate, especially towards the pinna apex, the transverse veins in ca. 15–30 rows between the costa and the margin, the costae and veins pilosulous; sori elongate, the sporangia glabrous; indusia absent.

Terrestrial in cypress sloughs and swamps. Very rare. Highlands, Martin, and Palm Beach counties, Florida.

Not cultivated.

268 Thelypteris tetragona (Swartz) Small
Free-tip Star-hair Fern

Rhizomes short-creeping, 2–3 mm in diam., scaly, the scales lanceate, 3–4 mm long, dark reddish-brown, rather densely covered with pale, stellate hairs. Stipes approximate, (6)10–40 cm long, straw-colored above the brown base, with minute, short-armed, stellate hairs, especially in the adaxial groove. Laminae oblong to broadly lanceolate, 15–37 cm long, 10–25 cm wide, pinnate-pinnatifid, the lowest pinna pair often reflexed; lobes somewhat ascending, round at the apex, with stiff, acicular hairs up to 0.25 mm long especially on the abaxial axes and veins; sori round, inframedial, the sporangia with a few, short, acicular hairs; indusia absent.

Terrestrial in wet, circumneutral soil. Rare. Hernando to Marion counties, Florida.

Cultivated in moist garden soil or potting mix in partial sun.

269 Thelypteris reptans (Gmel.) Morton
Creeping Star-hair Fern

Rhizomes short-creeping to ascending, 2–3 mm in diam., scaly, the scales lanceate, 2–3 mm long, dark reddish-brown, rather densely covered with pale, stellate hairs. Stipes approximate, 2–35 cm long, greenish above the pale brown base, with minute, stellate hairs, especially in the adaxial groove, and a few, long, acicular hairs. Laminae decumbent or pendent, narrowly elliptic-lanceolate, 3–32 cm long, 1–6.5 cm wide, pinnate, gradually tapered and often proliferous along the flagelliform apex, truncate or abruptly tapered at the base; pinnae entire or with broad, shallow, round lobes, with stiff, acicular hairs up to ca. 0.5 mm long on especially the abaxial axes and veins and a few, small, stellate hairs on the axes, veins, and lamina tissue; sori round, slightly inframedial, the sporangia glabrous; indusia rudimentary, long-pilose.

Epipetric on the walls of limestone sinks. Occasional. Peninsular Florida.

Cultivated in moist garden soil or potting mix in partial sun. Suitable for subtropical rock gardens.

270 Thelypteris sclerophylla (Kunze in Spreng.) Morton
Stiff Star-hair Fern

Rhizomes erect, ca. 5–8 mm in diam., densely scaly, the scales lanceate, 5–10 mm long, dark brown to purplish-black, sparsely covered with pale, stellate hairs. Stipes approximate, 5–14 cm long, straw-colored above the dark reddish-brown base, with minute, evenly distributed, stellate hairs. Laminae narrowly rhombic, 15–40 cm long, 4–9.5 cm wide, pinnate, gradually tapered at the apex and base; pinnae with broad, shallow, ascending, rather pointed lobes, with many, minute, stellate hairs on the axes, veins, and lamina tissue; sori round, medial, the sporangia glabrous; indusia rudimentary, bearing stellate hairs.

Terrestrial in limestone hammocks. Very rare. Dade Co., Florida.

Not cultivated.

271   Thelypteris pilosa var. alabamensis Crawford
Alabama Streak-sorus Fern

Rhizomes short-creeping, 1.5–2.5 mm in diam., scaly, the scales lanceate, dark reddish-brown, slightly contorted, bearing a few, acicular hairs. Stipes approximate, 1.5–7.5 cm long, straw-colored above the dark brown base, pilose with acicular hairs. Laminae narrowly elliptic-lanceolate, 3.5–15 cm long, 1.3–3.3 cm wide, pinnate, usually slightly narrowed and truncate at the base, gradually narrowed to an acute, pinnatifid apex; pinnae entire, crenate, or rarely crenately lobed, with many, acicular hairs on the axes, veins, and lamina tissue; sori elongate, somewhat irregular, the sporangia with acicular hairs; indusia absent.

Epipetric on sandstone cliffs in river gorges. Very rare. Known in the United States only from northwestern Alabama.

Not cultivated. Short and Freeman (1978) reported the rediscovery of this fern in Alabama some years after the original locality had been obliterated.

*272   Thelypteris resinifera (Desv.) Proctor
Glandular Maiden Fern

Rhizomes erect and forming a small trunk in age, (3)5–12 mm in diam., clothed with old, adherent stipe bases, mostly scaly at the apex, the scales 3–7 mm long, lanceate, pale yellowish-brown, thin. Stipes congested, 7–15 cm long, straw-colored above the dark reddish-brown base, pilosulous and with scales like those of the rhizome near the base. Laminae rhombic, 45–80 cm long, (10)15–25 cm wide, pinnate-pinnatifid, attenuate at the base with the lowest pinnae reduced to auricles, evenly narrowed to an acute, pinnatifid apex; pinnae deeply pinnatifid, ascending, the segments strongly ascending at an angle of ca. 45°, often somewhat falcate, pilose on especially the axes of the abaxial surface, and with scattered, sessile, spherical, brownish or reddish glands on the abaxial surface of the lamina; sori round, the sporangia mostly glabrous; indusia erose, sparsely pilose and glandular.

Terrestrial in damp woods and swamps in subacid soil. Rare. Central peninsular Florida.

Cultivated in moist garden soil or potting mix in partial shade.

273 Thelypteris totta (Thunb.) Schelpe

Hottentot Fern

Rhizomes very long-creeping, 3–5 mm in diam., scaly only at the apex, the scales lanceolate from a cordate base, blackish. Stipes 3–6 cm distant, 25–80(105) cm long, straw-colored above the black lower portion and base, glabrous. Laminae lanceolate, 30–95(125) cm long, 15–30(50) cm wide, pinnate-pinnatifid, obtuse at the base, abruptly narrowed to a pinnatifid apex; pinnae with ascending, rather triangular lobes, glabrous or with acicular hairs on the axes, veins, and lamina tissue, mostly on the abaxial side; sori round, the sporangia glabrous; indusia absent.

Terrestrial in roadside ditches, swamps, riverbanks, and wet woods. Occasional. Southern and central peninsular Florida.

Not cultivated because of its weediness. This species is part of a pantropical complex that needs cytological and morphological study. The New World specimens seem more like the South African ones than like specimens from India, and there appear to be chromosome differences as well between the Indian and other specimens. Therefore, it is perhaps best to adopt the oldest non-Indian epithet for American material, which is *totta* (based on material from South Africa), rather than to use the name *T. interrupta* (Willd.) Iwatsuki, which applies with certainty only to Indian material.

274 Thelypteris limbosperma (All.) H. P. Fuchs

Mountain Fern

Rhizomes short-creeping, 5–10 mm in diam., clothed with old, adherent stipe bases, scaly at the apex, the scales 5–8 mm long, lanceate, pale brown, thin. Stipes congested, especially thick at the base, 5–15 cm long, straw-colored above the dark brown base, with ovate-lanceolate to linear-lanceolate scales like those of the rhizome. Laminae rhombic, (25)45–65 cm long, (6)8–16(20) cm wide, pinnate-pinnatifid, acute to attenuate at the base with the lowest pinnae reduced to auricles, evenly tapered to an acute, pinnatifid apex; pinnae pinnatifid, slightly falcate or ascending, the segments slightly ascending and sometimes slightly falcate, scaly on the abaxial surface of the rachis and slightly so on the abaxial surface of the costae, with narrow to linear scales like those of the stipes; sori round; indusia minute, erose-ciliate, deciduous.

Terrestrial in open, rocky woods and subalpine meadows in acid soil. Rare. Coastal Alaska, British Columbia, and Washington. Disjunct at one locality in Newfoundland, according to Bouchard and Hay (1976).

Not cultivated.

275 Thelypteris palustris var. pubescens (Laws.) Fern.

Marsh Fern

Rhizomes long-creeping, 1–2 mm in diam., with the fronds distant for several cm, then closely spaced, scaly mostly at the apex, the scales 2–4 mm long, broadly ovate-lanceate, pale brown, thin. Stipes approximate to distant, 9–45 cm long, straw-colored above the dark brown base, glabrous or with a very few, scattered scales like those of the rhizome. Laminae oblong-lanceolate, 10–40(50) cm long, 5–15(20) cm wide, pinnate-pinnatifid, usually the fertile laminae somewhat longer and narrower than the sterile ones, slightly tapered and obtuse to truncate at the base or the basal pinnules slightly reflexed, evenly tapered to an acute, pinnatifid apex; pinnae deeply pinnatifid to pinnatisect, very sparsely to sparsely pilose on the axes, and sometimes with small scales like those of the rhizome on the abaxial surface of the costae; sori round; indusia pilose.

Terrestrial in marshes, swamps, meadows, riverbanks, lake shores, roadside ditches, and wet woods. Abundant. Newfoundland to Florida west to Manitoba, the Dakotas, Nebraska, Kansas, Oklahoma, and Texas.

Cultivated in moist garden soil or potting mix in partial shade, but difficult in the garden because of its aggressively weedy habit. For some years, this species was called *T. thelypteroides* (Michx.) Holub, but A. F. Tryon et al. (1980) have shown that name to be incorrect and based on a mistypification.

*276 Thelypteris simulata (Davenp.) Nieuwl.

Massachusetts Fern

Rhizomes long-creeping, 1.5–2.5 mm in diam., with the fronds distant for several cm, then closely spaced, scaly mostly at the apex, the scales 3–5 mm long, broadly ovate- lanceate, pale brown, thin. Stipes approximate to somewhat distant, 7–40 cm long, straw-colored or greenish above the dark brown base, glabrous except for a very few, scattered scales like those of the rhizome. Laminae oblong, 14–30 cm long, 6–14 cm wide, pinnate-pinnatifid, the fertile laminae usually somewhat longer than the sterile ones, slightly tapered and truncate at the base or the basal pinnae deeply pinnatifid, with a few, acicular hairs on the axes and lamina tissue, especially on the adaxial side, plus scattered, sessile, spherical, reddish glands on the abaxial side; sori round, the sporangia glabrous; indusia slightly erose and glandular.

Terrestrial in bogs and swamps in very acid soil, usually among sphagnum moss. Occasional. Nova Scotia to New York, Pennsylvania, Maryland, Virginia, and probably North Carolina and Tennessee. Disjunct in the driftless area of southwestern Wisconsin.

Not cultivated.

277   Thelypteris noveboracensis (L.) Nieuwl.

New York Fern

Rhizomes long-creeping, 1.5–2.5 mm in diam., with the fronds distant for several cm, then closely spaced and clothed with old, adherent stipe bases, scaly mostly at the apex, the scales 1–3 mm long, lanceolate, pale or golden brown, thin. Stipes 4–30 cm long, straw-colored above the reddish-brown to dark brown base, with a few scales like those of the rhizome. Laminae narrowly rhombic, 15–35(55) cm long, 5.5–14 cm wide, pinnate-pinnatifid, usually rather abruptly tapered and then attenuate at the base with the lowest pinnae reduced to auricles, evenly tapered to an acute-acuminate, pinnatifid apex; pinnae pinnatifid, spreading to slightly ascending, the segments slightly ascending, not falcate, sparsely pilose on the abaxial surface of the rachis, costae, and sometimes the costules and veins; sori round; indusia small, subentire to erose, sometimes deciduous.

Terrestrial in woods and swamps in rich, subacid soil. Abundant. Newfoundland to Ontario, Michigan, and Illinois south to Georgia, Alabama, Mississippi, and Tennessee.

Cultivated in moist garden soil in partial sun. Rather easily grown.

278   Thelypteris nevadensis (Baker) Clute ex Morton

Nevada Marsh Fern

Rhizomes long-creeping, 1.5–3 mm in diam., with the fronds distant or absent for several cm, then closely spaced and clothed with old, adherent stipe bases, scaly mostly at the apex, the scales 3–4 mm long, lanceate, pale brown to reddish-brown, thin. Stipes 2.5–20(35) cm long, straw-colored above the dark, reddish-brown base, with a few scales ca. 2 mm long like those of the rhizome. Laminae rhombic to narrowly rhombic, 15–50(65) cm long, 4–15(18) cm wide, pinnate-pinnatifid, usually evenly tapered to an attenuate base, evenly tapered to an acuminate, pinnatifid apex; pinnae pinnatifid, spreading to slightly ascending or falcate, the segments ascending, lacking hairs or very sparsely pilosulous on the abaxial surface of the costae; sori round; indusia short-ciliate to subentire, usually not deciduous.

Terrestrial in woods, meadows, and on stream banks in moist to wet soil. Occasional. British Columbia to California.

Cultivated in moist to wet garden soil or potting mix in partial sun.

279   Thelypteris dentata (Forsk.) E. P. St. John

Downy Maiden Fern

Rhizomes short-creeping, 3–5 mm in diam., scaly mostly at the apex, the scales ca. 5 mm long, linear-lanceate, yellowish to dark reddish-brown, sparsely pilosulous. Stipes 12–30(35) cm long, usually purplish throughout, with a few scales like those of the rhizome at the base. Laminae rhombic-lanceolate, 25–60(70) cm long, 10–25(28) cm wide, pinnate-pinnatifid, slightly tapered towards the base and then abruptly tapered to 1 or 2 smaller, but not auriculiform, pinna pairs, abruptly tapered to an acuminate, pinnatifid apex; pinnae lobed, spreading or the distal ones ascending, the lobes ascending, pilosulous on both surfaces and all axes, the basal veins of adjacent pinna lobes always joined with an excurrent vein to the sinus; sori round; indusia pilose.

Terrestrial in woods, limestone sinks, along riverbanks, and sometimes in disturbed places in circumneutral soil. Rare. Coastal plain of South Carolina, Georgia, and Florida to Louisiana.

Cultivated in moist garden soil or potting mix in partial sun. Common as a greenhouse weed under benches and in pots.

280 Thelypteris hispidula var. versicolor (R. P. St. John in Small) Lellinger

Hairy Maiden Fern

Rhizomes short-creeping, 2–4 mm in diam., scaly mostly at the apex, the scales 3–4 mm long, linear-lanceate, yellowish-brown to brown, sparsely pilosulous. Stipes (10)15–40 cm long, straw-colored above the brown base, lanceolate, 20–60 cm long, (7)10–27 cm wide, pinnate-pinnatifid, somewhat tapered and truncate at the base, the basal pinnae often reflexed, evenly or abruptly tapered to an acuminate, pinnatifid apex; pinnae pinnatifid, spreading or the distal ones ascending, the lobes ascending, sometimes sparsely pilosulous on the lamina tissue of both surfaces and sparsely pilose on the axes of both surfaces, at least a few, but never all, of the basal veins of adjacent pinna lobes joined with an excurrent vein to the sinus; sori round; indusia pilose.

Terrestrial in moist soil, often weedy in disturbed places. Frequent. South Carolina to Florida and Texas.

Cultivated in moist garden soil or potting mix in partial sun. The fronds of this species are variable in having the basal veins from adjoining segments free, connivent below the sinus, or joined below the sinus with an excurrent veinlet leading to the sinus. In the last case, the excurrent vein is shorter than it is in *T. dentata*.

281 Thelyperis kunthii (Desv.) Morton

Widespread Maiden Fern

Rhizomes long-creeping, 3–5 mm in diam., scaly mostly at the apex, the scales 3–6 mm long, linear-lanceate, yellowish-brown, very sparsely pilosulous mostly along the scale margin. Stipes 10–50 cm long, straw-colored above the reddish-brown base, with a few scales like those of the rhizome at and above the base. Laminae lanceolate, lanceate, or triangular, (15)20–50(70) cm long, (7)12–35 cm side, pinnate-pinnatifid, not or slightly tapered at the truncate base, the basal pinnae not reflexed, evenly to abruptly tapered to a pinnatifid apex; pinnae pinnatifid, spreading to somewhat falcate, occasionally ascending, the lobes ascending, often falcate, pilose on the axes and veins on the abaxial surface and on the axes of the adaxial surface, the basal veins of adjacent pinna lobes free or connivent at the sinus, but never joined below the sinus and producing an excurrent vein; sori round; indusia pilose.

Terrestrial or sometimes epipetric in moist to dry woods, occasionally weedy. Common. South Carolina to Florida west to southeastern Arkansas and eastern Texas. This species has been known as *T. normalis* (C. Chr.) Moxley.

Cultivated in moist garden soil or potting mix in partial sun.

282 Thelypteris grandis A. R. Smith var. grandis
Stately Maiden Fern

Rhizomes long-creeping, 6–8 mm in diam., scaly throughout, the scales 2–3 mm long, lanceate, brown to dark brown, sparsely pilosulous. Stipes 0.9–1.3 m long, straw-colored above the brown base, with a few scales like those of the rhizome at the base. Laminae lanceate, 75–130 cm long, 45–90 cm wide, pinnate-pinnatifid, not or slightly tapered at the obtuse base, evenly or abruptly tapered to a narrow, sometimes subconform, pinnatifid apex; pinnae pinnatifid, ascending, rather straight, the lobes falcate to ascending, pilosulous on the costae and on the abaxial surface of the costules; sori round; indusia finely and sparsely pilosulous.

Terrestrial in wet swamps. Very rare. Recently discovered in Collier Co., Florida.

Not cultivated.

283 Thelypteris augescens (Link) Munz & Johnston
Abrupt-tip Maiden Fern

Rhizomes long-creeping, 2.5–4 mm in diam., scaly throughout, the scales 2–4 mm long, lanceate, brown to dark brown, nearly glabrous. Stipes 20–55 cm long, straw-colored above the dark brown base, with a few scales like those of the rhizome at the base. Laminae oblong, 20–50 cm long, (8)15–25 cm wide, pinnate-pinnatifid, obtuse at the base, very abruptly tapered to a narrow, sometimes subconform pinnatifid apex; pinnae pinnatifid, ascending, straight, the lobes ascending, with a few, lanceate, clathrate, brownish scales, pilosulous on the costae and on the abaxial surface of the costules and veins; sori round; indusia pilose.

Terrestrial or epipetric in neutral soil. Rare. Dade Co., Florida.

Not cultivated. Occasionally this species hybridizes with *T. kunthii* and *T. ovata* var. *ovata* in Florida.

284 Thelypteris puberula var. sonorensis A. R. Smith

Sonoran Maiden Fern

Rhizomes long-creeping, 3–8 mm in diam., scaly throughout, the scales lanceate, 2–4 mm long, mostly dark reddish-brown, sparsely pilosulous along the margin. Stipes 20–30 cm long, straw-colored above the pale brown base, glabrous. Laminae lanceolate or rhombic-lanceolate, 35–65 cm long, 15–35 cm wide, pinnate-pinnatifid, more or less truncate at the base, the basal pinnae reflexed, abruptly tapered to a pinnatifid apex; pinnae pinnatifid, ascending or sometimes the largest ones spreading, straight, the lobes ascending, sparsely and evenly pilosulous throughout, especially on the abaxial side; sori round; indusia small, pilose.

Terrestrial on riverbanks. Rare. Southern California to southern Arizona.

Cultivated in moist garden soil or potting mix in partial sun.

*285 Thelypteris ovata R. P. St. John in Small var. ovata

Ovate Maiden Fern

Rhizomes long-creeping, 4–6 mm in diam., scaly throughout, the scales 2–3 mm long, lanceate, mostly dark reddish-brown, sparsely pilosulous along the margin. Stipes 10–60 cm long, straw-colored above the dark reddish-brown base, scaly towards the base with pale brown scales like those of the rhizome. Laminae ovate-lanceolate to lanceolate-oblong, (15)25–65 cm long, (6)12–30(35) cm wide, pinnate-pinnatifid, obtuse to truncate at the base, the basal pinnae sometimes reflexed, abruptly tapered to a pinnatifid apex; pinnae pinnatifid, spreading to falcate-ascending, the lobes ascending, pilosulous on the costae and especially on the costae and costules of the abaxial surface; sori round; indusia large, pilose.

Terrestrial in circumneutral soil or epipetric on limestone. Occasional. Coastal plain of South Carolina, Georgia, and Alabama to southern Florida.

Not cultivated. Epipetric specimens tend to be much smaller than terrestrial ones.

286 Thelypteris ovata var. lindheimeri (C. Chr.) A. R. Smith

Lindheimer's Maiden Fern

Rhizomes long-creeping, 4–6 mm in diam., sparsely scaly throughout, the scales 2–3 mm long, lanceate, pale to dark brown, sparsely pilosulous along the margin. Stipes 15–60 cm long, straw-colored above the dark reddish-brown to blackish base, scaly towards the base with pale brown scales like those of the rhizome. Laminae ovate-lanceate, (20)30–50 cm long, (10)15–30 cm wide, pinnate-pinnatifid, truncate at the base, the basal pinnae usually only sightly shorter than the supra-basal ones, usually abruptly tapered to a pinnatifid apex; pinnae pinnatifid, spreading or somewhat ascending, the lobes falcate-ascending, pilosulous on the costae and on the costules and veins of the abaxial surface; sori round; indusia large, sparsely pilose.

Terrestrial or occasionally epipetric, often in wet soil along riverbanks. Occasional. Central and southwestern Texas.

Not cultivated.

ASPLENIACEAE
The Spleenwort Family

The Aspleniaceae, used here in the strict sense, includes the very large genus *Asplenium* plus about nine other small genera, of which only *Phyllitis* occurs in the United States. Among the United States species of *Asplenium*, *A. rhizophyllum* is often placed in the segregate genus *Camptosorus*, and hybrids between this species and other species of *Asplenium* are sometimes called *Asplenosorus* to indicate their hybridity. *Asplenium dalhousiae* has been considered to be a *Ceterach*, but this species differs from true *Ceterach*, which is entirely Old World in distribution and has pinnatifid laminae that are densely scaly throughout. The species of Aspleniaceae are distributed world-wide, mostly in tropical and subtropical regions.

The plants of the Spleenwort Family are small to medium-sized. They have short-creeping to erect rhizomes. Their rhizome scales are one cell thick and strongly to weakly clathrate; i.e., the walls joining adjacent cells are thick and usually dark brown to black, but the walls forming the surface of the scale are thin and translucent to transparent, resulting in scales which look like leaded windows. The stipes are brown or reddish-brown throughout or only at the base, and many species have narrowly alate (winged) stipes. The laminae are thin in most species and range from simple to 3-pinnate; a few species have slightly dimorphic fronds, with the fertile ones more erect and usually a little larger or longer than the sterile ones. The sori are always elongate and usually are several to many times longer than wide. They are protected by an oblong to linear, translucent to opaque, usually entire indusium.

The Aspleniaceae are mostly epiphytic in the tropics and epipetric in temperate regions. They thrive in partial sun in moist habitats and are abundant in mid-elevation cloud forests. Many more species are adaptable to greenhouse cultivation than are suitable for rock gardens; among the most popular are the Birds-nest Ferns (*Asplenium nidus* and its allies) and the Mother Ferns (*A. bulbiferum* and its allies). The epiphytic species usually are easy to grow either as epiphytes or as pot plants, especially if atmospheric conditions are not too dry.

Key to the Genera of Aspleniaceae
  1. Sori single along a vein, provided with an elongate indusium, *Asplenium*, p. 229
  1. Sori in pairs along adjacent veins, each provided with an elongate indusium, the indusia facing each other and enclosing the double sorus, *Phyllitis*, p. 228

PHYLLITIS
The Hart's-tongues

Phyllitis, which is by some authors united with *Asplenium*, is a genus of eight mostly tropical and subtropical species found on all continents except South America. The common name refers to the tongue-shaped lamina. Uniting this genus with *Asplenium* can be justified because the two genera are known to hybridize in Europe. On the other hand, the double sori and the lamina shape are amply distinct from all North American species of *Asplenium*, and the horticultural importance of the genus makes it useful to distinguish it from *Asplenium*.

Hart's-tongue plants are small to medium-sized, with erect rhizomes bearing a crown of simple, linear fronds that are subauriculate at the base and acute at the apex. The sori lie medially in closely set pairs, each protected by a single, elongate indusium. The indusia face each other, and so appear to enclose the young sori.

Among the species of *Phyllitis*, only *P. scolopendrium* (L.) Newm. var. *scolopendrium*, the European Hart's-tongue, is easily cultivated. Horticulturally, it is much more vigorous than the American Hart's-tongue, var. *americana*. Several fancy varieties of the European Hart's-tongue with variously cut or deformed laminae are known in cultivation.

287 Phyllitis scolopendrium var. americana Fern.
American Hart's-tongue

Rhizomes erect, 3–5 mm in diam., not branched; scales lanceolate, 3–6 mm long, 1–1.5 mm wide, brown, shiny, weakly clathrate with very narrow adjoining cell walls. Stipes 3–12 cm long, brown to dark brown, not alate, densely covered with narrow, brownish scales like those of the rhizome. Laminae linear, 8–30 cm long, 2–4.5 cm wide, subauriculate at the base, tapering below the apex to an acute apex, the margins entire, the midrib brown on the abaxial surface toward the base of the lamina, straw-colored toward the apex; sori (2)4–18 mm long, 2–4 mm distant from the midrib and the margin, at nearly a right angle to the midrib;

indusia translucent, pale tan to whitish, paired with 1 on each side of a double sorus, commonly hidden by the sporangia at maturity.

Epipetric, in sink holes in the southern part of the range. Very rare. Bruce Peninsula, Ontario, upper peninsula of Michigan, central New York, and eastern Tennessee and northern Alabama.

Cultivated with difficulty on moist to wet limestone rocks in full shade. The few, scattered populations of this poorly reproducing variety are watched anxiously by fern specialists (Faust, 1960; Futyma, 1980). Recently, two new localities have been discovered by cave explorers in sink holes in northern Alabama (Short, 1980).

ASPLENIUM
The Spleenworts

Asplenium is a very large, world-wide genus of approximately 650 mostly tropical and subtropical species. Nearly half of the 35 species and named hybrids native to the United States and Canada belong to the Appalachian Asplenium complex. Another six belong to the *Asplenium verecundum* complex, and two others hybridize to form a third hybrid species. The details of the species complexes are given on pp. 314–318. It is likely that similar complexes are formed in the tropics, e.g., in Hawaii. Only 10 United States species are not known to hybridize; some of these are tropical species found in Florida, and others are from the drier parts of the southwestern United States, where opportunities for hybridization are slight.

The Spleenworts are small to medium-sized ferns. Some of the tropical species and hybrids, including a few from Florida, reproduce vegetatively by root proliferations. Buds produced at intervals on the long, creeping roots form rhizomes and fronds. This results in a mat of genetically identical plants that gives the misleading appearance of propagation by spores and sexual means, even when the plants are hybrids. The rhizomes usually are short-creeping or ascending and bear tufted fronds. The rhizomes scales are conspicuously clathrate. The laminae are mostly glabrous and range from simple to 3-pinnate in the North American species. The temperate species are light to dark green and papery to leathery, whereas the tropical, epiphytic ones are mostly pale green and often are thin in texture. The sori are single, elongate, and follow the straight or slightly curved veins on the abaxial surface of the laminae. The indusia are long, thin, opaque to translucent, and usually are entire.

Most of the North American Spleenworts are epipetric. Some of the tropical members of the genus that have become established in peninsular Florida are epiphytic. A few temperate species may be either epipetric or terrestrial, but when growing on the ground, commonly are associated with rocks.

The tropical species mostly can be grown in pots in greenhouses. Their diversity makes them interesting, more so than the native species. Among the native species, *Asplenium platyneuron* and *A. trichomanes* are relatively easy to grow, and both have some unusual cut varieties that are of interest to woodland and rock gardeners in temperate areas. *Asplenium pinnatifidum* and *A. rhizophyllum* are readily cultivated in terraria. The *Asplenium trichomanes* group was monographed by Maxon (1913, pp. 134–153).

Key to Asplenium

1. Laminae pinnate or more divided, sometimes merely lobed at the apex, **7**

1. Laminae simple, entire or lobed, sometimes pinnate at the base, **2**

2(1). Fronds grass-like, linear, sometimes forked, 3.5–15 cm long; old and young stipes in large numbers, tightly clustered, greenish, dark reddish-brown at the base, W, WV. *288. A. septentrionale*

2(1). Fronds not grass-like; stipes not tightly clustered in large numbers, **3**

3(2). Laminae at least 30 cm long, 6 cm wide, not lobed, attenuate at the base and apex, forming a tall, spreading, vase-like rosette; stipes straw-colored or greenish; FL. *289. A. serratum*

3(2). Laminae up to 20(30) cm long, 5 cm wide, simple or lobed, not attenuate at the base of forming a vase-like rosette; stipes dark reddish-brown or brown, at least at the base, **4**

4(3). Stipes up to 1 cm long, not obvious; laminae elliptic, widest at the middle; AZ. *290. A. dalhousiae*

4(3). Stipes 1–10 cm long, obvious; laminae narrowly lanceate, widest at the base, **5**

5(4). Laminae simple, usually entire except for a pair of basal lobes, with a prolonged apex usually terminated by a rooting, apical bud; E. *308. A. rhizophyllum*

5(4). Laminae lobed to pinnatifid, sometimes pinnate at the base, with an attenuate apex not rooting at the tip, **6**

6(5). Stipes green at the apex; lamina lobes about as long as wide, round or sometimes acute at the apex, uniformly smaller toward the lamina apex; E. *309. A. ×pinnatifidum*

6(5). Stipes dark reddish-brown at the apex, the dark color passing into the rachis; lamina lobes usually much longer than wide, acute to acuminate or sometimes round at the apex, variable in size; E. *307. A. ×ebenoides*

7(1). Laminae 2–3-pinnate, **20**

7(1). Laminae 1-pinnate (rarely 2-pinnate in *A. pumilum*), the pinnae crenate to entire (up to pinnatifid or pinnate in some rare forms of *A. platyneuron*), **8**

8(7). Laminae linear-rhombic, widest at the middle; pinnae 2–4 mm wide, **11**

8(7). Laminae narrowly to broadly triangular, widest at the base; pinnae 5–15 mm wide, **9**

9(8). Pinnae 1–4 pairs; sori in 2 or more series on each side of the costa; laminae usually with a few whitish hairs on the veins of both surfaces; FL. *291. A. pumilum*

9(8). Pinnae (4)5–30 pairs; sori in 1 series on each side of the costa; laminae lacking whitish hairs on the veins of both surfaces, **10**

10(9). Pinnae (4)5–8 pairs, with a low, acroscopic basal lobe or the lobe lacking; indusia translucent, pale tan; FL. *297. A. abscissum*

10(9). Pinnae (7)15–30 pairs, with a prominent, acroscopic basal lobe; indusia opaque, whitish; FL. *292. A. auritum*

11(8). Rachises purplish-black or dark brown; pinnae mostly (2)3–4 times longer than wide (only 1–2 times longer than wide in *A. trichomanes*), **13**

11(8). Rachises green; pinnae rhombic or oblanceolate, 1–2 times longer than wide, crenately lobed, **12**

12(11). Fronds monomorphic; pinnae rhombic, appearing dimidiate, nearly obtuse at the base, the upper and outer margins crenately lobed; rhizomes short-creeping; N. *293. A. trichomanes-ramosum*

12(11). Fronds slightly dimorphic, the shorter, sterile ones forming an arching rosette around the taller, more erect fertile ones; pinnae oblanceolate, symmetrical, acute at the base, the outer, round margin crenately lobed; rhizomes erect; FL. *294. A. trichomanes-dentatum*

13(11). Rachises prolonged, with a proliferous bud at the apex; SWB. *299. A. palmeri*

13(11). Rachises not prolonged nor with an apical bud, **14**

14(13). Fronds slightly dimorphic, the sterile fronds prostrate or arching, much shorter than the erect, fertile fronds; E. *306. A. platyneuron*

14(13). Fronds monomorphic, **15**

15(14). Sori 1(rarely 2 or 3) per pinna, borne along the basiscopic margin; AZ, SC. *300. A. monanthes*

15(14). Sori several per pinna, not confined to the basiscopic margin, **16**

16(15). Pinnae nearly oval, not much longer than wide; rachises thin, flexible, not straight; WIDESPREAD. *305. A. trichomanes*

16(15). Pinnae oblong, usually more than 2 times longer than wide; rachises rather thick, straight, **17**

17(16). Median and apical fertile veins mostly forked; pinnae subentire to crenate; S. *301*. *A. resiliens*

17(16). Median and apical fertile veins usually simple (0–4 forked in *A. ×heteroresiliens*); pinnae shallowly to deeply crenate or crenate-serrate or crenately lobed, **18**

18(17). Stipes and rachises purplish-black to reddish-brown, greatly curved at the base; pinnae deeply crenate to crenately lobed; CA. *297*. *A. vespertinum*

18(17). Stipes and rachises black to purplish-black, almost straight at the base; pinnae shallowly crenate or crenate-serrate to deeply crenate-serrate, **19**

19(18). Pinnae lacking a basiscopic auricle in the basal ⅓ of the lamina, the margins deeply crenate-serrate; laminae herbaceous, the veins visible, yellow- green, somewhat shiny; spores 64 per sporangium; FL. *303*. *A. heterochroum*

19(18). Pinnae with a slight basiscopic auricle in the lower ⅓ of the lamina, the margins shallowly crenate or crenate-serrate; laminae subcoriaceous, the veins not visible, medium green, rather dull; spores 32 per sporangium; FL. *302*. *A. ×heteroresiliens*

20(7). Laminae lanceate or lanceolate, widest at or near the base, obtuse to truncate at the base, **22**

20(7). Laminae narrowly rhombic, widest near the middle, attenuate at the base, **21**

21(20). Stipes reddish-brown at the base, greenish toward the apex; pinnae and often the rachis terminating in a small bud; AZ. *314*. *A. exiguum*

21(20). Stipes gray-brown throughout; buds absent; FL. *295*. *A. verecundum*

22(20). Fronds mostly less than 15(20) cm long; laminae mostly less than 4 cm wide (up to 7(10) cm wide in *A. montanum*); plants of the temperate United States, **25**

22(20). Fronds mostly more than (10)15 cm long; laminae mostly more than 4 cm wide; plants of tropical and subtropical Florida, **23**

23(22). Pinnae attenuate at the apex, inequilateral at the base; sori 2–4 mm long; FL. *292*. *A. auritum*

23(22). Pinnae round or obtuse at the apex, equilateral at the base; sori 1–2 mm long, **24**

24(23). Pinnae ascending, tapering to an acute apex; segment apices mostly subobtuse, not pointed; FL. **296*. *A. ×curtissii*

24(23). Pinnae at a right angle to the rachis, not much tapering, the apex obtuse or round; segment apices acute, slightly pointed; FL. *298*. *A. cristatum*

25(22). Suprabasal pinnae usually stalked 2–5 mm; ultimate segments obovate, often angular; NE. *312. A. ruta-muraria*

25(22). Suprabasal pinnae sessile or stalked up to 2 mm; ultimate segments usually not obovate or angular, **26**

26(25). Laminae shorter than the stipes, usually deltate and no more than 2 times longer than wide; stipes somewhat swollen at the base; SW. *313. A. adiantum-nigrum*

26(25). Laminae longer than the stipes, usually lanceolate and at least 2 times longer than wide; stipes not swollen at the base, **27**

27(26). Reddish-brown color of the stipe extending into the rachis; laminae oblong, almost parallel-sided; E. *311. A. bradleyi*

27(26). Reddish-brown color of the stipe not extending into the rachis; laminae mostly lanceate, not parallel-sided; E. *310. A. montanum*

288 Asplenium septentrionale (L.) Hoffm.
Forked Spleenwort

Rhizomes multicipital, ca. 1 mm in diam., much branched, the fronds very densely clustered; scales linear-lanceate, ca. 3 mm long, 0.5 mm wide. Stipes 2.5–12 cm long, dark reddish-brown at the base, greenish toward the apex, with two abaxial grooves. Laminae linear, 1–3 cm long, 0.75–1.5 mm wide, usually simple, sometimes forked, lacerate with 1–several distant, acicular lobes; sori linear in each groove; indusia thin, translucent, pale tan, entire.

Epiphytic in crevices often in granitic rocks, around boulders, and rarely forming mats on flat rocks. Rare. Southwestern South Dakota, Wyoming, Colorado, western Oklahoma, western Texas, New Mexico, Arizona, and the Sierra Nevada mountains of California to southwestern Oregon. Disjunct on shale in Monroe Co., West Virginia.

Cultivated in moist potting mix in partial sun. This species is known from widely scattered localities. It may well be overlooked because of its grass-like fronds.

289 Asplenium serratum L.
New World Bird's-nest Fern

Rhizomes erect or ascending, 0.5–1.5 cm in diam., rarely branched; scales narrowly lanceolate, 5–10 mm long, 1–1.5 mm wide, grayish, not strongly clathrate. Stipes 1–8 cm long, alate to or nearly to the base. Laminae narrowly rhombic, 40–80 cm long, 6–12 cm wide, simple, acuminate to attenuate at the base, acuminate to acute at the apex, the margins finely serrate; sori confined to the central ½–⅔ of the lamina width; indusia opaque, whitish, entire.

Epiphytic on the base of trees and on fallen logs and stumps. Occasional. Southern peninsular Florida.

290 Asplenium dalhousiae Hooker

Countess Dalhousie's Spleenwort

Rhizomes erect, ca. 2 mm in diam., not branched; scales lanceate, 2–5 mm long, 1 mm wide, black with brown, sparsely short-toothed margins, clathrate. Stipes up to 1 cm long, brown at the base, straw-colored above, not alate, sparsely to densely covered with small scales like those of the rhizome. Laminae oblanceolate, 4–15 cm long, 1.8–5 cm wide, acuminate to attenuate at the base, acute to round at the apex, widest above the middle, pinnatifid, the lobes oblong to triangular, round at the apex; sori 1–8 mm long, in basically 1 somewhat irregular series on the lobes and along the sparsely scaly lamina midrib, slightly sunk in the thick lamina tissue; indusia thin, pale tan, entire, often hidden by the sporangia at maturity.

Terrestrial among and at the bases of rocks. Rare. Southeastern Arizona.

Cultivated in terraria. This species commonly is called *Ceterach dalhousiae* (Hooker) C. Chr. However, the genus *Ceterach*, should be restricted to species with pinnatifid laminae that are densely scaly throughout.

291 Asplenium pumilum Swartz

Dwarf Spleenwort

Rhizomes erect, ca. 1 mm in diam., not branched; scales linear, 1.5–3 mm long, ca. 0.1 mm wide, mostly 1 cell wide, blackish, strongly clathrate. Stipes 1.5–10(13) cm long, narrowly alate in the distal half, purplish-black to brown at the base, green adaxially and brown abaxially toward the apex. Laminae lanceolate, 1.25–5(9) cm long, 1.25–4(5) cm wide, pinnate or rarely 2-pinnate, the pinnae 0.5–2.5 cm wide and long, rhombic to lanceolate, entire to irregularly crenate, often with a few, whitish, several-celled hairs on the veins of both surfaces, the lateral pinnae 1(3) pairs, the larger ones with a basiscopic basal lobe, the apical pinna with 1–several pairs of basal lobes; sori 2–8 mm long in 2 or more irregular series on each lobe; indusia thin, whitish, entire.

Epipetric on calcareous, usually limestone, outcrops and boulders. Rare. Alachua, Citrus, Hernando, and Marion counties, northern peninsular Florida.

Not cultivated.

292 Asplenium auritum Swartz

Auricled Spleenwort

Rhizomes erect, ca. 2 mm in diam., not branched; scales broadly lanceolate, 3–4 mm long, 1 mm wide, brownish, clathrate. Stipes 6–12 cm long, narrowly alate to near the base, purplish-black throughout, except greenish adaxially toward the apex. Laminae linear-lanceate, 6–35 cm long, 3–12 cm wide, 1–2-pinnate, the pinnae lanceolate, with a prominent, acroscopic basal auricle or pinnule, the lateral pinnae (7)15–30 pairs, the apex gradually tapered, pinnatifid, acute to acuminate or caudate; sori 1.5–6 mm long, in 1 series on each pinna or pinnule; indusia opaque, whitish, entire.

Epiphytic on tree trunks and logs in swamps and hammocks. Occasional. Central and southern peninsular Florida.

Cultivated in moist potting mix in partial sun. Both pinnate and 2-pinnate fronds are found on Florida plants. These forms are but a small part of the variation of this aggregate species, which is in need of cytological and chemical study.

293   Asplenium trichomanes-ramosum L.
Green Spleenwort

Rhizomes short-creeping, ca. 1.5 mm in diam., occasionally branched; scales linear, 2–3.5 mm long, 0.25 mm wide, blackish, strongly clathrate with transparent, iridescent lumina. Stipes 1–6 cm long, entirely exalate or with a narrow ala at the apex, reddish-brown at the base, greenish above. Laminae linear-lanceate, 2–8(10) cm long, 0.7–1.2 cm wide, pinnate, the pinnae rhombic (nearly round near the base of the lamina), appearing dimidiate, crenately lobed on the upper and outer edges; sori 0.5–1(1.5) mm long; indusia thin, whitish, entire, often deciduous.

Epipetric in crevices of limestone and other basic rocks and on talus slopes. Frequent. Newfoundland to Alaska south to Vermont, northern New York, northern Michigan, Door Co., Wisconsin, Montana, South Dakota, Wyoming, Colorado, Utah, northeastern Nevada, Oregon, and northern California.

Not cultivated. This species long has been known as A. viride Hudson, but there appears to be no substantial reason why Linnaeus' earlier name, even though it is a compound, should not be used, as are A. adiantum-nigrum and A. ruta-muraria (Lellinger, 1981).

294   Asplenium trichomanes-dentatum L.
Toothed Spleenwort

Rhizomes erect, ca. 1 mm in diam., not branched; scales 1–2 mm long, ca. 0.5 mm wide, blackish, strongly clathrate. Stipes 1–7 cm long, narrowly alate nearly to the base, gray-brown at the base, green at the apex. Laminae slightly dimorphic, the sterile fronds forming a spreading rosette with laminae 2.5–6 cm long, 0.8–1 cm wide, the fertile fronds erect, with laminae 7–15 cm long, 1–1.7 cm wide; laminae nearly linear, truncate to acute at the base, acute to acuminate at the apex, pinnate, the pinnae crenately lobed on the outer edge; sori 1–4 mm long; indusia translucent, whitish, entire, not deciduous.

Epipetric on outcropping rocks and in sinks on limestone. Rare. Broward and Dade counties, southern peninsular Florida.

Not cultivated. As in the case of *A. trichomanes-ramosum*, Linnaeus' compound name should stand in favor of the later name *A. dentatum* L. (Lellinger, 1981). This species hybridizes with *A. verecundum* to form *A. ×biscayneanum* (D. C. Eaton) A. A. Eaton (see p. 315).

295 Asplenium verecundum Chapm. ex Underw.
Modest Spleenwort

Rhizomes erect, ca. 2 mm in diam., not branched; scales narrowly lanceate, 2–3 mm long, ca. 0.3 mm wide, blackish, clathrate. Stipes 1–3 cm long, narrowly alate nearly to the base, gray-brown throughout. Laminae rhombic, (3)6–25 cm long, (1)2.5–5 cm wide, attenuate at the base, acuminate at the apex, 3-pinnate, the pinnae oblong-lanceate, with pinnate, bifid, or simple pinnules, the simple pinnules and ultimate segments mostly oblanceolate, slightly asymmetrical, broadly attached; sori 1–3 mm long; indusia translucent, whitish, slightly erose.

Epipetric in lime sinks and on shaded boulders. Frequent. Peninsular Florida.

Not cultivated. This species hybridizes with *A. abscissum* to form *A. ×curtisii* and with *A. trichomanes-dentatum* to form *A. ×biscayneanum* (D. C. Eaton) A. A. Eaton (see p. 315). The spores of this species, which is a tetraploid, consistently are larger than those of the very similar *A. myriophyllum* (Swartz) Presl from the West Indies, which presumably is a diploid (Lellinger, 1981).

*296 Asplenium ×curtissii Underw.
Curtiss' Spleenwort

Rhizomes erect, ca. 2 mm in diam., not branched; scales lanceate, 1.5–2 mm long, 0.3 mm wide, black with brown margins, clathrate. Stipes (3)4–18 cm long, narrowly alate about half way to the base, gray-brown throughout. Laminae oblong-lanceolate, (9)12–26(32) cm long, (2.5)4–7(8) cm wide, obtuse at the base, narrowly acute at the apex, 2-pinnate-pinnatifid to 3-pinnate, the pinnae oblong, tapering at the apex, with pinnate, bifid, or simple pinnules, the simple pinnules and ultimate segments mostly elliptic, symmetrical, slightly pointed at the apex, broadly attached; sori 1–2 mm long; indusia translucent, whitish, entire.

Epipetric on limestone rocks and in sink holes. Rare. Peninsular Florida.

Not cultivated. This is the apogamous hybrid of *A. abscissum* and *A. verecundum* (see p. 315).

297 Asplenium abscissum Willd.

Cut Spleenwort

Rhizomes erect, ca. 2 mm in diam., not branched; scales lanceate, 2–3.5 mm long, 0.5 mm wide, blackish with a brown margin, clathrate. Stipes (2)5–20 cm long, narrowly alate to near the base, gray-brown throughout on the abaxial side, green adaxially above the base. Laminae lanceolate, 5–18 cm long, 2.5–8 cm wide, pinnate, the pinnae lanceolate, 2–6 cm long, 0.8–1.5 cm wide, often with a low, acroscopic, basal auricle, the lateral pinnae (4)5–8 pairs, the apical pinna pinnatifid, tapering to an acuminate apex; sori 2–7 mm long, in 1 series on each side of the costa; indusia translucent, pale tan, entire.

Epipetric on calcareous rocks or sometimes terrestrial on soils derived from calcareous rocks. Occasional. Peninsular Florida.

Not cultivated. This species hybridizes with *A. verecundum* to form *A. × curtissii* and backcrosses with *A. × curtissii* to form *A. × plenum* E. P. St. John ex Small (see p. 315).

298 Asplenium cristatum Lam.

Hemlock Spleenwort

Rhizomes erect, ca. 3 mm in diam., not branched; scales lanceate, ca. 3 mm long, 0.5 mm wide, black, clathrate. Stipes (3)5–12 cm long, narrowly alate to near the base, gray-brown throughout. Laminae lanceolate, (5)7–16 cm long, (2)4–6 cm wide, obtuse to truncate at the base, narrowly acute at the apex, 2-pinnate-pinnatifid to 3-pinnate, the pinnae oblong, nearly round at the apex, with pinnate, bifid, or simple pinnules, the simple pinnules and ultimate segments elliptic, symmetrical, acute at the apex, broadly attached; sori 1–2 mm long; indusia translucent, whitish, entire, usually hidden by the sporangia at maturity.

Epipetric on limestone boulders and ledges. Rare. Sumter and Citrus counties, peninsular Florida.

Not cultivated.

299 Asplenium palmeri Maxon

Palmer's Spleenwort

Rhizomes erect-ascending, ca. 1.5 mm in diam., probably multicipital; scales linear, ca. 3 mm long, 0.1 mm wide, black with brown margins, clathrate. Stipes 1–3 cm long, very narrowly alate to the base, black throughout. Laminae linear- rhombic, 3–16 cm long, 0.7–1.7 cm wide, attenuate at the base and apex, the rachis fragile, prolonged, terminating in a proliferous bud, the median pinnae oblong, up to 7 mm long, 3 mm wide, crenate on the upper and outer margins; sori ca. 1 mm long; indusia translucent, whitish, entire.

Epipetric or terrestrial near rocks. Rare. Western Texas to southeastern Arizona.

Not cultivated.

300 Asplenium monanthes L.
Single-sorus Spleenwort

Rhizomes erect, ca. 2 mm in diam., not branched; scales linear-lanceolate, ca. 3 mm long, very narrowly alate at the apex, reddish-brown throughout. Laminae linear-rhombic, 7–23 cm long, 0.8–2.3 cm wide, attenuate at the base, acuminate to acute at the apex, pinnate, the median pinnae nearly oblong, tapering a little toward the apex, up to 2.5 mm wide, crenately lobed on the upper and outer margins; sori 1.5–3 mm long, 1(3) per pinna along or near the basiscopic margin of the pinna; indusia translucent, whitish, entire.

Epipetric on cliffs and boulders. Very rare. Huachuca Mountains, Cochise Co., Arizona, Transylvania Co., North Carolina, Oconee Co., South Carolina, and Jackson Co., Alabama.

Not cultivated.

301 Asplenium resiliens Kunze
Black-stemmed Spleenwort

Rhizomes ascending, ca. 2 mm in diam., sometimes multicipital; scales linear-lanceate, 3–5 mm long, 0.05–1 mm wide, black, clathrate. Stipes 1.5–5 cm long, straight and stiff, obscurely alate about half way to the base on each side of the adaxially flattened stipe, purplish-black through-out. Laminae linear-rhombic, 5–22(30) cm long, 1–2.5 cm wide, atten-uate at the base, acute at the apex, pinnate, the median pinnae oblong, usually with a broad, acroscopic auricle, slightly tapering toward the round to subacute apex, up to 4 mm wide, mostly 3–4 times longer than wide, subentire to crenate on the acroscopic, outer, and distal portions of the basiscopic margin; sori ca. 1 mm long; indusia opaque, greenish, en-tire or slightly erose.

Epipetric on limestone or other basic rocks, on cliffs, and in sinkholes. Frequent. Florida to Arizona north to Virginia, southern Pennsylvania, Kentucky, southern Illinois, Missouri, southeastern Kansas, Oklahoma, Texas, New Mexico, southeastern Colorado, Utah, and southern Nevada.

Not cultivated. In Florida this apogamous, 32-spored triploid hybrid-izes with sexual, 64-spored, tetraploid *A. heterochroum* to form penta-ploid *A.* ×*heteroresiliens*.

302   Asplenium × heteroresiliens Wagner

Morzenti's Spleenwort

Rhizomes erect, ca. 2 mm in diam., rarely branched; scales ca. 2 mm long, 0.05–0.1 mm wide, black, clathrate. Stipes 0.5–1.5 cm long, obscurely alate to the base on each side of the slightly adaxially flattened stipe, black to purplish-black throughout. Laminae linear-rhombic, 7–15 cm long, 1.3–2 cm wide, attenuate at the base, acute or acute-caudate at the apex, pinnate, the median pinnae nearly oblong, slightly tapering toward the apex, with a sharp and pronounced acroscopic basal auricle and a very low basiscopic basal auricle 2–3 mm wide, shallowly crenate or crenate-serrate on the margins; sori 1–1.5 mm long; indusia opaque, greenish, entire.

Epipetric on shaded boulders. Rare. Atlantic coastal plain from North Carolina to northern Florida. This is an apogamous, 32-spored hybrid between sexual, tetraploid *A. heterochroum* and apogamous, triploid *A. resiliens*. Detailed studies of the morphology and cytology of the parents and hybrid were made by Morzenti (1966).

Not cultivated.

303   Asplenium heterochroum Kunze

Bicolored Spleenwort

Rhizomes erect or ascending, ca. 1.5 mm in diam., rarely branched; scales linear, ca. 3 mm long, 0.1 mm wide, black, clathrate. Stipes 1–5 cm long, obscurely alate nearly to the base on each side of the adaxially flattened stipe, black to purplish-black throughout. Laminae linear-rhombic, (3)6–25(33) cm long, 1.2–1.8(2.3) cm wide, attenuate at the base, acute or acute-caudate at the apex, pinnate, the median pinnae oblong, up to 4(5) mm wide, deeply crenate-serrate on the margins; sori 1–1.5 mm long; indusia opaque, greenish, slightly erose.

Epipetric on boulders, outcrops, and in sinkholes. Frequent. Northern peninsular Florida.

Not cultivated. This 64-spored, fertile species hybridizes with apogamous *A. resiliens* to form *A. × heteroresiliens*.

304   Asplenium vespertinum Maxon

Western Spleenwort

Rhizomes short-creeping, ca. 2.5 mm in diam., seldom branched, the fronds greatly clustered; scales narrowly lanceate, ca. 3 mm long, 0.25 mm wide, black, with distantly toothed margins, clathrate. Stipes 2–5 cm long, entirely exalate, purplish-black to reddish-brown throughout, greatly curved at the base. Laminae linear-rhombic, 6–14(20) cm long, 1–1.7(2.3) cm wide, somewhat attenuate at the base, acute at the apex, pinnate, the median pinnae nearly oblong, round at the apex, up to 2.5(3) mm wide, deeply crenate to crenately lobed on the upper and outer margins, less lobed on the lower margin; sori 0.5–1 mm long; indusia opaque, greenish, suberose.

Epipetric under overhanging rocks. Rare. Southern California.

Not cultivated.

305   Asplenium trichomanes L.
Maidenhair Spleenwort

Rhizomes short-creeping, ca. 1 mm in diam., much branched or multicipital, the fronds clustered in large groups; scales narrowly lanceate, 2–3 mm long, ca. 0.25 mm wide, black with brown margins, clathrate. Stipes 1–7 cm long, thin and flexible, very narrowly alate nearly to the base on each side of the adaxially flattened stipe, reddish-brown to purplish-black throughout. Laminae linear-rhombic, 3–15 cm long, 0.6–1.3 cm wide, attenuate at the base, narrowly acute at the apex, pinnate, the median pinnae oblong, with a low, acroscopic basal auricle, round at the apex, up to 3 mm wide, crenately lobed on the upper and outer margins; sori ca. 1 mm long; indusia opaque, greenish, suberose to entire.

Epipetric in rock crevices of limestone and usually other basic rocks. Common. Newfoundland, Quebec, Ontario, and Alaska south to Georgia, Alabama, Mississippi, Louisiana, Texas, New Mexico, Arizona, Utah, Idaho, Oregon, and northern California.

Cultivated in moist, basic potting mix in partial sun. Several fancy cultivated varieties are known, which are of more horticultural interest than is wild material. This species hybridizes with *A. ruta-muraria* to form *A. × clermontiae* Syme, with *A. pinnatifidum* to form *A. × herb-wagneri* Taylor & Mohl., and with *A. rhizophyllum* to form *A. × shawneense* (Moran) H. E. Ballard.

306   Asplenium platyneuron (L.) B.S.P.
Ebony Spleenwort

Rhizomes creeping, 1–2.5 mm in diam.; scales lanceate, ca. 3–4 mm long, 0.5 mm wide, black, clathrate. Stipes 1–10 cm long, not alate, reddish-brown throughout. Laminae narrowly linear-rhombic, slightly dimorphic, the sterile ones 4–10 cm long, 1–2.5 cm wide, spreading, the fertile ones 9–50 cm long, 1.5–5(7) cm wide, erect, attenuate at the base, narrowly acute at the apex, pinnate, the median pinnae oblong with an acroscopic basal auricle, 3–12 times longer than wide, usually slightly crenate or finely serrate on the margins; sori 1–2 mm long; indusia translucent, whitish, slightly erose-toothed.

Epipetric on rock ledges, terrestrial in subacid soil, and on masonry and rock walls. Abundant. Quebec, Ontario, southeastern Minnesota, Iowa, and southeastern Colorado south to Florida, Georgia, Alabama, Mississippi, Louisiana, eastern and western Texas, Oklahoma, and northwestern New Mexico. Disjunct in northeastern Arizona.

Cultivated in moist, subacid garden soil in partial sun. Many fancy forms exist in cultivation and in nature that have incised to pinnatifid pinnae. These were described and illustrated by Taylor, Mohlenbrock, and Burton (1976). Plants in the southern states tend to be more serrately incised than do those farther north. Wagner and Johnson (1981) demonstrated that this species is becoming more common in the northern part of its range. This species hybridizes with *A. montanum* to form *A.* × *bradleyi* D. C. Eaton, with *A. pinnatifidum* to form *A.* × *kentuckiense,* with *A. rhizophyllum* to form *A.* × *ebenoides,* and with *A. trichomanes* to form *A.* × *virginianum* Maxon (see p. 314).

307 Asplenium × ebenoides R. R. Scott
Scott's Spleenwort

Rhizomes erect or ascending, ca. 1 mm in diam., rarely branched; scales linear, 2–3 mm long, 0.25–0.5 mm wide, blackish, strongly clathrate. Stipes 1–10 cm long, not alate, purplish-black or reddish-brown throughout, the dark color continuing 1/2–2/3 of the way toward the lamina apex. Laminae irregularly lanceate, 2–15(20) cm long, 1–4(8) cm wide, simple, mostly lobed, truncate at the base, often with basal pinnae, acuminate to attenuate at the apex (juvenile laminae partially lobed, acute at the apex), the lobes mostly much longer than wide, irregular in length, acute to acuminate; sori mostly 1–2 mm long, 1–several on each lobe; indusia thin, whitish, irregularly crenate.

Epipetric on sandstone, conglomerate, and limestone cliffs. Rare. Scattered localities in New Jersey, Pennsylvania, Ohio, Kentucky, southern Illinois, Missouri, south to the mountains of Alabama, Tennessee, and Arkansas. Disjunct in Rutland Co., Vermont.

Cultivated outdoors and in terraria in soil to which rock chips have been added. Except for one fertile, polyploid population in Alabama (Walter et al., 1982), this species is the sterile hybrid of *A. platyneuron* and *A. rhizophyllum* (see p. 314).

308 Asplenium rhizophyllum L.
Walking Fern

Rhizomes erect or ascending, 1–1.5 mm in diam., rarely branched; scales lanceolate from a rather broad base, 2–3 mm long, 0.5–1 mm wide, blackish, strongly clathrate. Stipes 0.5–12(15) cm long, narrowly alate, dark reddish-brown at the base, greenish toward the apex. Laminae narrowly triangular, 2–20(30) cm long, 1–2(5) cm wide, simple and mostly unlobed, usually with round or rarely acute or acuminate lobes at the base, attenuate and rooting at the apex, with a proliferous terminal bud (juvenile laminae round to acute), the margins entire; sori mostly 1–4 mm long, in several irregular series; indusia thin, whitish, entire.

Epipetric on usually limestone rocks and ledges, occasionally epiphytic or on fallen tree trunks. Frequent. Southern Quebec, Ontario, and southeastern Minnesota south to northern Georgia, Alabama, and Mississippi, Tennessee, Arkansas, Oklahoma, eastern Kansas, and Iowa.

Cultivated in moist, basic potting mix or in soil to which chips of limestone rock have been added, in partial sun. Attractive in terraria and bottle gardens. Frequent. This species hybridizes with *A. montanum* to form *A.* ×*pinnatifidum*, with *A. platyneuron* to form *A.* ×*ebenoides*, with *A. ruta-muraria* to form *A.* ×*inexpectatum* (E. L. Braun) Morton, and with *A. trichomanes* to form *A.* ×*shawneense* (Moran) H. E. Ballard (see p. 314).

309 Asplenium pinnatifidum Muhl.

Lobed Spleenwort

Rhizomes short-creeping or ascending, ca. 1 mm in diam., branched; scales linear-lanceate, 3–4 mm long, 0.5 mm wide, blackish, strongly clathrate. Stipes 2–10 cm long, narrowly alate to near the base, dark reddish-brown at the base, greenish toward the apex. Laminae narrowly lanceate, (2)6–20 cm long, (1)1.5–4 cm wide, simple and mostly lobed, sometimes pinnate at the base, truncate at the base with round or sometimes elongate basal lobes or pinnae, lobed in the median portion, acute, acuminate, or even attenuate and occasionally with a proliferous terminal bud (juvenile laminae entire, round to acute at the apex), the lobes ca. as long as wide, round at the apex; sori mostly 1–2 mm long, 1–several on each lobe; indusia thin, whitish, entire.

Epipetric on usually sandstone cliffs and rocks. Frequent. New Jersey, Pennsylvania, Maryland, southern Ohio, Indiana, Illinois, and Missouri south to northern Georgia, Alabama, Mississippi, Arkansas, and eastern Oklahoma.

Cultivated outdoors and in terraria in soil to which chips of sandstone rock have been added. This species arose as a sterile hybrid of *A. montanum* and *A. rhizophyllum*, and occurs both as a sterile hybrid and as a fertile polyploid. The latter, a tetraploid species, hybridizes with several members of the Appalachian Asplenium complex, including with *A.* ×*bradleyi* to form *A.* ×*gravesii* Maxon and with *A. montanum* to form *A.* ×*trudellii* Wherry (see p. 314).

310 Asplenium montanum Willd.

Mountain Spleenwort

Rhizomes short-creeping or ascending, ca. 1 mm in diam., occasionally branched; scales narrowly lanceate, 2–3 mm long, 0.3 mm wide, dark brown, strongly clathrate, entire. Stipes (1)2–9 cm long, not alate, brown or dark brown at the base, green toward the apex. Laminae lanceate, (2.5)3–11 cm long, (1)1.5–7(10) cm wide, 1–2-pinnate-pinnatifid, obtuse to truncate at the base, acute to acuminate at the apex, the pinnae lanceate to oblong, equilateral or nearly so; sori 0.5–1.5 mm long; indusia translucent, pale tan, somewhat erose, often hidden by the sporangia at maturity.

Epipetric in crevices in acid rocks. Common. Massachusetts, Rhode Island, Connecticut, New York, Ohio, and Kentucky south to Georgia and Alabama.

Cultivated outdoors or in terraria in soil to which acidic rock chips have been added. This species hybridizes with many others in the Appalachian Asplenium complex, especially with *A. platyneuron* to form *A.* × *bradleyi* and with *A. rhizophyllum* to form *A. pinnatifidum*. It backcrosses with *A. pinnatifidum* to form *A.* × *trudellii*.

311 Asplenium bradleyi D. C. Eaton
Bradley's Spleenwort

Rhizomes short-creeping or ascending, ca. 1 mm in diam., occasionally branched; scales narrowly lanceate with a filiform apex, 2–4 mm long, ca. 0.25 mm wide, blackish, strongly clathrate, slightly toothed along the margins. Stipes 1.5–10 cm long, not alate, dark reddish-brown throughout. Laminae narrowly oblong or oblong-lanceate, 3–15(20) cm long, 1–4(5) cm wide, pinnate-pinnatifid to 2-pinnate, truncate at the base, acute at the apex, the pinnae ovate-oblong to lanceate, nearly equilateral, often with a slightly enlarged acroscopic basal lobe or pinnule; sori 1–2 mm long; indusia mostly opaque, whitish to pale tan, entire.

Epipetric in crevices of granite, sandstone, or other acid rocks. Rare. Maryland, Pennsylvania, Ohio, Kentucky, southern Illinois, Missouri, and Oklahoma south to Georgia, Alabama, Tennessee, and Arkansas.

Not cultivated. This species arose as a sterile diploid hybrid between *A. montanum* and *A. platyneuron*, but fertile tetraploids have been formed by autopolyploidy which hybridize infrequently with other members of the Appalachian Asplenium complex (see p. 314).

312 Asplenium ruta-muraria L.
Wall-rue

Rhizomes short-creeping, ca. 1.5 mm in diam., branched; scales lanceate with 1–several large teeth near the base, ca. 2 mm long, 0.25 mm wide, black, clathrate. Stipes 1.5–8 cm long, not alate. Laminae ovate, lanceolate, oblanceolate, obtuse to truncate at the base, round to acute at the apex, 2–6 cm long, 1–3.5 cm wide, 2-pinnate to 2-pinnate-pinnatifid, the pinnae angular-ovate, with simple pinnules, the simple pinnae and pinnules mostly angular-ovate, symmetrical, acute at the base, round to acute at the apex, the outer margin often finely serrate, decidedly stalked; sori 1–3 mm long; indusia translucent, whitish to tan, erose-fimbriate.

Epipetric on limestone and calcareous shale. Frequent. Vermont, Ontario, and the upper peninsula of Michigan south to New York, Pennsylvania, Maryland, Ohio, the mountains of Virginia, North Carolina, Tennessee, and northern Alabama, and Missouri.

Cultivated with difficulty in moist, neutral, or subalkaline soil in partial sun. This species hybridizes with *A. trichomanes* to form *A.* × *clermontiae* Syme and with *A. rhizophyllum* to form *A.* × *inexpectatum* (E. L. Braun) Morton.

313   Asplenium adiantum-nigrum L.
Black Spleenwort

Rhizomes short-creeping or ascending, ca. 2 mm in diam., occasionally branched; scales narrowly lanceate with a filiform apex, 2–4 mm long, 0.25 mm wide, blackish, strongly clathrate, short-toothed along the margins. Stipes 2–10 cm long, narrowly alate at the apex, dark reddish-brown at the base, greenish toward the apex, swollen at the very base. Laminae usually deltate, 1–1.5(2) times longer than wide, 3–10 cm long, 3–6 cm wide, 2–3-pinnate, truncate at the base, acute to acuminate at the apex, the pinnae inequilateral, especially the lower ones with an enlarged basiscopic basal pinnule; sori 1–3 mm long; indusia nearly translucent, pale tan, entire.

Epipetric in crevices in cliffs. Very rare. Boulder Co., Colorado, Zion National Park in southwestern Utah, and Coconino Co., Arizona.

Cultivated in moist potting mix in partial sun. This species is widespread in Eurasia and Africa. Whether American material should be considered a distinct variety is still unclear (Maxon, 1912).

314   Asplenium exiguum Bedd.
Little Spleenwort

Rhizomes erect, ca. 2 mm in diam., not branched; scales 2–3 mm long, 0.25 mm wide, black, strongly clathrate. Stipes 1–3 cm long, narrowly alate about half way to the base, dark reddish-brown at the base, brown or sometimes greenish above the base, especially on the adaxial side, sparsely scaly with linear scales like those of the rhizome. Laminae rhombic, (4)6–10 cm long, (1)1.2–2 cm wide, attenuate at the base and apex, 2-pinnate to 2-pinnate-pinnatifid (juveniles sometimes only pinnate-pinnatifid), the apex sometimes bearing a proliferous bud, the pinnae oblong, with pinnate, bifid, or simple pinnules, usually emarginate at the apex with a small, dormant bud; sori 1–1.5 mm long; indusia translucent, whitish, entire.

Terrestrial. Very rare. Sycamore Canyon, Sta. Cruz Co., and the Huachuca Mountains, Cochise Co., Arizona.

Not cultivated. The United States and northern Mexican populations of this species are disjunct from the center of distribution in the Himalaya Mountains of Asia.

WOODSIACEAE
The Cliff Fern Family

The Woodsiaceae, used here to include *Matteuccia, Onoclea, Athyrium, Diplazium, Gymnocarpium, Cystopteris, Woodsia,* and related genera, includes about 660 species in 16 genera. About half the genera, mostly small ones, are exclusively Old World. *Diplazium* (ca. 400 species) and *Athyrium* (ca. 180 species) are the only large genera in the family. Both genera are largely tropical, and *Diplazium* is especially diverse in the New World tropics. Several of the smaller genera are subtropical or temperate, and *Woodsia* is largely circumboreal.

The plants of the Woodsiaceae are mostly small or medium-sized, with some tropical species that are large. They have long-creeping to erect rhizomes, with non-clathrate, pale to brown, lanceolate scales having inconspicuous cell walls. The stipes are typically dark at the base and paler above. Often they are scaly at the base and sometimes also above the base. The laminae are rather thin in most species, and in the temperate species most are pinnate-pinnatifid to 2-pinnate-pinnatifid. The laminae usually are glabrous. *Matteuccia* and *Onoclea* have fully dimorphic fronds; the other genera are entirely monomorphic or have a few species with partially dimorphic fronds. The sori lie along or sometimes also across the veins. *Gymnocarpium, Matteuccia,* and one species of *Athyrium* in the United States and Canada lack indusia; the other genera have flap-like or pocket-like indusia covering the sporangia or cup-like indusia surrounding them, although *Onoclea* appears to be exindusiate and the bead-like segments provide most of the protection for the young sori.

The species of the Cliff Fern family are mostly terrestrial or epipetric, especially in temperate regions. They occur in moist regions or in moist situations like swampy woods, seeps, and wet cliffs in dry regions. Many are useful garden or greenhouse plants. The terrestrial species generally are easier to cultivate than the epipetric ones.

Key to the Genera of Woodsiaceae
   1. Fertile and sterile fronds monomorphic or only slightly dimorphic, **3**
   1. Fertile and sterile fronds strongly dimorphic, the fertile laminae contracted, **2**
   2(1). Laminae gradually narrowed at the base; rachises of sterile laminae not alate; veins free; frond-bearing portions of the rhizomes erect, the fronds forming a vase-shaped rosette, the stipe bases straight, *Matteuccia,* p. 246

2(1). Laminae truncate at the base; rachises of sterile laminae broadly alate toward the apex, narrowly alate or free at the base; veins anastomosing; rhizomes entirely long-creeping, the fronds scattered, the stipe bases curved, *Onoclea*, p. 247

3(1). Laminae ternate or nearly so with 1(2) pairs of pinnate pinnae, the distal pinnae merely pinnatifid, *Gymnocarpium*, p. 254

3(1). Laminae pinnate, with all but the apical pinnae about equally divided, **4**

4(3). Sori round or nearly so; indusia present or absent, **6**

4(3). Sori elongate to linear; indusia flap-like, along a vein, opening laterally, **5**

5(4). Sori all or partially back-to-back, *Diplazium*, p. 252

5(4). Sori never back to back (somewhat hooked over the vein in some species), *Athyrium*, p. 248

6(4). Sori submarginal, exindusiate, *Athyrium* (*alpestre* subsp. *americanum*), p. 250

6(4). Sori medial or nearly so, indusiate (the indusia difficult to see in mature fronds of *Woodsia* and in some of *Cystopteris*), **7**

7(6). Stipes deciduous, not forming a tuft; indusia pocket-like, above the sporangia, *Cystopteris*, p. 255

7(6). Stipes persistent, forming a tuft; indusia cup-like or reduced nearly to long hairs, below the sporangia, *Woodsia*, p. 261

MATTEUCCIA
The Ostrich Ferns

Matteuccia is a small genus native to the temperate parts of the United States, Canada, Europe, and northern Asia. Two species are found in eastern Asia and one in Europe and North America.

The Ostrich Ferns are large. Their rhizomes are dimorphic, with long-creeping, horizontal portions having at intervals stout, erect portions that bear a vase-shaped crown of fronds. The straight stipe bases are persistent and are dark brown to blackish. Above the base, the stipes are bright green or straw-colored, as are the rachises. The sterile laminae are pinnate-pinnatifid and are obtuse at the apex, with a small, acute tip, rather like ostrich feathers in outline. The fertile laminae are linear-oblanceolate, pinnate, and have short, thick, narrow, contracted, brown pinnae.

Ostrich Ferns grow in swamps, river bottoms, and moist, wooded slopes in the northeastern United States and adjacent Canada. This fern was widely used as a foundation planting around houses in the early part of the 20th century, but is less commonly used now.

Fiddleheads of the Ostrich Fern are the most commonly eaten ferns in North America (see p. 38). *Matteuccia* was monographed by Lloyd (1971).

315 Matteuccia struthiopteris var. pensylvanica (Willd.) Morton

Ostrich Fern

Rhizomes erect, 2–9 cm in diam. including the closely spaced, persistent stipe bases clothed with lanceolate, pale brown scales. Fronds strongly dimorphic. Sterile stipes 8–25 cm long, blackish to reddish-brown at the base, bright green adaxially, adaxially grooved. Sterile laminae oblanceolate, 50–150(250) cm long, 15–30(60) cm wide, attenuate at the base, obtuse at the apex, pinnate-pinnatifid, with ca. 30–60 pinnae, the pinnae lanceate-oblong, ascending, 1–20(30) cm long, 1.25–2.5(3) cm wide, with up to 30(40) pairs of ascending lobes and free veins. Fertile stipes 12–30 cm long, dark brown at the base, reddish-brown above, adaxially grooved. Fertile laminae narrowly oblanceolate, 15–35 cm long, 3–7 cm wide, attenuate at the base, obtuse at the apex, pinnate-pinnatifid, the lobes short, the pinnae thick, brown at maturity, underrolled; sori on very long receptacles standing at right angles to the abaxial surface of the fertile segments; indusia none.

Terrestrial in swamps, river bottoms, and moist, wooded slopes. Common. Newfoundland to Alaska south to Maryland, Virginia, West Virginia, Ohio, Indiana, northern Illinois, northern Missouri, Iowa, South Dakota, North Dakota, Saskatchewan, Alberta, and British Columbia. Elsewhere probably persistent or escaped from cultivation.

Easily cultivated in moist garden soil or potting mix in partial shade. The American variety differs from the European *M. struthiopteris* (L.) Tod. var. *struthiopteris* in having concolorous, rather than bicolorous scales with a black central stripe, according to Morton (1950).

ONOCLEA
The Sensitive Ferns

Onoclea is a monotypic genus containing only *O. sensibilis* L. It is found in northern Asia and the United States. The common name refers to the plants sensitivity to frost; its fronds shrivel and turn brown. *Onoclea* was monographed by Lloyd (1971). See *O. sensibilis* for a description and notes.

316 Onoclea sensibilis L.

Sensitive Fern

Rhizomes long-creeping, 2–9 mm in diam., occasionally forked, reddish-brown to brown, with scattered stipes. Fronds strongly dimorphic.

Sterile stipes 10–50 cm long, reddish-brown or brown at the base, straw-colored above; adaxially with 2 grooves. Sterile rachises broadly alate at the apex, the ala narrower to the basal or suprabasal pinna pair. Sterile laminae ovate-lanceate to deltate, 10–50 cm long, 15–45 cm wide, obtuse to truncate at the base, usually obtusely narrowed to an acute tip at the apex, pinnate-pinnatifid at the base, pinnatifid toward the apex, with 5–11(14) pinna pairs or lobes, these 3–18 cm long, 1–5 cm wide, entire, crenate, or with ascending, somewhat acute lobes and veins anastomosing to form elongate, polygonal areolae. Fertile stipes 15–35 cm long, reddish-brown to straw-colored at the base, straw-colored above the base, adaxially flattened. Fertile laminae nearly linear, 8–15 cm long, 1.5–2.5 cm wide, acute at the base, obtuse at the apex, 2-pinnate-pinnatifid, the pinnule lobes round, the pinnae thick, brown at maturity, underrolled; sori on very long receptacles standing at right angles to the abaxial surface of the fertile segments; indusia minute, hidden by the bead-like segments.

Terrestrial in marshes, swamps, damp woodlands, and along river banks in wet, usually subacid soil. Abundant. Labrador to Manitoba south to Florida, Georgia, Alabama, Mississippi, Louisiana, Texas, Colorado, Nebraska, and the Dakotas.

Cultivated in moist garden soil in partial sun, but tends to be weedy because of its long-creeping rhizomes.

ATHYRIUM
The Lady Ferns and Glade Ferns

Athyrium is a large and somewhat confusing genus of about 180 species. Several genera, such as *Lunathyrium* and *Cornopteris*, have been separated from *Athyrium* recently. The Glade Ferns, which are less divided than the Lady Ferns, sometimes are placed in the segregate genus *Allantodia*.

The Lady Ferns and Glade Ferns are medium-sized to large. Their rhizomes are stout and ascending to erect or sometimes creeping. The stipe bases are blackish and adhere persistently to the rhizome. Above the slightly scaly bases, the stipes are straw-colored and have a few scales. The laminae are pinnate or pinnate-pinnatifid in the Glade Ferns and are 2–3-pinnate-pinnatifid in the Lady Ferns, usually are rather pale green, and are deciduous. The sori follow the veins in most species and are protected by a short to long and often hooked indusium.

Athyrium grows in moist to wet places, usually in woods or thickets, or swamps where it receives only partially sun. The various North American species are suitable for the woodland garden, although they will spread fairly rapidly because of their creeping rhizomes. Several cultivated varieties, both of the North American and Eurasiatic species, are known and are better in the garden than wild stock. The North American species of *Athyrium* were monographed by Liew (1972).

Key to Athyrium

1. Pinnae 2–3-pinnate-pinnatifid; sori often 1–3 times longer than wide, **3**

1. Pinnae simple or deeply pinnatifid; sori usually (2)3–5(6) times longer than wide, **2**

2(1). Pinnae simple, shallowly crenate to entire, the veins 1-forked just above the base and the branches themselves forked above their base; stipes sparsely hairy to glabrous; E. *317. A. pycnocarpon*

2(1). Pinnae deeply pinnatifid, crenate-serrate to entire, the veins simple or 1-forked well above the base; stipes with narrowly lanceolate scales; E. *318. A. thelypterioides*

3(1). Laminae narrowly rhombic to nearly linear, 3–6 cm wide, 15–30 cm long; indusia absent; sori round, submarginal; W, QUE. *319. A. alpestre* subsp. *americanum*

3(1). Laminae oblanceolate, rhombic, or lanceolate, (6)10–30(50) cm wide, (18)25–90(110) cm long; indusia present, elongate, not submarginal, **4**

4(3). Indusia short, strongly recurved, sometimes almost circular, bearing marginal hairs as long or longer than the width of the indusium; W. *320. A. filix-femina* subsp. *cyclosorum*

4(3). Indusia long, slightly curved, not circular, bearing marginal hairs shorter than the width of the indusium, **5**

5(4). Stipe base scales lanceolate, medium to dark brown; spores yellow; rachises mostly a little less than 1 mm in diam.; laminae nearly rhombic, broadest well above the base and tapering toward the base; NE. *321. A. filix-femina* subsp. *angustum*

5(4). Stipe base scales linear-lanceolate, pale to medium brown; spores dark brown; rachises mostly a little more than 1 mm in diam.; laminae lanceolate, broadest just above the base; E. *322. A. filix-femina* subsp. *asplenioides*

317 Athyrium pycnocarpon (Spreng.) Tidestr.
Narrow-leaved Glade Fern

Rhizomes creeping, ca. 5 mm in diam., with broadly lanceolate, tan scales, especially at the apex. Stipes mostly 1–2 cm distant, 15–35 cm long, dark reddish brown at the base, straw-colored above the base, with a few scales like those of the rhizome near the base. Laminae oblong-lanceolate, 35–75 cm long, 13–25 cm wide, acute at the base, widest above the base, acute-acuminate at the apex, pinnate, the pinnae linear, truncate at the base, shallowly crenate to entire, acuminate at the apex, the veins forked at or near the base and 0–2 branches again forked above the base; sori elongate, several times longer than wide, nearly straight, not recurved, at ca. a 60° angle to the costae; indusia translucent, brownish, entire.

Terrestrial in swampy thickets and glades in moist, neutral soil. Frequent. Southern Quebec, southern Ontario, and southeastern Minnesota south to Florida, Georgia, Alabama, Mississippi, Louisiana, Arkansas, northwestern Kansas, and eastern Iowa.

Cultivated in rich, moist, basic soil or potting mix in partial sun.

318   Athyrium thelypterioides (Michx.) Desv.
Silvery Glade Fern

Rhizomes creeping, ca. 15 mm in diam. including the stipe bases, with lanceolate to narrowly lanceolate, pale tan scales especially at the apex. Stipes mostly less than 1 cm distant, 10–45 cm long, dark reddish-brown at the base, straw-colored above the base, with a few scales like those of the rhizome throughout. Laminae rhombic-lanceolate, 30–75 cm long, (12)15–25(30) cm wide, acute at the base, widest near the middle, acuminate at the apex, pinnate-pinnatifid, the pinnae oblong, truncate at the base, deeply pinnatifid, the segments entire to slightly lobed in the very largest specimens, acuminate at the apex, the veins simple or 1-forked well above the base; sori elongate, several times longer than wide, nearly straight to conspicuously recurved across a vein; indusia opaque, pale tan, subentire.

Terrestrial in moist woods, often on slopes, in subacid to circumneutral soil. Frequent. Nova Scotia to Ontario south to Georgia, Alabama, Tennessee, Arkansas, Louisiana, Missouri, Illinois, eastern Iowa, and Minnesota.

Cultivated in moist garden soil or potting mix in partial shade.

319   Athyrium alpestre subsp. americanum (Butters) Lellinger
American Alpine Lady Fern

Rhizomes erect or ascending, 20–40 mm in diam. including the stipe bases, with lanceolate, bronzy to tan scales, especially at the apex. Stipes approximate, (7)10–20(32) cm long, blackish at the base, reddish-brown or pale brown above, with sparse scales like those of the rhizome throughout. Laminae narrowly rhombic to nearly linear, 15–30 cm long, 3–6 cm wide, tapering slightly to an obtuse base, widest near the middle, acute at the apex, 2–3-pinnate-pinnatifid, the pinnae lanceate, spreading to ascending, obtuse at the base, acute at the apex; sori round, submarginal near the end of a vein that terminates in a reflexed tooth slightly protecting the sori; indusia none.

Terrestrial on wet talus slopes and rocky hillsides, and in alpine meadows. Occasional. Alaska, British Columbia, Washington, Oregon, and the Sierra Nevada of California east to Montana, Wyoming, Colorado, and northeastern Nevada. Disjunct in Newfoundland and the Gaspé Peninsula, Quebec.

Cultivated in moist garden soil or potting mix in partial to full sun. This subspecies formerly was called *A. alpestre* var. *americanum* Butters.

320 Athyrium filix-femina subsp. cyclosorum (Rupr.) C. Chr.

Western Lady Fern

Rhizomes erect or ascending, 20–50 mm in diam. including the stipe bases, with tan to brown, large, lanceate scales. Stipes approximate, 15–35 cm long, black at the base, straw-colored above, with scales like those of the rhizome, especially at the base. Laminae rhombic, (25)35–90(110) cm long, 10–30(50) cm wide, very gradually tapered at the base, acute at the base and apex, 2-pinnate-pinnatifid, the pinnae oblong-lanceate, obtuse at the base, quite parallel-sided, acute at the apex; sori strongly recurved, short, almost circular; indusia bearing flattened marginal hairs much longer than the width of the indusia.

Terrestrial in moist forests and swampy places. Abundant. Alaska, British Columbia, Alberta, Montana, Wyoming, western South Dakota south to southern California, Arizona, New Mexico, and Colorado. Disjunct in southern Ontario and Quebec.

Cultivated in moist to wet garden soil in partial sun. According to Liew (1972, pp. 200–204), specimens from the southwestern United States are not sufficiently distinct to be separated from those of the northwest, although some authors have done so as var. *californicum* Butters.

321 Athyrium filix-femina subsp. angustum (Willd.) Clausen

Northern Lady Fern

Rhizomes erect or ascending, 15–35 mm in diam. including the stipe bases, with brown to dark brown, large, lanceolate scales. Stipes approximate, 15–35 cm long, black at the base, straw-colored above the base, with a few, pale brown scales like those of the rhizome, especially near the base. Laminae rhombic, (25)30–75 cm long, (8)10–30 cm wide, gradually tapered to an acute to obtuse base, acute at the apex, 2-pinnate-pinnatifid, the pinnae truncate at the base, lanceolate-oblong, usually widest at the middle and not parallel-sided, acute-acuminate at the apex; sori straight to slightly curved, long; indusia bearing marginal hairs almost as long as the indusia are wide; spores yellow.

Terrestrial in moist woods, swamps, and thickets in usually subacid soil.

Abundant. Newfoundland to Manitoba south to Virginia, West Virginia, Ohio, Indiana, Illinois, Missouri, Iowa, and South Dakota.

Cultivated in moist to wet garden soil in partial sun.

322 Athyrium filix-femina subsp. asplenioides (Michx.) Hultén
Southern Lady Fern

Rhizomes creeping to ascending, 20–30 mm in diam. including the stipe bases, with brown to bronzy, large, lanceolate scales. Stipes approximate, 15–50 cm long, black at the base, straw-colored above, with tan or reddish scales like those of the rhizome, especially at the base. Laminae lanceolate, (18)25–50 cm long, (6)10–25 cm wide, slightly reduced and truncate at the base, acute at the apex, 2-pinnate-pinnatifid, the pinnae oblong, truncate at the base, nearly parallel-sided, acuminate at the apex; shorter sori straight, the longer ones conspicuously recurved; indusia bearing marginal hairs almost as long as the indusia are wide; spores dark brown.

Terrestrial in moist woods and thickets, swamps, and seeps in moderately to strongly acid soil. Abundant. Florida to eastern Texas north to Rhode Island, southeastern New York, New Jersey, Delaware, Maryland, southeastern Pennsylvania, West Virginia, Kentucky, southern Indiana, southern Illinois, Missouri, Oklahoma, and southeastern Kansas.

Cultivated in moist to wet garden soil in partial sun.

DIPLAZIUM
The Twin-sorus Ferns

Diplazium is a large genus of about 400 species found mostly in the New World tropics. Only two naturalized species are indisputably part of the United States flora at present. Other species may occur as escapes or as non-persisting accidentals.

The Twin-sorus ferns are medium to large in size. Their rhizomes are erect, short-creeping, or long-creeping and bear narrow to broad, pale brown scales. The stipes are straw-colored or brown to blackish at the base. The laminae usually are lanceolate, 1–2-pinnate, or are even more divided in some tropical species. The sori are short to long, usually back-to-back, and straight or slightly curved. Commonly they are in several series on rather broad, shallowly cut pinnae or in one series on pinnules or segments. Indusia are present, except for a few tropical species in which they are rudimentary or absent.

Diplazium grows in moist, sheltered ravines in Florida, southern Georgia, and southeastern Alabama. Being a tropical genus, it barely survives in the United States, and perhaps will disappear in time. Many species are interesting greenhouse plants. Being terrestrial, they do well in moist potting mix in partial sun.

Key to Diplazium

1. Pinnae broadest at the middle, equilateral at the base; rhizomes long-creeping, the fronds scattered; FL, GA, AL. *323. D. japonicum*

1. Pinnae broadest at the base, inequilateral at the base, the acroscopic lobe enlarged, the basiscopic lobe cut away; rhizomes erect or ascending, the fronds clustered; LA. *324. D. lonchophyllum*

323 Diplazium japonicum (Thunb.) Bedd.
Japanese Twin-sorus Fern

Rhizomes long-creeping, ca. 5 mm in diam., the stipes mostly 0.5–1 cm distant; scales linear-lanceate, ca. 8 mm long, 1.25 mm wide, pale tan. Stipes 10–20 cm long, greenish above the dark brown to blackish base. Laminae ovate-lanceolate, 15–40 cm long, 6–25 cm wide, obtuse at the base, abruptly contracted to an acuminate, pinnatifid apex, pinnate-pinnatifid, the pinnae 4–8 subopposite pairs, lanceate-oblong, 3–14 cm long, 1–3 cm wide, with ascending, slightly serrate to subentire lobes, bearing scattered, short, multicellular hairs on the axes of both surfaces; sori 1.5–3 mm long, slightly curved; indusia whitish, erose-ciliate when young, pale tan at maturity.

Terrestrial in moist ravines. Rare. Northern Florida to central Georgia and southern Alabama.

Cultivated in moist potting mix in partial sun. This species is naturalized from southeastern Asia.

324 Diplazium lonchophyllum Kunze
Lance-leaved Twin-sorus Fern

Rhizomes erect or ascending, ca. 15 mm in diam. including the crowded stipe bases; scales lanceate, ca. 5 mm long, 1 mm wide, dark brown. Stipes 15–20 cm long, straw-colored above the dark brown base. Laminae lanceolate, 20–30 cm long, 8–15 cm wide, obtuse at the base, somewhat abruptly contracted to an acuminate, pinnatifid apex, pinnate-pinnatifid, the pinnae (5)7–15 subopposite to alternate pairs, lanceate or lanceate-oblong, 3.5–7 cm long, 1–2(2.5) cm wide, with ascending, entire, sometimes shallow lobes, glabrous or nearly so; sori 4–6 mm long, slightly curved; indusia brownish, entire.

Terrestrial. Very rare. Iberia Parish, Louisiana.

Not cultivated.

GYMNOCARPIUM
The Oak Ferns

Gymnocarpium is a small genus of four species and several hybrids in mostly boreal North American and Eurasia and another two species in the mountains of Taiwan, New Guinea, and the Phillippines. The genus was long confused with *Dryopteris*, but differs strongly in its small, delicate, tripartite laminae with long-stalked basal pinnae.

The Oak Ferns are small or very small. They have thin, long-creeping, black rhizomes with distant stipes. The very thin, wiry stipes are straw-colored or greenish above the blackish base, and have a few scales. They are longer to much longer than the laminae. The laminae are deltate, tripartite, have long-stalked basal pinnae, and are pinnate-pinnatifid above the 2-pinnate-pinnatifid basal pinnae. The pinnae are weakly articulate to the rachis. The sori are round, lack indusia, and are close to the segment and pinnule margins at the fork of free veins.

Gymnocarpium is terrestrial, often among rocks, in shady places. Some of the species are cultivated in woodland gardens. *Gymnocarpium* is more complex in North America than is usually supposed. Recent cytological and phytochemical papers (Sarvela, 1978, 1980; Sarvela, Britton & Pryer, 1981; Pryer, Britton & McNeill, 1983) do not account for all the morphological forms, according to W. H. Wagner, Jr. (pers. comm.). More than the entities discussed below exist, but their morphological distinctions and status as species or subspecies is still uncertain.

Key to Gymnocarpium
1. Stipe, rachis, and axes glabrous or obscurely glandular; suprabasal pinna pair divided more like the distal pinnae than the basal ones; stalks of the basal pinnae (0.5)1–2.5 cm long; N, W. 325. *G. dryopteris*

1. Stipe, rachis, and axes with many very small, stalked, capitate, white glands; suprabasal pinna pair usually divided more like the basal pinnae than the distal ones; stalks of the basal pinnae 0.5–1(2) cm long; N. 326. *G. robertianum*

325 Gymnocarpium dryopteris (L.) Newm.
Oak Fern

Rhizomes very long-creeping, ca. 1 mm in diam., blackish, bearing scattered stipes; scales lanceolate, ca. 2 mm long, very thin, pale reddish-tan. Stipes 7–30 cm long, ca. 1 mm in diam., straw-colored, with scales like those of the rhizome especially at the base, with few or no short, capitate glands. Laminae deltate, tripartite, obtuse at the base, broadly acute at the apex, the pinnae weakly articulate to the usually eglandular rachis, the basal pinnae stalked (0.5)1–2.5 cm; sori round, submarginal; indusia absent.

Terrestrial in rocky woods and swamps and on talus slopes in rich, usually subacid soil, and epipetric on cliffs. Abundant. Labrador to Alaska south to New York, the mountains of Pennsylvania, Virginia, Ashe Co., North Carolina, and West Virginia, eastern Ohio, Michigan, Illinois, eastern Iowa, Minnesota, western South Dakota, Wyoming, Colorado, New Mexico, Arizona, Utah, Nevada, and Oregon.

Cultivated in moist potting mix or rich garden soil in partial sun. A beautiful fern for the woodland garden. Wagner (1966) upholds var. *disjunctum* (Rupr.) Ching for large, diploid, small-spored specimens from Washington and Alaska, but the morphological limits of the several taxa and their cytology are not yet completely understood. The diploids of this species hybridize with *G. robertianum* to form *G.* ×*heterosporum* Wagner, a synonym of which is *G. dryopteris* f. *glandulosa* Tryon. The hybrids were shown by Root (1961) and by Wagner (1966) to have irregular spores and to be intermediate between the parents in several characters, most noticeably in having sparse glands, rather than copious or no glands, on the rachises above the basal pinna pair. Scattered hybrid populations have been found in Alaska, Pennsylvania, Wisconsin, Michigan, and Minnesota. The plants are especially abundant in southwestern Ontario.

326 Gymnocarpium robertianum (Hoffm.) Newm.

Limestone Oak Fern

Rhizomes very long-creeping, 1–2 mm in diam., blackish, bearing scattered stipes; scales broadly lanceolate, ca. 2 mm long, very thin, pale reddish-tan. Stipes 5–20(28) cm long, 0.5–1 mm in diam., with scales like those of the rhizome especially at the base, with many, minute, capitate glands. Laminae deltate, tripartite, obtuse at the base, acute to broadly acute at the apex, the pinnae weakly articulate to the minutely glandular rachis, the basal pinnae stalked 0.5–1(2) cm; sori round, submarginal; indusia absent.

Terrestrial on wooded slopes and in swamps in circumneutral soil, andepipetric on cliffs. Rare. Newfoundland to Alaska south to Ontario, northern Michigan, Wisconsin, Minnesota, northeastern Iowa, northern Idaho, and British Columbia.

Cultivated in moist, circumneutral garden soil in partial sun. Limited to cool climates. This species hybridizes to form *G.* ×*heterosporum* Wagner, which is discussed under the other parent, *G. dryopteris*.

CYSTOPTERIS

The Bladder Ferns

Cystopteris is a genus of 17–20 species found mostly in the temperate regions of the Northern Hemisphere. Most of the species are polyploids, and many are fertile hybrids. The common name refers to the extrorse, inflated, bladder-like young indusia.

The Bladder Ferns are small plants and usually have short-creeping rhizomes with crowded to somewhat distant stipes. Epipetric plants commonly have more crowded stipes than do terrestrial plants. The rhizomes and stipe bases have narrow, lanceolate, pale tan or pale reddish scales. In most species, the laminae are equal to or are longer than the stipes. The laminae mostly are lanceolate or lanceate, 2–3-pinnate, rather pale green, and have sori dorsal on the veins protected by a pocket-like or scale-like, whitish, thin, commonly ciliate indusium.

Cystopteris is epipetric or terrestrial, and the habitat is often rather constant for the species. All grow in moist to wet places. They are cultivated in cool greenhouses and gardens. The genus was monographed by Blasdell (1963), which stimulated considerable study that has led to a better understanding of its biosystematics. The North American species are notable for forming a polyploid complex in which the species have high chromosome numbers and are biologically distinct, but are often difficult to distinguish morphologically (see p. 318).

Key to Cystopteris

1. Laminae deltate, ⅓–½ as long as the stipes; rhizomes long-creeping, the stipes distant; CAN, MT, CO. *327. C. montana*

1. Laminae ovate-lanceolate to linear-lanceate, usually equalling or longer than the stipes; rhizomes creeping to short-creeping, the stipes approximate (in terrestrial specimens) to congested (in epipetric specimens), **2**

2(1). Laminae lanceate or lanceolate; bulblets absent; indusia eglandular, **5**

2(1). Laminae linear-lanceate; persistent or deciduous bulblets or abortive bulblets sometimes present distally on the rachis; indusia densely to sparsely (very sparsely in *C. tennesseensis*) glandular, the glands short, capitate, white, **3**

3(2). Veins in the laminae all terminating in minute emarginations or sinuses; laminae linear-lanceate; rachises with ovoid to bilobed bulblets; NE. *328. C. bulbifera*

3(2). Veins in the laminae terminating variously in minute emarginations or short teeth; laminae lanceate; rachises usually with abortive, scaly bulblets, **4**

4(3). Laminae widest at the base; indusia cup-shaped, truncate at the apex; SE. *329. C. tennesseensis*

4(3). Laminae widest above the base or at the middle; indusia ovate-lanceolate, often lacerate at the apex; ONT, NO. **330. C. laurentiana*

5(2). Laminae lax, broad, mostly 2–2.5(3) times longer than wide; basal pinnules short-stalked to sessile, obtuse to cuneate at the base; indusia round to ovate, 7

5(2). Laminae compact, narrow, mostly (2.5)3–4 times longer than wide; basal pinnules sessile, truncate to obtuse at the base; indusia lanceolate, 6

6(5). Spores echinate, appearing slightly spiny at 60× magnification; N, SW. *331. C. fragilis*

6(5). Spores rugose-verrucose, appearing smooth at 60× magnification; CAN, W. *332. C. dickieana*

7(5). Rhizomes long-creeping, somewhat scaly and often densely villous, extending 1–several cm beyond the rather distant stipe base, especially during late spring and summer; E. *333. C. protrusa*

7(5). Rhizomes rather short-creeping, scaly (and slightly villous in *C. tenuis*), not extending beyond the approximate stipe bases, 8

8(7). Pinnules with a broad, uncut center; segments mostly round at the apex; laminae pinnate-pinnatifid to 2(3)-pinnate-pinnatifid; basal pinnules cuneate in less divided forms, obtuse in more divided ones; plants usually epipetric, sometimes terrestrial; N, E, S, W. *334. C. tenuis*

8(7). Pinnules lacking a broad, uncut center; segments mostly acute at the apex; laminae 2–3-pinnate-pinnatifid; basal pinnules mostly cuneate at the base; plants usually terrestrial; SW. *335. C. reevesiana*

327 Cystopteris montana (Lam.) Bernh. ex Desv.

Mountain Bladder Fern

Rhizomes very long-creeping, blackish, the stipe bases 1–2 cm distant. Stipes 10–32 cm long, (1)2–3 times longer than the laminae, blackish at the base, sparsely scaly, the scales broadly lanceolate. Laminae deltate, 6–14 cm long and wide, 3(4)-pinnate-pinnatifid at the base, 2(3)-pinnate-pinnatifid and less divided toward the apex, the basal pinnae basiscopically developed, especially in large laminae; indusia shallowly cup-shaped, eglandular.

Terrestrial in wet woods among rocks. Very rare. Labrador to Alaska south to Ontario, Newfoundland, Quebec, Ontario, Alberta, Montana, and British Columbia. Disjunct in Summit and Pitkin counties, Colorado.

Not cultivated. This species does not hybridize in North America, although it may do so in Europe.

328 Cystopteris bulbifera (L.) Bernh.

Bulblet Fern

Rhizomes short-creeping, the stipe bases very congested, blackish or dark brown, sparsely scaly, the scales lanceolate. Stipes 8–20(25) cm long, usually ½ – ⅓ as long as the laminae, dark reddish-brown at the base, often purplish throughout, sparsely scaly. Laminae linear-lanceate,

(10)14–45(53) cm long, 5–10(14) cm wide, truncate at the base, attenuate at the apex, 2-pinnate-pinnatifid nearly throughout, the basal pinnae slightly basiscopically developed, the suprabasal pinnae equilateral; veins in the laminae all terminating in emarginations of the teeth; ovoid or lobed bulblets usually present on the distal portion of the rachis; indusia and lamina axes with scattered, short, stalked, yellowish glands.

Epipetric on rocks and talus slopes and terrestrial around rocks or in hardwood and white cedar swamps in the northern part of the range. Common. Newfoundland to Ontario and Minnesota south to Alabama, North Carolina, Tennessee, Arkansas, Oklahoma, Missouri, eastern Nebraska, and eastern South Dakota. Disjunct in Utah, central Arizona, New Mexico, and western Texas.

Cultivated in moist to wet garden soil among limy rocks. This species hybridizes with *C. protrusa* to form *C. tennesseensis*, with *C. tenuis* to form *C.* × *illinoensis* Moran, with *C. fragilis* to form *C. laurentiana*, and with *C. reevesiana* (see p. 318).

329 Cystopteris tennesseensis Shaver
Hybrid Bladder Fern

Rhizomes short-creeping, the stipe bases very congested, brown. Stipes 4–15(20) cm long, usually about equalling the laminae, dark brown or dark reddish-brown at the base. Laminae lanceate, 6–25 cm long, 3.5–11 cm wide, widest at the obtuse base, acute to acuminate at the apex, 2-pinnate-pinnatifid at and above the base, pinnate-pinnatifid below the pinnatifid apex; veins in the laminae terminating in marginal sinuses and emarginations of the teeth; abortive, often scaly bulblets occasionally present on the distal portion of the rachis; indusia cup-shaped, truncate at the apex, with a few, scattered, short, stalked, white glands.

Epipetric on limestone and sandstone cliffs and rocks. Common. North Carolina, Kentucky, Illinois, Missouri, Iowa, and Kansas south to Tennessee, Arkansas, and western Oklahoma. Disjunct in the Guadalupe Mountains, Culberson Co., western Texas.

Not cultivated. This species is the fertile hybrid between *C. bulbifera* and *C. protrusa*. It hybridizes with *C. tenuis* to form *C.* × *wagneri* Moran (see p. 318).

*330 Cystopteris laurentiana (Weath.) Blasdell
Laurentian Bladder Fern

Rhizomes short-creeping, the stipe bases very congested. Stipes 6–24 cm long, usually ca. ⅔ as long as the laminae, brown to reddish-brown, with lanceolate scales. Laminae narrowly elliptic-lanceolate, 9–21(27) cm long, 3.5–8(12) cm wide, widest near the middle, obtuse at the base, acute to acuminate at the apex, the basal pinna pair often spaced rather distantly from the suprabasal pair, 2-pinnate-pinnatifid at and above the base, pinnate-pinnatifid below the pinnatifid apex; veins in the laminae terminating in teeth and emarginations of teeth; abortive, scaly bulblets occasionally present on the distal portion of the sparsely glandular rachis; indusia ovate-lanceolate, often lacerate at the apex, with a few, scattered, short, stalked, white glands.

Epipetric on limestone, dolomite, conglomerate, shale, and diabase cliffs and rocks. Rare. Newfoundland to southern Ontario south to northern Michigan, northern Wisconsin, and northern Minnesota. Disjunct in Centre Co., central Pennsylvania.

Not cultivated. This species is the fertile hybrid between *C. bulbifera* and *C. fragilis* (see p. 318).

331 Cystopteris fragilis (L.) Bernh.
Brittle Fern

Rhizomes short-creeping, the stipe bases very congested. Stipes 2–15(18) cm long, usually ca. ⅔ as long as the laminae, dark reddish-brown at the base, reddish-brown, brown, or pale brown toward the apex, scaly at the base, the scales lanceolate. Laminae narrowly lanceate, 4–23 cm long, 1.5–6 cm wide, widest near the base, obtuse to truncate at the base, acute at the apex, the basal pinna pair usually spaced rather distantly from the suprabasal pair, usually 2-pinnate or 2-pinnate-pinnatifid at and above the base, rarely up to 3-pinnate-pinnatifid; basal pinnules sessile, truncate to obtuse at the base; veins terminating in usually entire teeth; indusia lanceolate, not glandular.

Epipetric on rocks and cliffs or sometimes on sandy soil. Abundant. Newfoundland to Alaska south to Massachusetts, Connecticut, New York, New Jersey, Maryland, the mountains of Virginia and West Virginia, Kentucky, Illinois, Missouri, Oklahoma, Texas, New Mexico, and Arizona. Usually rare in the southern part of the range.

Cultivated in moist to wet, basic potting mix in partial sun. This species is a fertile tetraploid. It hybridizes with *C. bulbifera* to form *C. laurentiana* and with *C. tenuis*. See p. 318 for a discussion of the origins of *C. fragilis*.

*332 Cystopteris dickieana Sim
Dickie's Brittle Fern

Rhizomes short-creeping, the stipe bases very congested. Stipes 3–25 cm long, usually ca. ⅔ as long as the laminae, dark reddish-brown at the base, reddish-brown to pale brown or straw-colored toward the apex, scaly at the base, the scales lanceolate. Laminae narrowly lanceolate, (2)5–20 cm long, (0.8)2–4(5) cm wide, widest above the base, obtuse to truncate at the base, acute at the apex, the basal pinna pair usually decidedly distant from the suprabasal pair, usually 2-pinnate-pinnatifid, sometimes 2-pinnate at and above the base; basal pinnules sessile, truncate to obtuse at the base; veins terminating in usually entire teeth; indusia lanceolate, eglandular.

Epipetric on rocks and cliffs. Frequent. Newfoundland to Quebec, northern New York, Michigan, and Wisconsin. Also Alaska to Saskatchewan south to Nebraska, Colorado, northern Arizona, and southern California.

Cultivated in moist to wet potting mix in partial sun. There seems to be no reliable character other than spore ornamentation to separate this species from *C. fragilis* (Profumo, 1969; Profumo & Raggi, 1968). The stipes and rachises typically are paler, but the amount of overlap between the two species precludes using this as a taxonomic character. C. Haufler (pers. comm.) believes that some of the American material may be only a developmental phase of *C. fragilis* and may not be conspecific with material from the type locality of *C. dickieana* along the coast of England.

333   Cystopteris protrusa (Weath.) Blasdell
Lowland Brittle Fern
Rhizomes long-creeping, often densely villous throughout, scaly only at the apex, the stipe bases rather distant, the rhizome apex extending 1–several cm beyond the stipe bases, especially in late spring and early summer. Stipes 4–22 cm long, ca. equalling the laminae, reddish-brown at the base, sometimes brown but usually straw-colored above the base, scaly at and often above the base, the scales lanceolate. Laminae lanceolate, 8–20(24) cm long, (3.5)4–10 cm wide, widest above the base, obtuse at the base, acute or sometimes acuminate at the apex, the basal pinna pair usually not or only slightly distant from the suprabasal pair, 2-pinnate to 2(3)-pinnate-pinnatifid at and above the base; basal pinnules sessile, truncate to obtuse at the base; veins terminating in entire or sometimes slightly emarginate teeth; indusia ovate, eglandular.

Terrestrial in soil in mesic woods. Abundant. New York, Ontario, southern Michigan, southern Wisconsin, and southern Minnesota south to Georgia, Alabama, Mississippi, Louisiana, Arkansas, eastern Kansas, eastern Nebraska, and Iowa.

Cultivated in moist to wet potting mix in partial sun. This species has been called *C. fragilis* var. *protrusa* Weath. It hybridizes with *C. bulbifera* to form *C. tennesseensis* and with an unknown diploid to form *C. tenuis* (see p. 318).

334   Cystopteris tenuis (Michx.) Desv.
Mackay's Brittle Fern
Rhizomes short-creeping, the stipes approximate. Stipes 4–20 cm long, ca. ⅔ as long to equalling the laminae, dark brown at the base, reddish-brown or straw-colored above the base, scaly at the base, the scales lanceolate. Laminae lanceolate, 6–24 cm long, 2.5–9(12) cm wide, widest

above the base, obtuse at the base, acuminate or acute at the apex, the basal pinna pair slightly distant from the suprabasal pair, pinnate-pinnatifid to 2(3)-pinnate-pinnatifid at and above the base; basal pinnules cuneate in less divided forms, obtuse in more divided ones; veins terminating in entire or emarginate teeth; indusia ovate, often lacerate at the apex, not glandular.

Epipetric or sometimes terrestrial, especially in the southern part of the range. Abundant. Newfoundland to Alaska south to Georgia, Alabama, Mississippi, Louisiana, Oklahoma, New Mexico, Arizona, and California.

Cultivated in moist to wet potting soil in partial sun. This is the fertile hybrid between *C. protrusa* and an unknown diploid species. This species has been called *C. fragilis* var. *mackayii* Laws. It hybridizes with *C. bulbifera* to form *C.* ×*illinoensis* Moran (see p. 318).

*335 Cystopteris reevesiana Lellinger
Southwestern Brittle Fern

Rhizomes rather long-creeping, the fronds somewhat distant. Stipes 4–19 cm long, ca. ½–⅔ as long as the laminae, dark brown at the base, paler brown or sometimes reddish-brown above the base, slightly scaly at the base, rarely scaly above, the scales narrowly lanceolate. Laminae lanceolate, 10–27(30) cm long, (4)6–10(14) cm wide, widest above the base, obtuse at the base, acuminate at the apex, the basal pinna pair distinctly distant from the suprabasal pair, 2–3-pinnate-pinnatifid at and above the base; basal pinnules mostly cuneate at the base; veins terminating in entire or slightly emarginate teeth; indusia nearly round, sometimes ovate, not glandular.

Usually terrestrial, especially on soils derived from quartzite, according to M. Windham (pers. comm.). Rare. Southern Utah to Arizona and New Mexico.

Not cultivated. This species has been called *C. fragilis* var. *tenuifolia* (Clute) Broun or subsp. *tenuifolia* Clute. It hybridizes with *C. bulbifera* and may be a parent of *C. fragilis* (see p. 318).

WOODSIA
The Cliff Ferns

Woodsia is a genus of 23–25 species found mostly in the cool and cold portions of the northern hemisphere, with extensions into Central America, one species in South America, and another in South Africa. The plants are almost exclusively epipetric, hence the common name.

The Cliff Ferns are small plants and usually have short-creeping, scaly rhizomes bearing tufts of fronds. The stipes are scaly at the base, articulate in a few species, and with dark (eventually fading), persistent stipe bases in all species. The laminae are linear-lanceolate to ovate, as long as or longer than the stipes, pinnate-pinnatifid to 2-pinnate, have the lower proximal pinnae gradually more distant from each other than the distal pinnae, and bear many pairs of short pinnae with submedial, sometimes glandular sori surrounded from beneath by a cup-like indusium or one that has been reduced nearly to a series of hairs.

Woodsia grows most frequently in crevices on rocks and cliffs, and less frequently on talus slopes, in damp places in cool and cold climates. A few species are cultivated on rocks in woodland gardens. Several hybrids exist, and several species appear to have two chromosome levels (W. H. Wagner, pers. comm.). The cytology of the North American species is so poorly known that a full understanding of the interspecific relationships is not possible at present. Plants of *Woodsia* sometimes are confused with those of *Cystopteris*; they differ in indusium form and in having persistent stipe bases. The genus was monographed very carefully by Brown (1964).

Key to Woodsia
1. Stipes not articulate above the base, fracturing irregularly and leaving persistent stipe bases of various lengths crowded about the rhizomes; rhizome scales bicolorous, with a dark central band; laminae with unicellular, sessile glands (and also multicellular, elongate glands in *W. scopulina*), 4

1. Stipes articulate above the base, mostly fracturing evenly and leaving persistent stipe bases of similar length crowded about the rhizomes; laminae eglandular, 2

2(1). Stipes and rachises greenish to straw-colored; laminae nearly glabrous on the abaxial surface, bipinnatifid, the pinnae with ca. 1–4 lobes on a side; N. *336*. *W. glabella*

2(1). Stipes and rachises straw-colored to brown or purplish-black; scaly or pilose on the abaxial surface, 3

3(2). Laminae pinnate-pinnatifid to 2-pinnate, scaly on the abaxial surface; median pinnae with 3–6 lobes on a side; N. *338*. *W. ilvensis*

3(2). Laminae pinnate-pinnatifid, with pilose hairs among the sporangia; median pinnae with ca. 3 lobes on a side; N. *337*. *W. alpina*

4(1). Pinnae and rachises with articulated hairs and sessile and multicellular, elongate glands; N, *W. 339*. *W. scopulina*

4(1). Pinnae and rachises lacking articulated hairs, with only sessile, unicellular glands or more or less glabrous, 5

5(4). Indusia strongly ciliate; lamina segments with broadly and shallowly incised segments, appearing toothed, 6

5(4). Indusia not ciliate, entire, fragmenting into several broad segments; lamina segments with narrowly and usually deeply incised segments, appearing somewhat lacerate, 7

6(5). Stipes pale almost to the brown or dark brown base; SW. *342*. *W. mexicana*

6(5). Stipes dark brown or dark reddish-brown at and above the base; N, W. *340*. *W. oregana*

7(5). Laminae usually only slightly glandular, the indusia eglandular; E. *341*. *W. obtusa*

7(5). Laminae usually copiously glandular throughout, even on the indusia; SW. *343*. *W. plummerae*

336   Woodsia glabella R. Brown in Richards.
Smooth Cliff Fern

Stipes 1–3 cm long, articulate, with pale brown scales. Laminae narrowly linear-oblanceolate, 4–11 cm long, 4–10 mm wide, widest above the middle, tapering gradually at the base, acute at the long, congested, pinnatifid apex, pinnate-pinnatifid, the pinnae ca. 8–12 pairs, all short, oblong, glabrous or nearly so; indusia small, bearing a few, very long, fine hairs on the margins.

Epipetric in crevices of cliffs. Rare. Newfoundland to Alaska south to Maine, New Hampshire, Vermont, New York, Ontario, Minnesota, Manitoba, Saskatchewan, Alberta, Northwest Territories, and Yukon Territory.

Not cultivated. This species hybridizes with *W. ilvensis* to form *W. alpina*. Among the *Woodsia* species of the United States and Canada, this species has the smallest and narrowest laminae.

337   Woodsia alpina (Bolton) S. F. Gray
Alpine Cliff Fern

Stipes 2–6(9) cm long, articulate, with pale brown scales. Laminae narrowly elliptic-lanceolate, 2–13(18) cm long, 0.4–2.4 cm wide, widest at or below the middle, not much tapering at the base, acute at the rather short, slightly congested apex, barely pinnate-pinnatifid in dwarf forms, subbipinnate above the base in large forms, the pinnae ca. (6)8–15 pairs, often short, the smallest ones nearly flabellate, the larger ones oblong, bearing long, fine hairs on the laminae and margins of the small indusia.

Epipetric in exposed and sheltered crevices of cliffs and occasionally on talus slopes. Rare. Newfoundland to Alaska south to Maine, Vermont, northern New York, Michigan, Minnesota, Northwest Territories, and Yukon Territory.

Not cultivated. This species is the fertile tetraploid hybrid of *W. glabella* and *W. ilvensis*. It is intermediate in lamina size between its parents. It, in turn, backcrosses with *W. ilvensis* to form the sterile triploid hybrid *W. ×gracilis* (Laws.) Butters, known from scattered localities in Quebec, Maine, Vermont, Ontario, and Minnesota.

338 Woodsia ilvensis (L.) R. Brown
Rusty Cliff Fern

Stipes 2–11 cm long, articulate, with pale brown to reddish-brown, distantly toothed scales. Laminae lanceolate or elliptic-lanceolate, 3–15 cm long, 1.2–4(5) cm wide, widest at or below the middle, tapering to a reduced, distant, often deciduous basal pinna pair, acute at the rather short, slightly congested apex, pinnate-pinnatifid to 2-pinnate-pinnatifid in larger pinnae, the pinnae ca. 7–15 pairs, sometimes short, the smallest ones nearly flabellate, the larger ones oblong, bearing long, often somewhat twisted hairs on the laminae and in the sori plus long, narrow, tan scales on the axes of the abaxial surface of the laminae; indusia small, bearing long, straight, fine hairs on the margins.

Epipetric in exposed and sheltered crevices of subacidic cliffs and occasionally on talus slopes. Common. Newfoundland to Alaska south to North Carolina, Virginia, West Virginia, northeastern Ohio, Michigan, northern Illinois, northwestern Iowa, Minnesota, Manitoba, Saskatchewan, Alberta, and British Columbia.

Cultivated in moist to wet, acidic garden soil or potting mix, especially in rock gardens in cool climates. This species hybridizes with *W. glabella* to form *W. alpina*, with *W. alpina* to form *W.* ×*gracilis* (see *W. alpina*), and with *W. scopulina* to form the sterile diploid *W.* ×*abbeae* Butters known from Ontario, upper Michigan, Wisconsin, and Minnesota.

339 Woodsia scopulina D. C. Eaton
Mountain Cliff Fern

Stipes 4–12 cm long, not articulate, with concolorous, pale brown scales or bicolorous scales having pale brown margins and a dark brown central stripe. Laminae elliptic-lanceolate, (5)8–20 cm long, (1)2–5 cm wide, widest at or below the middle, tapering to an often greatly reduced, distant basal pinna pair, acute at the rather short, slightly congested apex, 1–2-pinnate-pinnatifid, the pinnae ca. 10–15(20) pairs, lanceolate-oblong, bearing long, sometimes flattened hairs and short-stalked, hyaline glands on the laminae; indusia small, bearing short, inconspicuous marginal hairs.

Epipetric in rock crevices, on ledges, and on talus slopes in subacid soil. Frequent. Quebec to British Columbia and coastal Alaska south to South Dakota, Wyoming, Colorado, northern and eastern New Mexico, Arizona, and California. Disjunct in Virginia, North Carolina, West Virginia, Tennessee, and Arkansas.

Cultivated in moist to wet garden soil or potting mix in partial sun, especially in rock gardens in cool climates. This species hybridizes with *W. ilvensis* to form the sterile diploid *W.* ×*abbeae* Butters known from Ontario, upper Michigan, Wisconsin, and Minnesota, and probably with tetraploid plants of *W. oregana* to form the sterile triploid *W.* ×*maxonii*

Tryon known from Ontario. According to Brown (1964, p. 98), *W. scopulina* var. *appalachiana* T. M. C. Taylor is not consistently different in any significant way from var. *scopulina,* and so should be considered a synonym of var. *scopulina.*

340   Woodsia oregana D. C. Eaton
Western Cliff Fern

Stipes 2–8(10) cm long, not articulate, with concolorous, pale brown scales or irregularly bicolorous scales having pale brown margins and dark, reddish-brown central portions. Laminae narrowly rhombic, 5.5–17 cm long, 1–4 cm wide, gradually tapering at both ends to a truncate base and an acute apex, 2-pinnate-pinnatifid, the pinnae ca. 10–14 pairs, borne at uniformly increasing distances from the lamina apex to the base, lanceolate or lanceolate-oblong, bearing few to many elongate glands on the laminae; indusia small, bearing conspicuous marginal hairs.

Epipetric in rock crevices, on ledges and boulders, and on talus slopes. Frequent. Quebec to British Columbia south to northern Vermont, central New York, the upper peninsula of Michigan, Wisconsin, Iowa, Nebraska, Kansas, Oklahoma, New Mexico, Arizona, and California.

Cultivated in moist to wet potting soil or garden soil among rocks in partial sun. This species contains not only diploid plants but cryptic tetraploid ones that have more globose spores and clear, enlarged cells along the segment margins (the latter best seen in cleared specimens). The tetraploids have been called *W. cathcartiana* B. L. Robins. or *W. oregana* var. *cathcartiana* (B. L. Robins.) Morton. The nature and origin of their tetraploidy is as yet unknown, and the plants are difficult to distinguish with certainty from diploid plants. Brown (1964, p. 129) detected tetraploids only in eastern Minnesota and adjacent Wisconsin, but I believe they may have a wider range, perhaps around Lake Superior. The tetraploids may be parents, along with *W. scopulina,* of *W.* ×*maxonii* Tryon.

341   Woodsia obtusa (Spreng.) Torrey
Blunt-lobed Cliff Fern

Stipes 4–15(21) cm long, not articulate, with concolorous, pale reddish-brown scales and bicolorous scales having pale reddish-brown margins and broad, dark brown central portions at and above the base of the stipe. Laminae rhombic to narrowly rhombic, 8–35(50) cm long, 3.5–8(10) cm wide, attenuate to a sometimes truncate base, rather abruptly tapered to an acute to acuminate apex, pinnate-pinnatifid in small specimens, 2-pinnate-bipinnatifid in large ones, the pinnae ca. 8–15 pairs, borne at usually uniformly increasing distances from the crowded lamina apex to the base, bearing few to many elongate glands on the laminae and multicellular hairs on the stipes; indusia large, lacking marginal hairs.

Epipetric in rock crevices, on ledges and boulders, on talus slopes, and terrestrial in sandy, loess, and probably other types of soil. Abundant. Maine, Quebec, New York, Michigan, Wisconsin, Minnesota, eastern Nebraska, Kansas, northern Oklahoma south to South Carolina, Georgia, Alabama, Mississippi, Louisiana, and Texas.

Cultivated in moist, neutral to acidic garden soil or potting mix in partial sun. The scaly rachises distinguish this species from members of the genus *Cystopteris*.

342   Woodsia mexicana Fée
Mexican Cliff Fern

Stipes 1.5–9 cm long, not articulate, with concolorous, pale brown scales and bicolorous scales having pale brown margins and usually broad, dark brown central portions at the base of the stipe. Laminae rhombic, 5–21 cm long, 1–5 cm wide, attenuate and sometimes rather truncate at the base, acute-acuminate at the apex, pinnate-pinnatifid in small specimens, 2-pinnate-pinnatifid at the base of the pinnae in large ones, the pinnae ca. 8–20 pairs, only the lowest few basal pairs increasingly distant, lanceate to nearly oblong, with lobes that often are truncate at the apex, bearing few to many elongate glands on the lamina and stipe and some multicellular marginal hairs; indusia small, bearing conspicuous marginal hairs.

Epipetric in crevices in cliffs and at the base of rocks. Occasional. Southeastern Colorado to western Texas, New Mexico, Arizona, and southern California.

Not cultivated. Presumably this species hybridizes with the Mexican *W. mollis* (Kaulf.) J. Smith to form the tetraploid hybrid *W. plummerae*.

343   Woodsia plummerae Lemmon
Plummer's Cliff Fern

Stipes 2–10 cm long, not articulate, with concolorous, pale reddish-brown scales and bicolorous scales having pale reddish-brown margins and usually broad, purplish-black central portions at the base of the stipe. Laminae lanceolate (in small specimens) to rhombic (in larger ones), 5–18(23) cm long, 2–5(6) cm wide, acute to acuminate, or occasionally forked at the apex, 2-pinnate-pinnatifid, the pinnae ca. 6–12 pairs, increasingly distant from below the lamina apex, lanceate to oblong, with lobes that are round to truncate at the apex, bearing elongate glands on the lamina and stipe and some multicellular hairs on the stipe; indusia large, bearing short marginal hairs.

Epipetric on shaded ledges and in rock crevices, occasionally terrestrial among broken rocks. Rare. Western Texas to Arizona.

Not cultivated. Presumably this species is a fertile tetraploid hybrid of *W. mexicana* and *W. mollis* (Kaulf.) J. Smith.

DRYOPTERIDACEAE
The Wood Fern Family

The Dryopteridaceae is used here to include the Tectarioideae and Dryopteridoideae of Crabbe, Jermy, and Mickel (1975, pp. 150–151). The family includes about 850 species in 32 genera; half of the genera are exclusively Old World, and most of the New World genera are entirely tropical. The principal genera in the family are *Arachniodes*, *Ctenitis*, *Dryopteris*, *Polystichum*, and *Tectaria*; all of which are found in the United States, as are *Cyrtomium* and *Phanerophlebia*.

The plants of the Dryopteridaceae are mostly medium to large in size, especially the tropical species. Their rhizomes are erect, ascending, or short-creeping and have pale to dark brown or sometimes reddish-brown lanceolate to linear scales with inconspicuous cell walls. The stipes are usually pale throughout and have a tuft of scales at the base or are scaly throughout. The mostly monomorphic laminae are papery to leathery, pinnate to more than 3-pinnate, and often are slightly scaly or hairy on the abaxial surface of the rachis and costae. The margins in some genera typically are spinulose, thickened, or both. The venation may be free or anastomosing with or without free included veinlets. The sori are round in most genera and species and usually are protected by a reniform or peltate indusium, although some species are exindusiate.

Most species of the Wood Fern Family are terrestrial; a few are epipetric or facultatively epipetric. Plants of *Dryopteris* and *Polystichum* are excellent in cool-climate woodland gardens. *Cyrtomium* and *Arachniodes* are suitable for greenhouse cultivation or in rock gardens in the southern United States. The small species of *Tectaria* also make excellent greenhouse plants.

Key to the genera of Dryopteridaceae
1. Veins free, **3**
1. Veins copiously anastomosing, with or without free included veinlets, **2**

2(1). Pinna margins not thick or pale; areolae irregularly polygonal, with or without free included veinlets; pinnae without a low acroscopic basal auricle, *Tectaria*, p. 269

2(1). Pinna margins thick and pale; areolae regular, between closely spaced main side veins; pinnae with a low, acroscopic auricle, *Cyrtomium*, p. 280

3(1). Pinna margins not thick or pale, sometimes spinulose; indusia reniform or absent, **6**

3(1). Pinna margins thick and pale, usually spinulose; indusia peltate or reniform, **4**

4(3). Laminae subpentagonal; apical pinna as long or longer than the rest of the lamina, *Arachniodes*, p. 283

4(3). Laminae not subpentagonal; apical pinna much shorter than the rest of the lamina, **5**

5(4). Sori in 2 or 3 rows on each side of the pinna costa; lamina apex a barely lobed, subconform pinna; pinnae simple, not lobed, *Phanerophlebia*, p. 281

5(4). Sori in 1(2) rows on each side of the pinna costa or pinnule costule; lamina apex pinnatifid, not subconform; pinnae simple, lobed, or more divided, *Polystichum*, p. 272

6(3). Stipe bases with broad, lanceolate scales; indusia reniform and large; laminae rather coriaceous; articulate hairs absent on the lamina axes, *Dryopteris*, p. 284

6(3). Stipe bases with narrow, hair-like scales; indusia absent; articulate hairs common on the lamina axes, *Ctenitis*, p. 268

CTENITIS
The Comb Ferns

Ctenitis is a genus of about 150 species found in the New and Old World tropics. Two species that are common in tropical America are known from southern Florida. The common name of the genus refers to the pectinate pinnae or pinnules found in most species.

The Comb Ferns are medium to large-sized plants with short-creeping or erect rhizomes. Many have a crown of fronds emanating from a short, erect or ascending rhizome, and so look a little like a tree fern. Typically, the stipe bases bear a mass of narrow, almost hair-like scales. The laminae are thin, usually bright, pale, or medium green, and are pinnate-pinnatifid or more divided. The adaxial side of the axes are hairy, usually with articulate hairs. The sori are round and are usually borne medially between the axis and the margin. The sori are exindusiate or have a small, reniform indusium in many tropical species.

Ctenitis grows in moist to wet woods in full sun to full shade. Given sufficient warmth and humidity, they make good greenhouse plants or garden plants in tropical regions.

Key to Ctenitis

1. Laminae oblong, pinnate-pinnatifid; pinnae 1.5–2.7 cm wide, all equilateral; FL. *344. C. submarginalis*

1. Laminae ovate-lanceolate, 2–3-pinnate-pinnatifid; pinnae 3–15 cm wide; especially the basal ones inequilateral, the basiscopic pinnules much longer than the acroscopic ones; FL. *345. C. sloanei*

344 Ctenitis submarginalis (Langsd. & Fisch.) Copel.

Brown-hair Comb Fern

Rhizomes short-creeping; stipes 20–45 cm long, straw-colored, densely covered at and above the base with long, narrowly lanceate, reddish-brown to brown scales with a filiform apex. Laminae oblong, 30–60 cm long, 15–35 cm wide, parallel-sided, slightly tapered at the truncate base, abruptly tapered to an acuminate, pinnatifid apex, pinnate-pinnatifid, thin, bright pale green, with small scales like those of the stipe scattered on the axes; pinnae oblong-lanceate, 6–16 cm long, 1.5–2.7 cm wide, with many subopposite pairs of round-truncate, subentire lobes, the veins free, simple; sori round, medial, exindusiate.

Terrestrial in swamps and wet woods, usually in hammocks, in circum-neutral soil. Frequent. Central and southern peninsular Florida.

Not cultivated.

345 Ctenitis sloanei (Poepp.) Morton

Florida Tree Fern

Rhizomes erect; stipes 30–100 cm long, pale reddish-brown, densely covered at and above the base with long, narrowly linear, reddish-brown scales with a filiform apex; laminae ovate-lanceate, 40–80 cm long, 30–80 cm wide, obtuse at the base, acute-acuminate at the apex, 3-pinnate-pinnatifid at the base, 2-pinnate-pinnatifid toward the apex, thin, medium green, the axes with short hairs scattered on the abaxial surface of the axes; pinnae oblong-lanceate, 15–40 cm long, 3–15 cm wide, the basal pinnae much the widest and especially basiscopically developed, the basiscopic pinnules ca. twice as long as the acroscopic pinnules, the veins free, simple; sori round, exindusiate, but protected by a few short paraphyses.

Terrestrial in circumneutral humus over limestone in hammock woods. Frequent. Southern peninsular Florida.

Cultivated in moist basic potting mix in full sun or partial shade. Formerly this species erroneously was called *C. ampla* (Humb. & Bonpl. ex Willd.) Ching, a rather rare South American species.

TECTARIA
The Halberd Ferns

Tectaria is a large genus of tropical ferns totalling about 200 species. The genus is rather diverse, and many segregate genera have been proposed. Those species with acrostichoid fertile laminae do belong to other genera, but segregates founded on sterile lamina shape or venation mostly should not be recognized because the fronds are so variable. Most species of *Tectaria* are tropical.

The Halberd Ferns mostly are medium-sized plants. The terrestrial species generally have stout, erect or short-creeping rhizomes bearing brownish-black scales. The stipes are mostly straw-colored above a brown base and have a few, often deciduous scales, especially at the base. The laminae are about as long as the stipes and are pinnate to 2-pinnate in most species, although a few species are more dissected and fewer have simple or lobed laminae. The laminae usually are glabrous and have anastomosing veins with or without free included veinlets. The sori are round or sometimes elongate and are dorsal on the veins or at the intersection of veins; they may be exindusiate or indusiate with a reniform or peltate indusium.

Tectaria grows in moist to wet places, mostly in the lowland tropics. A few species, including most of those occurring in the United States, are epipetric. Many of the species are rather large and coarse, but some of the smaller and more delicate ones are suitable for greenhouse growing. Several common tropical species are in cultivation. Both *Tectaria* and the genera segregated from it are in need of monographic study to determine rational limits of the genera.

Key to Tectaria
  1. Laminae up to 8(15) cm wide, ca. 5–30 cm long; stipes delicate, ca. 1 mm in diam., **3**
  1. Laminae ca. 15–30 cm wide, ca. 15–50 cm long; stipes coarse, at least 2 mm in diam, **2**
  2(1). Lateral pinnae shallowly lobed, often the basiscopic pair with a series of basiscopic lobes; FL. *346. T. heracleifolia*
  2(1). Lateral pinnae mostly entire, the basiscopic pair usually with a single pair of basiscopic lobes; FL. *347. T. incisa*
  3(1). Basal pinnae (if any) inequilateral, cut away at the lower base, usually adnate to the rachis at the upper base; hairs on the stipes mostly less than 1 mm long; FL. *348. T. lobata*
  3(1). Basal pinnae equilateral, not cut away at the lower base, never adnate to the rachis at the upper base; hairs on the stipes mostly 1–3 mm long; FL. *349. T. coriandrifolia*

346   Tectaria heracleifolia (Willd.) Underw.
Broad Halberd Fern
Rhizomes erect or ascending; stipes 15–45 cm long, reddish-brown or pale brown above a dark brown base; laminae variable, the smaller ones unlobed, the larger ones usually pentagonal, 15–40 cm long, (10)15–30 cm wide, the lateral pinnae 1 or 2 pairs, commonly shallowly lobed, usually with a basal basiscopic lobe, especially on the basal pair, the terminal pinna usually with 1–several pairs of basal lobes, shallowly lobed toward the acuminate apex; venation of polygonal areolae with a few included

veinlets between straight side veins; sori round, in a single row on either side of the side veins; indusia peltate.

Epipetric or terrestrial on or around limestone, in lime sinks and in hammocks. Common. Peninsular Florida. Also formerly known from Uvalde Co., Texas.

Cultivated in moist garden soil or potting mix in partial sun. Some plants of this species are slightly dimorphic, with tall, narrow fertile fronds.

347 Tectaria incisa Cav.
Incised Halberd Fern

Rhizomes short-creeping; stipes 50 cm long, pale brown above a dark brown base; laminae oblong, ca. 50 cm long, 30 cm wide, the lateral pinnae ca. 5 pairs, mostly entire except the basal pair with a single pair of basiscopic lobes, the terminal pinna with 1–several pairs of basal lobes, abruptly tapered to an entire, acuminate apex; venation of polygonal areolae with many included veinlets between ascending side veins; sori round, in a single row close to either side of the side veins; indusia reniform.

Terrestrial in wet hammocks. Rare. Known only from Dade and Broward counties Florida.

Cultivated in moist potting mix or garden soil in partial sun. The United States specimens are referable to var. *incisa*; this and other varieties are widespread in tropical America.

348 Tectaria lobata (Poir.) Morton
Least Halberd Fern

Rhizomes short-creeping; stipes 4–20(28) cm long, pale brown above a dark brown base; laminae lanceolate to deltate, 4–11(14) cm long, 2–8(15) cm wide, the smaller laminae simple, lanceolate, shallowly to deeply lobed, the larger laminae deltate, deeply pinnatifid or with 1 pair of free basal pinnae and a deeply lobed terminal pinna gradually tapered to an acuminate apex; venation of polygonal areolae with a few to many included veinlets between side veins; sori round, in a single row close to either side of the side veins; indusia reniform.

Epipetric in lime sinks and solution holes. Rare. Central and southern peninsular Florida.

Not cultivated. This species has been known as *T. minima* Underw. It hybridizes with *T. coriandrifolia* to form the sterile *T.* ×*amesiana* A. A. Eaton.

349   Tectaria coriandrifolia (Swartz) Underw.
Hairy Halberd Fern

Rhizomes short-creeping; stipes 3–10 cm long, pale brown or reddish-brown above a dark brown base; laminae lanceolate-oblong, 5–10 cm long, 2.5–4 cm wide, the lateral pinnae 2 or 3 pairs, with 1–several pairs of lobes, the large terminal pinna deeply lobed at the base, more shallowly lobed toward the acute apex; buds sometimes present at the base of the pinnae; venation of curving, polygonal areolae with no included veinlets, the side veins poorly developed; sori round, in a single row on either side of the side veins; indusia reniform.

Epipetric on lime sinks. Very rare. Known only from Dade Co., Florida, but not seen for several years and perhaps extirpated.

Not cultivated. This species hybridizes with *T. lobata* to form *T.* × *amesiana* A. A. Eaton.

POLYSTICHUM
The Holly Ferns

Polystichum is a large genus that includes about 135 species found principally in the North Temperate region; a few species occur at high elevations in the tropics or in the South Temperate region. The common name refers to the spinulose margins of the fronds, which resemble in a small way the spine-like protuberances on Holly leaves. The genus is close to *Phanerophlebia* and yet closer to *Cyrtomium*, which may prove to be inseparable from *Polystichum*; W. H. Wagner (1979) has shown that the anastomosing veins found in *Cyrtomium* and in some species of *Phanerophlebia* arose in two separate ways that, when compared with the anastomosing veins found in a few species of *Polystichum*, may shed further light on the limits of these genera.

The Holly Ferns have erect to ascending rhizomes bearing a cluster of fronds at their apex. The stipes are stout, usually short in relation to the length of the laminae, and are densely covered at and above the base with large, lanceate or lanceolate scales. The laminae are longer than the stipes, rhombic to lanceolate, pinnate or more divided, and commonly are rather stiff and harsh. Their rachises usually are scaly with paler, smaller scales than those of the stipe bases. The laminae often have narrow scales or hair-like scales on the costae or the abaxial surface. The veins are free and hidden by the coriaceous texture of the laminae. The indusia are peltate, usually persistent, and commonly erose-toothed or ciliate.

Polystichum grows in moist woods or among rocks, and a few species are found in crevices or on ledges of cliffs. Many species are in cultivation in woodland gardens or as plantings in cool climates. In Victorian times, fancy sports of the European *P. setiferum* (Forsk.) Woyn. and *P. aculeatum* (L.) Schott were much in demand by gardeners. Unfortunately, many of the eagerly sought fancy types no longer are in cultivation. *Polystichum* was monographed for the western United States by D. H. Wagner (1979).

Key to Polystichum

1. Laminae partially dimorphic, the distal portion contracted and fertile; E. *350*. *P. acrostichoides*

1. Laminae entirely monomorphic, the upper portion not contracted, the laminae fertile more or less throughout, **2**

2(1). Pinnae lobed to pinnate, **6**

2(1). Pinnae entire to serrate, not lobed, **3**

3(2). Laminae narrowly oblanceolate, attenuate at the base, widest above the middle; stipes ca. ⅕–1/10 as long as the laminae; N, W. *362*. *P. lonchitis*

3(2). Laminae nearly oblong, truncate at the base, widest about the middle; stipes ca. ¼–⅓ as long as the laminae, **4**

4(3). Scales on the rachis many, persistent, reddish-brown, lanceolate, more than 1 mm wide; W. *352*. *P. munitum*

4(3). Scales on the rachis few, deciduous, usually pale brown, acicular, less than 1 mm wide, **5**

5(4). Pinnae less than 5 times longer than wide; laminae not plane, the crowded pinnae held horizontally in life, commonly imbricate when pressed; W. *358*. *P. imbricans* subsp. *imbricans*

5(4). Pinnae more than 5 times longer than wide; laminae plane, the less crowded pinnae not held horizontally in life, usually not imbricate when pressed; CA. **357*. *P. imbricans* subsp. *curtum*

6(2). Segments not spinulose; laminae usually only 10–15 cm long; P. *360*. *P. lemmonii*

6(2). Segments spinulose; laminae usually more than 15 cm long (9–15 cm in *P. aleuticum*), **7**

7(6). Pinnules or lobes broadly adnate to the costule or costa, **9**

7(6). Pinnules stalked or sessile, not or scarcely adnate to the costule or costa, **8**

8(7). Laminae rhombic, greatly tapered at the base; basal acroscopic pinnules lobed, not cut to the costule; stipes usually less than 15 cm long, N. *356*. *P. braunii*

8(7). Laminae lanceolate, not much tapered at the base; basal acroscopic pinnules fully pinnate, cut to the costule; stipes at least 15 cm long; CA. *355*. *P. dudleyi*

9(7). Largest scales above the base of the stipe mostly 2.5–5 mm wide, ovate-lanceolate; laminae mostly more than 5 cm wide, **12**

9(7). Largest scales above the base of the stipe mostly less than 2 mm wide, narrowly ovate-lanceolate to linear-lanceolate; laminae mostly less than 5 cm wide, **10**

10(9). Stipes purplish-black to brown, the scales entire or very sparsely toothed, acuminate at the apex; AK. *363*. *P. aleuticum*

10(9). Stipes straw-colored above the base, the scales noticeably toothed, filiform at the apex, **11**

11(10). Median pinnae (2)3–4 times longer than wide, slightly spinulose; QUE, W. *359*. *P. scopulinum*

11(10). Median pinnae mostly 1.5–2.5 times longer than wide, decidedly spinulose; W. **361*. *P. kruckebergii*

12(9). Rachises usually bearing 1 subapical, proliferous bud; NW. *351*. *P. andersonii*

12(9). Rachises never bearing a proliferous bud, **13**

13(12). Pinnules shallowly to deeply lobed; lower portion of the stipes densely covered with golden-brown scales; AK. **364*. *P. microchlamys*

13(12). Pinnules scarcely or not lobed; lower portion of the stipes sparsely covered with reddish-brown or pale brown scales, **14**

14(13). Basal pinnules scarcely adnate to the costa; rachises with few to many linear-lanceolate scales; costae with a few linear scales; larger stipe scales dark reddish-brown; P. *354*. *P. californicum*

14(13). Basal pinnules distinctly adnate to the costa; rachises with many lanceolate scales; costae with few to many linear-lanceolate scales; larger stipe scales pale brown; AK, BC. *353*. *P. setigerum*

350 Polystichum acrostichoides (Michx.) Schott
Christmas Fern

Stipes 6–30 cm long; laminae narrowly lanceolate-oblong, 15–55 cm long, 5–12(14) cm wide, slightly reduced to a truncate base, the basal pinnae sometimes reflexed, contracted toward the apex ca. ⅓ in fertile specimens, tapering to an acute-acuminate apex, simply pinnate, the pinnae inconspicuously to conspicuously serrate (or more divided in several trivial fancy forms), with a single, spinulose lobe at the upper base, slightly excavate at the lower base; sori in 1 or 2 rows on each side of the costa, the indusia often deciduous at maturity and the sporangia then appearing acrostichoid.

Terrestrial in well-drained, cirumneutral to subacid soil in partial sun. Abundant. Nova Scotia, Quebec, Ontario, and southeastern Minnesota south to Florida, Alabama, Mississippi, Louisiana, Texas, Oklahoma, southeastern Kansas, Missouri, and southeastern Iowa.

Cultivated in moist garden soil or potting mix in full shade. This species hybridizes with *P. braunii* in Pennsylvania and New York and with *P. lonchitis* in Ontario to form *P. ×hagenahii* Cody. Several forms and varieties of this species have been described that appear to be based on developmental abnormalities; these have crisped, cristate, emarginate, tapered, or twisted pinnae. For instance, Wagner, Farrar, and McAlpin (1970) have shown that *P. acrostichoides* f. *incisum* (Gray) Gilbert is not genetically fixed, for fronds of this "form" appear sporadically on normal plants of *P. acrostichoides*.

351   Polystichum andersonii Hopkins

Anderson's Holly Fern

Stipes 5–20 cm long, with concolorous, reddish-brown, slightly toothed scales at and above the base and on the rachis and with pale reddish-brown, narrow scales toward the stipe apex and on the rachis; rachises usually bearing 1 subapical, proliferous bud; laminae rhombic, 17–75(90) cm long, (4)6–16(20) cm wide, gradually tapered to the base, evenly tapered to an acute-acuminate apex, 2-pinnate or nearly so; pinnae lanceate or lanceate-oblong, deeply lobed to nearly pinnate, the basal lobes or pinnules broadly attached to the costae; indusia erose-toothed.

Terrestrial in woods and thickets, sometimes among rocks. Alaska to Oregon and Montana.

Cultivated in moist potting mix in partial sun. Rare. This species presumably is of hybrid origin between an undescribed diploid from British Columbia and *P. munitum* (see p. 328 and D. H. Wagner, 1979, p. 43). Backcrosses between *P. andersonii* and *P. munitum* are known from Washington.

352   Polystichum munitum (Kaulf.) Presl

Sword Fern

Stipes 6–55 cm long, with small, concolorous, pale brown and large (up to ca. 2 cm long), weakly bicolorous, golden, dark brown, or dark reddish-brown scales, especially at the base; laminae linear-lanceolate, sometimes subrhombic in small specimens, (15)25–110 cm long, (5)6–22 cm wide, usually subtruncate at the base, usually obtusely tapered to a short, acuminate apex, pinnate; pinnae entire to serrate, strongly spinulose, excavate at the lower base, auriculate at the upper base; indusia ciliate.

Terrestrial in moist to seasonally dry woods. Abundant. Alaska to Idaho, Montana, Oregon, and California. Disjunct in the Black Hills of South Dakota.

Cultivated in moist potting mix in full shade. This species hybridizes with *P. dudlyei* to form *P. californicum*, with *P. braunii* to form *P. setigerum*, and with an unknown diploid species to form *P. andersonii* (see p. 328).

353 Polystichum setigerum (Presl) Presl
Alaska Holly Fern

Stipes 6–20 cm long, with concolorous, wide, pale brown scales at and above the base and with few to many, straw-colored, lanceolate scales toward the stipe apex and on the rachis; laminae rhombic, 25–90 cm long, (6)8–20(24) cm wide, gradually tapered at the base and at the acute-acuminate apex, pinnate-pinnatifid to nearly 2-pinnate; pinnae oblong, the distal ones lanceate, deeply lobed to subpinnate at the base, the basal pinnules decidedly adnate; indusia distinctly ciliate, deciduous.

Terrestrial in woods. Very rare. Panhandle of Alaska to southern coastal British Columbia.

Not cultivated. This species is a hybrid of *P. braunii* and *P. munitum* (see p. 328).

354 Polystichum californicum (D. C. Eaton) Diels
California Holly Fern

Stipes 6–35 cm long, with concolorous, long, dark reddish-brown, entire scales at and above the base and with few to many, straw-colored to pale brown, linear-lanceolate scales toward the stipe apex and on the rachis; laminae linear-lanceate, 15–60(75) cm long, 4–15(22) cm wide, slightly tapered above the truncate base, gradually tapered to an acuminate apex, 2-pinnate or nearly so; pinnae oblong-lanceate, deeply lobed to pinnate at the base, the basal pinnules scarcely adnate; indusia erose-toothed, ciliate when young.

Terrestrial in woods or epipetric in crevices and on ledges of cliffs. Occasional. Vancouver Island, British Columbia to central California.

Not cultivated. This species is a tetraploid hybrid between *P. dudleyi* and *P. munitum*. It backcrosses with both parents (see p. 328).

355 Polystichum dudleyi Maxon
Dudley's Holly Fern

Stipes 15–40 cm long, with concolorous, pale to dark reddish-brown, slightly toothed scales at and above the base, and with straw-colored, linear scales toward the stipe apex and on the rachis; laminae lanceolate, 20–60 cm long, 6–25(30) cm wide, the lowest pinnae (1.5)4–11 cm long, evenly acuminate at the apex, 3-pinnate; pinnae oblong, the basal and median pinnules of the median pinnae short-stalked to sessile, lobed to pinnate (in large specimens), the distal pinnule somewhat adnate, all pinnules strongly dimidiate; indusia long-ciliate.

Terrestrial in woods. Rare. Coast ranges of central California.

Cultivated in moist potting soil in partial sun. This species hybridizes with *P. munitum* to form *P. californicum* (see p. 328).

356   Polystichum braunii (Spenner) Fée
Braun's Holly Fern

Stipes 4–18 cm long, with concolorous, pale brown or slightly reddish-brown entire scales at and above the base and with straw-colored, linear scales toward the stipe apex and on the rachis; laminae rhombic, (15)30–75 cm long, (6)10–22 cm wide, gradually tapered at the base, the lowest pinnae usually no more than 2 cm long, evenly acute-acuminate at the apex, 2-pinnate-pinnatifid; pinnae oblong, the basal and median pinnules of the median pinnae sessile, lobed, the distal pinnules somewhat adnate, all pinnules strongly dimidiate; indusia erose-toothed to entire.

Terrestrial in moist woods and thickets, occasionally among rocks. Occasional. Nova Scotia to Ontario south to Maine, New Hampshire, Vermont, New York, Pennsylvania, Michigan, Wisconsin, and northern Minnesota. Disjunct in Alaska, British Columbia, and northern Idaho.

Cultivated in moist potting mix in partial sun or in cool, woodland gardens. This species hybridizes with *P. munitum* to form *P. setigerum* and with *P. acrostichoides* (see p. 328). American material of this species sometimes is distinguished from the European var. *braunii* as var. *purshii* Fern., but the differences between the two are slight.

*357   Polystichum imbricans subsp. curtum (Ewan) D. H. Wagner
Narrow-leaved Sword Fern

Stipes 8–26 cm long, with long, lanceolate, concolorous, dark reddish-brown scales at and above the base and sometimes small, linear, pale brown scales toward the stipe apex and on the rachis; laminae nearly linear, (15)20–50 cm long, (5)6–11 cm wide, almost truncate at the base, evenly tapered to an acuminate apex, pinnate; pinnae (2.5)3–5 cm long, entire, short-spinulose, excavate at the lower base, auriculate at the upper base; indusia irregularly erose-toothed.

Terrestrial in moist woods. Rare. Central to Southern California.

Cultivated in moist potting mix in partial sun.

358   Polystichum imbricans (D. C. Eaton) D. H. Wagner subsp. imbricans
Narrow-leaved Sword Fern

Stipes 5–22(28) cm long, with long, concolorous, dark reddish-brown scales at and above the base and sometimes with paler brown similar scales toward the stipe apex and on the rachis; laminae nearly linear, (15)21–45(55) cm long, 4–9(12) cm wide, almost truncate at the base, evenly tapered to an acute or acuminate apex, pinnate; pinnae 2–4.5(5.5) cm long, entire, short-spinulose, excavate at the lower base, auriculate at the upper base; indusia entire.

Terrestrial in rather dry, rocky woods. Occasional. British Columbia to southern California.

Cultivated in moist potting mix in partial sun. This subspecies hybridizes with *P. lemmonii* to form *P. scopulinum;* backcrosses with the latter species are known (see p. 328).

359 Polystichum scopulinum (D. C. Eaton) Maxon
Crag Holly Fern

Stipes 3–17 cm long, with long, concolorous, pale to medium reddish-brown toothed scales at and above the base and with straw-colored, linear scales toward the stipe apex and on the rachis; laminae narrowly rhombic to narrowly lanceolate, 9–25(30) cm long, 1.5–4(5) cm wide, tapered abruptly or gradually at the base, acute at the apex, pinnate-pinnatifid to 2-pinnate in larger specimens; pinnae lanceolate-oblong, deeply pinnatifid or with a single pinnule at the acroscopic base, lobed to pinnatifid elsewhere, the margins indistinctly spinulose; indusia entire.

Terrestrial among rocks. Occasional. Southern British Columbia, Idaho, and northwestern Wyoming south to southern California and southeastern Arizona. Disjunct on the Gaspé Peninsula, Quebec.

Not cultivated. This species is a hybrid between *P. imbricans* subsp. *imbricans* and *P. lemmonii.* It backcrosses with both parents (see p. 328).

360 Polystichum lemmonii Underw.
Lemmon's Holly Fern

Stipes 4–12(17) cm long, with concolorous, pale reddish-brown distantly toothed scales at and above the base and with smaller, pale brown, almost linear scales toward the stipe apex and on the rachis; laminae almost linear, 6–23(26) cm long, (1.5)2–4(5) cm wide, slightly tapered above the truncate base, rather abruptly but evenly tapered to an acute apex, 2-pinnate-pinnatifid; pinnae not spinulose, the segment margins with few to many low lobes terminating in broad teeth, the basal pinnules of the median pinnae sessile, lobed, the other pinnules somewhat adnate, lobed to entire, none strongly dimidiate; indusia entire.

Terrestrial in serpentine soils among rocks. Occasional. Washington to central California.

Said to be cultivated in moist potting mix in partial sun, but probably difficult due to the need for soil derived from selenium-bearing rocks. This species hybridizes with *P. imbricans* subsp. *imbricans* to form *P. scopulinum;* backcrosses with that species are known (see p. 328).

*361 Polystichum kruckebergii W. H. Wagner
Kruckeberg's Holly Fern

Stipes 2–11 cm long, with long, concolorous, pale to medium brown, slightly toothed scales at and above the base and with pale, narrow scales toward the stipe apex and on the rachis; laminae linear-lanceolate, 7–23 cm long, 1.5–3 cm wide, scarcely tapered to a truncate base, the lower pinnae rather distant from the median ones, acute at the crowded apex, pinnate-pinnatifid; pinnae oblong, short, with a large, acroscopic basal auricule, lobed; indusia entire.

Epipetric in crevices in cliffs or on talus slopes often, but not exclusively, on serpentine rocks. Very rare. British Columbia to southern California east to western Montana, Idaho, and northwestern Utah.

Cultivated among rock in cool-climate gardens. This species is the hybrid between *P. lemmonii* and *P. lonchitis* (see p. 328).

362   Polystichum lonchitis (L.) Roth
Northern Holly Fern

Stipes 1–6 cm long, with pale brown or reddish-brown, concolorous scales; laminae narrowly oblanceolate, 10–55 cm long, 2–6 cm wide, attenuate at the base, acute or sometimes acuminate at the very apex, pinnate; pinnae strongly serrate-spinulose, the lower and median sterile ones excavate at the lower base, the fertile upper ones dimidiate and often somewhat falcate, not or only slightly different in length from the lower ones, auriculate at the upper base; indusia entire.

Terrestrial among rocks or on talus slopes in circumneutral soil associated with basic rocks. Nova Scotia to northern Michigan and adjacent Ontario. Alaska to Alberta south to the mountains of Montana, Wyoming, Colorado, Arizona, Utah, Idaho, Oregon, and northern California.

Cultivated in moist potting mix in partial sun. Frequent. This species hybridizes with *P. lemmonii* to form *P. kruckebergii* and with *P. acrostichoides* to form the sterile hybrid *P.* × *hagenahii* Cody, found in Ontario (see p. 328).

363   Polystichum aleuticum C. Chr. in Hultén
Aleutian Holly Fern

Stipes 2–6 cm long, purplish-black to brown throughout, with concolorous, pale to medium brown, nearly entire scales at and above the base and with straw-colored, linear scales on the rachis; laminae nearly linear, (6)9–15 cm long, (1)1.5–2 cm wide, slightly tapered at the base, acute at the apex, pinnate-pinnatifid; pinnae nearly ovate, lobed at the base, rather weakly spinulose; indusia erose-toothed.

Presumably terrestrial. Very rare. Aleutian Islands.

Not cultivated.

*364 Polystichum microchlamys (Christ) Matsumura
Attu Holly Fern

Stipes 25–30 cm long, with concolorous, brown to golden-brown, slightly toothed scales at and above the base and on the rachis and with abundant, pale golden-brown, narrow to wide scales toward the stipe apex and on the rachis; laminae elliptic-lanceolate, ca. 80 cm long, 15 cm wide, abruptly tapered at the base, abruptly tapered at the apex to a short, small, pinnatifid, acuminate apex, 2-pinnate-pinnatifid; pinnae lanceolate-oblong, the pinnules deeply lobed, their ultimate segments broadly attached to the costules; indusia slightly erose-toothed.

Terrestrial in woods. Very rare. Attu Island, Alaska.

Not cultivated.

CYRTOMIUM
The Net-veined Holly Ferns

Cyrtomium is an Old World genus of about 12 species, most of which occur in Japan and China. *Cyrtomium caryotideum* (Wall. ex. Hook. & Grev.) Presl and *C. falcatum* L. f.) Presl extend into the Pacific Islands and Africa, perhaps by introduction; and the latter, along with *C. fortunei* J. Smith, has been introduced and is becoming naturalized in the United States. W. H. Wagner (pers. comm.) has found correspondences between the patterns of anastomosing veins of *Cyrtomium* and certain species of *Polystichum* with broad, undivided pinnae. Further work along this line may demonstrate that *Cyrtomium* would be better treated as a section or subgenus of *Polystichum*.

The Net-vein Holly Ferns have erect or ascending rhizomes bearing a few fronds at the apex. The stipes are shorter than the laminae and have large, dark brown, erose-toothed scales at and above the base. The laminae are oblong, 1-pinnate, truncate or only slightly narrowed at the base, and are not much tapered at the apex below the subconform, basally lobed, apical pinna. The pinnae are lanceate with a slight acroscopic basal lobe, falcate, crenate at the thickened, pale margin, and have closely spaced lateral veins with anastomosing branch veins. The round sori in 2–8 rows between the main lateral veins are protected by peltate indusia.

Cyrtomium in the United States grows mostly as an escape on north-facing brick or stone walls. A few naturalized occurrences are known. *Cyrtomium caryotideum*, *C. falcatum* and several of its cultivated varieties, and *C. fortunei* all are cultivated as greenhouse plants or are planted outdoors with suitable protection in subtropical portions of the country.

Key to Cyrtomium
1. Adaxial surface of the coriaceous laminae shiny, dark green; pinnae 1.5–3 cm wide, 4–10(12) pairs per lamina; SE. *365. C. falcatum*

1. Adaxial surface of the papyraceous laminae dull, pale green; pinnae 1–2 cm wide, 10–25 pairs per lamina; SE *366. *C. fortunei*

365   Cyrtomium falcatum (L. f.) Presl
Asian Net-veined Holly Fern

Stipes 15–30 cm long, with concolorous or weakly bicolorous, blotchy, pale and dark brown, erose-ciliate scales at and above the base; laminae oblong-lanceolate, 15–35 cm long, 10–15 cm wide, nearly truncate at the base, slightly tapered to a simple apical pinna bearing a single basal lobe, pinnate, the rachis and costae with small, contorted, pale, toothed, hair-like scales; pinnae 4–10(12) oblong-lanceolate pairs, 1.5–3 cm wide, somewhat abruptly tapered below the falcate, acuminate apex; indusia erose-toothed, crowded, the submarginal ones often almost touching.

Epipetric on cliffs, and rocks and terrestrial on clay soil in woods. Rare. Escaped and perhaps naturalized from South Carolina to Florida (especially St. Augustine and St. Johns counties) and Louisiana. A disjunct population was known at La Jolla, San Diego Co., California.

Cultivated in moist to dry garden soil or potting mix in partial shade. Several cultivated varieties, including cv. *Mayi* and cv. *Rochefordianum*, are currently grown.

*366   Cyrtomium fortunei J. Smith
Fortune's Net-veined Holly Fern

Stipes 15–30 cm long, with concolorous or weakly bicolorous, blotchy, pale and dark brown, erose-ciliate scales at and above the base; laminae oblong-lanceolate, 25–60 cm long, (12)15–20 cm wide, slightly tapered to a truncate base, somewhat tapered to a simple apical pinna bearing a single basal lobe, pinnate, the rachis and costae with small, contorted, pale, toothed, hair-like scales; pinnae 10–25 lanceolate pairs, 1–2 cm wide, falcate, with an acuminate apex; indusia entire or slightly erose, uniformly somewhat distant.

Epipetric on brick or stone walls and terrestrial on clay banks in woods. Very rare. Naturalized in southwestern Mississippi and adjacent Louisiana. Escaped and apparently naturalized in South Carolina, Georgia, and perhaps elsewhere.

Cultivated in moist to dry potting mix in partial shade.

PHANEROPHLEBIA
The Mexican Holly Ferns

Phanerophlebia includes only eight species, most of which grow in Mexico and Central America. The genus is related to *Polystichum*, although less closely than is *Cyrtomium*, with which it has been combined by some authors. Like *Polystichum*, most of the species are free-veined and a few have anastomosing veins, but the anastomosing vein pattern is not like that of *Cyrtomium* in origin and development, according to W. H. Wagner (pers. comm.).

The Mexican Holly Ferns have erect or ascending rhizomes bearing a few fronds at the apex. The stipes are rather thin, about equal to the laminae in length, and have pale reddish-brown, linear-lanceate to linear scales at and above the base, with smaller, linear scales also present on the rachis and costae. The laminae are pinnate, lanceolate-oblong or oblong, truncate at the base, and acute at the apex with a conform, unlobed terminal pinna. The pinnae are lanceolate to linear-lanceolate, sometimes somewhat falcate, commonly spinulose along the thickened, pale margin, and have rather distant, pinnately branched lateral veins which anastomose irregularly near the margin in some species. The round sori in 1–4 rows mostly rather distant from the costae are protected by peltate indusia.

Phanerophlebia grows on or among rocks, mostly in shaded canyons in otherwise rather dry localities. None of the species seems to be in cultivation. The genus was monographed by Underwood (1899).

Key to Phanerophlebia
1. Larger pinnae with an acroscopic basal auricle or partially free segment, the fertile ones 1.5–2.5 cm wide, mostly lanceolate and 3–5 times longer than wide; indusia plane; SW. *367. P. auriculata*

1. Larger pinnae without an acroscopic basal auricle or free segment, the fertile ones 1–2 cm wide, mostly linear-lanceolate and 4–6 times longer than wide; indusia with a central protuberance or indentation; TX. *368. P. umbonata*

367 Phanerophlebia auriculata Underw.
Eared Mexican Holly Fern
Stipes 6–25(40) cm long, with concolorous, pale brown or brown, erose-ciliate scales at and above the base; laminae oblong, 20–35 cm long, (6)8–15 cm wide; pinnae (2)3–7(8) lanceolate pairs, the larger ones with an acroscopic basal lobe or partially free segment, the basiscopic base somewhat cut away in a smooth curve; indusia plane.

Epipetric in crevices of damp, shady canyon walls and cliffs. Occasional. Western Texas to central and southern Arizona.

Not cultivated.

368 Phanerophlebia umbonata Underw.
Umbonate Mexican Holly Fern
Stipes 20–55 cm long, with concolorous, pale brown, entire to erose-ciliate scales at and above the base; laminae oblong, 20–50 cm long, 9–15

cm wide; pinnae 9–16 mostly alternate pairs, lacking an acroscopic basal lobe or segment, the basiscopic base only slightly cut away; indusia with a central protuberance or indentation.

Epipetric in crevices of damp, shady canyon walls and cliffs. Very rare. Chisos Mountains, Brewster Co., western Texas.

Not cultivated.

ARACHNIODES
The East Indian Holly Ferns

Arachniodes includes about 30 species, three in the New World and the remainder in the tropics and subtropics of Asia and the Pacific Islands, with a few species in Australia, the Philippines, and Africa. The genus differs from *Dryopteris* and *Polystichum* in being continuously sulcate on the adaxial surface of the costules, costae, and rachis.

The East Indian Holly Ferns have densely scaly, creeping rhizomes with rather distant stipes. The stipes are covered, especially toward the base, with narrowly lanceate to nearly linear, dark brown, fibrous scales. The laminae are usually somewhat pentagonal with a large, terminal pinna, 2–3-pinnate, evergreen, coriaceous, and have a pale, thickened, often spinulose margin. Small, hair-like scales with an expanded base occur on the abaxial surface of the continuously grooved rachis, costae, and costules. Sori are borne in 1 or 2 rows on or at the tips of the free, forked veins; the indusia are thick, persistent, and reniform.

Several Asiatic species of *Arachniodes* are commonly cultivated in greenhouses or outdoors in tropical and subtropical regions. Morton (1960) published notes on *Arachniodes* and related genera.

*369   Arachniodes simplicior (Makino) Ohwi
Simpler East Indian Holly Fern

Rhizomes creeping, 5–8 mm in diam., densely scaly, the scales narrowly lanceate with a dilated base, tan to cinnamon-brown. Stipes 15–46 cm long, sulcate, subscabrous, with scales like those of the rhizome especially at and above the base, the scales smaller toward the apex of the stipes. Laminae evergreen, deltate-pentagonal, 24–39 cm long, 26–34 cm wide, 2–3-pinnate, the terminal pinna as long or longer than the rest of the laminae; lateral pinnae ca. 5 pairs, pinnate except the proximal pinnae 2-pinnate at the base, the adaxial surface glossy, green, glabrous, the adaxial surface not glossy, pale green, glabrous; pinnules spinulose, free-veined, sori in 1 submarginal row; indusia 0.5–1 mm in diam., orbicular-reniform, with a deep sinus and often overlapping lobes.

Terrestrial in ravines. Very rare. In the United States known only from one locality in North Augusta, Aiken Co., South Carolina, according to Gordon (1981). Presumably this species has been naturalized in its present location for 20–25 years.

Not cultivated.

DRYOPTERIS
The Wood Ferns

Dryopteris is a cosmopolitan genus of about 150 species. It is well represented in the United States, where most of the species are members of a large species complex (see p. 000). In many older Floras, *Gymnocarpium* and *Thelypteris* were united with *Dryopteris*, but these genera differ in having ternate laminae and in having small, awl-shaped hairs in or on the groove of the rachis, respectively.

The Wood Ferns are mostly medium-sized plants. Their stout rhizomes are erect, ascending, or short-creeping, and so their stipes are always closely spaced and typically form a vase-shaped cluster. The stipes and to some extent the rachises are covered with large, pale to medium brown, usually lanceolate scales. Minute, capitate, colorless glands are present on the axes and sometimes the laminae of some of the species; hairs are uncommon, but narrow to wide scales often are present on the abaxial surface of the costae. The pinnate-pinnatifid to 4-pinnate laminae are thin, not usually evergreen, and bear a single series of usually medial sori on each side of the segment midrib. The sori are round and are protected by a reniform indusium.

Even casual observers may stumble on hybrid plants of *Dryopteris*, several of which are quite common in the northeastern and upper midwestern states, especially where two or more species of Wood Ferns grow close together (Montgomery, 1976). Hybrids can be distinguished by their abortive spores and also often by their abortive sporangia. The spores will be of varying sizes, misshapen, or absent, and the sporangia may lack a dark-colored annulus or may be undeveloped. Since the key to *Dryopteris* has not been designed to be used with most sterile hybrids, many hybrids will key to a name that is incorrect for them. However, Montgomery (1982) has published a reliable key to the hybrids.

Dryopteris grows for the most part in moist to wet places, usually in fully or partially shaded woods or swamps. Many of the North American species are good subjects for the woodland garden, and most are in cultivation and are available in the trade. Several Asiatic species, like *D. erythrosora* (D. C. Eaton in Perry) Kuntze, are hardy with minimal protection in all but the coldest parts of the United States.

Key to Dryopteris

1. Laminae pinnate-pinnatifid to sometimes 2-pinnate-pinnatifid at the base of the lower pinnae, **7**

1. Laminae 3–4 pinnate, at least at the base, **2**

2(1). Laminae usually more than 30 cm long; plants terrestrial, **4**

2(1). Laminae usually less than 30 cm long; plants epipetric, **3**

3(2). Pinnules obtuse to round at the apex, with a broad, relatively undissected apical portion; laminae broadly ovate-lanceolate, 1.5–2 times longer than wide; AZ. *370. D. rossii*

3(2). Pinnules acute at the apex, with a narrow, usually dissected apical portion; laminae lanceolate, (1.5)2–3 times longer than wide; TX. *371. D. cinnamomea*

4(2). Basal basiscopic pinnule of the basal and suprabasal pinnae shorter than or equal to the adjacent distal basiscopic pinnules; pinnules in the middle and distal portion of the laminae narrowly attached nearly perpendicularly to the costae; axes and indusia glandular; fronds evergreen; NE, NO. *374. D. intermedia*

4(2). Basal basiscopic pinnule of the basal and suprabasal pinnae longer than the adjacent distal basiscopic pinnules; pinnules in the middle and distal portion of the laminae broadly attached at an oblique angle to the costae; axes eglandular; fronds not evergreen, **5**

5(4). Basal basiscopic pinnules of the basal pinnae usually less than 2 times longer than the basal acroscopic pinnules; stipe scales concolorous, pale brown; laminae long-deltate; N. *375. D. carthusiana*

5(4). Basal basiscopic pinnules of the basal pinnae more than 2 times longer than the basal acroscopic pinnules; stipe scales weakly bicolorous, at least some of them with a darker brown central stripe or basal portion; laminae broadly ovate, **6**

6(5). Stipe base scales pale brown to pale reddish-brown, usually with a slightly darkened, broad area at the base; basal basiscopic pinnules of the basal pinnae (2)3–4(5) times longer than the basal acroscopic pinnules; indusia slightly glandular; NE. *373. D. campyloptera*

6(5). Stipe base scales pale brown, usually with a distinctly darkened, broad central stripe or basal area; basal basiscopic pinnules of the basal pinnae 2–3 times longer than the basal acroscopic pinnules; indusia eglandular; N. *372. D. expansa*

7(1). Laminae persistent, up to 5(6) cm wide, usually tapering as gradually at the base as at the apex, densely covered on the abaxial surface with scales; N. *382. D. fragrans*

7(1). Laminae not persistent, usually more than 8 cm wide (sometimes less in *D. cristata*), tapering more gradually at the apex than at the base, not at all covered with scales on the abaxial surface, **8**

8(7). Sori submarginal; laminae leathery, evergreen; E. *381. D. marginalis*

8(7). Sori submedial to supramedial; laminae papery, evergreen or not, **9**

9(8). Pinnae in the basal half of the laminae divided into segments that are broadly attached and scarcely or not contracted at the base, **11**

9(8). Pinnae in the basal half of the laminae divided into pinnules that are narrowly attached to the costae and decidedly contracted at the base, **10**

10(9). Pinnules and segments serrately lobed, barely spinulose; costae with hair-like scales; NE, W. *383. D. filix-mas*

10(9). Pinnules and segments decidedly spinulose; costae with narrow, lanceate scales; P. *384. D. arguta*

11(9). Laminae decidedly dimorphic, the fertile laminae longer and more erect than the sterile ones, 3–4(5) times longer than wide; pinnae lanceate, mostly 1.5–3 times longer than wide; N. *376. D. cristata*

11(9). Laminae monomorphic or nearly so, 2–3 times longer than wide; pinnae oblong to lanceate, mostly 3–4 times longer than wide, **12**

12(11). Laminae fertile only in the distal half, the fertile pinnae and segments narrower and more distant than the sterile ones; stipe base scales pale brown, not shiny; ECP. *378. D. ludoviciana*

12(11). Laminae fertile throughout, the fertile pinnae and segments not narrower or more distant than the sterile ones; stipe base scales medium to dark brown, often shiny, at least in the center, **13**

13(12). Laminae rarely more than 18(20) cm wide; basal pinnae triangular, 1.5–2 times longer than wide; NE. **377. D. clintoniana*

13(12). Laminae rarely less than 20 cm wide; basal pinnae lanceolate, usually 3–4 times longer than wide, **14**

14(13). Fertile pinna segments approximate, with very narrow sinuses, not more decurrent than surcurrent on the costae; sori medial, touching the costule at maturity; laminae abruptly narrowed and obtuse below the apex; NE, NC. *380. D. goldiana*

14(13). Fertile segments distant, with broad sinuses, usually more decurrent than surcurrent on the costae; sori submedial, not touching the costule at maturity; laminae usually almost evenly narrowed and subobtuse or acute below the apex; E. *379. D. celsa*

370 Dryopteris rossii C. Chr. in H. Ross
Ross' Wood Fern

Stipes 5–25 cm long, with narrow, reddish or sometimes nearly black-tipped scales; laminae rather broadly lanceolate, 15–25 cm long, 8–20 cm wide, obtuse at the base, acute at the apex, 3-pinnate to 3-pinnate-pinnatifid, the pinnae and pinnules somewhat inequilateral, the pinnule lobes with acute lobes or teeth, the laminae gray-green on the abaxial surface, sparsely covered throughout with minute, clavate, clear or pale yellow glands; indusia plane, ca. 0.75 mm in diam. entire.

Epipetric on crevices of exposed quartzite cliffs. Very rare. Southeastern Arizona.

Not cultivated.

*371   Dryopteris cinnamomea (Cav.) C. Chr.
Cinnamon Wood Fern

Stipes 7–15 cm long, with narrow, reddish scales; laminae lanceate, 15–25 cm long, 6–12 cm wide, broadest at or just above the obtuse base, acuminate at the apex, 3-pinnate-pinnatifid; pinnae and pinnules nearly equilateral, the pinnule lobes entire, the laminae eglandular or sparsely covered with minute, subcapitate, clear glands; indusia plane to slightly vaulted, ca. 1 mm in diam., entire.

Epipetric in crevices of sheltered rocks in a cave. Very rare. In the Flora area known only from near Comstock, Val Verde Co., southwestern Texas.

Not cultivated.

372   Dryopteris expansa (Presl) Fraser-Jenkins & Jermy
Spreading Wood Fern

Stipes 10–40 cm long, with pale brown scales usually having a darker brown, broad, central stripe or sometimes basal area; laminae lanceolate to ovate-lanceolate, (15)20–60 cm long, (12)15–30 cm wide, broadest above the base, acute-acuminate at the apex, 3-pinnate-pinnatifid at the base, acute-acuminate at the base, 2-pinnate-pinnatifid above the base, the pinnae and pinnules nearly equilateral, except the basal pinnae expanded, the basal basiscopic pinnules 2–3 times longer than the basal acroscopic ones, the pinnule segments and lobes spinulose, the laminae eglandular or slightly glandular; indusia medial or submedial, eglandular.

Terrestrial, often among rocks, in moist woods and exposed places. Common. Labrador, Quebec, southern Ontario, the upper peninsula of Michigan, northern Wisconsin, and northwestern Minnesota. Also Alaska south to Oregon, central California, northern Idaho, western Montana, northwestern Wyoming, and northern Colorado.

Cultivated in moist garden soil or potting mix in partial sun. Probably restricted to cool climates. This species hybridizes with *D. marginalis* and with *D. intermedia* to form *D. campyloptera* (see p. 319). This species was formerly called *D. dilatata* (Hoffm.) A. Gray.

373 Dryopteris campyloptera Clarkson
Mountain Wood Fern

Stipes 10–35(40) cm long, with pale brown to pale reddish-brown scales usually having a darker brown, broad area at the base; laminae ovate-lanceolate, 15–60 cm long, (12)15–35 cm wide, broadest above the base, acute-acuminate at the apex, 3-pinnate-pinnatifid, the pinnae and pinnules equilaterla, except the basal pinnae expanded with the basal basiscopic pinnules (2)3–4(5) times longer than the basal acroscopic ones and usually as wide at the base as the two opposing acroscopic pinnules, the pinnule segments and lobes finely spinulose, the lamine eglandular; indusia supramedial, glandular or eglandular.

Terrestrial or among rocks in woods and exposed places. Frequent. Labrador and Newfoundland to southern Quebec south to New Hampshire, western Massachusetts, New York, and northern Pennsylvania. Disjunct in the Appalachian Mountains from southern Pennsylvania to western North Carolina and eastern Tennessee.

Cultivated in moist to garden soil or potting mix in partial sun. This species hybridizes with *D. marginalis* and backcrosses with *D. intermedia* (see p. 319).

374 Dryopteris intermedia (Muhl.) A. Gray
Fancy Fern

Stipes 12–30 cm long, with broad, pale brown scales having an irregular, darker central area; laminae evergreen, oblong-lanceolate, 20–40(50) cm long, (8)10–20 cm wide, broadest just above the obtuse base, abruptly and acutely tapered below the acuminate apex, 3-pinnate-pinnatifid; pinnae and pinnules nearly equilateral, except the basal pinnae slightly expanded, with the basal basiscopic pinnules a little larger than the basal acroscopic ones, the pinnule segments or lobes finely spinulose, the laminae sparsely to rather noticeably covered with minute, capitate, clear glands; indusia medial, with similar glands.

Terrestrial in moist, sometimes rocky woods and swamps. Abundant. Newfoundland to southern Quebec and southern Ontario south to North Carolina, the mountains of Georgia, Alabama, and eastern Tennessee, Kentucky, eastern Missouri, Illinois, Iowa, Wisconsin, and eastern Minnesota.

Cultivated in moist, rich, subacid to circumneutral soil in full shade or partial sun. This species hybridizes with *D. expansa* to form *D. campyloptera*, and backcrosses with *D. campyloptera*. Unlike *D. campyloptera* and *D. expansa*, it also hybridizes with many other species (see p. 319), e.g., with *D. celsa* to form *D.* × *separabilis* Small, with *D. carthusiana* to form *D.* × *triploidea* Wherry, with *D. clintoniana* to form *D.* × *dowellii* (Farw.) Wherry, and with *D. cristata* to form *D.* × *boottii* (Tuckerm.) Underw. It also hybridizes with an unknown diploid species to form *D. carthusiana*.

375   Dryopteris carthusiana (Villars) H. P. Fuchs
Toothed Wood Fern

Stipes 5–50 cm long, with entirely pale brown scales; laminae lanceolate-oblong to deltate-ovate, 10–65 cm long, (5)10–30(40) cm wide, broadest above the obtuse base to near the middle of the lamina, acute-acuminate at the apex, (2)3-pinnate-pinnatifid, the pinnae and pinnules nearly equilateral, the pinnule segments or lobes finely spinulose, the laminae eglandular; indusia medial, eglandular.

Terrestrial in moist to wet woods and swamps. Abundant. Labrador to British Columbia south to North Carolina, South Carolina, Kentucky, Arkansas, eastern Missouri, Iowa, Nebraska, eastern South Dakota, Manitoba, Alberta, western Montana, northern Idaho, and Washington.

Cultivated in moist, subacid garden soil in full shade to partial sun. This species has been called *D. spinulosa* (O. F. Muell.) Watt. It hybridizes with many other species, including with *D. clintoniana* to form *D. × benedictii* Wherry, with *D. cristata* to form *D. × uliginosa* Druce, with *D. intermedia* to form *D. × triploidea* Wherry, with *D. marginalis* to form *D. × pittsfordensis* Slosson, and with *D. goldiana*.

376   Dryopteris cristata (L.) A. Gray
Crested Wood Fern

Stipes 5–35 cm long, with concolorous, very pale brown scales; laminae subdimorphic, nearly oblong, the fertile ones erect, deciduous, 30–60 cm long, 8–12(14) cm wide, the sterile ones spreading, evergreen, ca. ½–⅓ shorter, obtuse at the base, uniformly acute at the apex, pinnate-pinnatifid with none of the segments contracted at the base the segments subentire to distantly and shallowly serrately lobed, spinulose, the laminae eglandular; indusia medial, eglandular.

Terrestrial in wet woods and swamps. Common. Newfoundland to southern British Columbia south to North Carolina, Tennessee, West Virginia, Ohio, Indiana, northern Illinois, Iowa, Kansas, Minnesota, North Dakota, Manitoba, Saskatchewan, western Montana, and northern Idaho.

Cultivated in moist garden soil or potting mix in partial sun. This species is the fertile autoallotetraploid of *D. ludoviciana* and an unknown diploid species (see p. 319). It hybridizes with *D. carthusiana* to form *D. × uliginosa* Druce, with *D. marginalis* to form *D. × slossoniae* Wherry ex Lellinger (see Lellinger (1984) for a discussion of the complex nomenclatural history of this hybrid), with *D. goldiana* to form *D. clintoniana*, and with *D. intermedia* to form *D. × boottii* (Tuckerm.) Underw. It also backcrosses with *D. clintoniana* and with *D. celsa*. Wagner and Musselman

(1979) have discovered that *D. atropalustris* Small is a variant of *D. celsa*, and is not a hybrid between that species and *D. cristata*.

*377 Dryopteris clintoniana (D. C. Eaton) Dowell
Clinton's Wood Fern

Stipes 20–40 cm long, with concolorous, pale brown or weakly bicolorous, pale brown scales with a broad, dark brown central area at the base; laminae oblanceolate to oblong, 25–70 cm long, (12)15–18(20) cm wide, usually tapered to an obtuse base, acute to nearly obtuse below the apex with an acuminate tip, pinnate-pinnatifid with a few basal segments contracted at the base, the segments subentire to shallowly serrately lobed, scarcely spinulose, the laminae eglandular; indusia medial, eglandular.

Terrestrial in wet woods and swamps. Frequent. Southern Quebec, southern Ontario, and the lower peninsula of Michigan south to northern New Jersey, northern Pennsylvania, northern Ohio, and northern Indiana.

Cultivated in moist garden soil in partial to full shade. This species often has subdimorphic fronds, with the sterile fronds shorter than the fertile, a characteristic more strongly expressed in its parent *D. cristata*. The other parent of this species is *D. goldiana*. This species also hybridizes with *D. carthusiana* to form *D.* × *benedictii* Wherry, with *D. marginalis* to form *D.* × *burgessii* Boivin, with *D. intermedia* to form *D.* × *dowellii* (Farw.) Wherry, and with *D. celsa*. It backcrosses with *D. goldiana* (see p. 319).

378 Dryopteris ludoviciana (Kunze) Small
Southern Wood Fern

Rhizomes short-creeping; stipes (10)15–40 cm long, with concolorous, long, pale to medium brown or bronzy scales; laminae evergreen, subdimorphic, rhombic or rhombic-lanceolate, 25–90 cm long, 10–22 cm wide, fertile on contracted pinnae in the distal half, tapered to an obtuse base, acute below the acuminate apex, pinnate-pinnatifid with the fertile segments sometimes contracted at the base, the segments subentire to distantly serrate, not spinulose, the laminae eglandular; indusia supramedial, eglandular.

Epipetric on limestone rocks or terrestrial in wet woods. Frequent. Florida north on the coastal plain to North Carolina and west to eastern Texas.

Cultivated in woodland gardens as far north as Pennsylvania. This species hybridizes with *D. celsa* to form *D.* × *australis* (Wherry) Small, with *D. marginalis* to form *D.* × *leedsii* Wherry, and with an unknown diploid to form *D. cristata* (see p. 319). *Dryopteris* × *australis* is subdimorphic like *D. ludoviciana*.

379 Dryopteris celsa (W. Palmer) Small
Log Fern

Stipes 30–50 cm long, with large, bicolorous scales with a broad, dark, reddish-brown central stripe and pale brown margins and with small, almost hair-like, concolorous, pale brown scales; laminae not evergreen, oblong, 35–60(85) cm long, (15)22–32 cm wide, not or only slightly tapered at the obtuse base, obtuse below the acuminate tip at the apex, pinnate-pinnatifid with a few basal segments contracted at the base, the segments subentire, distantly serrate, or serrately lobed, scarcely spinulose, the laminae eglandular; indusia submedial, eglandular.

Terrestrial on rotting logs and in humus-rich, moderately to strongly acid soils in swamps, wet woods, and drainage ditches. Rare. Scattered localities in northeastern New Jersey and northeastern New York to Maryland, Virginia, and southern Illinois south to South Carolina, northern Georgia, Alabama, Tennessee, northern Louisiana, Arkansas, and eastern Missouri. Disjunct in western New York and western Michigan.

Not cultivated. This species is a fertile allotetraploid between *D. goldiana* and *D. ludoviciana*. Fertile pinnae of *D. celsa*, unlike those of *D. ludoviciana*, and *D. × australis*, are not at all contracted compared to the sterile pinnae. This species hybridizes with *D. cristata*, with *D. intermedia* to form *D. × separabilis* Small, and with *D. marginalis* to form *D. × leedsii* Wherry. It also backcrosses with *D. ludoviciana* to form *D. × australis* (Wherry) Small and with *D. goldiana*.

380 Dryopteris goldiana (Hooker) A. Gray
Goldie's Wood Fern

Stipes 15–45 cm long, with concolorous, pale brown scales and bicolorous scales with a broad, dark, reddish-brown central stripe and narrow, pale brown margins; laminae not evergreen, oblong, (20)25–70 cm long, (15)20–30(35) cm wide, only slightly tapered above the obtuse base, obtuse below the apex with an abruptly acuminate tip, pinnate-pinnatifid, with a few basal segments contracted at the base, the segments remotely serrate, scarcely spinulose, the laminae eglandular; indusia medial, eglandular.

Terrestrial in damp woods and on stream banks, often among rocks, occasionally epipetric at the base of cliffs and on talus slopes. Frequent. Southern Quebec, southern Ontario, Michigan, Wisconsin, and Minnesota south to Connecticut, New York, New Jersey, northern Delaware, Maryland, Virginia, North Carolina, the mountains of Georgia and Alabama, Tennessee, Kentucky, Illinois, eastern Missouri, and Iowa.

Cultivated in moist garden soil or potting mix in full shade or partial sun. This species hybridizes with *D. cristata* to form *D. clintoniana*, with *D. ludoviciana* to form *D. celsa*, with *D. marginalis* to form *D. × neowherryi* Wagner, and with *D. carthusiana*, which has erroneously been called *D. poyseri* Wherry, according to Wagner and Wagner (1982a). It also backcrosses with *D. celsa* and *D. clintoniana*. It also hybridizes with *D. intermedia* (Evans & Wagner, 1964); see p. 319.

381 Dryopteris marginalis (L.) A. Gray
Marginal Wood Fern
Stipes 10–30 cm long, with a tuft of linear-lanceate, concolorous, pale reddish-brown scales at the base and smaller, scattered scales above the base; laminae evergreen, oblong-lanceolate, (20)30–45 cm long, (10)12–20 cm wide, broadest just above the obtuse base, uniformly acute at the apex in narrow laminae, nearly obtuse with an acuminate apex in broad laminae, pinnate-pinnatifid with the basal pinnules somewhat contracted at the base, the segment margins subentire to somewhat crenate, the laminae eglandular, coriaceous, with a few hair-like scales; indusia submarginal, eglandular.

Epipetric or terrestrial on rock ledges, talus slopes, and on soil in shade and exposed places. Abundant. Newfoundland to Ontario south to South Carolina, Georgia, Alabama, Tennessee, Arkansas, eastern Oklahoma, eastern Kansas, Iowa, and Wisconsin.

Cultivated in moist but well-drained garden soil in partial shade. This species hybridizes with *D. campyloptera*, with *D. carthusiana* to form *D. ×pittsfordensis* Slosson, with *D. celsa* to form *D. ×leedsii* Wherry, with *D. clintoniana* to form *D. ×burgessii* Boivin, with *D. cristata* to form *D. ×slossoniae* Wherry ex Lellinger, with *D. expansa*, with *D. goldiana* to form *D. ×neo-wherryi* Wagner, with *D. fragrans* to form *D. ×algonquinensis* Britton, and with *D. intermedia*. Large fronds with deeply lobed segments or crested pinnae are occasionally found in nature.

382 Dryopteris fragrans (L.) Schott
Fragrant Wood Fern
Rhizomes bearing persistent dead fronds; stipes (1)2–11 cm long, sparsely glandular and with large, concolorous, pale reddish-brown scales; laminae elliptic or sometimes linear-lanceolate, (4)6–25(35) cm long, 1–5(6) cm wide, usually broadest near the middle of the lamina, usually acute at the base, acute to narrowly acute at the apex, pinnate-pinnatifid, or in large specimens barely 2-pinnate-pinnatifid near the rachis, the laminae aromatic when fresh, slightly glandular, and also scaly on the abaxial surface; indusia medial, eglandular, often imbricate.

Epipetric and on talus slopes in shady locations. Frequent. Labrador to Alaska south to Maine, New Hampshire, Vermont, the mountains of New York, Ontario, the upper peninsula of Michigan, northern Wisconsin and Minnesota, the Northwest Territories, northern British Columbia, and Alaska.

Not cultivated. In aspect, this species resembles the genus *Woodsia;* it is by far the smallest of the North American Wood Ferns. This species hybridizes with *D*. *marginalis* to form *D*. × *algonquinensis* Britton in Ontario. Larger plants with more distant pinnae found especially in the northeastern United States sometimes are distinguished as var. *remotiuscula* Komarov.

383   Dryopteris filix-mas (L.) Schott
Male Fern

Stipes 8–35 cm long, with concolorous, long, pale reddish-brown scales, especially at the base; laminae oblanceolate to rhombic, 20–80 cm long, 10–30 cm wide, commonly widest above the middle, tapering to a truncate or obtuse base, broadly acute or obtuse below the acute-acuminate apex, 2-pinnate or 2-pinnate-pinnatifid with many segments contracted at the base, the segments serrate to lobed, barely spinulose, the laminae eglandular; indusia medial, eglandular.

Terrestrial or among rocks in woods and on talus slopes in circumneutral soil. Frequent. Nova Scotia to northern British Columbia south to Quebec, Vermont, the upper peninsula of Michigan, western South Dakota, Wyoming, Colorado, New Mexico, western Oklahoma, western Texas, Arizona, southern California, Nevada, Oregon, and Idaho. Disjunct in northern Illinois.

Cultivated in moist garden soil or potting mix in partial sun. This species hybridizes with *D*. *marginalis* (see p. 319); in Europe, it hybridizes with *D*. *carthusiana* to form *D*. × *brathaica* Fraser-Jenkins & Reichstein, which should be sought in eastern Canada and the northwestern United States and adjacent Canada wherever the parental species occur together.

384   Dryopteris arguta (Kaulf.) Watt
Coastal Wood Fern

Rhizomes short-creeping; stipes 10–45 cm long, with concolorous or weakly bicolorous, pale reddish-brown scales sometimes having a broad, darker area near the base; laminae lanceolate to elliptic-lanceolate, (15)30–55 cm long, (8)12–30 cm wide, obtuse to truncate at the base, uniformly acute-acuminate or acute below the apex with an acuminate tip, 1(2)-pinnate-pinnatifid with many segments contracted at the base, the segments shallowly serrately lobed decidedly spinulose, the laminae glandular, especially on the rachis; indusia medial, eglandular.

Terrestrial in rather dry, open woods or sometimes epipetric on sheltered ledges. Frequent. Vancouver Island, British Columbia, the coast ranges from Washington to southern California. Disjunct in central Arizona.

Cultivated in well-drained garden soil or potting mix in partial shade. Hybrids are not known between this species and other species of North American *Dryopteris*.

LOMARIOPSIDACEAE
The Vine Fern Family

There are seven to nine genera in this tropical family, including the very large genus *Elaphoglossum*. The only genus of the family occurring in the United States is *Lomariopsis*, where one species is confined to a few localities in southern Florida.

Plants of the Vine Fern Family are small to large. The scaly rhizomes are erect, short-creeping, or very long-creeping. Most genera are partially to fully dimorphic, with fertile laminae that differ from the sterile ones in size, shape, or dissection. The sterile laminae are thin and have anastomosing veins or are thick and free-veined. Usually the laminae are glabrous, but some species have narrow or even hair-like scales on the laminae or axes, and many species of the tropical genus *Elaphoglossum* are very scaly. The sporangia are acrostichoid, spread over the surface of the contracted fertile laminae, and are exindusiate.

The Vine Fern Family contains both terrestrial and epiphytic species, and also a few species, like those of *Lomariopsis*, which are hemiepiphytes in the tropics: they have long-creeping rhizomes that remain rooted in the ground, but climb tree trunks, and so bear their sterile fronds where light is more favorable than on the forest floor and their fertile fronds where slight breezes can scatter their spores. A few species of *Elaphoglossum* and *Lomariopsis* are cultivated in greenhouses, but for the most part, members of this family are not in cultivation.

385   Lomariopsis kunzeana (Presl ex Underw.) Holtt.
Holly Vine Fern

Rhizomes creeping, dorsiventrally flattened, woody, somewhat contorted, straw-colored, bearing scattered, lanceolate, brown scales; stipes borne at 0.5–2 cm intervals on either side of the rhizome, 3–12 cm long, adaxially grooved, narrowly alate, straw-colored, bearing a few scales like those of the rhizome; laminae linear-oblanceolate, 7–25 cm long, 3–6 cm wide, broadest above the middle, gradually tapered below to an obtuse base, obtuse at the apex, with a conform terminal pinna, the rachises uniformly and narrowly alate throughout, the pinnae alternate; sterile pinnae lanceolate to nearly oblong, serrate, with free, usually 1-forked veins, pale green on the abaxial surface, dark green on the adaxial surface; fertile pinnae contracted, linear, entire, covered on the abaxial surface with bronzy sporangia.

Epipetric in dark lime sinks. Rare. Dade Co., Florida.

Not cultivated. Florida specimens are smaller than those from the Greater Antilles and are mostly somewhat juvenile, with more deeply serrate sterile pinna margins than are characteristic of mature specimens. In addition, the rhizomes do not climb trees, but bear both the sterile and fertile fronds at ground level.

DAVALLIACEAE
The Boston Fern Family

The Davalliaceae, used here to include both the davallioid and nephrolepioid ferns, contains about 220 tropical species in 14 or 15 genera. The principal genera are *Davallia, Humata, Nephrolepis,* and *Oleandra*. Most of the genera are confined to the Old World; only *Nephrolepis, Oleandra,* and *Rumohra* occur in the New World, and only *Nephrolepis* in the United States.

The plants of the Boston Fern Family are small (in Old World epiphytic genera) to rather large (in some *Nephrolepis* species with pendent fronds). Their rhizomes are long-creeping and conspicuously scaly in several genera, although they are short and inconspicuous in *Nephrolepis*. In several genera, the point of articulation is above the base of the stipe, and so a short to long, cylindrical stipe base called a phyllopodium is left attached to the rhizome after the frond has fallen. Stipes, rachises, and laminae may have short, multicellular hairs or, more often, narrow, often ciliate scales. The laminae range from simple (in *Oleandra*) to several times pinnate (in *Davallia* and related genera). Those species that are branch epiphytes growing in direct sunlight have thick laminae; those trunk epiphytes growing in the shade, as *Nephrolepis* often does, have thinner laminae. The indusia in some genera are pouches facing the margin; other genera have dorsal sori usually protected by reniform indusia.

Most of the genera of the Davalliaceae are epiphytic. *Nephrolepis* also is terrestrial or epipetric. Several genera, especially *Nephrolepis* and *Davallia*, the Rabbit's-foot Fern, are widely grown in greenhouses, often in hanging baskets.

NEPHROLEPIS
The Boston Ferns

This pan-tropical genus includes about 30 species, many of which are in cultivation and have given rise to fancy cultivated varieties. The generic name refers to the kidney-shaped indusia, which characterize most species of the genus.

The Boston Ferns are medium to rather large-sized plants with inconspicuous rhizomes bearing clusters of erect, arching, or pendent fronds. Reproductive stolons are produced by the rhizomes of many species, and in *N. cordifolia* these stolons may bear round tubers. The stipes and rachises are often wiry. The laminae are thin, pale green, and pinnate (in wild material, although many cultivated varieties are highly divided). The pinnae are articulate to the rachis, free-veined, and bear a single row of usually submarginal, round sori that are protected by a reniform indusium.

Being entirely tropical, *Nephrolepis* is found only in Florida. The species occurring there have been monographed by Nauman (1981). Both native and naturalized species are grown in greenhouses and outdoors in Florida and southern California. Although several non-native species have given rise to cultivated varieties, *N. exaltata* var. *bostoniensis* has produced over 100 fancy sports over the years, many of them named and in cultivation. These cultivated varieties are the easiest of the Boston Ferns to grow in an ordinary household environment, for they are more tolerant of low humidity than are the other species of the genus. The name Boston Fern came about because the original variety appeared spontaneously among plants of *N. exaltata* grown in nurseries in and around Boston (Benedict, 1916).

Key to Nephrolepis
1. Indusia round or nearly so, with a narrow or closed sinus at the base, the sporangia protruding in all directions; adaxial surface of the costae with few to many, short, multicellular, jointed hairs; laminae 8–24 cm wide, 3
1. Indusia narrowly reniform with an open sinus at the base, the sporangia mostly protruding toward the pinna margin; adaxial surface of the costae glabrous or with a few scales; laminae 4–10(11) cm wide, 2
2(1). Pinnae equilateral, the costa equidistant from the acroscopic and basiscopic lateral margins in the proximal portion of the pinna; acroscopic basal auricle commonly overlapping the rachis; tubers absent from the stolons; FL. *386. N. exaltata*
2(1). Pinnae inequilateral, the costa farther from the acroscopic than the basiscopic lateral margin in the proximal portion of the pinna; acroscopic basal auricle usually not overlapping the rachis; tubers usually present on the stolons; FL. *387. N. cordifolia*
3(1). Abaxial surface of the laminae with true hairs and some narrow, linear scales lacking an expanded base; FL. *388. N. biserrata*
3(1). Abaxial surface of the laminae with narrowly lanceolate scales with an expanded, ciliate base; FL. *389. N. multiflora*

386 Nephrolepis exaltata (L.) Schott

Wild Boston Fern

Stipes 10–25 cm long, bearing pale brown to reddish-brown, linear-lanceate, subentire scales with a slightly enlarged, ciliate base; laminae narrowly rhombic-oblanceolate, 50–100 cm long, 5.5–10(11) cm wide, widest at or above themiddle; rachises with linear, hair-like scales with a greatly enlarged, strongly ciliate base; pinnae oblong-lanceolate, not or only slightly falcate, round at the lower base, with a low, acute auricle at the upper base, glabrous on the adaxial side, with a few linear, hair-like scales with a greatly enlarged, strongly ciliate base on the abaxial side; indusia narrowly reniform with an open sinus at the base.

Terrestrial on fallen tree trunks, epiphytic, or epipetric. Frequent. Southern and central peninsular Florida.

Cultivated in moist potting mix in full sun or partial shade. This species hybridizes with *N. biserrata* to form *N.* × *averyi* Nauman from central and southern peninsular Florida.

387 Nephrolepis cordifolia (L.) Presl

Tuberous Sword Fern

Rhizomes often producing tuber-bearing stolons, the tubers up to 15 mm in diam., densely scaly; stipes 5–15 cm long, bearing pale brown, linear-lanceate, subentire scales with a slightly ciliate base; laminae oblong-rhombic, 20–60 cm long, 2.5–7 cm wide, parallel-sided in the middle ⅓–½ of the lamina; rachises with linear, hair-like scales with an enlarged, ciliate base; pinnae lanceate, slightly falcate, round at the small lower base, with a low, acute auricle at the upper base, glabrous on the adaxial side, glabrous or with a few, minute hairs on the abaxial side; indusia narrowly reniform with an open sinus at the base.

Terrestrial, epiphytic on Palmettos, or epipetric on old walls. Rare. According to Nauman (1981), this species usually persists from cultivation and is naturalized only at one locality in Palm Beach Co., Florida.

Cultivated in moist garden soil or potting mix in full sun to partial shade.

388 Nephrolepis biserrata (Swartz) Schott

Giant Sword Fern

Stipes 15–25 cm long, bearing pale brown, linear, subentire scales with a slightly ciliate base; laminae rhombic, 50–100 cm long, 10–20(28) cm wide, widest at the middle; rachises with a few, linear, hair-like scales with an enlarged, subciliate base plus many short, multicellular hairs; pinnae oblong to lanceate, not falcate, obtuse or with a very low auricle at the lower base, with a small, acute or sometimes round auricle at the upper base, with a few short, multicellular hairs especially on the costa on the adaxial side, with many, short, multicellular hairs on the costa and lamina surface on the abaxial side; indusia round, with a narrow closed sinus at the base.

Terrestrial or sometimes epiphytic or epipetric. Rare. Central and southern peninsular Florida.

Cultivated in moist to rather dry potting mix in full sun or partial shade. This species hybridizes with *N. exaltata* to form *N.* ×*averyi* Nauman known from central and southern peninsular Florida.

389   Nephrolepis multiflora (Roxb.) Jarrett ex Morton
Asian Sword Fern

Stipes 15–30 cm long, bearing bicolorous, lanceolate, long-ciliate scales with a dark brown central stripe and pale brown edges; laminae rhombic, 50–100 cm long, 8–15 cm wide, widest at the middle; rachises with bicolorous and concolorous, linear to narrowly lanceolate, long-ciliate scales, the cilia causing the rachises to appear hairy as well as scaly; pinnae oblong to lanceate, not falcate, round or with a very low, round auricle at the lower base, with a long, narrow, acute auricle at the upper base, with abundant, multicellular hairs on the costa on the adaxial side, with many small, lanceolate scales having enlarged, long-ciliate bases on the costae and lamina surface of the abaxial side; indusia round, with a narrow or closed sinus at the base.

Terrestrial. Naturalized in central and southern peninsular Florida.

Cultivated in moist garden soil or potting mix in full sun.

BLECHNACEAE
The Chain Fern Family

The Blechnaceae includes about 250 species in eight genera. Most occur in the tropics and subtropics of the southern hemisphere, Asia, and the Pacific Islands. Only *Blechnum* and *Woodwardia* (including *Anchistea* and *Lorinseria*) are found in the New World and in the United States.

The plants of the Chain Fern Family are small to large; those of the Hawaiian endemic genus *Sadleria* are small tree ferns, and some of the tropical species of *Blechnum* also have a small, tree-like habit. The scaly rhizomes are creeping to erect and usually bear a terminal cluster of fronds. The stipe base scales usually are pale to reddish-brown, but are dark brown or have a dark brown stripe in some species. In small species, the scales are small and lanceolate, but in the larger species they are sometimes several centimeters long and linear. The laminae are pinnatifid to pinnate-pinnatifid and usually lanceolate or oblong. Many species are dimorphic, with contracted fertile laminae often longer and more erect than the sterile laminae. The laminae usually are glabrous, although a few species are slightly scaly or hairy on the abaxial costae or rachis. The veins are free to areolate. The sori are linear or merely elongate in some species and lie in a single row on each side of the costae or costules. They are protected by elongate, often inconspicuous or deciduous indusia that open toward the costae or costules.

Most species of the Blechnaceae are terrestrial; a few tropical ones are epiphytic. Various species of *Blechnum, Doodia, Sadleria,* and *Stenochlaena* are cultivated in temperate greenhouses or in lathhouses in southern California and Florida.

Key to the Genera of Blechnaceae
1. Sori (and indusia) on each pinna elongate, numerous, in a paired series, 1 on each side of the costae or costules; laminae entirely pinnate-pinnatifid or pinnatifid, *Woodwardia,* p. 301
1. Sori (and indusia) on each pinna linear, only a single, continuous pair, 1 on each side of the costae; laminae pinnate at the base, pinnatifid only at the apex or above the base, *Blechnum,* p. 299

BLECHNUM
The Deer Ferns

Blechnum is a genus of about 220 species found in the tropics and subtropics of the New and Old World. The genus is divided into subgenera, considered genera by some, with monomorphic fronds (subg. *Blechnum*) and with dimorphic fronds (subg. *Lomaria*) having the fertile laminae greatly contracted.

The Deer Ferns are small to large-sized plants with long-creeping to erect (sometimes trunk-like) rhizomes bearing lanceolate to linear, concolorous or bicolorous scales. The laminae are pinnatifid or pinnate, monomorphic or dimorphic, and sometimes scaly or hairy on the abaxial surface of the costae or rachises. In dimorphic species, the fertile laminae are reduced almost to the line of attachment of the indusia, and so the segments or pinnae are very narrow. The sori are linear and protected by linear, introrse indusia that are close to and parallel with the costae or costules.

Blechnum grows in moist to dry soil in full sun to partial shade. Some strictly tropical species are epiphytic. About a dozen species of *Blechnum* are in cultivation. Young, sterile fronds are attractive because of their pink to pale reddish-brown color.

Key to Blechnum
1. Fronds dimorphic, the erect, fertile ones longer than the spreading, sterile ones and the fertile pinnae narrower than the sterile ones; PN. 390. *B. spicant*
1. Fronds monomorphic, the fertile and sterile alike, 2

2(1). Laminae pinnate throughout, much more than 30 cm long; pinnae finely serrulate; FL. *391*. *B. serrulatum*

2(1). Laminae pinnatifid except pinnate at the base, less than 30 cm long; pinnae or segments entire or nearly so; FL. *392*. *B. occidentale*

390 Blechnum spicant (L.) J. Smith
Deer Fern

Rhizomes short-creeping or ascending with a cluster of stipes at and near the apex; fertile stipes stiffly erect, 15–60 cm long, purplish-black, glossy; fertile laminae narrowly rhombic, 25–65 cm long, (3)6–10(15) cm wide, with narrow, widely spaced pinnae; sterile stipes spreading, reddish-brown, 2–30 cm long; sterile laminae narrowly oblanceolate, 20–75 cm long, 3–10(14) cm wide, with approximate, fully adnate, falcate pinnae.

Terrestrial in wet woods and swamps. Common. Alaska to British Columbia, Oregon, northern Idaho, and northern California, mostly along the coast and in the coastal mountain ranges.

Cultivated in garden soil or moist potting mix in full or partial shade.

391 Blechnum serrulatum L. C. Rich.
Swamp Fern

Rhizomes short- to long-creeping deep in the soil, with erect to ascending branches bearing 1–several fronds near the apex; stipes 10–55 cm long, pale brown; laminae oblong-lanceate, 25–70 cm long, (5)7–28 cm wide, the pinnae alternate, ascending, not falcate, sharply serrate, the basal and supra-basal pinnae rarely if ever fertile, the upper, fertile pinnae slightly narrower than the lower, sterile ones.

Terrestrial in wet woods and hammocks. Frequent. Peninsular Florida.

Cultivated in moist to wet garden soil or potting mix in partial shade.

392 Blechnum occidentale L.
Hammock Fern

Rhizomes erect or ascending; stipes 4–28 cm long, straw-colored, sometimes with a few reddish scales; laminae narrowly lanceolate, 13–30 cm long, 3–10 cm wide, the pinnae and segments opposite at the base, alternate toward the apex, decidedly falcate, entire, usually fertile throughout, the fertile pinnae and segments not narrower than the sterile ones.

Terrestrial in forests, often among or over rocks, in moist soil. Rare. Central peninsular Florida, Echols Co., Georgia, Iberville Parish, La., and Llano Co., Texas. All the wild material found in Florida seems to be f. *pubirachis* (Rosenst.) Lellinger, which is smaller than f. *occidentale*, has at least slightly puberulous rachises on the abaxial surface, and which grows at higher altitudes in the tropics than does f. *occidentale*.

WOODWARDIA
The Chain Ferns

Woodwardia is a genus of 12 species found mostly in the temperate and subtropical regions of the northern hemisphere, with a few species extending into the southern hemisphere tropics of the Old World. The genus is named for Thomas Jenkinson Woodward, an English botanist of the late 18th and early 19th century.

The Chain Ferns are medium to large-sized plants with long-creeping, deeply subterranean or ascending rhizomes. Their stout stipes commonly have large, reddish-brown scales at the base. The laminae are pinnate-pinnatifid and monomorphic or dimorphic, with contracted fertile laminae. The pinnae are often rather thick and have anastomosing veins. The elongate sori are borne in a single series on either side of the costae, or costules if any are present, and are protected by elongate indusia which face the costae or costules.

Several species of *Woodwardia* are in cultivation. They are easy to grow in warm regions in full to partial sun in moist garden soil, but must have adequate room, for those with long-creeping rhizomes tend to spread.

Key to Woodwardia
1. Laminae dimorphic, the sterile ones usually less than 30 cm long, pinnate at the base, pinnatifid toward the apex, the fertile pinnae greatly contracted, pinnate; E. *393. W. areolata*

1. Laminae monomorphic, all usually more than 30 cm long, pinnate-pinnatifid, 2

2(1). Rhizomes long-creeping, deeply subterranean, the fronds scattered; sterile pinna lobes 0.6–1.5 cm long, round at the apex; laminae up to ca. 50 cm long, 30 cm wide; E. *394. W. virginica*

2(1). Rhizomes ascending, not entirely subterranean, the fronds clustered at the apex; sterile pinna lobes 2–6 cm long, acute at the apex; laminae mostly larger than 50 cm long, 30 cm wide; P. *395. W. fimbriata*

393 · Woodwardia areolata (L.) Moore
Netted Chain Fern

Rhizomes long-creeping, blackish, slightly subterranean; fronds dimorphic; stipes distant, sparsely scaly, the sterile ones (7)10–40 cm long, reddish-brown at the base, straw-colored above the base, often narrowly alate at the apex, the fertile ones 13–60 cm long, dark reddish-brown or purplish-black, not alate at the apex; sterile laminae ovate-lanceate to oblong, 10–37 cm long, 5.5–20 cm wide, pinnate at the base, pinnatifid above the base, the rachises narrowly to broadly alate, the pinnae and segments narrowly elliptic to oblong, slightly undulate, acute at the apex;

fertile laminae oblong, 15–35 cm long, 6–18 cm wide, pinnate through-out, the rachises not alate, the pinnae linear.

Terrestrial in wet woods, swamps, along streams, and in bogs in acid soil. Common. Nova Scotia to Florida and west to Texas, especially on the coastal plain, and at scattered locations inland to New Hampshire, New York, Michigan, Ohio, Kentucky, southern Illinois, Tennessee, southern Missouri and Arkansas.

Cultivated in wet, acidic garden soil or potting mix in partial sun to full shade. This species is also known as *Lorinseria areolata* (L.) Presl. The fertile–sterile dimorphism in this species is often incomplete, resulting in laminae that are fertile at the apex and sterile at the base. This shows that the character of dimorphism is insufficient to maintain *Lorinseria* as a genus separate from *Woodwardia*.

394   Woodwardia virginica (L.) J. E. Smith
Virginia Chain Fern

Rhizomes long-creeping, blackish, subterranean; stipes distant, sparsely scaly at the base with some reddish-brown scales, 10–50 cm long, reddish-brown to purplish-black at the base, straw-colored above the base; laminae oblong-lanceolate, (15)25–72 cm long, (9)14–30 cm wide, pinnate-pinnatifid throughout, except for a very small pinnatifid apex, the pinnae oblong-lanceolate, pinnatifid.

Terrestrial in bogs, swamps, marshes, and at the edge of ponds, in wet, acid to subalkaline soil. Common. New Brunswick and southern Quebec to Florida west to southern Ontario, Michigan, Ohio, Indiana, Illinois, Arkansas, and eastern Texas.

Cultivated in wet garden soil in partial to full sun. Because of its creeping rhizomes and aggressive growth, this species is not suitable for small gardens.

395   Woodwardia fimbriata J. E. Smith
Giant Chain Fern

Rhizomes ascending, only the basal portion subterranean; stipes clus-tered, scaly at the base with large, pale reddish-brown scales, 15–85 cm long, straw-colored throughout or reddish-brown at the base; laminae el-liptic-lanceolate, up to ca. 150 cm long, 50 cm wide, pinnate-pinnatifid throughout except for a very small pinnatifid apex, the pinnae oblong-lanceate, pinnatifid.

Terrestrial in moist woods, often near streams. Common. Southern British Columbia to southern California. Disjunct in southeastern Arizona and northeastern Nevada.

Cultivated in moist garden soil in full sun or partial shade.

MARSILEACEAE
The Water-clover Family

The Marsileaceae includes only *Marsilea* (world-wide), *Pilularia* (north and south temperate zones), and *Regnellidium* (southern Brazil), a total of about 67 species.

The plants of this family are quite unlike other ferns. They have thin, long-creeping, usually glabrous rhizomes with fronds at the nodes. The long stipes bear small, round laminae of four segments (*Marsilea*) or two segments (*Regnellidium*), or the laminae may be absent and the stipes alate (*Pilularia*). Sporangia are borne within hard, nearly spherical or bean-shaped sporocarps that are attached by a short stalk to a node or a stipe near its base. The sporocarps, and in many cases the laminae, are hairy (at least when young) with pale, long, straight or wavy, usually multiseriate hairs. The sporangia are of two types and bear large, immobile megaspores and small, motile microspores (antherozoids).

The Marsileaceae are aquatic and either float or are rooted in deep water or they are terrestrial and rooted in shallow water or on land. Most pass the dry or cold season as sporocarps. All species are commonly overlooked, unless present in large masses. A few species of *Marsilea* are cultivated in aquaria or decorative pools.

Key to Marsileaceae

    1. Laminae of 4 cuneate to roughly oblanceolate segments; stipes not alate; sporocarps somewhat elongate, *Marsilea*, p. 303

    1. Laminae absent; stipes alate, ca. 0.5 mm wide; sporocarps spherical, *Pilularia*, p. 307

MARSILEA
The Water-clovers

Marsilea includes about 60 species widely distributed in the temperate and warm regions of both hemispheres. Most of the United States species are confined to Texas, but *M. quadrifolia* is northeastern and *M. vestita* is western. Most parts of the United States and Canada have but one or two species. However, five species grow in Texas, and the keys and habitat notes of Correll and Correll (1975, pp. 53–57) will be helpful in distinguishing them.

The Water-clovers are small ferns with thin, long-creeping rhizomes. In water forms, single fronds are given off at widely spaced nodes. In land forms, a short side branch bearing 1–several closely spaced fronds also is produced at each node, giving the plants a tufted appearance. The fronds consist of a long stipe topped by a lamina 0.5–3.5(5.5) cm in diameter that is divided into four segments like a clover leaf. Slightly elongate, subglobose sporocarps are borne on an unbranched or branched stalk at or near the stipe base. The hard, dark sporocarps split open and, through the absorption of water, a gelatinous, thread-like, sporangium-bearing structure is extruded.

The water forms of the Water-clovers grow floating or rooted in deep water. The land forms are rooted in shallow water or grow on land after the water has dried up. Probably all species (except *M. quadrifolia* and *M. vestita*) that are subject to freezing weather overwinter as sporocarps, in the manner of annual seed plants. A few species are cultivated in aquaria or decorative pools.

The conversion of the fronds of water forms to land forms may be accomplished by changes in light quality that accompany lowering water levels (Gaudet, 1963), but presumably only if certain nutritional requirements are met (White, 1966). Apparently abscisic acid produced within the plant causes the conversion, but the chemical pathway that causes the acid to form is not yet known (Liu, 1984). Like most aquatic plants, the species of *Marsilea* are variable in their morphology, which makes it difficult to prepare a satisfactory key to them.

Key to Marsilea

1. Laminae usually sparsely pilose or sericeous at maturity (sometimes glabrous in old plants of *M. vestita* and often entirely so in large plants of *M. uncinata*); lateral margins of the segments slightly concave, sharply rounded to the round or truncate segment apex; sporocarps solitary on unbranched stalks (except grouped or paired on branched pedicels in *M. macropoda*); short branches at the rhizome nodes many, well developed, the fronds mostly clustered in groups along the rhizome, **3**

1. Laminae glabrous at maturity (sparsely pilose when young in some species); lateral margins of the segments straight, broadly curved to the round segment apex; sporocarps grouped or paired on branched stalks; short branches at the rhizome nodes few, poorly developed, the fronds mostly distant along the rhizome, **2**

2(1). Abaxial surface of old laminae usually lacking conspicuous, reddish-brown stripes between the veins; sporocarps on paired stalks; NE. 396. *M. quadrifolia*

2(1). Abaxial surface of old laminae with conspicuous, reddish-brown stripes between the veins; sporocarps on branched stalks; TX. 397. *M. mexicana*

3(1). Lamina segments 3–7.5 times longer than wide, irregularly lacerate-toothed at the apex, obliquely cuneate; TX. *398. *M. tenuifolia*

3(1). Lamina segments mostly 1–2 times longer than wide, entire at the apex, broadly acute at the base, **4**

4(3). Fronds mostly more than (10)15 cm long; laminae mostly more than 2 cm wide; sporocarps grouped on paired stalks; TX. *399. M. macropoda*

4(3). Fronds mostly less than 10(15) cm long; laminae mostly less than 2(2.5) cm wide; sporocarps solitary on unbranched stalks, **5**

5(4). Upper tooth on the sporocarp straight or slightly bent; stalk no longer than the sporocarp; abaxial surface of the laminae always at least slightly hairy; SE, W. *400. M. vestita*

5(4). Upper tooth on the sporocarp conspicuously bent or hooked; stalk usually twice as long as the sporocarp; abaxial surface of the laminae glabrous or slightly hairy; TX. *401. M. uncinata*

396 Marsilea quadrifolia L.
European Water-clover

Rhizomes with poorly developed short branches at the nodes, the fronds distant along the rhizome. Stipes (2)5–20(35) cm long, the usually 1-branched stalks ca. 1 cm long, bearing a pair of sericeous, glabrescent sporocarps. Laminae 1–3.5(5) cm in diam., glabrous at maturity, the segments with straight lateral margins, broadly curved to the round segment apex.

Aquatic, either submerged or emergent, or sometimes on wet ground bordering ponds. Naturalized from Ontario and New England south to Maryland, Pennsylvania, Ohio, Michigan, Kentucky, Indiana, Illinois, Missouri, Kansas, and Iowa.

Cultivated in aquaria and decorative pools.

397 Marsilea mexicana A. Braun
Mexican Water-clover

Rhizomes with poorly developed short branches at the nodes, the fronds distant along the rhizome. Stipes (5)7–25 cm long, the pinnately branched stalks ca. 1.5 cm long, bearing several glabrescent sporocarps. Laminae (1)2–3.5 cm in diam., glabrous and with conspicuous reddish-brown stripes on the abaxial surface between the veins at maturity, the segments with straight lateral margins, broadly curved to the round segment apex.

Aquatic in shallow water on mud bottoms of ponds and ditches. Very rare. In the United States known only from Aransas Co., Texas.

Not cultivated. For a comment on reddish-brown stripes in *M. vestita*, see that species.

*398 Marsilea tenuifolia Engelm. ex Kunze
Narrow-leaved Water-clover

Rhizomes with well-developed short branches at the nodes, the fronds clustered. along the rhizome. Stipes 3–19 cm long, the stalks 3–8 mm long, bearing 1 appressed-pilose sporocarp. Laminae 2–4 cm in diam., sparsely sericeous, the segments slightly asymmetrical, narrow (3–7.5 times longer than wide), irregularly lacerate-toothed at the apex.

Aquatic in shallow lakes and streams and in periodically inundated depressions. Rare. Central and western Texas.

Not cultivated.

399 Marsilea macropoda Engelm. ex A. Braun
Bigfoot Water-clover

Rhizomes with well-developed short branches at the nodes, the fronds clustered along the rhizome. Stipes 3–27 cm long, the stalks ca. 1.5 cm long, forked or pinnately branched, bearing 2–several woolly sporocarps. Laminae (1)1.5–4(5.5) cm in diam., sericeous with commonly curved hairs, the segments symmetrical, the lateral margins distinctly concave, the apex entire, broadly round.

Terrestrial in wet sand or soil at the edges of swamps, ditches, streams, and lakes. Occasional. Central Texas.

Not cultivated.

400 Marsilea vestita Hook. & Grev.
Hairy Water-clover

Rhizomes with well-developed short branches at the nodes, the fronds clustered along the rhizome. Stipes 1.5–21 cm long, the pedicels 3–5 mm long, bearing 1 appressed-pilose to sericeous sporocarp. Laminae 0.8–2.7 cm in diam., sparsely to rather densely appressed-pilose and rarely with reddish-brown stripes between the veins, the segments usually somewhat asymmetrical, the lateral margins plane or concave, the apex entire, round.

Aquatic in temporary pools or at the edge of ponds, occasionally terrestrial in wet soil. Frequent. British Columbia to California east to Saskatchewan, the Dakotas, Iowa, Missouri, Arkansas, Tennessee, Louisiana. Escaped in Mobile Co., Alabama, according to Kral (1976, p. 439).

Cultivated in aquaria and decorative pools. Cronquist et al. (1972, p. 220) has included *M. mucronata* A. Braun and *M. oligospora* Goodd. in this species, which is followed here. Although typical *M. mucronata* has shorter, straighter, and coarser hairs on the laminae and sporocarps than do *M. vestita* and *M. oligospora*, many specimens of these species can be found with coarse hairs on the sporocarps and fine ones on the laminae, or vice-versa. *Marsilea oligospora* seems to be an extreme form of *M. vestita*. Water forms of *M. vestita* and rarely of *M. quadrifolia* occasionally have reddish-brown stripes between the veins on the abaxial surface that look much like those of *M. mexicana*. If such plants are sterile, they may be difficult to distinguish from the latter species, although the veins seem to be a little more obscure in *M. mexicana* than they do in *M. vestita* and *M. quadrifolia*.

401   Marsilea uncinata A. Braun
Hooked Water-clover

Rhizomes with well-developed short branches at the nodes, the fronds clustered along the rhizome. Stipes 3–21 cm long, the stalks 8–25 mm long, bearing 1 appressed-pilose sporocarp having a conspicuous, hooked tooth above the stalk. Laminae 1–3(4.5) cm in diam., sparsely appressed-pilose to glabrous, the segments asymmetrical, the lateral margins plane or concave, the apex entire, round.

Aquatic along edges of lakes, streams, and ditches in permanently wet situations. Occasional. Arkansas, Louisiana, and Texas.

Not cultivated.

PILULARIA
The Pillworts

Pilularia includes six species in temperate regions of the northern and southern hemispheres. Only one species is native to the United States; it grows principally in California.

The Pillworts are very small ferns with thin, long-creeping rhizomes. Single fronds are given off from rather closely spaced nodes. A short side branch with several closely spaced fronds also is produced at each node. The fronds consist only of a long, alate stipe; the lamina is absent. Spherical sporocarps are borne on an unbranched stalk at the node. The hard sporocarp contains four sori each containing microsporangia or megasporangia.

The Pillworts grow rooted in shallow water. They pass the dry or cold season as sporocarps, at least in cold climates. They are not cultivated and are seldom collected, for they look like young grasses or rushes. Their young stipes are curled at the apex like typical fiddleheads, and so they can be distinguished in the field by that character or by their sporocarps.

402   Pilularia americana A. Braun
American Pillwort

Rhizomes with well-developed short branches at the nodes, the fronds clustered along the rhizome. Stipes 1–7.5 cm long, ca. 0.5 mm wide including the alae, the stalks ca. 1 mm long, bearing one spherical, villous sporocarp ca. 3 mm in diam. Laminae absent.

Aquatic in the mud of temporary pools and pond margins. Rare. Oregon to southern California, Nebraska to Texas, and disjunct in Arkansas, Tennessee, and Georgia.

Readily cultivated in wet potting soil if kept uncrowded.

SALVINIACEAE
The Floating Fern Family

The Salviniaceae includes only one genus, *Salvinia*, with about 10 species in warm-temperate to tropical regions of the New and Old World. Only *S. minima* occurs in the United States.

The plants of this family are very peculiar, small, floating ferns. They have long, thin rhizomes bearing at their closely spaced nodes fronds in groups of three, two of which are simple, nearly orbicular, and float on the surface of the water, and one of which is highly dissected, irregular, hangs down in the water, serves as roots for the plant, and bears the sporocarps. The simple, floating fronds have obvious, whitish, multicellular hairs in rows on the upper surface that are divided at the apex into four branches; the branch tips unite in species of the *S. auriculata* group, but are free in other species. By trapping air among them, the hairs cause the plants to right themselves if they are turned over in the water. The globose to ovoid or flattened sporocarps, which are highly modified indusia, bear within them several megasporangia or microsporangia. The development of these structures is very complex (see Eames, 1936, pp. 232–242).

The species of Salviniaceae all are aquatic. Usually they are found floating in quiet water, but as water levels fall, they may be found on freshly exposed mud. *Salvinia auriculata* Aubl. commonly is cultivated in aquaria; it is not native to the United States. *Salvinia molesta* D. S. Mitchell, a sterile pentaploid hybrid, occasionally is grown in aquaria and decorative pools. It poses some threat to the waters of Florida and the Gulf Coast, should it escape from cultivation. *Salvinia* fronds tend to diminish in size under crowded or low-light conditions, making identification to species difficult.

403 Salvinia minima Baker
Water Spangles

Rhizomes 1–4(6) cm long, 0.5–0.75 mm in diam., straw-colored, bearing dark, multicellular, jointed hairs; floating fronds elongate-orbicular, 7–15 mm long, 6–13 mm wide, pale green on the upper surface with straw-colored to whitish hairs up to ca. 2 mm long, the hairs quadrifid at the apex, the branches free, dark green on the lower surface; submerged fronds up to ca. 3 cm long, bearing hairs like those of the rhizome.

Aquatic or on mud in ponds and lakes, occasionally in swamps. Frequent. Florida and coastal Georgia.

Cultivated in aquaria and decorative pools. *Salvinia rotundifolia* Willd. is a commonly used synonym.

AZOLLACEAE
The Mosquito Fern Family

The Azollaceae includes only one genus, *Azolla*, with about six species in tropical to temperate regions of the New and Old World. The plants, which usually are floating on water, are reputed to grow so densely that mosquitos cannot penetrate the mass of fronds, hence the common name.

Plants of the Mosquito Fern Family are somewhat moss-like. In their details, they resemble the Salviniaceae, but the fronds are much smaller and more crowded. The fragile, branched rhizomes bear crowded, alternate fronds. Each frond is divided into a thick, photosynthetic, aerial upper lobe and a somewhat larger, non-photosynthetic, submerged, lower lobe. The lower surface of the upper lobe contains a cavity that bears the blue-green alga *Anabaena azollae* (Holst & Yopp, 1979; Lumpkin & Plucknett, 1980). Roots are borne along the rhizomes. Papillae on the upper surface of the aerial portions of the fronds and air trapped in small spaces between the fronds keep the plants from sinking when they are disturbed. Short-stalked, thin-walled sporocarps are formed in the axil of the upper lobe of the fronds. The megasporocarps are nearly globular; the microsporocarps are globular to rhomboid. The megasporocarps contain at maturity a single megasporangium bearing a single megaspore with a roughly conical, divided apical massula (usually called a float). The microsporocarps contain microsporangia. The microspores, instead of being released singly as in terrestrial ferns, are trapped together in 4–6 globular structures called massulae, which bear on their surface, harpoon-like glochidia. These latter structures serve to anchor the massulae near the megasporangia, to assure fertilization and the subsequent development of gametophytes. The development and function of these structures are similar to that of *Salvinia* (see Eames, 1936, pp. 244–255).

The Mosquito Ferns are free floating in quiet water or grow on mud near the water's edge. When given good opportunity to grow, they are noxious weeds. Because of their symbiontic relationship with *Anabaena azollae*, which fixes atmospheric nitrogen, *Azolla* is encouraged to grow in rice paddies (Moore, 1969).

The only United States monograph (Svenson, 1944) is in need of revision, considering the large number of specimens that have accumulated in recent years. Scanning electron microscopy of the megaspores may prove to be the most reliable character (Bates & Browne, 1981), but investigations have scarcely begun. As in most aquatic genera, the species are rather variable and are decidedly influenced by environmental factors. The key will work best with well-grown, mature material.

Key to Azolla
1. Plants usually 0.5–1 cm long, dichotomously branched almost throughout; fronds not or scarcely imbricate, the upper lobes usually 0.5–0.6 mm long; glochidia of the massulae lacking septae; megaspores unknown; E. *404. A. caroliniana*

1. Plants usually more than 1 cm long, pinnately branched from a central axis, dichotomously branched only at the periphery of the plant; fronds slightly to greatly imbricate, the upper lobes usually at least 0.7 mm long, **2**

2(1). Plants 1–1.5 cm long; glochidia of the massulae with many septae; megaspores pitted in the basal region; W, NO. *405. A. mexicana*

2(1). Plants 2–6 cm long; glochidia with 0–(2) septae; megaspores reticulate in the basal region; P, E. *406. A. filiculoides*

404   Azolla caroliniana Willd.
Eastern Mosquito Fern
Plants usually 0.5–1 cm long, dichotomously branched almost throughout; fronds rather widely spaced, scarcely imbricate, the upper lobes usually 0.5–0.6 mm long; massulae ca. 0.3 mm in diam.; glochidia nonseptate; megaspores unknown in United States plants.

Floating in still water. Rare. Massachusetts and New York on the coastal plain to Florida west to Louisiana. Also in Mississippi, Tennessee, Kentucky, and perhaps Illinois, along the east side of the Mississippi River valley.

Cultivated commonly in aquaria and decorative pools. According to T. Lumpkin (pers. comm.), this species becomes fertile when it is crowded and exhibits 3-dimensional growth away from the surface of the water, but not so markedly as in *A. filiculoides*.

405   Azolla mexicana Presl
Mexican Mosquito Fern
Plants usually 1–1.5 cm long, pinnately branched from a central axis at least in large plants, dichotomously branched only at the periphery of the plant; fronds imbricate, often densely so, the upper lobes usually 0.7–0.9 mm long; massulae 0.2–0.3 mm in diam.; glochidia multiseptate; megaspores conspicuously shallowly pitted at the base.

Floating in still water. Rare. Southern British Columbia to southern California east to Nevada, Utah, Colorado, Nebraska, Iowa, Minnesota, Wisconsin, Illinois, Missouri, Arkansas, central Texas, and southern New Mexico.

Cultivated occasionally in aquaria and decorative pools. According to T. Lumpkin (pers. comm.), this species usually becomes fertile while uncrowded and exhibiting 2-dimensional growth.

406 Azolla filiculoides Lam.

Large Mosquito Fern

Plants usually 2–6 cm long, pinnately branched from a central axis at least in large plants, dichotomously branched only at the periphery of the plant; fronds usually densely imbricate, the upper lobes 0.8–1 mm long; massulae 0.5–0.6 mm in diam.; glochidia non-septate or rarely with 1 or 2 septae; megaspores reticulate with raised hexagons at the base.

Floating in still water. Rare. Washington to southern California and Arizona. Disjunct on Long Island, New York, Sapelo Island, Georgia, and perhaps other localities along the eastern seaboard, according to Bates and Browne (1981). Introduced or disjunct and perhaps not persisting in southern Idaho.

Cultivated commonly in aquaria and decorative pools. According to T. Lumpkin (pers. comm.), this species becomes fertile when it is very crowded and exhibits strong, 3-dimensional growth away from the surface of the water.

HYBRID COMPLEXES

The modern era of study of hybrid complexes in the ferns and fern-allies dates from Manton's book *Problems of Cytology and Evolution in the Pteridophyta* (1950), which was the first comprehensive survey of pteridophyte cytology. The book also popularized the acetocarmine squash method of preparing sporangia and root tips for cytological examination. For the first time, a rapid and accurate method for counting chromosomes was made available to botanists, who heretofore had to make laborious paraffin sections that often yielded erroneous counts. Needless to say, the amount of data and the number of species known cytologically increased dramatically after 1950. The interest in fern hybrids (Wagner, 1968) and the increase in the number of cytologically investigated species (Löve, Löve & Pichi Sermolli, 1977) continues to the present time. The data accumulated for so many genera and species have been helpful in developing modern phylogenies in the pteridophytes, both within genera and at higher levels of classification. Recent biosystematic work in the pteridophytes has been summarized by Lovis (1977).

Sexual diploid species (and sexual polyploid species of hybrid origin) are the carriers of genetic material over long periods of geological time through their sexual reproduction. However, asexual hybrids, both diploids and polyploids, also occur in a number of pteridophyte genera found in the United States and Canada. These plants have unbalanced sets of chromosomes (genomes), usually cannot form spores because of the failure of meiosis (see Life Cycle), and rarely play an important role in evolution. However, by investigating interspecific hybrids, much can be learned about the taxonomy, patterns of morphological development, processes of reproduction, and pathways of evolution in plants. Many sterile hybrids occur between isolated pairs of species (e.g., *Aspidotis* × *carlotta-halliae*, *Nephrolepis* × *averyi*, and *Osmunda* × *ruggii*), with no hybrid complex built up of a number of parental species and hybrids. In other cases, extensive, reticulate complexes occur, which are summarized in this chapter. Unless they reproduce asexually and are widespread, sterile hybrids mostly have been omitted from the keys and are merely mentioned in the discussions of the sexual species in this book.

Asexual hybrids tend to be uncommon or rare and are sporadic in distribution. A few form large, local colonies or clones by vegetative means (see Life Cycle). Sterile hybrids are able to move long distances only by fragmentation and spread of parts like rhizomes. Even so, some have been found growing hundreds of miles from their parents. The separation normally is longitudinal and not latitudinal; hybrids tend to occur within the north–south limits of their parents. However, many primarily Canadian species and their hybrids occur at high altitudes far to the south along the Blue Ridge from Virginia to the Carolinas and in the Rocky Mountains.

Finding and identifying pteridophyte hybrids is a special challenge. They may be only subtly different from their parents and difficult to detect. Because so many are rare and in need of study, sterile hybrids should not be collected until living plants have been studied in the field; if necessary for identification, a frond without a rhizome can be detached carefully and sent to an expert for evaluation. Hybrids with unbalanced genomes usually form few or no spores and sometimes only a few, malformed sporangia. The sori consequently are smaller and paler than those of species that form viable spores. In rare cases, mostly in *Dryopteris*, the annuli of the sporangia are not indurated. These clues to hybridity can be seen with the aid of a hand lens. Lastly, hybrids do tend to be intermediate between their parents, usually in proportion to the number of genomes contributed by each parent. (For instance, triploid hybrids that inherit two genomes from one parent and one from the other are likely to look more like the parent from which they inherited the two genomes, rather than the one from which they inherit only one.) Knowing the frond shape and division and other characteristics of the parents well is a definite aid in detecting odd, potentially hybrid descendents.

The charts in this chapter include only species and hybrids native to the United States and Canada. Many North American species also occur in Eurasia. Some hybrids found there shed light on the complexes as they exist in North America. The sets of chromosomes (genomes) are represented by capital letters. The chromosomes themselves are indicated by the number of paired chromosomes (bivalents, II) and unpaired chromosomes (univalents, I) to be expected during meiosis. In fact, nature is not fastidious, especially in hybrids, and chromosome pairing is not necessarily so clear as the neat formulae would make it seem. In several places, the charts are the best educated guess that could be made at the present time, and errors of interpretation doubtless have occurred. The names of sexual diploid species are highlighted by a rectangle, those of sexual polyploid species by an oval. Conjectural genomes or chromosome counts are marked (?). This chapter must be used with caution and with the knowledge that some parts of it will need to be revised and expanded as new information and new hybrids are discovered.

APPALACHIAN ASPLENIUM COMPLEX

This complex is the second largest in the United States, after the North American *Dryopteris* complex. It is also one of the best known and longest studied; even so, new discoveries are still being made (Moran, 1981). The basic outline of this complex was reported by Wagner (1954). In subsequent years, further investigations by Wagner and his associates resulted in a number of papers reporting additional information. Wagner and Darling (1957) included a key to many hybrids in the complex. Wagner (1963a, pp. 143–145) showed that *Asplenium ruta-muraria* var. *cryptolepis* (Fern.) Massey and var. *ohionis* (Fern.) Wherry were inconsequential variants of *A. ruta-muraria*. Wagner and Wagner (1969) described what is now known as *A. herb-wagneri* Tayl. & Mohlenbr. and reduced *A. ×stotleri* Wherry to synonymy under *A. ×bradleyi*.

As originally defined, the Appalachian *Asplenium* complex included *A. montanum, platyneuron, rhizophyllum*, and the hybrids between them, which are diagrammed in a triangle. *Asplenium ×kentuckiense* McCoy, which lies near the center of the diagram, is notable because it theoretically could be formed by a cross between any one of three diploid species at the corners of the triangle and the tetraploid hybrid species lying directly opposite the diploid. Whether, in fact, it is formed other than as a hybrid between *A. pinnatifidum* and *A. platyneuron* is not known. The relationships between the ploidy levels of *A. trichomanes* are not clearly understood. Wagner and Wagner (1976) have found irregular pairing in tetraploid *A. ×clermontiae*, which apparently means that all *A. ruta-muraria* chromosomes are paired and that some from tetraploid *A. trichomanes* are also. The latter species is mostly diploid in the United States, although some tetraploids and a few triploids are known (Moran, 1982).

ASPLENIUM VERECUNDUM COMPLEX

Several basically tropical species in Florida hybridize to form a small complex. These hybrids all spread vegetatively by root proliferations, which Appalachian Aspleniums are not known to do, and so persist even though they rarely or never form viable spores and probably are not created anew by hybridization very often because of the rarity of their parents. The hybrids are Florida endemics, although *A. ×plenum* could occur in the Antilles, Central America, and northern and western South America. Both *A. ×curtissii* and *A. ×plenum* are apogamous and presumably reproduce by unreduced spores. Neither *A. trichomanes-dentatum* nor *A. verecundum* is understood cytologically. Possibly both are of hybrid origin; if so, a search for their likely parents could be very rewarding. At present, it is possible only to represent them with tentative genomic formulae. Fortunately, Morzenti (1967) published a highly detailed paper describing most of the other details of the complex. She suggested that *A. verecundum* could be an autotetraploid, but this hypothesis is as yet unproven.

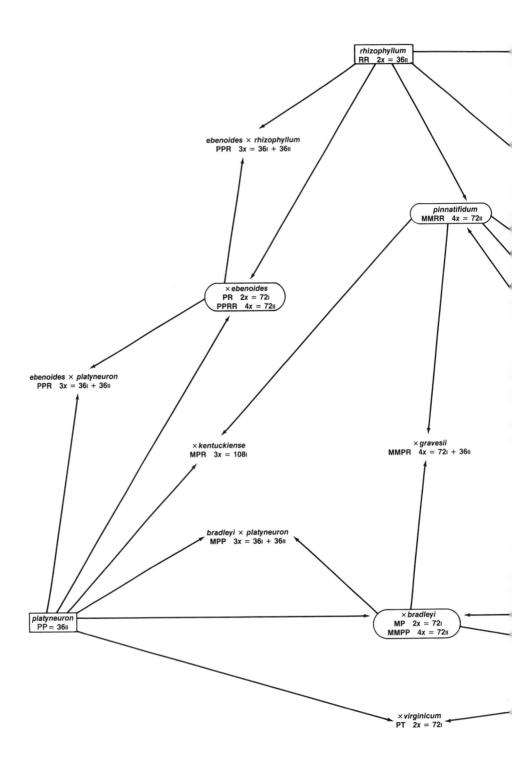

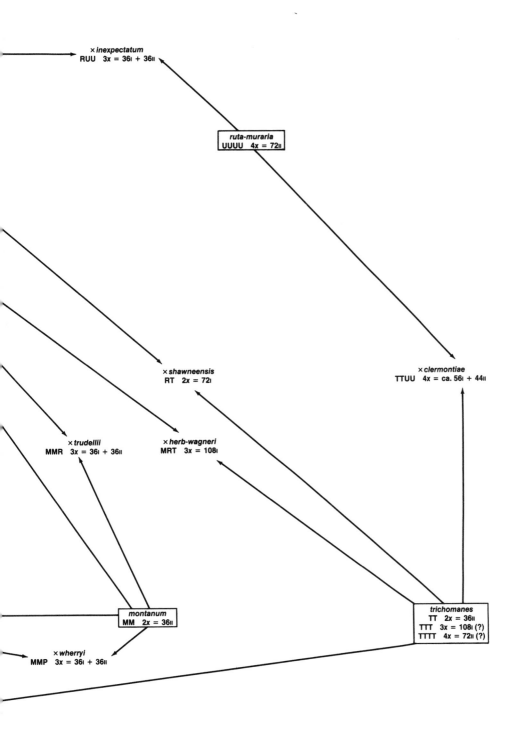

Fig. 6. Appalachian Asplenium complex.

317

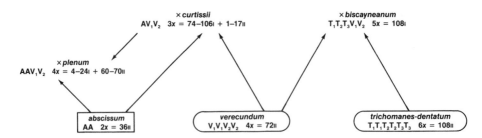

Fig. 7. Asplenium verecundum complex.

CYSTOPTERIS FRAGILIS COMPLEX

Lovis (1977, p. 356) has called this "perhaps the most formidable bio-systematic problem in the ferns." The scheme presented here depends greatly upon data from T. Reeves and A. M. Evans (both pers. comm.)

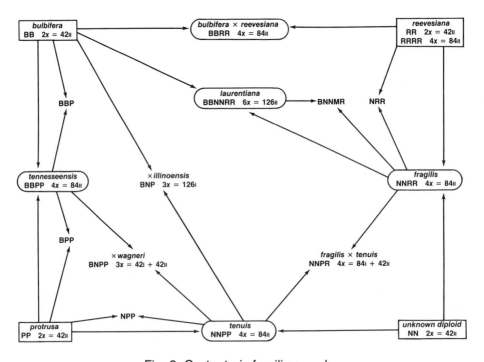

Fig. 8. Cystopteris fragilis complex.

and from Haufler (1985) and Moran (1983); it may be modified as additional data become available. The conclusions are confirmed in part by chemical evidence (Haufler, 1985). The polyploids presumably arose from sterile hybrids as a result of chromosome doubling. The unnamed back-crosses are important in that their chemistry and chromosome behavior are consistent with the hybrids' presumed parents and so demonstrate the distinctness of the parents, some of which have been considered varieties or subspecies of *C. fragilis* in the past. The discovery and analysis of hybrids between *C. fragilis* and its possible parents are especially important.

The origin of *C. fragilis* remains uncertain at the present time. Vida (1974) synthesized several hybrids between European species and *C. protrusa*, his chromosome data demonstrated that the latter species could not be a parent of *C. fragilis*. Three current hypotheses accounting for the origin of *C. fragilis*, which is a tetraploid, include: (1) a scarce or extinct, presumably northern American, diploid may have moved south during the Wisconsinin glaciation to hybridize with *C. reevesiana*, (and with *C. protrusa*) and presumably became extinct at the end of that glaciation; (2) a second, unknown diploid, rather than *C. reevesiana*, was one parent of *C. fragilis*; or (3) *C. fragilis* arose as an autotetraploid from a scarce or extinct diploid, with no involvement from *C. reevesiana* or another unknown diploid.

This is the first complex in the pteridophyta of the United States and Canada in which isozyme data have been critically used. Although the technique is difficult (Soltis et al., 1983), in this case the rewards have been ample; by coupling isozyme and cytological data, Haufler has greatly advanced knowledge of species relationships.

NORTH AMERICAN DRYOPTERIS COMPLEX

Most of the North American species of *Dryopteris* fall into one large biosystematic complex. Several species from Eurasia are part of the complex, but are not considered here. Much is yet to be learned about the species relationships; Wagner (1971b), Widén et al. (1975), Lovis (1977, pp. 343–350), Montgomery and Paulton (1981), and Montgomery (1982) are the most recent summaries. Carlson (1979) has studied the frequency of various *Dryopteris* hybrids with respect to the comparative ecology of these plants. The principal remaining problem in the complex is the identity of the unknown diploid that is presumed to be a parent of both *D. carthusiana* and *D. cristata*. This species has entirely escaped detection. Its morphology can be inferred from that of *D. ludoviciana, cristata, carthusiana*, and *intermedia*. The two tetraploids are likely to be intermediate between the unknown diploid and their other parent in each case. For instance, because *D. cristata* has narrower laminae than does *D. ludoviciana*, it is highly likely that the unknown diploid is narrower than *D. cristata*. The search for the unknown diploid in North America has been fruitless. However, it is entirely possible that it is a Eurasian species, perhaps extant or perhaps extinct, that is present in North America only in the genomes that it contributed in Eurasia to *D. cristata* and *D. carthusiana*.

Chromosome pairing in this complex is straightforward, except for some of the *D. celsa* and *D. clintoniana* hybrids (Wagner, 1971b) and for *D.*

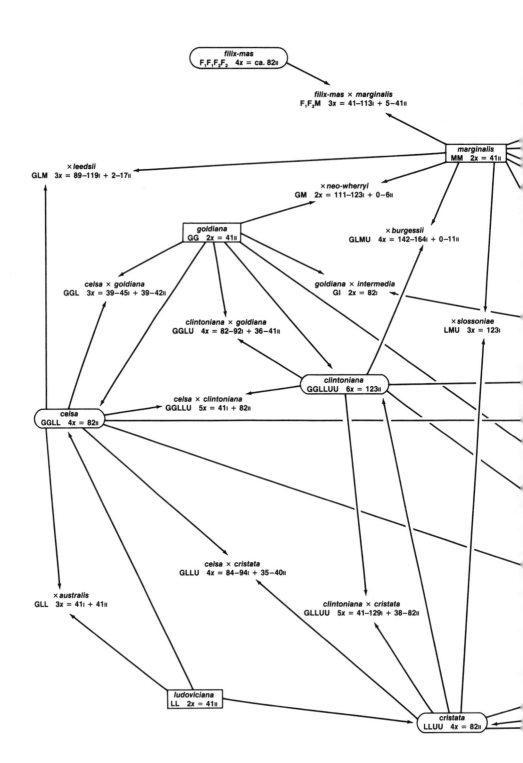

320

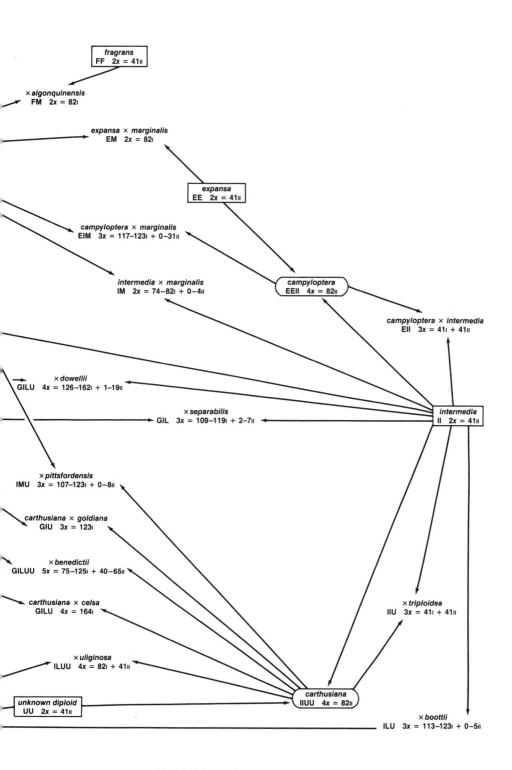

Fig. 9. North American Dryopteris complex.

filix-mas, its progenitors, and its hybrids. According to Fraser-Jenkins (1976), European *D. filix-mas* is an autoallotetraploid hybrid of *D. caucasica* and *D. oreades*. The diploid hybrid from which *D. filix-mas* arose shows some pairing at meiosis, which indicates that the two genomes are partially homologous. Wagner (1971b) reported irregular pairing in hybrids between *D. filix-mas* and *D. marginalis*, which indicates a cytology similar to that of European *D. filix-mas*, and which increases the probability that American and European specimens are in fact one species.

NORTH AMERICAN EQUISETUM COMPLEX

Of the native Scouring-rushes (*Equisetum* subg. *Hippochaete*), all but *E. scirpoides* form a complex. Although the hybrids are not well known cytologically, all appear to be diploid with 216 univalent chromosomes, half contributed by each parent. The characteristics of the hybrids have been studied in detail by Hauke (1963). The hybrids are sterile and have abortive spores, sporangia, or cones, making them fairly easy to detect. Despite their sterility, extensive hybrid colonies develop by rhizome growth and stem fragmentation (Peck, 1980).

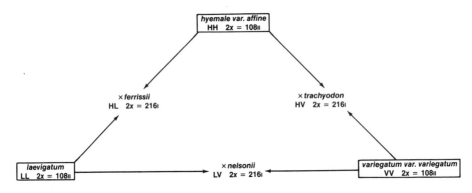

Fig. 10. North American Equisetum complex.

EASTERN AMERICAN ISOËTES COMPLEX

In contrast to the *Cystopteris fragilis* complex, diploids are abundant in *Isoëtes*. Hybrids, however, are just beginning to be recognized; few have been studied cytologically (Boom, 1979, p. 4) or chemically. Therefore, no attempt has been made on the chart to indicate genomes or cytological data for most hybrids. Boom (1979) has distinguished hybrid specimens on the basis of their intermediate morphology. He found that the widespread *I. engelmannii* is a parent of several hybrids in the southeastern and eastern United States. W. C. Taylor (pers. comm.) has brought several native *Isoëtes* species and hybrids into cultivation in order to study their cytology based on root tip squashes. He considers *I. echi-*

nospora subsp. *muricata,* × *eatonii, engelmannii,* and *riparia* to fall into one group on the basis of spore morphology and *I. acadiensis, hieroglyphica, macrospora,* and *tuckermanii* to fall into a second group. The parentage of the latter group, even the tetraploids, is unknown at the present time. He has found intermediates between *I. acadiensis* and *I. tuckermanii,* and he believes the two species may be despeciating. The decaploids appear to be related to the tetraploids in some way; *I. hieroglyphica* could be a hybrid involving pentaploid European *I. lacustris* L. Taylor's groups are joined by hybrids that, along with hybrids within the groups, are often characterized by polymorphic spores.

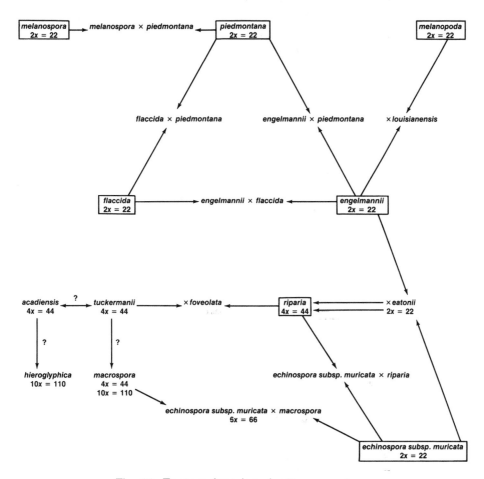

Fig. 11. Eastern American Isoëtes complex.

LYCOPODIUM INUNDATUM COMPLEX

The *Lycopodium inundatum* complex was first described in detail by Gillespie (1962). The parents form hybrids readily; the only combination not recorded is the one between *L. inundatum* and *L. prostratum*, which do not grow together. Additional data appear in an unpublished dissertation by Bruce (1975), who found several cryptic, undescribed tetraploids and triploids involving *L. inundatum* in the Great Lakes region. Bruce also found that the sterile diploid hybrids, which are rare as a rule, have a single set of chromosomes from each parent, that these chromosomes somehow pair, and that the plants thus produce well-formed, viable spores that are capable of being dispersed widely, for colonies of the hybrids are known at considerable distances from their parents. Such pairing and spore formation are not known in the true ferns. Backcrosses from these diploid hybrids to their parents are unknown.

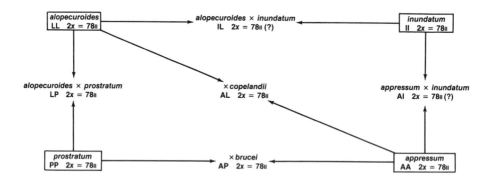

Fig. 12. Lycopodium inundatum complex.

LYCOPODIUM TRISTACHYUM COMPLEX

As in the *L. inundatum* complex, all the species and hybrids investigated so far are diploid (F. S. Wagner, 1980) and chromosome pairing and spore formation occur. Those hybrids with binomial names are found infrequently, and those represented only by formula names are very rare. According to Wilce (1965, p. 88), the sterility barriers between parents and hybrids are not complete; she suggested that some introgression may be taking place, as shown by less than 100% viable spores in the parental species and less than 100% spore abortion in the hybrids. F. S. Wagner (1980), however, found little or no spore abortion and no introgression or backcrossing.

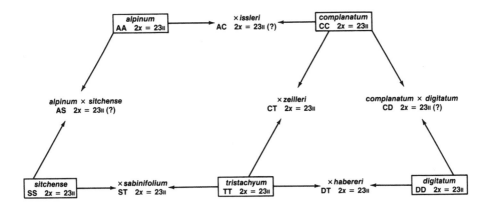

Fig. 13. Lycopodium tristachyum complex.

PELLAEA GLABELLA COMPLEX

The basic data on this complex were developed by A. F. Tryon (1957). The species in this complex have dark stipes and, except for *P. ternifolia*, have concolorous, reddish-brown rhizome scales. The relationships between the species in this complex are entirely conjectural, for neither the cytological evidence nor the morphological evidence is sufficiently strong to prove the relationships. Since *P. atropurpurea* is an apogamous triploid, it is most likely to be a hybrid between a diploid and a tetraploid. The only other extant Mexican or North American *Pellaea* that is at all sericeous on the rachis and costae is *P. ternifolia*, and so it is likely to be the diploid parent. The only available tetraploid seems to be *P. glabella*. Of course, it is possible that either or both parents are extinct, rather than extant, species. *Pellaea × suksdorfiana* is intermediate in many morphological characters between *P. × atropurpurea* and *P. occidentalis* (A. F. Tryon, 1957, p. 147), and the illustration of its chromosomes (A. F. Tryon & Britton, 1958, fig. 1D) seems to show 58 univalents and 29 bivalents.

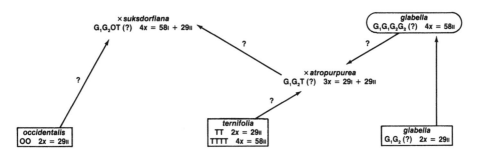

Fig. 14. Pellaea glabella complex.

PELLAEA MUCRONATA COMPLEX

The species in this complex have dark stipes, like those of the *P. glabella* complex, but differ in having bicolorous rhizome scales. *Pellaea ternifolia*, which presumably played a role in the *P. glabella* complex, surely is a member of this complex, for it has bicolorous rhizome scales. Wagner (1965) has shown that *P. wrightiana* is an autoallotetraploid that back-crosses with *P. truncata* to form sterile triploid hybrids. W. H. Wagner (pers. comm.) has demonstrated that *P. bridgesii* is a member of this complex, and Wagner, Smith, and Pray (1983) have shown that it hybridizes with *P. mucronata* var. *mucronata* to form *P.* ×*glaciogena*.

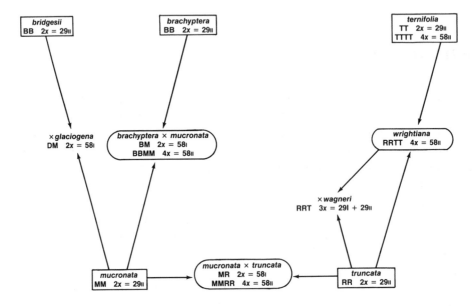

Fig. 15. Pellaea mucronata complex.

326

POLYPODIUM HESPERIUM COMPLEX

This complex is centered in California, where recent discoveries indicate that it is more involved than was formerly realized. S. Whitmore (pers. comm.) has succeeded in finding hybrids involving *P. californicum*, *P. glycyrrhiza*, and perhaps *P. scouleri*. The characters are subtle and require detailed observations. The triploid hybrids that have *P. hesperium* as one parent are known only from one or a few localities in British Columbia. Published accounts of this complex include those of Lang (1971) and Lloyd (1975), who summarized the morphological differences between the species in this complex.

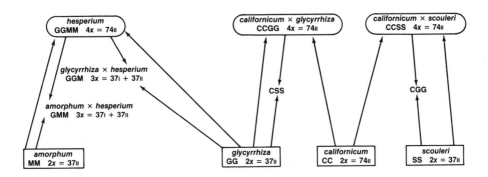

Fig. 16. Polypodium hesperium complex.

NORTH AMERICAN POLYSTICHUM COMPLEX

This complex was first worked out by W. H. Wagner (1973). His scheme was modified by D. H. Wagner (1979). Data from both investigators form the basis for the diagram. The North American *Polystichum* complex differs from most other complexes in that the sterile diploids underlying the fertile tetraploids are quite commonly encountered. However, they can be distinguished from the tetraploids only by their spore abortion, and so are rather difficult to detect. The cytology of *P. braunii* is based on European material; presumably plants from North America do not differ. D. H. Wagner (1979, pp. 26–27) found that *P. andersonii* is an amphidiploid with one parent *P. munitum* and the other an unknown species. He predicted the morphology of the other parent and found a herbarium specimen from British Columbia of that parent. Living material of the new species is being sought so that it can be investigated cytologically and described adequately.

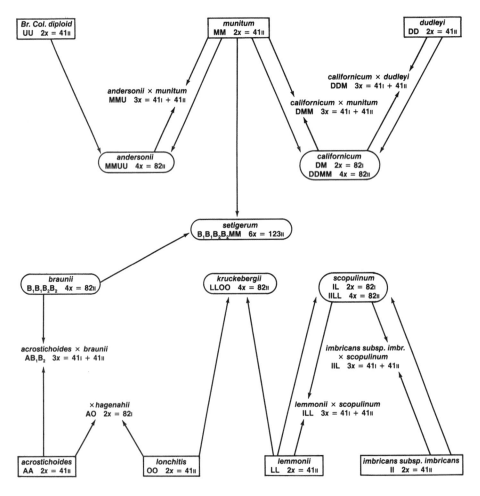

Fig. 17. North American Polystichum complex.

Glossary

abaxial: facing away from the axis. *Ant.* adaxial.

abortive: distorted or developed incompletely; not well formed. Said especially but not exclusively of reproductive structures like sporangia and spores.

abrupt: suddenly narrowed or cut off. *Ant.* gradual, tapered.

acicular: needle-shaped (Fig. 21J).

acroscopic: facing the apex of the axis on which it is borne (Fig. 20). *Ant.* basiscopic.

acrostichoid: having sporangia borne like those of *Acrostichum*, apparently scattered on the surface of the fertile lamina, usually densely so.

acuminate: forming an angle of less than 30° with the sides somewhat concave (Fig. 22C).

acute: forming an angle of 30–90° with the 2 sides straight or slightly convex (Fig. 22G).

adaxial: facing toward the axis. *Ant.* abaxial.

adjacent: next to each other, but not touching or overlapping.

adnate: fused, usually laterally, to an unlike structure, as lamina to rachis. *Ant.* separate. *See* connate.

adventitious: in roots, those that arise from stems, rather than from the primary root. All roots of mature pteridophytes are adventitious.

aerial: above ground; epigeous. *Ant.* subterranean.

agamosporous: having a life cycle in which chromosome segregation and recombination have been circumvented.

ala: a wing, usually a long, narrow membrane laterally bordering a stipe, rachis, or costa. *Pl.* **alae.**

alate: bearing an ala.

alternate: one part inserted at a single point along an axis; neither in pairs (opposite) nor whorled.

anastomosing: joining together; in the case of veins, usually to form networks and enclose areolae.

angular: being angled.

annulus: the row of thick- and thin-walled cells of the leptosporangium (the sporangium of higher ferns), which causes the sporangium to open and to discharge its spores. *Pl.* **annuli.**

antheridium: the male sex organ borne on the underside of the gametophyte and producing spermatozoids. *Pl.* **antheridia.**

antrorse: pointed forward and upward. *Ant.* retrorse.

apex: terminal portion of a structure.

apical: pertaining to the apex.

apiculate: abruptly terminated in a small, sharp apex (Fig. 23J).

apogamous: having the condition of apogamy.

apogamy: the formation of a sporophyte from a gametophyte by asexual means such as budding, rather than by egg formation and fertilization.

apomixis: lacking fertilization.

aposporous: having the condition of apospory.

apospory: the formation of a gametophyte from a sporophyte by asexual means without meiosis or spore formation.

appressed: tightly pressed against something. *Ant.* spreading.

approximate: closely spaced, and so nearly touching. *Ant.* distant.

arachnoid: like cobwebs.

archegonium: female sex organ borne on the underside of the gametophytes and producing eggs. *Pl.* **archegonia.**

areola: the area enclosed by anastomosing veins when they form a mesh or network. *Pl.* **areolae.**

articulate: having a swollen or discolored place of separation or weakness in a stipe or stem.

ascending: inclined upward.

asymmetrical: having a different outline on each side of a central axis. *Ant.* symmetrical.

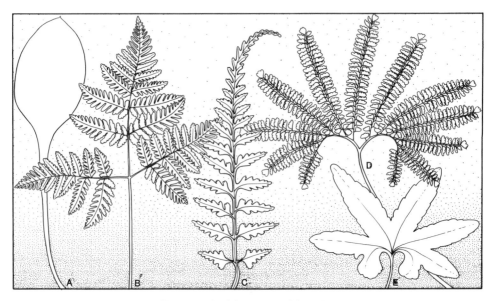

Fig. 18. Architecture of fronds.
A = simple, B = tripartite, C = pinnate, D = pedate, E = palmate.

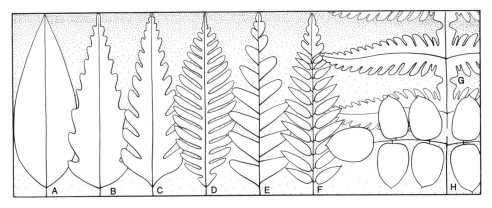

Fig. 19. Division of fronds.
A = entire, B = lobed, C = pinnatifid, D = pectinate, E = pinnatisect, F = pinnate,
G = bipinnatifid, H = bipinnate.

attenuate: forming an angle of less than 15°; narrower than acute (Fig. 22A).

auriculate: bearing 1 or 2 auricles (Figs. 22D, F).

auricle: a low, basal lobe.

auriculiform: having the shape of an auricle.

axil: the acroscopic angle formed at the point of insertion of a minor axis on a major one (Fig. 20). *Pl.* **axils.**

axis: the central line or structure along which parts or organs are arranged. *Pl.* **axes.**

basal: of or pertaining to the base.

base: the proximal portion of a structure, that part nearest the point of attachment.

basiscopic: facing the base of the axis on which it is borne (Fig. 20). *Ant.* acroscopic.

biauriculate: having 2 auricles (Fig. 22F).

bicolorous: having two colors, often said of scales (Fig. 25I).

bifid: forked or cut into 2 narrow teeth.

bipinnate or **2-pinnate:** divided into pinnae bearing pinnules (Fig. 19H).

bipinnatifid: pinnatifid with pinnatifid lobes (Fig. 19G).

bivalent: a pair of chromosomes, usually 1 contributed from each parent.

blunt: not apiculate or pointed.

branch: a division of a main stem or adventitious root; in *Equisetum*, one of few to many small stems forming whorls at intervals along the larger, main stem.

branchlet: a small branch.

bristle: a stiff, usually straight hair sometimes 2 or 3 cells wide at the base (Fig. 25H).

bristly: bearing bristles.

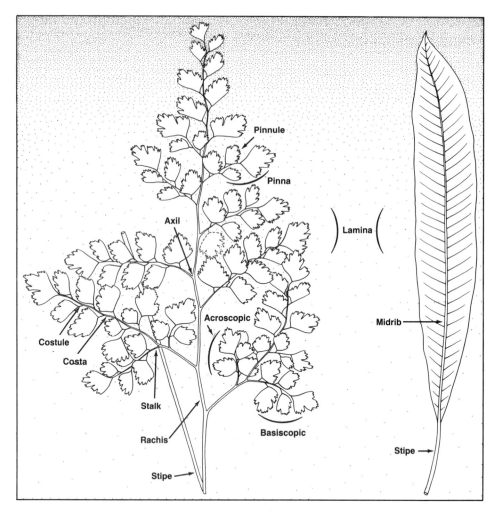

Fig. 20. Parts of fronds.

bud: *See* bulblet.

bulblet: a small, globular, sometimes hairy or scaly, asexual propagule borne along the rachis or costa and capable of forming a new plant before or after separation from the mother plant.

bulbous: swollen; nearly spherical.

capitate: terminated by a bulbous, swollen area or cell (Fig. 25L).

carnose: fleshy.

caudate: bearing a narrow, elongate tail (Fig. 23K).

central: pertaining to or of the center.

cilium: a short, usually stiff, usually unicellular, marginal hair. *Pl.* **cilia.**

ciliate: bearing cilia (Fig. 24F).

circular: having the shape of a circle.

clathrate: lattice-like; having thick lateral (adjacent) cell walls and thin surficial walls, especially said of rhizome scales (Fig. 25J).

clavate: club-shaped, round at the apex, widest just below the apex, and tapering slightly to the base (Fig. 25K).

compact: pressed together or closely joined; in rhizomes, those with short internodes and closely spaced stipes.

concolorous: uniform in color.

cone: in pteridophytes, a compact reproductive structure borne at the tip of a branch, consisting of a central axis bearing closely spaced, spirally arranged sporangia each subtended by a sporophyll.

confluent: running together. *Ant.* discrete.

conform: similar in shape and size to others; usually said of an apical pinna in comparison with the lateral pinnae of a lamina.

congested: close together.

conical: cone-shaped.

connate: fused, usually laterally, to a similar structure, as one pinna to another. *See* adnate.

connivent: coming together, but not fused; usually said of veins in a lamina.

continuous: not interrupted.

contorted: irregularly twisted; distorted.

cordate: with a sinus and broadly rounded, sometimes overlapping lobes (Fig. 22H).

coriaceous: leathery in texture.

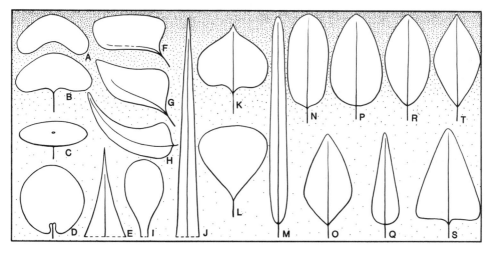

Fig. 21. Outlines of fronds and structures.
A = lunulate, B = reniform, C = peltate, D = orbiculate, E = subulate, F = dimidiate, G = trapeziform, H = falcate, I = spathulate, J = acicular, K = deltate, L = flabellate, M = linear, N = oblong, O = ovate-lanceolate, P = ovate, Q = lanceolate, R = elliptic, S = triangular, T = rhombic.

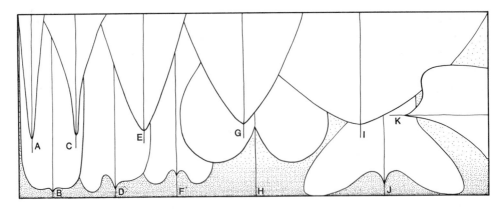

Fig. 22. Outlines of lamina bases.

A = attenuate, B = truncate, C = acuminate, D = uniauriculate, E = cuneate,
F = biauriculate, G = acute, H = cordate, I = obtuse, J = hastate, K = excavate.

corm: a solid, globular rootstock, in pteridophytes found only in *Isoëtes*.
cortex: in rhizomes and other axes, the tissue between the stele and the epidermis.
costa: the major axis of a pinna (Fig. 20). *See* midrib, rachis. *Pl.* **costae.**
costule: an axis that is a branch of a costa or another costule (Fig. 20).
creeping: extending horizontally in or on the soil.
crenate: shallowly scalloped, with rounded teeth (Fig. 24B).
crenulate: minutely crenate.
crest: in spores, a tall, irregular ridge; in fronds, an abnormally divided and elaborated frond, pinna, or pinnule apex.
crisped: irregularly curled.
cristate: bearing crests (Fig. 26A).
cuneate: forming an angle of 30–45° with the two sides straight (Figs. 22E, 23E).
cuspidate: rather abruptly constricted at the apex to a narrow, sharp-pointed tip (Fig 23F).
cylindrical: having the shape of a cylinder.
decaploid: having 10 sets of chromosomes.
deciduous: detaching. *Ant.* persistent.
decurrent: extending downward on and adnate to an axis.
delicate: fragile; easily broken.
deltate: broadly triangular with an obtuse apex (Fig. 21K).
dentate: bearing teeth that usually are directed outward from the margin, rather than forward (Fig. 24C).
denticulate: finely dentate.
depauperate: dwarfed due to poor growing conditions.
dichotomous: equal-forked.
dimidiate: halved diagonally, with usually one half rudimentary or absent (Fig. 21F).

dimorphic: having two shapes; in ferns usually referring to fertile versus sterile laminae or portions of laminae. *Ant.* monomorphic.

diploid: having 2 sets of chromosomes.

discrete: separate. *Ant.* confluent.

disjunct: separated geographically, especially a population of restricted area lying outside a main range.

distal: towards the apex in position. *Ant.* proximal.

distant: similar parts that are well separated and not overlapping or touching at the edges; stipes that are widely spaced. *Ant.* approximate.

distichous: occurring in 2 ranks in a single plane, 1 on each side of an axis.

dorsal: the upper side of a horizontal structure.

echinate: bearing spines, especially said of spores (Fig. 26F).

egg: the female sex cell (gamete).

eglandular: not glandular.

elater: strap-shaped appendages of *Equisetum* spores.

elliptic: having the outline of an elongate circle (Fig. 21R).

elongate: much longer than wide.

emarginate: having an emargination (Fig. 23A).

emargination: a V-shaped sinus at the apex of a lobe or tooth.

endodermis: the thin sheath of cells bounding the stele and separating it from the cortex.

endophytic: growing within the tissue of a plant.

entire: an even or smooth margin, not toothed or lobed, and with or without marginal hairs or cilia (Figs. 19A, 24A).

epidermis: the outermost layer(s) of cells of the plant, which retard water loss by exuding a wax-like cuticular layer or by being impregnated with wax-like substances.

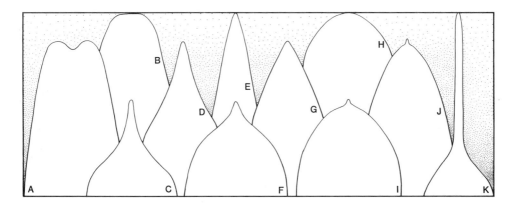

Fig. 23. Outlines of lamina apices.
A = emarginate, B = truncate, C = attenuate, D = acuminate, E = cuneate, F = cuspidate, G = acute, H = round, I = mucronate, J = apiculate, K = caudate.

epipetric: growing on rocks.

epiphytic: growing on shrubs or trees, either on the trunks or the branches.

equilateral: equal on both sides of an axis. *Ant.* inequilateral.

erect: vertical or upright.

erose: irregularly cut away and appearing eroded (Fig. 24G).

eusporangium: a thick-walled sporangium originating from several epidermal cells.

exalate: lacking an ala.

excavate: cut away, usually in a smooth curve, usually said of pinna bases (Fig. 22K).

excurrent: running or pointing outward or away from the point of origin.

exindusiate: lacking indusia.

expanded: increased in area or size.

exserted: projecting beyond another structure.

exstipitate: lacking a stipe, and so having the lamina and rachis joined directly to the rhizome.

extrorse: opening toward the margin and away from a central axis.

falcate: curved and tapered; sickle-shaped (Fig. 21H).

false indusium: *See* indusium.

false vein: *See* vein.

farina: a white, yellow, or other colored, waxy-appearing exudate of glands, in ferns especially in the Sinopteridaceae.

farinose: bearing farina.

fasciculate: in a closely set cluster.

fertile: bearing sporangia. *Ant.* sterile.

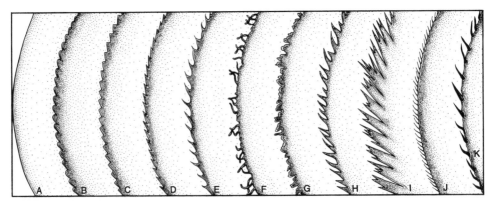

Fig. 24. Margins of laminae, scales, and indusia.
A = entire, B = crenate, C = dentate, D = serrate, E = toothed, F = ciliate,
G = erose, H = fimbriate, I = lacerate, J = setose, K = spinulose.

Fig. 25. Hair, scale, and gland types.

Hair types: A = pubescent, B = lanate, C = sericeous, D = pilose, E = villous,
F = strigose, G = stellate. Scale types: H = bristles, I = bicolorous, J = clathrate.
Gland types: K = clavate, L = capitate.

filamentous: wire-shaped.

filiform: thread-like.

fimbriate: fringed (Fig. 24H).

flabellate: fan-like with equal venation throughout and without a prominent central axis (Fig. 21L).

flexible: easily bent or twisted by hand; not stiff.

flexuous: bending in alternate directions; zig-zag.

fluted: bearing minute, longitudinal grooves. *See* striate.

foot: the portion of the young sporophyte that remains embedded in the gametophyte.

foveolate: pitted (Fig. 26D).

free: not connate or adnate; in veins, not anastomosing.

frond: the leaf of a fern.

fusiform: longer than wide and with tapered ends; spindle-shaped.

gamete: a sex cell, in pteridophytes called antherozoids or spermatozoids (male) and eggs (female).

gametophyte: the inconspicuous, non-vascular structures that bear male and female sex organs and sex cells (gametes). In homosporous pteridophytes, they are surficial, thin, chlorophyllous, and filamentous, ribbon-like, or heart-shaped or are subterranean, massive, achlorophyllous, and globular or cylindrical. In heterosporous pteridophytes, they are much reduced structures borne within spores.

gemma: a minute, readily detached, asexual propagule found on some gametophytes. *Pl.* **gemmae.**

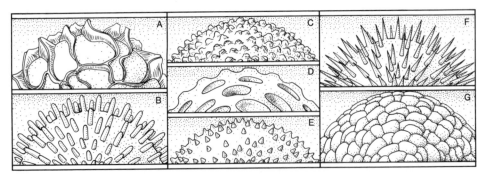

Fig. 26. Spore surface ornamentation types.
A = cristate, B = papillate, C = verrucose, D = foveolate, E = tuberculate,
F = echinate, G = rugose.

glabrescent: becoming glabrous in age.
glabrous: lacking glands, hairs, and scales.
gland: a unicellular or multicellular, filiform, clavate, capitate, or globular epidermal appendage secreting and/or containing resinous or wax-like, often highly colored substances. *See* farina.
glandular: bearing glands.
glaucous: having the surface very thinly covered and not obscured by a usually bluish or whitish, wax-like coating. *See* pruinose.
globular: nearly spherical.
glochidium: a minute, terminally barbed, spine-like hair present on the microspore-bearing structures of *Azolla*. *Pl.* **glochidia.**
hair: an epidermal outgrowth composed of a single elongate cell or a single file of cells.
heteroblastic series: a continuum of small to large and often differently divided fronds borne on juvenile to mature plants.
hastate: having the shape of an arrowhead, with outward-pointing basal lobes (Fig. 22J).
hemiepiphytic: remaining rooted in the ground but climbing tree trunks.
heterosporous: bearing spores of two sizes and sexes. *Ant.* homosporous.
hexaploid: having 6 sets of chromosomes.
homosporous: having spores of a single size.
hyaline: colorless and translucent. *See* scarious.
imbricate: having similar parts that overlap.
immersed: within lamina tissue, and so not readily seen upon superficial examination. *See* impressed, prominulous.
impressed: at a level below the surface of lamina tissue, but not completely immersed in it, thus readily seen upon superficial examination. *See* immersed, prominulous.
incised: deeply and sharply cut.
included: contained within, as a veinlet within an areola.

338

incurved: curved forward or upward toward an axis. *Ant.* recurved.

indusiate: bearing indusia.

indusium: a usually thin, often scale-like membrane or structure partially or fully covering or subtending the sorus and protecting the young sporangia. Especially in the Sinopteridaceae, the underrolled margin of the lamina is a modified frond margin, rather than an outgrowth of the lamina surface, and so is correctly called a **false indusium.** *Pl.* **indusia.**

inequilateral: not equal on both sides of an axis. *Ant.* equilateral.

inferior: basiscopic.

inframedial: below the middle; sori a little closer to the costa or costule than to the margin. *Ant.* supramedial.

internode: the portion of a stem between two nodes.

introgression: the formation of a range of intermediate plants by hybridization among parents and progeny; very rare in pteridophytes.

involucre: the tubular or bilabiate indusium found in *Hymenophyllum* and *Trichomanes*.

jointed: having obvious, thickened areas between cells, said especially of hairs.

juvenile: young; not adult in morphology. In ferns, juveniles may be precociously fertile.

lacerate: deeply and irregularly cut, appearing almost torn (Fig. 24I).

lamina: the expanded portion of a frond; the leaf blade of a fern. *Pl.* **laminae.**

lanate: wooly; densely clothed with long, tangled hairs (Fig. 25B).

lanceolate: lance-shaped, with a long, tapering apex and a short-tapering base (Fig. 21Q).

lateral: on or near the side.

lax: so weak as to be scarcely self-supporting.

leptosporangium: a thin-walled sporangium originating from a single epidermal cell.

ligule: In *Isoëtes*, a small, often triangular flap of leaf tissue located just distal to the sporangium on the adaxial surface of the leaf base.

linear: long, narrow, and of uniform or nearly uniform width (Fig. 21M).

lip: the apical portion of an involucre in *Hymenophyllum* and *Trichomanes*.

lobe: a portion of a lamina, pinna, pinnule, or segment that is fully connate and with a shallow sinus on either side that extends no more than half way from the lobe apex to the axis that the lobe is attached to. *See* segment.

lobed: having lobes (Fig. 19B).

long-creeping: growing horizontally for at least a few cm. In rhizomes, usually with the stipes distant.

lumen: the central cavity of a cell, especially in cells of clathrate rhizome scales. *Pl.* lumina.

lunulate: shaped like a small crescent or half-moon (Fig. 21A).

margin: an edge of a flat structure, usually a lamina.

marginal: pertaining to the margin.

massula: in *Azolla,* structures associated with megaspores or enclosing and trapping microspores to increase the probability of fertilization. *Pl.* **massulae.**

mat: a thick tangle.

matted: formed into a mat.

medial, median: pertaining to the middle; in sori, those positioned midway between the costa or costule and the margin.

megaspore: the large, female spore of the heterosporous pteridophytes *Azolla, Isoëtes, Salvinia,* and *Selaginella.*

meiosis: cell division, in pteridophytes usually leading to the formation of spores, in which the number of chromosomes in the daughter cells is half that of the parent cell. *See* mitosis.

membranaceous: like a membrane in thickness and texture.

megasporangium: in heterosporous pteridophytes, a female sporangium bearing megaspores. *Pl.* **megasporangia.**

microsporangium: in heterosporous pteridophytes, a male sporangium bearing microspores. *Pl.* **microsporangia.**

microspore: the small, male spore of heterosporous pteridophytes *Azolla, Isoëtes, Salvinia,* and *Selaginella.*

midrib: the major axis of a simple, lobed, or pinnatifid lamina. *See* costa, rachis.

mitosis: cell division in which the number of chromosomes in the daughter cells is the same as that of the parent cell. *See* meiosis.

monolete: in spores, having a single, unbranched scar or laesura. Characteristic of bilateral spores. *See* trilete.

monomorphic: having 1 shape, usually referring to fertile versus sterile laminae or portions of laminae. *Ant.* dimorphic.

monoploid: having 1 set of chromosomes.

mucronate: having a short, stiff, bristle-like apical projection (Fig. 23I).

multicellular: formed of more than 2 cells.

multicipital: many headed; a cluster of short, ascending rhizome branches.

multiseptate: bearing more than 2 septae.

neotenic: retaining juvenile characteristics throughout the life span.

node: the point at which a leaf is attached to a stem; also a swelling on the stipe of a fern frond, especially in *Danaea.*

oblanceolate: the inverse of lanceolate; gradually narrowed toward the base.

oblique: unequal-sided; slanting.

oblong: longer than wide with the long sides mostly parallel (Fig. 21N).

obovate: the inverse of ovate; ovate with the narrow end toward the base and a round to obtuse apex.

obscure: hidden. *Ant.* obvious.

obsolete: not very apparent; vestigial or rudimentary.

obtuse: forming an angle of 90° or more with the 2 sides straight or slightly convex (Fig. 22I).

octoploid: having 8 sets of chromosomes.

opaque: not capable of transmitting light. *Ant.* translucent, transparent.

opposite: two parts inserted opposite each other at a single point along an axis.

orbiculate: circular in outline, or nearly so (Fig. 21D).

ovate: having the outline of a longitudinal section of a hen's egg; similar to elliptic except broadest toward the base, rather than at the middle (Fig. 21P).

ovate-lanceolate: between ovate and lanceolate in outline (Fig. 21O).

ovoid: a solid that is ovate in longitudinal outline.

palmate: having 3 or more divisions radiating from a single point (Fig. 18E).

papilla: a minute, nipple-shaped projection.

papillate: bearing papillae (Fig. 26B).

papyraceous: like paper in texture and thickness.

paraphysis: a minute, unicellular or multicellular, usually hair-like structure borne on the soral receptacle or on the sporangium stalk or case. *Pl.* paraphyses.

parenchyma: unspecialized, thin-walled cells found throughout plant bodies.

pectinate: pinnatisect with narrow, linear segments; comb-like (Fig. 19D).

pedate: having 3 or more divisions arising from a single point with the 2 lateral divisions more divided than the others, especially on the basiscopic side (Fig. 18D).

peltate: round or nearly so and attached by a central stalk; said of indusia and certain scales (Fig. 21C).

pendent: hanging down.

pentagonal: five-sided.

pentaploid: having 5 sets of chromosomes.

pericycle: the tissue of the stele lying just inside the endodermis.

persistent: remaining attached. *Ant.* deciduous.

petiolulate: having a petiolule.

phloem: tissue specialized for the transport of food elaborated by the fronds downward through the plant.

phyllopodium: in species with articulate stipes, that portion of the stipe proximal to the articulation that remains attached to the rhizome, especially in *Elaphoglossum* and *Oleandra*.

pilose: bearing long, soft, rather straight, but flexible hairs (Fig. 25D).

pilosulous: minutely pilose.

pinna: a stalked or sessile, primary division of a compound lamina that is narrowed at the base (Fig. 20). *See* segment.

pinnate: divided into pinnae (Fig. 18C, 19F).

pinnatifid: deeply lobed, but not cut to the axis, and the lobes not contracted at their base (Fig. 19C). *See* pinnatisect, pinnate.

pinnatisect: lobed all the way to the axis, and the lobes not contracted at their base (Fig. 19E). *See* pinnate, pinnatifid.

pinnule: a stalked or sessile division of a pinna that is narrowed at the base (Fig. 20).

plane: flat; level.

plantlet: a small plant, usually one produced vegetatively from a rhizome or lamina bulblet.

polygonal: having several straight sides at an angle to each other.

polyploidy: having more than 2 sets of chromosomes in cells of the sporophyte or more than 1 set in cells of the gametophyte.

primary: the first or principal order of veins or axes in a branching system.

proliferous: bearing bulblets or plantlets.

prolonged: extended.

prominent: noticeable because of contrasting color and/or raised position with respect to surrounding tissue.

prominulous: slightly raised above the lamina tissue, and so readily seen upon superficial examination of the lamina.

prostrate: lying on the substrate.

proximal: toward the base in position. *Ant.* distal.

pruinose: having the surface obscured by a rather thick, bluish or whitish, wax-like coating. *See* glaucous.

pseudolamina: a false lamina, one usually formed by the lateral expansion of a rachis, and so lacking a rachis itself.

pubescent: downy with minute, straight, erect, soft hairs (Fig. 25A).

quadrangular: *See* oblong.

quadrifid: divided into 4 parts.

rachis: the principal, central axis of a pinnatisect or more compound lamina (Fig. 20). *See* costa, midrib.

radial: radiating from a central point.

receptacle: the lamina tissue, often thickened and amply supplied by 1 or more veins, to which the sporangia are attached.

recurved: curved backward or downward. *Ant.* incurved.

reflexed: bent abruptly downward or backward.

reniform: kidney-shaped (Fig. 21B).

repand: having an undulating margin.

reticulate: joined together to form a mesh-like network.

reticulum: a mesh-like network. *Pl.* **reticula.**

revolute: having the lateral margins rolled abaxially, thus exposing the adaxial surface and covering the abaxial surface.

rhizome: the rootstock or stem, an erect or creeping, usually scaly or hairy organ bearing fronds and adventitious roots.

rhombic: diamond-shaped, often much longer than wide (Fig. 21T).

rhomboid: a solid having the shape of 2 cones placed face-to-face.

ridge: a narrow, longitudinal projection.

rooted: anchored by roots to the substrate.

rootstock: a usually subterranean stem bearing fronds and adventitious roots. *See* rhizome.

rosette: a circular, radiating cluster of fronds borne horizontally at ground level from a largely subterranean rhizome.

round: having a round margin or shape.

rudimentary: partially developed.

rugose: wrinkled (Fig. 26G).

scabrous: rough to the touch.

scale: a multicellular, usually plane and elongate epidermal outgrowth 2 to typically many cells wide.

scaly: bearing scales.

scarious: thin and membranaceous, not green. *See* hyaline.

secondary: the next order after primary of veins or axes in a branching system.

segment: a portion of a lamina, pinna, or pinnule that is fully adnate and with a deep sinus on each side that extends more than half way from the segment apex to the axis that the segment is attached to. *See* lobe, pinna.

septa: a partition or cross-wall in certain kinds of hairs, especially glochidia. *Pl.* **septae.**

septate: bearing septae.

sericeous: bearing fine, usually straight, appressed, hairs (Fig. 25C).

serrate: having forward-pointing saw teeth on the margin (Fig. 24D).

serrulate: finely serrate.

sessile: borne without a stipe, petiolule, or stalk.

seta: a long, thin, straight, stiff, usually terete hair. *Pl.* **setae.**

setose: bearing setae (Fig. 24J).

setulose: minutely setose.

sheath: a more or less tubular structure closely and completely or partially surrounding another structure.

shiny: reflecting light well because of a smooth surface. *Ant.* dull.

short-creeping: growing horizontally a few cm. at most, usually said of rhizomes, which then have the stipe bases approximate.

simple: not divided, compound, or branched. In laminae, without segments or pinnae (subdivisions that are petiolulate or narrowed at the base; Fig. 18A); in pinnae, without pinnules.

sinus: the space between two lobes.

sorus: a cluster of sporangia having a distinct shape.

spathulate: spatula-shaped (Fig. 21I).

spermatozoid: male sex cell (gamete).

spherical: having the shape of a sphere.

spine: a strong usually narrowly conical, pointed projection from the epidermis.

spinulose: minutely spiny; in ferns, bearing short, spine-like teeth along the lamina margin (Fig. 24K).

sporangiophore: in *Equisetum,* a greatly transformed, peltate sporophyll bearing a ring of ca. 6 sporangia facing the axis of the cone.

sporangium: the spore-case of pteridophyta. *Pl.* **sporangia.**

spore: a usually unicellular, commonly spherical, tetrahedral, or bean-shaped, often highly ornamented reproductive structure produced by the sporangia and germinating to form a gametophyte. *Pl.* **spores.**

sporocarp: a structure containing sporangia in *Azolla, Marsilea,* and *Salvinia.*

sporophyll: a fertile leaf bearing sporangia or subtending a sporangium.

sporophyte: in pteridophytes, the conspicuous plants that bear spores. *See* gametophyte.

sport: a genetically fixed, although sometimes rather unstable, mutant occurring randomly, usually in cultivated plants.

spreading: directed away from the structure to which it is attached. *Ant.* appressed.

stalk: a short, supporting axis, as the petiolule of a pinna or segment; or the structure attaching a sporangium or synangium to its receptacle (Fig. 20).

stalked: joined to an axis or receptacle with a stalk.

stele: the axial vascular and associated tissues from the endodermis inward.

stellate: bearing lateral arms radiating from a central point, as in some hairs (Fig. 25G).

sterile: lacking sporangia. *Ant.* fertile.

stiff: rigid and unbending, not flexible or brittle.

stipe: the stalk of a frond from the base of the lamina to the point of attachment to the rhizome; the petiole of a fern leaf (Fig. 20).

stolon: a spreading or horizontal, asexual reproductive stem that roots along its length or at its tip to form new plants.

stoma: a minute, epidermal pore that usually is bordered by a pair of relatively large and conspicuous (under the microscope) guard cells.

stout: thick and short.

striate: marked with fine, longitudinal ridges. *See* fluted.

strigose: having stiff, straight, usually somewhat appressed hairs (Fig. 25F).

strigulose: minutely strigose.

sub-: a prefix indicating a lesser degree of a characteristic or indicating a proximal position.

subtend: growing close to but slightly lower on an axis.

subterranean: below ground; hypogeous. *Ant.* aerial. **subulate:** awl-shaped; very narrow and tapered from the base to apex (Fig. 21E).

superficial: on the surface.

suprabasal: above the base, usually referring to pinnae or pinnules.

supramedial: beyond the middle; sori a little closer to the margin than the costa or costule. *Ant.* inframedial.

surcurrent: extending upward on and adnate to an axis.

suture: the elongate, sometimes branched line on the surface of pteridophyte spores through which the germinating spore expands.

symmetrical: having a similar outline on both sides of a central axis. *Ant.* asymmetrical.

synangium: an oblong group of fused sporangia found in the Marattiaceae. *Pl.* **synangia.**

tapered: gradually narrower or thinner.

terete: round in cross-section.

terminal: apical.

ternate: divided into 3 equal or subequal parts.

terrestrial: growing in soil.

tetragonal: four-sided.

tetraploid: having 4 sets of chromosomes.

toothed: with marginal teeth (Fig. 24E).

translucent: thin enough to pass light, but not an image.

transparent: thin enough to pass an image.

transverse: cross-wise in position.

trapeziform: having the outline of a trapezoid, with 4 unequal sides, none of them parallel (Fig. 21G).

triangular: having the outline of a triangle (Fig. 21S).

tripartite: divided into 3 parts, such as the laminae of *Pteridium* (Fig. 18B).

triploid: having 3 sets of chromosomes.

truncate: appearing as if cut off perpendicular to the axis (Fig. 22B).

tubercle: a low, rounded or conical protuberance that is not sharply pointed at the apex.

tuberculate: bearing tubercles (Fig. 26E).

twisted: turned about a longitudinal axis.

ultimate: of the lowest order; the smallest division.

uniauriculate: bearing 1 auricle (Fig. 22D).

univalent: a single, unpaired chromosome. *See* bivalent.

unreduced: not having undergone meiosis, and so with the number of chromosomes per cell that is characteristic of a sporophyte.

vascular bundle: a group of conducting cells (xylem tracheids and phloem sieve cells) that serve to conduct mostly water distally and sugars in solution proximally.

vein: a strand of vascular tissue. An elongate region of thickened cells appearing to be a vein, but not connected to true veins and not functioning as a vein, is termed a **false vein** or **venuloid.**

veinlet: a subdivision or branch of a vein.

velum: in *Isoëtes,* a thin covering over the sporangium on the abaxial surface of the leaf base.

ventral: the lower side of a horizontal structure.

verrucose: having a warty surface, said especially of spores (Fig. 26C).

villous: having long, soft, irregularly twisted or curled, non-matted hairs (Fig. 25E).

viscid: sticky.

whorl: 3 or more parts inserted at a single point along an axis.

whorled: having a whorl.

xylem: tissue specialized for the transport of water and minerals upward through the plant. *See* vascular bundle.

zygote: cell formed by the union of a spermatozoid and an egg; the first cell of the sporophyte.

Bibliography

Adams, D. C. 1977. Ciné analysis of the medullary bundle system in Cyathea fulva. Amer. Fern J. 67:73–80.

———, and P. B. Tomlinson. 1979. Acrostichum in Florida. Amer. Fern J. 69:42–46.

Aderkas, P. von. 1984. Economic history of the Ostrich Fern, Matteuccia struthiopteris, the edible fiddlehead. Econ. Bot. 38:14–23.

Allen, D. E. 1969. The Victorian Fern Craze. Hutchinson, London.

Alt, K. S., and V. Grant. 1960. Cytotaxonomic observations on the Goldback Fern. Brittonia 12:153–170.

Balick, M. J., D. G. Furth, and G. Cooper-Driver. 1978. Biochemical and evolutionary aspects of arthropod predation on ferns. Oecologia (Berlin) 35:55–89.

Banerjee, R. D. and S. P. Sen. 1980. Antibiotic activity of pteridophytes. Econ. Bot. 34:284–298.

Barclay, A. S. and R. E. Perdue, Jr. 1976. Distribution of anticancer activity in higher plants. Cancer Treat. Rep. 60:1081–1113.

Bates, V. M., Jr., and E. T. Browne, Jr. 1981. Azolla filiculoides new to the southeastern United States. Amer. Fern J. 71:33–34.

Benedict, R. C. 1916. The origin of new varieties of Nephrolepis by orthogenetic saltation, I. Progressive variations. Bull. Torrey Bot. Club 43:207–234.

Berglund, B., and C. E. Bolsby. 1971. The Edible Wild. Scribners, New York.

Bierhorst, D. W. 1968. Observations on Schizaea and Actinostachys spp., including A. oligostachys, sp. nov. Amer. J. Bot. 55:87–108.

———. 1971. Morphology of Vascular Plants. Macmillan, New York.

———. 1977. The systematic position of Psilotum and Tmesipteris. Brittonia 29:3–13.

Birdseye, C., and E. G. Birdseye. 1951. Growing Woodland Plants. Oxford Univ. Press, New York. [also 1972 paperback reprint by Dover, New York.]

Blasdell, R. F. 1963. A monographic study of the fern genus Cystopteris. Mem. Torrey Bot. Club 21(4):1–102.

Boom, B. M. 1979. Systematic Studies of the Genus Isoetes in the Southeastern United States. M. S. Thesis, University of Tennessee, Knoxville, TN.

———. 1980. Intersectional hybrids in Isoëtes. Amer. Fern J. 70:1–4.

Bouchard, A., and S. G. Hay. 1976. Thelypteris limbosperma in eastern North America. Rhodora 78:552–553.

Brown, D. F. M. 1964. A monographic study of the fern genus Woodsia. Nova Hedw. Beih. 16:i–x, 1–154, *pl. 1–40.*

Bruce, J. G. 1975. Systematics and morphology of subgenus Lepidotis of the genus Lycopodium (Lycopodiaceae). Ph. D. Thesis, Univ. of Michigan, Ann Arbor, MI.

––––––. 1976a. Comparative studies in the biology of Lycopodium carolinianum. Amer. Fern J. 66:125–137.

––––––. 1976b. Gametophytes and subgeneric concepts in Lycopodium. Amer. J. Bot. 63:919–924.

Buck, W. R. 1977. A new species of Selaginella in the S. apoda complex. Canadian J. Bot. 55:366–371.

Carlson, T. J. 1979. The comparative ecology and frequencies of interspecific hybridization of Michigan woodferns. Michigan Bot. 18:47–56.

Clausen, R. T. 1938. A monograph of the Ophioglossaceae. Mem. Torrey Bot. Club 19(2):1–177.

Cooper-Driver, G. A., and C. Haufler. 1983. The changing role of chemistry in fern classification. Fern Gaz. 12:283–294.

Correll, D. S. 1939. Trichomanes membranaceum in Mississippi? Amer. Fern J. 29:103.

––––––, and H. B. Correll. 1975. Aquatic and Wetland Plants of Southwestern United States, vol. 1. Stanford Univ. Press, Stanford, CA.

Crabbe, J. A., A. C. Jermy, and J. T. Mickel. 1975. A new generic sequence for the pteridophyte herbarium. Fern Gaz. 11:141–162.

Crist, K. C., and D. R. Farrar. 1983. Genetic load and long-distance dispersal in Asplenium platyneuron. Canadian J. Bot. 61:1809–1814.

Cronquist, A., A. H. Holmgren, N. H. Holmgren, and J. L. Reveal. 1972. Intermountain Flora, vol. 1. Hafner, New York.

Darling, T., Jr. 1982. The deletion of Nephrolepis pectinata from the flora of Florida. Amer. Fern J. 72:63.

Dyer, A. F., ed. 1979. The Experimental Biology of Ferns. Academic Press, London & New York.

Eames, A. J. 1936. Morphology of Vascular Plants: Lower Groups (Psilophytales to Filicales). McGraw-Hill, New York.

Evans, A. M. 1964. Ameiotic alternation of generations: a new life cycle in the ferns. Science 143:261–263.

––––––. 1968. The Polypodium pectinatum–plumula complex in Florida. Amer. Fern J. 58:169–175.

––––––. 1969. Interspecific relationships in the Polypodium pectinatum–plumula complex. Ann. Missouri Bot. Gard. 55:193–293.

––––––. 1975. Cheilanthes in Florida. Amer. Fern J. 65:1–3.

––––––, and W. H. Wagner, Jr. 1964. Dryopteris goldiana × intermedia—a natural Woodfern cross of noteworthy morphology. Rhodora 66:255–266.

Evans, I. A. 1970. Naturally occurring chemical carcinogens: Bracken fern toxin. 10th Intl. Cancer Congr., Houston. [Mimeographed report.]

Eysinga, F. W. B. van. 1975. Geological Time Table, 3rd ed. Elsevier Sci. Publ., Amsterdam.

Farnsworth, N. R. et al. 1976. Oncogenic and tumor-promoting speratophytes and pteridophytes and their active principles. Cancer Treat. Rep. 60:1171–1214.

Farrar, D. R. 1967. Gametophytes of four tropical fern genera reproducing independently of their sporophytes in the southern Appalachians. Science 155:1266–1267.

————. 1968. A culture chamber for tropical rain forest plants. Amer. Fern J. 58:97–102.

————. 1978. Problems in the identity and origin of the Appalachian Vittaria gametophytes, a sporophyteless fern of the eastern United States. Amer. J. Bot. 65:1–12.

————, and R. D. Gooch. 1975. Fern reproduction at Woodman Hollow, Central Iowa: Preliminary observations and a consideration of the feasibility of studying fern reproductive biology in nature. Proc. Iowa Acad. Sci. 82:119–122.

————, J. C. Parks, and B. W. McAlpin. 1983. The fern genera Vittaria and Trichomanes in the northeastern United States. Rhodora 85:83–91.

Faust, M. A. 1960. Survival of Harts-tongue fern in central New York. Amer. Fern J. 50:55–62.

Fernald, M. L. 1950. Adiantum capillus-veneris in the United States. Rhodora 52:201–208.

Foster, A. S., and E. M. Gifford, Jr. 1974. Comparative Morphology of Vascular Plants, ed. 2. Freeman, San Francisco.

Fraser-Jenkins, C. R. 1976. Dryopteris caucasica, and the cytology of its hybrids. Fern Gaz. 11:263–267.

Futyma, R. P. 1980. The distribution and ecology of Phyllitis scolopendrium in Michigan. Amer. Fern J. 70:81–87.

Gastony, G. J. 1977. Chromosomes of the independently reproducing Appalachian gametophyte: a new source of taxonomic evidence. Syst. Bot. 2:43–48.

————. 1980. The deletion of Vittaria graminifolia from the flora of Florida. Amer. Fern J. 70:12–14.

Gaudet, J. J. 1963. Marsilea vestita: conversion of the water form to the land form by darkness and by far-red light. Science 140:975–976.

Gerson, U. 1979. The associations between pteridophytes and arthropods. Fern Gaz. 12:29–45.

Gillespie, J. P. 1962. A theory of relationships in the Lycopodium inundatum complex. Amer. Fern J. 52:19–26.

Gleason, H. A., and A. Cronquist. 1964. The Natural Geography of Plants. Colombia Univ. Press, New York.

Gordon, J. E. 1981. Arachniodes simplicior new to South Carolina and the United States. Amer. Fern J. 71:65–68.

Haufler, C. H. 1979. A biosystematic revision of Bommeria. J. Arnold Arb. 60:445–476.

————. 1985. Pteridophyte evolutionary biology: the electrophoretic approach. Proc. Royal Soc. Edinburgh 86:315–323.

Hauke, R. L. 1963. A taxonomic monograph of the genus Equisetum subgenus Hippochaete. Nova Hedw. Beih. 8:1–123, *table 1–9, graph 1–3, pl. 1–22.*

————. 1966. A systematic study of Equisetum arvense. Nova Hedw. 13:81–109, *pl. 1–9.*

————. 1978. A taxonomic monograph of Equisetum subgenus Equisetum. Nova Hedw. 30:385–455.

————. 1979. Equisetum ramosissimum in North America. Amer. Fern J. 69:1–5.

Hendrix, S. D. 1980. An evolutionary and ecological perspective of the insect fauna of ferns. Amer. Nat. 115:171–196.

Hennipman, E. 1968. The mucilage secreting hairs on the young fronds of some leptosporangiate ferns. Blumea 16:97–103.

Hevly, R. H. 1963. Adaptations of cheilanthoid ferns to desert environments. J. Arizona Acad. Sci. 2:164–175.

––––––. 1965. Studies of the Sinuous Cloak-fern (Notholaena sinuata) complex. J. Arizona Acad. Sci. 3:205–208.

Hickey, R. J. 1977. The Lycopodium obscurum complex in North America. Amer. Fern J. 67:45–48.

––––––, and J. M. Beitel. 1979. A name change for Lycopodium flabelliforme. Rhodora 81:137–140.

Hodge, W. H. 1973. Fern foods of Japan and the problem of toxicity. Amer. Fern J. 63:77–80.

Hollenbeak, K. H., and M. E. Kuehne. 1974. The isolation and structure determination of the fern glycoside osmundalin and the synthesis of its aglycone osmundalactone. Tetrahedron 30:2307–2316.

Holst, R. W., and J. H. Yopp. 1979. Studies of the Azolla–Anabaena symbiosis using Azolla mexicana, I. Growth in nature and laboratory. Amer. Fern J. 69:17–25.

Holttum, R. E. 1959. Flora Malesiana II, 1(1):1–64.

––––––. 1971. Studies in the family Thelypteridaceae III. A new system of genera in the Old World. Blumea 19:17–52.

Holub, J. 1964. Lycopodiella, nový rod řádu Lycopodiales. Preslia 36:16–22.

––––––. 1975a. Diphasiastrum, a new genus in Lycopodiaceae. Preslia 47:97–110.

––––––. 1975b. Notes on some species of Diphasiastrum. Preslia 47:232–240.

Horner, H. T., Jr., and H. J. Arnott. 1963. Sporangial arrangement in North American species of Selaginella. Bot. Gaz. 124:371–383.

Hoshizaki, B. J. 1970. The genus Adiantum in cultivation [Polypodiaceae]. Baileya 17:145–191.

––––––. 1975. Fern Growers Manual. Knopf, New York.

Jermy, A. C., J. A. Crabbe, and B. A. Thomas, eds. 1973. The Phylogeny and Classification of the Ferns. Academic Press, London.

Keeley, J. E. 1981. Diurnal acid metabolism in vernal pool Isoetes (Isoetaceae). Madroño 28:167–171.

Klekowski, E. J. 1966. Evolutionary significance of polyploidy in the pteridophyta. Science 153:305–307.

Knobloch, I. W., and D. B. Lellinger. 1969. Cheilanthes castanea and its allies in Virginia and West Virginia. Castanea 34:59–61.

––––––, and D. M. Britton. 1982. A comparative study of sporophyte morphology of the three cytotypes of Polypodium virginianum in Ontario. Canad. J. Bot. 60:1360–1370.

Kral, R. 1976. Additions to some notes on the flora of the southern states, particularly Alabama and middle Tennessee. Rhodora 78:438–456.

Kruckeberg, A. R. 1964. Ferns associated with ultramafic rocks in the Pacific northwest. Amer. Fern J. 54:113–126.

Lakela, O., and R. W. Long. 1976. Ferns of Florida. Banyan Books, Miami.

Lang, F. A. 1969. A new name for a species of Polypodium from northwestern North America. Madroño 20:53–60.

————. 1971. The Polypodium vulgare complex in the Pacific northwest. Madroño 21:235–254.

Lellinger, D. B. 1981. Notes on North American ferns. Amer. Fern J. 71:90–94.

————1984. Notes on North American ferns, II. Amer. Fern J. 74:62–63.

Leonard, S. W. 1972. The distribution of Thelypteris torresiana in the southeastern United States. Amer. Fern J. 62:97–99.

Liew, F. S. 1972. Numerical taxonomic studies on North American Lady Ferns and their allies. Taiwania 17:190–221.

Liu, B.-L. L. 1984. Abscisic acid induces land form characteristics in Marsilea quadrifolia L. Amer. J. Bot. 71:638–644.

Lloyd, R. M. 1971. Systematics of the onocleoid ferns. Univ. Calif. Publ. Bot. 61:i–iv, 1–86, *pl. 1–5*.

————. 1974. Reproductive biology and evolution in the Pteridophyta. Ann. Missouri Bot. Gard. 61:318–331.

————. 1975. The California polypodies. Fremontia 3(1):18–21.

————, and J. E. Hohn. 1969. Occurrence of the European Polypodium australe Fée on San Clemente Island, California. Amer. Fern J. 59:56–60.

————, and F. A. Lang. 1962. The Polypodium vulgare complex in North America. Brit. Fern Gaz. 9:168–177.

Löve, Á. 1962. Cytotaxonomy of the Isoetes echinospora complex. Amer. Fern J. 52:113–123.

————, D. Löve, and B. M. Kapoor. 1971. Cytotaxonomy of a century of Rocky Mountain orophytes. Arctic Alpine Res. 3:139–165.

————, D. Löve, and R. E. G. Pichi Sermolli. 1977. Cytotaxonomical Atlas of the Pteridophyta. J. Cramer, Vaduz.

Lovis, J. D. 1977. Evolutionary patterns and processes in ferns. Pp. 229–415 *in* R. D. Preston and H. W. Woolhouse, eds. Advances in Botanical Research, vol. 4. Academic Press, London, New York, and San Francisco.

Lumpkin, T. A., and D. L. Plucknett. 1980. Azolla: botany, physiology, and use as a green manure. Econ. Bot. 34:111–153.

Manton, I. 1950. Problems of Cytology and Evolution in the Pteridophyta. Cambridge Univ. Press, Cambridge.

Mason, C. T., Jr., and G. Yatskievych. 1981. Notes on the flora of Arizona VI. Desert Pls. 3(1):29–30.

Matthews, J. F., and W. H. Murdy. 1969. A study of Isoetes common to the granite outcrops of the southeastern Piedmont, United States. Bot. Gaz. 150:53–61.

May, L. W. 1978. The economic uses and associated folklore of ferns and fern allies. Bot. Rev. 44:491–528.

Maxon, W. R. 1912. The relationship of Asplenium andrewsii. Contr. U. S. Natl. Herb. 16:1–3, *pl. 2*.

————. 1913. Studies of tropical American ferns–No. 4. Contr. U. S. Natl. Herb. 17:133–179.

————. 1937. Notes on American ferns–XXI. Amer. Fern J. 27:109–111.

Mickel, J. T., and E. Fiore. 1979. The Home Gardeners Book of Ferns. Holt Rinehart Winston, New York.

Miller, C. N., Jr. 1967. Evolution of the fern genus Osmunda. Contr. Mus. Paleontol. Univ. Michigan 21:139–203, *pl. I–IV*.

―――. 1971. Evolution of the fern family Osmundaceae based on anatomical studies. Contr. Mus. Paleontol. Univ. Michigan 23:105–169.

Montgomery, J. D. 1976. The distribution and abundance of Dryopteris hybrids in New Jersey. Amer. Fern J. 66:53–59.

―――. 1982. Dryopteris in North America, Part II: The hybrids. Fiddlehead Forum 9:23–30.

―――, and E. M. Paulton. 1981. Dryopteris in North America. Fiddlehead Forum 8:25–31.

Moore, A. W. 1969. Azolla: biology and agronomic significance. Bot. Rev. 35:17–34.

Moran, R. 1981. × Asplenosorus shawneensis, a new natural fern hybrid between Asplenium trichomanes and Camptosorus rhizophyllus. Amer. Fern J. 71:85–89.

―――. 1982. The Asplenium trichomanes complex in the United States and adjacent Canada. Amer. Fern J. 72:5–11.

―――. 1983. Cystopteris × wagneri: a new naturally occurring hybrid between C. × tennesseensis and C. tenuis. Castanea 48:224–229.

Morton, C. V. 1939. Our southwestern Resurrection-Plants. Amer. Fern J. 29:14–16.

―――. 1950. Notes on the ferns of the eastern United States. Amer. Fern J. 40:241–252.

―――. 1957. Observations on cultivated ferns. I. Amer. Fern J. 47:7–14.

―――. 1960. Observations on cultivated ferns. VI. The ferns currently known as Rumohra. Amer. Fern J. 50:145–155.

―――. 1963. The classification of Thelypteris. Amer. Fern J. 53:149–154.

―――. 1968. The genera, subgenera, and sections of the Hymenophyllaceae. Contr. U. S. Natl. Herb. 38:153–214.

Morzenti, V. M. 1962. A first report on pseudomeiotic sporogenesis, a type of spore reproduction by which "sterile" ferns produce gametophytes. Amer. Fern J. 52:69–78.

―――. 1966. Morphological and cytological data on southeastern United States species of the Asplenium heterochroum–resiliens complex. Amer. Fern J. 56:167–177.

―――. 1967. Asplenium plenum: a fern which suggests an unusual method of species formation. Amer. J. Bot. 54:1061–1068.

Mulligan, G. A., and W. J. Cody. 1979. Chromosome numbers in Canadian Phegopteris. Canadian J. Bot. 57:1815–1819.

Munther, W. E., and D. E. Fairbrothers. 1980. Allelopathy and autotoxicity in three eastern North American ferns. Amer. Fern J. 70:124–135.

Nardi, E. 1979. Commentaria pteridologica. II. De legitimo usu nominis Polypodii cambrici L. Webbia 33:425–433.

Nauman, C. E. 1981. The genus Nephrolepis in Florida. Amer. Fern J. 71:35–40.

―――, and D. F. Austin. 1978. Spread of the exotic fern Lygodium microphyllum in Florida. Amer. Fern J. 68:65–66.

Nobel, P. S. 1978. Microhabitat, water relations, and photosynthesis of a desert fern, Notholaena parryi. Oecologia (Berlin) 31:293–309.

Peck, J. H. 1980. Equisetum × litorale in Illinois, Iowa, Minnesota, and Wisconsin. Amer. Fern J. 70:33–38.

Petersen, R. L., and D. E. Fairbrothers. 1980. Reciprocal allelopathy between the gametophytes of Osmunda cinnamomea and Dryopteris intermedia. Amer. Fern J. 70:73–78.

Petrik-Ott, A. J. 1976. Two new sites for Ceratopteris thalictroides in Texas. Amer. Fern J. 66:111.

Pichi Sermolli, R. E. G. 1977. Tentamen pteridophytorum genera in taxonomicum ordinem redigendi. Webbia 31:313–512.

Pickett, F. L. 1923. An ecological study of Cheilanthes gracillima. Bull. Torrey Bot. Club 50:329–338.

Potts, R., and W. T. Penfound. 1948. Water relations of the Polypody Fern, Polypodium polypodioides (L.) A. S. Hitchcock. Ecology 29:43–53.

Pray, T. R. 1967. Notes on the distribution of some American cheilanthoid ferns. Amer. Fern J. 57:52–58.

————. 1968. The valid varieties of Pellaea andromedaefolia. Amer. Fern J. 58:54–64.

Profumo, P. 1969. The gametophytes of Cystopteris fragilis and C. dickieana. Webbia 23:317–328.

————, and A. Raggi. 1968. Morfologia e anatomia dello sporofito in Cystopteris fragilis e Cystopteris dickieana. Annal. Mus. Civ. Stor. Nat. Genova 77:329–337.

Pryer, K. M., D. M. Britton, and J. McNeill. 1983. A numerical analysis of chromatographic profiles in North American taxa of the fern genus Gymnocarpium. Canad. J. Bot. 62:2592–2602.

Root, E. E. 1961. Hybrids in North American Gymnocarpiums. Amer. Fern J. 51:15–22.

Rury, P. M. 1978. A new and unique, mat-forming Merlins-grass (Isoëtes) from Georgia. Amer. Fern J. 68:99–108.

Sarvela, J. 1978. A synopsis of the fern genus Gymnocarpium. Ann. Bot. Fennici 15:101–106.

————. 1980. Gymnocarpium hybrids from Canada and Alaska. Ann. Bot. Fennici 17:292–295.

————, D. M. Britton, and K. Pryer. 1981. Studies on the Gymnocarpium robertianum complex in North America. Rhodora 83:421–431.

Seigler, D. S., and E. Wollenweber. 1983. Chemical variation in Notholaena standleyi. Amer. J. Bot. 70:790–798.

Short, J. W. 1980. A second Alabama locality for the Harts tongue. Amer. Fern J. 70:137.

————, and J. D. Freeman. 1978. Rediscovery, distribution and phytogeographic affinities of Leptogramma pilosa in Alabama. Amer. Fern J. 68:1–2.

Smith, A. R. 1971. Systematics of the neotropical species of Thelypteris section Cyclosorus. Univ. Calif. Publ. Bot. 59:i–vi, 1–136, *pl. 1–5*.

————. 1974a. Taxonomic and cytological notes on ferns from California and Arizona. Madroño 22:376–378.

————. 1974b. A revised classification of Thelypteris subgenus Amauropelta. Amer. Fern J. 64:83–95.

————. 1975. The California species of Aspidotis. Madroño 23:15–24.

————. 1980a. New taxa and combinations of pteridophytes from Chiapas, Mexico. Amer. Fern J. 70:15–27.

————. 1980b. Taxonomy of Thelypteris subgenus Steiropteris, including Glaphyropteris (Pteridophyta). Univ. Calif. Publ. Bot. 76:1–38, *pl. 1–4.*

Smith, D. M. 1980. Flavonoid analysis of the Pityrogramma triangularis complex. Bull. Torrey Bot. Club 107:134–145.

Soltis, D. E., C. H. Haufler, D. C. Darrow, and G. J. Gastony. 1983. Starch gel electrophoresis of ferns: a compilation of grinding buffers, gel and electrode buffers, and staining schedules. Amer. Fern J. 73:9–27.

Somers, P., and W. R. Buck. 1975. Selaginella ludoviciana, S. apoda and their hybrids in the southeastern United States. Amer. Fern J. 65:76–82.

Sporne, K. R. 1975. The Morphology of Pteridophytes, ed. 4. Hutchinson, London.

Star, A. E., D. S. Siegler, T. J. Mabry, and D. M. Smith. 1975. Internal flavonoid patterns of diploids and tetraploids of two exudate chemotypes of Pityrogramma triangularis (Kaulf.) Maxon. Biochem. Syst. Ecol. 2:109–112.

Stevenson, D. W. 1975. Taxonomic and morphological observations on Botrychium multifidum (Ophioglossaceae). Madroño 23:198–204.

Svenson, H. K. 1944. The New World species of Azolla. Amer. Fern J. 34:69–84.

Taylor, T. M. C. 1967. Mecodium wrightii in British Columbia and Alaska. Amer. Fern J. 57:1–6.

Taylor, T. N. 1981. Paleobotany: An Introduction to Fossil Plant Biology. McGraw-Hill, New York.

Taylor, W. C., R. H. Mohlenbrock, and F. J. Burton. 1976. Variation in North American Asplenium platyneuron. Amer. Fern J. 66:63–68.

————, R. H. Mohlenbrock, and J. A. Murphy. 1975. The spores and taxonomy of Isoëtes butleri and I. melanopoda. Amer. Fern J. 65:33–38.

Thieret, J. W. 1980. Louisiana Ferns and Fern Allies. Lafayette Natural History Museum, Lafayette.

Troop, J. E., and J. T. Mickel. 1968. Petiolar shoots in the dennstaedtioid and related ferns. Amer. Fern J. 58:64–70.

Tryon, A. F. 1957. A revision of the fern genus Pellaea section Pellaea. Ann. Missouri Bot. Gard. 44:125–193.

————. 1968. Comparisons of sexual and apogamous races in the fern genus Pellaea. Rhodora 70:1–24.

————, and D. M. Britton. 1958. Cytotaxonomic studies on the fern genus Pellaea. Evolution 12:137–145.

————, R. Tryon, and F. Badré. 1980. Classification, spores, and nomenclature of the Marsh Fern. Rhodora 82:461–474.

Tryon, R. M., Jr. 1941. A revision of the genus Pteridium. Contr. Gray Herb. 134:1–70, *pl. 650–653.*

————. 1955. Selaginella rupestris and its allies. Ann. Missouri Bot. Gard. 42:1–99.

————. 1956. A revision of the American species of Notholaena. Contr. Gray Herb. 179:1–108.

————. 1960. A review of the genus Dennstaedtia in America. Contr. Gray Herb. 187:23–52.

————. 1962. Taxonomic fern notes. II. Pityrogramma (including Trismeria) and Anogramma. Contr. Gray Herb. 189:52–76.

————, and A. F. Tryon. 1982. Ferns and Allied Plants with Special Reference to Tropical America. Springer-Verlag, New York, Heidelberg, and Berlin.

Underwood, L. M. 1899. American ferns–II. The genus Phanerophlebia. Bull. Torrey Bot. Club 26:205–216.

Vida, G. 1974. Genome analysis of the European Cystopteris fragilis complex. I. Tetraploid taxa. Acta Bot. Acad. Sci. Hungar. 20:181–192.

Voss, E. G. et al., eds. 1983. International Code of Botanical Nomenclature. Bohn, Schletema & Holkema, Utrecht and Antwerp.

Wagner, D. H. 1979. Systematics of Polystichum in western North America north of Mexico. Pteridologia 1:1–64.

Wagner, F. S. 1980. Chromosome behavior in three interspecific hybrids of Diphasiastrum (Lycopodiaceae). Bot. Soc. Amer. Misc. Ser. Publ. 158:121.

Wagner, W. H., Jr. 1954. Reticulate evolution in the Appalachian Aspleniums. Evolution 7:103–118.

————. 1957. Heteroblastic leaf morphology in juvenile plants of Dicranopteris linearis (Gleicheniaceae). Phytomorphology 7:1–6.

————. 1960a. Periodicity and pigmentation in Botrychium subg. Sceptridium in the northeastern United States. Bull. Torrey Bot. Club 87:303–325.

————. 1960b. Evergreen grapeferns and the meanings of infraspecific categories used in North American grapeferns. Amer. Fern J. 50:32–45.

————. 1961. Roots and the taxonomic differences between Botrychium oneidense and B. dissectum. Rhodora 63:164–175.

————. 1963a. Pteridophytes of the Mountain Lake area, Giles County, Virginia, including notes from Whitetop Mountain. Castanea 28:113–150.

————. 1963b. Biosystematics and taxonomic categories in lower vascular plants. Pp. 63–71 in V. H. Heywood and Á. Löve, eds. Symposium on Biosystematics. Intl. Assn. for Plant Taxonomy, Utrecht.

————. 1965. Pellaea wrightiana in North Carolina and the question of its origin. J. Elisha Mitchell Sci. Soc. 81:95–103.

————. 1966. New data on North American oak ferns, Gymnocarpium. Rhodora 68:121–138.

————. 1968. Hybridization, taxonomy, and evolution. Chapter 9 in V. H. Heywood, ed. Modern Methods in Plant Taxonomy. Academic Press, London.

————. 1971a. The southeastern adders-tongue, Ophioglossum vulgatum var. pycnostichum, found for the first time in Michigan. Michigan Bot. 10:67–74.

————. 1971b. Evolution of Dryopteris in relation to the Appalachians. Pp. 147–192 in P. C. Holt, ed. The Distributional History of the Biota of the Southern Appalachians, Part II, Flora. Virginia Polytech. Inst. State Univ. Res. Div. Monogr. 2.

————. 1972. Disjunctions in homosporous vascular plants. Ann. Missouri Bot. Gard. 59:203–217.

————. 1973. Reticulation of Holly Ferns (Polystichum) in the western United States and adjacent Canada. Amer. Fern J. 63:99–115.

————. 1977. Systematic implications of the Psilotaceae. Brittonia 29:54–63.

————. 1979. Reticulate veins in the systematics of modern ferns. Taxon 28:87–95.

————. 1980. A probable new hybrid grapefern, Botrychium matricariifolium × simplex, from central Michigan. Michigan Bot. 19:31–36.

————, C. M. Allen, and G. P. Landry. 1984. Ophioglossum ellipticum Hook. & Grev. in Louisiana and the taxonomy of O. nudicaule L. f. Castanea 49:99–110.

————, and K. E. Boydston. 1978. A dwarf coastal variety of maidenhair fern, Adiantum pedatum. Canadian J. Bot. 56:1726–1729.

————, and T. Darling, Jr. 1957. Synthetic and wild Asplenium gravesii. Brittonia 9:57–63.

————, D. R. Farrar, and K. L. Chen. 1965. A new sexual form of Pellaea glabella var. glabella from Missouri. Amer. Fern J. 55:171–178.

————, D. R. Farrar, and B. W. McAlpin. 1970. Pteridology of the Highlands Biological Station area, southern Appalachians. J. Elisha Mitchell Sci. Soc. 86:1–27.

————, and W. E. Hammitt. 1970. Natural proliferation of floating stems of scouring-rush, Equisetum hyemale. Michigan Bot. 9:166–174.

————, and D. M. Johnson. 1981. Natural history of the ebony spleenwort, Asplenium platyneuron (Aspleniaceae) in the Great Lakes area. Canadian Field-Nat. 95:156–166.

————, and L. P. Lord. 1956. The morphological and cytological distinctness of Botrychium minganense and B. lunaria in Michigan. Bull. Torrey Bot. Club 83:261–280.

————, and L. J. Musselman. 1979. Log ferns (Dryopteris celsa) and their relatives in the Great Dismal Swamp. Pp. 127–139 in P. W. Kirk, Jr., ed. The Great Dismal Swamp. Univ. Press of Virginia, Charlottesville.

————, and C. E. Nauman. 1982. Pteris × delchampsii, a spontaneous fern hybrid from southern Florida. Amer. Fern J. 72:97–102.

————, A. R. Smith, and T. R. Pray. 1983. A Cliff Brake hybrid, Pellaea bridgesii × mucronata, and its systematic significance. Madroño 30:69–83.

————, and F. S. Wagner. 1969. A new natural hybrid in the Appalachian Asplenium complex and its taxonomic significance. Brittonia 21:178–186.

————, and F. S. Wagner. 1976. Asplenium × clermontae Sim from Clifton Gorge, Greene County, Ohio—a second North American record. Ohio J. Sci. 76:99–102.

————, and F. S. Wagner. 1977. Fertile–sterile leaf dimorphy in ferns. Gard. Bull. Singapore 30:251–267.

————, and F. S. Wagner. 1980. Polyploidy in pteridophytes. Pp. 199–214 in W. H. Lewis, ed. Polyploidy: Biological Relevance. Plenum, New York and London.

————, and F. S. Wagner. 1982a. The taxonomy of Dryopteris × poyseri Wherry. Michigan Bot. 21:51–63.

————, and F. S. Wagner. 1982b. Botrychium rugulosum (Ophioglossaceae), a newly recognized species of evergreen Grapefern in the Great Lakes region of North America. Contr. Michigan Herb. 15:315–324.

————, and F. S. Wagner. 1983. Two moonworts of the Rocky Mountains: Botrychium hesperium and a new species formerly confused with it. Amer. Fern J. 73:53–62.

————, F. S. Wagner, C. Haufler, and J. K. Emerson. 1984. A new nothospecies of moonwort (Ophioglossaceae, Botrychium). Canadian J. Bot. 62:629–634.

————, F. S. Wagner, S. W. Leonard, and M. R. Mesler. 1981. A reinterpretation of Ophioglossum dendroneuron E. P. St. John. Castanea 46:311–322.

————, F. S. Wagner, C. N. Miller, Jr., and D. H. Wagner. 1978. New observations on the royal fern hybrid Osmunda × ruggii. Rhodora 80:92–106.

————, and R. C. Woodside. 1967. Ferns for an indoor limestone boulder habitat. Amer. Hort. Mag. 46(4):219–223.

Walker, T. G. 1970. Species of Pteris commonly in cultivation. Brit. Fern Gaz. 10:143–151.

Walter, K. S., W. H. Wagner, Jr., and F. S. Wagner. 1982. Ecological, biosystematic, and nomenclatural notes on Scotts Spleenwort, × Asplenosorus ebenoides. Amer. Fern J. 72:65–75.

Warne, T. B., and R. M. Lloyd. 1980. The role of spore germination and gametophyte development in habitat selection: temperature responses in certain temperate and tropical ferns. Bull. Torrey Bot. Club 107:57–64.

Wherry, E. T. 1961. The Fern Guide: Northeastern and United States and Adjacent Canada. Doubleday, Garden City, NY.

————. 1964. The Southern Fern Guide. Doubleday, Garden City, NY.

White, R. A. 1966. The morphological effects of protein synthesis inhibition in Marsilea. Amer. J. Bot. 53:158–165.

Widén, C.-J., D. M. Britton, W. H. Wagner, Jr., and F. S. Wagner. 1975. Chemotaxonomic studies on hybrids of Dryopteris in eastern North America. Canadian J. Bot. 53:1554–1567.

Wilce, J. H. 1965. Section Complanata of the genus Lycopodium. Nova Hedw. Beih. 19:i–x, 1–233, *pl. I.–XL.*

————. 1972. Lycopod spores, I. General spore patterns and the generic segregates of Lycopodium. Amer. Fern J. 62:65–79.

Wollenweber, E., and V. H. Dietz. 1981. Scale insects feeding on farinose species of Pityrogramma. Amer. Fern J. 71:10–12.

Checklist

Acrostichum
aureum L.
danaeifolium Langsd. & Fisch.

Actinostachys
pennula (Swartz) Hooker

Adiantum
capillus-veneris L.
jordanii K. Muell.
jordanii × pedatum subsp. pedatum (*See* A. ×tracyi)
melanoleucum Willd.
pedatum L.
  subsp. aleuticum Rupr.
  subsp. calderi Cody
  subsp. pedatum
  subsp. subpumilum (Wagner in Wagner & Boydston) Lellinger
tenerum Swartz
×tracyi C. C. Hall (A. jordanii × pedatum subsp. pedatum)
tricholepis Fée

Anemia
adiantifolia (L.) Swartz
cicutaria Kunze
wrightii Baker

Arachniodes
simplicior (Makino) Ohwi

Aspidotis
californica (Hook.) Nutt. ex Copel.
californica × densa (*See* A. ×carlotta-halliae)
×carlotta-halliae (Wagner & Gilbert) Lellinger (A. californica × densa)
densa (Brack. in Wilkes) Lellinger

Asplenium
abscissum Willd.
abscissum × curtisii (*See* A. ×plenum)
abscissum × verecundum (*See* A. ×curtisii)
adiantum-nigrum L.
auritum Swartz
×biscayneanum (D. C. Eaton) A. A. Eaton (A. trichomanes-dentatum × verecundum)
×boydstoniae (Walter) Short (A. ebenoides × platyneuron)

×bradleyi D. C. Eaton (A. montanum × platyneuron)
×bradleyi × montanum (*See* A. ×wherryi)
×bradleyi × pinnatifidum (*See* A. ×gravesi)
×bradleyi × platyneuron
×clermontiae Syme (A. ruta-muraria × trichomanes)
cristatum Lam.
×curtissii Underw. (A. abscissum × verecundum)
dalhousiae Hooker
×ebenoides R. R. Scott (A. platyneuron × rhizophyllum)
×ebenoides × platyneuron (*See* A. ×boydstoniae)
×ebenoides × rhizophyllum)
exiguum Bedd.
×gravesii Maxon (A. bradleyi × pinnatifidum)
×herb-wagneri Tayl. & Mohl. (A. pinnatifidum × trichomanes)
heterochroum Kunze
heterochroum × resiliens (*See* A. heteroresiliens)
heteroresiliens Wagner (A. heterochroum × resiliens)
×inexpectatum (E. L. Braun) Morton (A. rhizophyllum × ruta-muraria)
×kentuckiense McCoy (A. pinnatifidum × platyneuron)
monanthes L.
montanum Willd.
montanum × pinnatifidum (*See* A. ×trudellii)
montanum × platyneuron (*See* A. ×bradleyi)
montanum × rhizophyllum (*See* A. ×pinnatifidum)
palmeri Maxon
×pinnatifidum Muhl. (A. montanum × rhizophyllum)
×pinnatifidum × platyneuron (*See* A. ×kentuckiense)
×pinnatifidum × trichomanes (*See* A. ×herb-wagneri)
platyneuron (L.) B.S.P.
platyneuron × rhizophyllum (*See* A. ×ebenoides)
platyneuron × trichomanes (*See* A. ×virginicum)
×plenum E. P. St. John ex Small (A. abscissum × curtissii)
pumilum Swartz
resiliens Kunze
rhizophyllum L.
rhizophyllum × ruta-muraria (*See* A. ×inexpectatum)
rhizophyllum × trichomanes (*See* A. ×shawneense)
ruta-muraria L.
ruta-muraria × trichomanes (*See* A. ×clermontiae)
septentrionale (L.) Hoffm.
serratum L.
×shawneense (Moran) H. E. Ballard (A. rhizophyllum × trichomanes)
trichomanes L.
trichomanes-dentatum L.
trichomanes-dentatum × verecundum (*See* A. ×biscayneanum)

trichomanes-ramosum L.
× trudellii Wherry (A. montanum × pinnatifidum)
verecundum Chapm. ex Underw.
vespertinum Maxon
× virginianum Maxon (A. platyneuron × trichomanes)
× wherryi D. M. Smith (A. bradleyi × montanum)

  Athyrium
alpestre subsp. americanum (Butters) Lellinger
filix-femina
  subsp. angustum (Willd.) Clausen
  subsp. asplenioides (Michx.) Hultén
  subsp. cyclosorum (Rupr.) C. Chr.
pycnocarpon (Spreng.) Tidestr.
thelypterioides (Michx.) Desv.

  Azolla
caroliniana Willd.
filiculoides Lam.
mexicana Presl

  Blechnum
occidentale L.
serrulatum L. C. Rich.
spicant (L.) J. Smith

  Bommeria
hispida (Mett.) Underw.

  Botrychium
ascendens Wagner
biternatum (Sav.) Underw.
campestre Wagner
crenulatum Wagner
dissectum Spreng.
echo Wagner
hesperium (Maxon & Clausen) Wagner & Lellinger
jenmanii Underw.
lanceolatum (Gmel.) Ångstr.
  subsp. angustisegmentum (Pease & Moore) Clausen
  subsp. lanceolatum
lunaria (L.) Swartz
lunarioides (Michx.) Swartz
matricariifolium A. Braun
matricariifolium × simplex
minganense Vict.
montanum Wagner
mormo Wagner
multifidum (Gmel.) Rupr.

oneidense (Gilb.) House
paradoxum Wagner
pedunculosum Wagner
pinnatum H. St. John
pumicola Coville
rugulosum Wagner
simplex E. Hitchc.
virginianum (L.) Swartz
× watertonense Wagner (B. hesperium × paradoxum)

Campyloneurum
angustifolium (Swartz) Fée var. angustifolium
costatum (Kunze) Presl
phyllitidis (L.) Presl

Ceratopteris
pteridoides (Hook.) Hieron.
thalictroides (L.) Brongn.

Cheilanthes
aemula Maxon
alabamensis (Buckl.) Kunze
arizonica (Maxon) Mickel
castanea Maxon
clevelandii D. C. Eaton
cooperae D. C. Eaton
covillei Maxon
covillei × Notholaena newberryi (*See* C. × fibrillosa (Davenp.) Davenp. ex Underw.)
covillei × Notholaena parryi (*See* C. × parishii Davenp.)
eatonii Bak. in Hook. & Bak.
feei Moore
fendleri Hooker
× fibrillosa (Davenp.) Davenp. ex Underw. (C. covillei × Notholaena newberryi)
gracillima D. C. Eaton
horridula Maxon
intertexta (Maxon) Maxon in Abrams
kaulfussii Kunze
lanosa (Michx.) D. C. Eaton
lendigera (Cav.) Swartz
leucopoda Link
lindheimeri Hooker
microphylla (Swartz) Swartz
× parishii Davenp. (C. covillei × Notholaena parryi)
pringlei Davenp.
tomentosa Link

villosa Davenp.
viscida Davenp.
wootonii Maxon
wrightii Hooker

Cheiroglossa
palmata (L.) Presl

Cryptogramma
acrostichoides R. Br. in Richards.
stelleri (Gmel.) Prantl

Ctenitis
sloanei (Poepp.) Morton
submarginalis (Langsd. & Fisch.) Copel.

Cyrtomium
falcatum (L. f.) Presl
fortunei J. Smith

Cystopteris
bulbifera (L.) Bernh.
bulbifera × fragilis (*See* C. laurentiana)
bulbifera × protrusa (*See* C. tennesseensis)
bulbifera × reevesiana
fragilis (L.) Bernh. (C. reevesiana × unknown diploid)
fragilis × tenuis
dickieana Sim
×illinoensis Moran (C. bulbifera × tenuis)
laurentiana (Weath.) Blasdell (C. bulbifera × fragilis)
montana (Lam.) Bernh. ex Desv.
protrusa (Weath.) Blasdell
protrusa × unknown diploid (*See* C. tenuis)
reevesiana Lellinger
reevesiana × unknown diploid (*See* C. fragilis)
tennesseensis Shaver (C. bulbifera × protrusa)
tennesseensis × tenuis (*See* C. ×wagneri)
tenuis (Michx.) Desv. (C. protrusa × unknown diploid)
×wagneri Moran (C. tennesseensis × tenuis)

Dennstaedtia
bipinnata (Cav.) Maxon
globulifera (Poir.) Hieron.
punctilobula (Michx.) Moore

Diplazium
japonicum (Thunb.) Bedd.
lonchophyllum Kunze

Dryopteris
×algonquinensis Britton (D. fragrans × marginalis)
arguta (Kaulf.) Watt

362

×australis (Wherry) Small (D. celsa × ludoviciana)
×benedictii Wherry (D. carthusiana × clintoniana)
×boottii (Tuckerm.) Underw. (D. cristata × intermedia)
×burgessii Boivin (D. clintoniana × marginalis)
campyloptera Clarkson (D. expansa × intermedia)
campyloptera × intermedia
campyloptera × marginalis
carthusiana (Villars) H. P. Fuchs
carthusiana × celsa
carthusiana × clintoniana (*See* D. ×benedictii)
carthusiana × cristata (*See* D. ×uliginosa)
carthusiana × goldiana
carthusiana × intermedia (*See* D. ×triploidea)
carthusiana × marginalis (*See* D. ×pittsfordensis)
celsa (W. Palmer) Small (D. goldiana × ludoviciana)
celsa × clintoniana
celsa × cristata
celsa × goldiana
celsa × intermedia (*See* D. ×separabilis)
celsa × ludoviciana (*See* D. ×australis)
celsa × marginalis (*See* D. ×leedsii)
cinnamomea (Cav.) C. Chr.
clintoniana (D. C. Eaton) Dowell (D. cristata × goldiana)
clintoniana × cristata
clintoniana × goldiana
clintoniana × intermedia (*See* D. ×dowellii)
clintoniana × marginalis (*See* D. ×burgesii)
cristata (L.) A. Gray (D. ludoviciana × unknown diploid)
cristata × goldiana (*See* D. clintoniana)
cristata × intermedia (*See* D. ×boottii)
cristata × marginalis (*See* D. ×slossoniae)
×dowellii (Farw.) Wherry (D. clintoniana × intermedia)
expansa (Presl) Fraser-Jenkins & Jermy
expansa × intermedia (*See* D. campyloptera)
expansa × marginalis
filix-mas (L.) Schott
filix-mas × marginalis
fragrans (L.) Schott
fragrans × marginalis (*See* D. ×algonquinensis)
goldiana (Hooker) A. Gray
goldiana × intermedia
goldiana × ludoviciana (*See* D. celsa)
goldiana × marginalis (*See* D. neo-wherryi)
intermedia (Muhl.) A. Gray
intermedia × marginalis

×leedsii Wherry (D. celsa × marginalis)
ludoviciana (Kunze) Small
marginalis (L.) A. Gray
×neo-wherryi Wagner (D. goldiana × marginalis)
×pittsfordensis Slosson (D. carthusiana × marginalis)
rossii C. Chr. in H. Ross
×separabilis Small (D. celsa × intermedia)
×slossoniae Wherry ex Lellinger (D. cristata × marginalis)
×triploidea Wherry (D. carthusiana × intermedia)
×uliginosa Druce (D. carthusiana × cristata)

  Equisetum
arvense L.
arvense × fluviatile (*See* E. ×litorale)
×ferrissii Clute (E. hyemale var. affine × laevigatum)
fluviatile L.
hyemale var. affine (Engelm.) A. A. Eaton
hyemale var. affine × laevigatum (*See* E. ×ferrissii)
hyemale var. affine × variegatum var. variegatum (*See* E. ×trachyodon)
laevigatum A. Braun
laevigatum × variegatum var. variegatum (*See* E. ×nelsonii)
×litorale Kuehlewein ex Rupr. (E. arvense × fluviatile)
×nelsonii (A. A. Eaton) Schaffn. (E. laevigatum × variegatum var. variegatum)
palustre L.
pratense Ehrh.
ramosissimum Desf. subsp. ramosissimum
scirpoides Michx.
sylvaticum L.
telmateia subsp. braunii (Milde) Hauke
×trachyodon A. Braun (E. hyemale var. affine × variegatum var. variegatum)
variegatum Schleich. ex Weber & Mohr var. variegatum

  Gymnocarpium
dryopteris (L.) Newm.
dryopteris var. disjunctum (Rupr.) Ching
dryopteris × robertianum (*See* G. ×heterosporum)
×heterosporum Wagner (G. dryopteris × robertianum)
robertianum (Hoffm.) Newm.

  Hymenophyllum
tunbrigense (L.) J. E. Smith
wrightii v. d. Bosch

  Hypolepis
repens (L.) Presl

  Isoëtes

acadiensis Kott
bolanderi Engelm.
butleri Engelm.
×eatonii Dodge (I. engelmannii × echinospora subsp. muricata)
echinospora subsp. muricata (Dur.) Löve & Löve
echinospora subsp. muricata × macrospora
echinospora subsp. muricata × riparia
engelmannii A. Braun
engelmannii × flaccida
engelmannii × melanopoda (*See* I. ×louisianensis)
engelmannii × piedmontana
engelmannii × riparia
flaccida Shuttlew. ex A. Braun
flaccida × piedmontana
×foveolata A. A. Eaton ex Dodge (I. engelmannii × tuckermanii)
hieroglyphica A. A. Eaton
howellii Engelm.
lithophila Pfeiffer
×louisianensis Thieret (I. engelmannii × melanopoda)
macrospora Dur.
melanopoda Gay & Dur.
melanospora Engelm.
melanospora × piedmontana
nuttallii A. Braun ex Engelm.
occidentalis Hend.
orcuttii A. A. Eaton
piedmontana (Pfeiffer) Reed
riparia Engelm. ex A. Braun
tegetiformans Rury
tuckermanii A. Braun ex Engelm. in A. Gray
virginica Pfeiffer

   Lomariopsis
kunzeana (Presl ex Underw.) Holtt.

   Lycopodium
alopecuroides L.
alopecuroides × inundatum
alopecuroides × prostratum (*See* L. ×copelandii)
alpinum L.
alpinum × sitchense
alpinum × tristachyum (*See* L. ×issleri)
annotinum L.
appressum (Chapm.) Lloyd & Underw.
appressum × inundatum
appressum × prostratum (*See* L. ×brucei)

× brucei (Cranfill) Lellinger (L. appressum × prostratum)
× buttersii Abbe (L. lucidum × selago)
carolinianum L.
cernuum L.
clavatum L.
complanatum L.
complanatum × digitatum
× copelandii Eiger (L. alopecuroides × prostratum)
dendroideum Michx.
dichotomum Jacq.
digitatum Dillen. ex A. Braun
digitatum × tristachyum (*See* L. × habereri)
× habereri House (L. digitatum × tristachyum)
inundatum L.
× issleri (Rouy) Lawalrée (L. alpinum × tristachyum)
lucidulum Michx.
lucidulum × selago (*See* L. × buttersii)
obscurum L.
  var. isophyllum Hickey
  var. obscurum
porophilum Lloyd & Underw.
prostratum Harper
× sabinifolium Willd. (L. sitchense × tristachyum)
selago L.
  var. appressum Desv.
  var. miyoshianum Makino
  var. selago
sitchense Rupr.
tristachyum Pursh
× zeilleri (Rouy) Beitel (L. complanatum × tristachyum)
  Lygodium
japonicum (Thunb.) Swartz
microphyllum (Cav.) R. Brown
palmatum (Bernh.) Swartz
  Marsilea
macropoda Engelm. ex A. Braun
mexicana A. Braun
quadrifolia L.
tenuifolia Engelm. ex Kunze
uncinata A. Braun
vestita Hook. & Grev.
  Matteuccia
struthiopteris var. pensylvanica (Willd.) Morton
  Microgramma

heterophylla (L.) Wherry
  Nephrolepis
×averyi Nauman (N. biserrata × exaltata)
biserrata (Swartz) Schott
biserrata × exaltata (*See* N. ×averyi)
cordifolia (L.) Presl
exaltata (L.) Schott
multiflora (Roxb.) Jarrett ex Morton
  Neurodium
lanceolatum (L.) Fée
  Notholaena
aliena Maxon
aschenborniana Klotzsch
aurea (Poir.) Desv.
californica D. C. Eaton
candida var. copelandii (C. C. Hall) Tryon
cochisensis Goodd.
cochisensis × sinuata var. sinuata (*See* N. ×integerrima)
dealbata (Pursh) Kunze
fendleri Kunze
grayi Davenp.
greggii (Mett. ex Kuhn) Maxon
incana Presl
  ×integerrima (Hook.) Hevly (N. cochisensis × sinuata var. sinuata)
jonesii Maxon
lemmonii D. C. Eaton var. lemmonii
limitanea Maxon
  var. limitanea
  var. mexicana (Maxon) Broun
neglecta Maxon
newberryi D. C. Eaton
parryi D. C. Eaton
parvifolia Tryon
schaffneri var. nealleyi (Seaton ex Coulter) Weath.
sinuata (Lag. ex Swartz) Kaulf. var. sinuata
standleyi Maxon
  Onoclea
sensibilis L.
  Ophioglossum
crotalophoroides Walter
engelmannii Prantl
lusitanicum subsp. californicum (Prantl) Clausen
nudicaule L. f.
petiolatum Hooker

pusillum Raf.
pycnostichum (Fern.) Löve & Löve
  Osmunda
cinnamomea L.
claytoniana L.
claytoniana × regalis var. spectabilis (*See* O. ×ruggii)
regalis var. spectabilis (Willd.) A. Gray
  ×ruggii Tryon (O. claytoniana × regalis var. spectabilis)
  Pellaea
andromedifolia (Kaulf.) Fée
  var. andromedifolia
  var. pubescens D. C. Eaton
×atropurpurea (L.) Link (P. glabella × ternifolia)
×atropurpurea × occidentalis (*See* P. ×suksdorfiana)
brachyptera (Moore) Baker
brachyptera × mucronata var. mucronata
breweri D. C. Eaton
bridgesii Hooker
bridgesii × mucronata var. mucronata (*See* P. ×glaciogena)
cordifolia (Sessé & Moc.) A. R. Smith
glabella Mett. ex Kuhn
glabella × ternifolia (*See* P. ×atropurpurea)
×glaciogena Wagner, Smith & Pray (P. bridgesii × mucronata var. mucronata)
intermedia Mett. ex Kuhn
mucronata (D. C. Eaton) D. C. Eaton
  var. californica (Lemmon) Munz & Johnston
  var. mucronata
mucronata var. mucronata × truncata
occidentalis (E. Nels.) Rydb.
ovata (Desv.) Weath.
×suksdorfiana Butters (P. atropurpurea × occidentalis)
ternifolia (Cav.) Link
ternifolia × truncata (*See* P. wrightiana)
truncata Goodd.
truncata × wrightiana (*See* P. ×wagneri)
×wagneri Windham (P. truncata × wrightiana)
wrightiana Hook. (P. ternifolia × truncata)
  Phanerophlebia
auriculata Underw.
umbonata Underw.
  Phlebodium
aureum (L.) J. Smith
  Phyllitis
scolopendrium var. americana Fern.

Pilularia
americana A. Braun
  Pityrogramma
pallida (Weath.) Alt & Grant
triangularis (Kaulf.) Maxon
  var. maxonii Weath.
  var. triangularis
trifoliata (L.) Tryon
viscosa (D. C. Eaton) Maxon
  Pleopeltis
astrolepis (Liebm.) Fourn.
erythrolepis (Weath.) Pic. Ser.
  Polypodium
amorphum Suksd.
amorphum × glycyrrhiza (*See* P. hesperium)
amorphum × hesperium
cambricum L.
californicum Kaulf.
californicum × glycyrrhiza
californicum × scouleri
dispersum A. M. Evans
glycyrrhiza D. C. Eaton
glycyrrhiza × hesperium
hesperium Maxon (P. amorphum × glycyrrhiza)
plumula Humb. & Bonpl. ex Willd.
polypodioides var. michauxianum Weath.
ptilodon var. caespitosum (Jenm.) A. M. Evans
scouleri Hook. & Grev.
thyssanolepis A. Braun ex Klotzsch
virginianum L.
  f. cambricoides F. W. Gray
  Polystichum
acrostichoides (Michx.) Schott
acrostichoides × braunii
acrostichoides × lonchitis (*See* P. ×hagenahii)
aleuticum C. Chr. in Hultén
andersonii Hopkins (P. munitum × unknown diploid)
andersonii × munitum
braunii (Spenner) Fée
braunii × munitum (*See* P. setigerum)
californicum (D. C. Eaton) Diels (P. dudleyi × munitum)
californicum × dudleyi
californicum × munitum
dudleyi Maxon
dudleyi × munitum (*See* P. californicum)

×hagenahii Cody (P. acrostichoides × lonchitis)
imbricans (D. C. Eaton) D. H. Wagner
  subsp. curtum (Ewan) D. H. Wagner
  subsp. imbricans
imbricans subsp. imbricans × scopulinum
kruckebergii Wagner (P. lemmonii × lonchitis)
lemmonii Underw.
lemonii × lonchitis (*See* P. kruckebergii)
lemmonii × scopulinum
lonchitis (L.) Roth
microchlamys (Christ) Matsumura
munitum (Kaulf.) Presl
munitum × unknown diploid (*See* P. andersonii)
scopulinum (D. C. Eaton) Maxon (P. imbricans subsp. imbricans
  × lemmonii)
setigerum (Presl) Presl (P. braunii × munitum)
  Psilotum
nudum (L.) Pal. Beauv.
  Pteridium
aquilinum
  var. latiusculum (Desv.) Underw. ex Heller
  var. pseudocaudatum (Clute) Heller
  var. pubescens Underw.
caudatum (L.) Maxon
  Pteris
bahamensis (Agardh) Fée
bahamensis × vittata (*See* P. ×delchampsii)
cretica L.
×delchampsii Wagner & Nauman (P. bahamensis × vittata)
ensiformis cv. Victoriae Hort.
multifida Poir.
tripartita (Swartz) Presl
vittata L.
  Salvinia
minima Baker
  Schizaea
pusilla Pursh
  Selaginella
apoda (L.) Spring
arenicola Underw.
arizonica Maxon
asprella Maxon
bigelovii Underw.
braunii Baker

cinerascens A. A. Eaton
densa Rydb.
  var. densa
  var. scopulorum (Maxon) Tryon
  var. standleyi (Maxon) Tryon
douglasii (Hook. & Grev.) Spring
eatonii Hieron. ex Small
eclipes Buck
eremophila Maxon
hansenii Hieron.
kraussiana (Kunze) A. Braun
lepidophylla (Hook. & Grev.) Spring
leucobryoides Maxon
ludoviciana A. Braun
mutica D. C. Eaton ex Underw.
  var. limitanea Weath.
  var. mutica
  var. mutica × rupincola (S. × neomexicana)
×neomexicana Maxon (S. mutica var. mutica × rupincola)
oregana D. C. Eaton in Watson
peruviana (Milde) Hieron.
pilifera A. Braun
  var. pilifera
  var. pringlei (Baker) Morton
rupestris (L.) Spring
rupincola Underw.
selaginoides (L.) Link
sibirica (Milde) Hieron.
tortipila A. Braun
uncinata Spring
underwoodii Hieron.
utahensis Flowers
viridissima Weath.
wallacei Hieron.
watsonii Underw.
weatherbiana Tryon
willdenovii (Desv. in Poir.) Baker
wrightii Hieron.
   Sphenomeris
clavata (L.) Maxon
   Tectaria
×amesiana A. A. Eaton (T. coriandrifolia × lobata)
coriandrifolia (Swartz) Underw.
coriandrifolia × lobata (*See* T. ×amesiana)
heracleifolia (Willd.) Underw.

incisa Cav.
lobata (Poir.) Morton

Thelypteris
augescens (Link) Munz & Johnston
augescens × kunthii
augescens × ovata var. ovata
dentata (Forsk.) E. St. John
grandis A. R. Smith var. grandis
hexagonoptera (Michx.) Weath.
hispidula var. versicolor (R. St. John in Small) Lellinger
kunthii (Desv.) Morton
limbosperma (All.) H. P. Fuchs
nevadensis (Baker) Clute ex Morton
noveboracensis (L.) Nieuwl.
ovata R. St. John in Small
  var. lindheimeri (C. Chr.) A. R. Smith
  var. ovata
palustris var. pubescens (Laws.) Fern.
phegopteris (L.) Slosson
pilosa var. alabamensis Crawford
puberula var. sonorensis A. R. Smith
reptans (Gmel.) Morton
resinifera (Desv.) Proctor
reticulata (L.) Proctor
sclerophylla (Kunze in Spreng.) Morton
serrata (Cav.) Alston
simulata (Davenp.) Nieuwl.
tetragona (Swartz) Small
torresiana (Gaud.) Alston
totta (Thunb.) Schelpe

Trichomanes
boschianum Sturm
holopterum Kunze
krausii Hook. & Grev.
petersii A. Gray
punctatum subsp. floridanum W. Boer

Vittaria
lineata (L.) J. E. Smith

Woodsia
× abbeae Butters (W. ilvensis × scopulina)
alpina (Boulton) S. F. Gray (W. glabella × ilvensis)
alpina × ilvensis (See W. × gracilis)
glabella R. Brown in Richards. in Franklin
  × gracilis (Laws.) Butters (W. alpina × ilvensis)

ilvensis (L.) R. Brown
ilvensis × scopulina (*See* W. × abbeae)
 × maxonii Tryon (W. oregana × scopulina)
mexicana Fée
mexicana × mollis (*See* W. plummerae)
obtusa (Spreng.) Torrey
oregana D. C. Eaton
oregana × scopulina (*See* W. × maxonii)
plummerae Lemmon (W. mexicana × mollis (Kaulf.) J. Smith)
scopulina D. C. Eaton
  Woodwardia
areolata (L.) Moore
fimbriata J. E. Smith
virginica (L.) J. E. Smith

Index to Common Names

Index to
Scientific Names

Boldface numbers = reference numbers given to species in text

glabella R. Brown in Richards. in Franklin, **336**, 14, 263, 264

× gracilis (Laws.) Butters, 263, 264

ilvensis (L.) R. Brown, **338**, 14, 263, 264

× maxonii Tryon, 264, 265

mexicana Fée, **342**, 266

mollis (Kaulf.) J. Smith, 266

obtusa (Spreng.) Torrey, **341**

oregana D. C. Eaton, **340**, 264

    var. cathcartiana (B. L. Robins.) Morton, 265

plummerae Lemmon, **343**, 266

scopulina D. C. Eaton, **339**, 264, 265

    var. appalachiana T. M. C. Taylor, 265

    var. scopulina, 265

Woodsiaceae, 9, 245

Woodwardia, 298, 301, 302

    areolata (L.) Moore, **393**, 14

    fimbriata J. E. Smith, **395**, 38

    radicans J. E. Smith, 11

    virginica (L.) J. E. Smith, **394**

Zalesskya, 31, 33

Zosterophyllopsida, 29, 30, 32

Zygopteridales, 31